INDIGENOUS DISPOSSESSION, ANTI-IMMIGRATION,
AND THE PUBLIC PEDAGOGY OF US EMPIRE

RACE AND MEDIATED CULTURES
Camilla Fojas, Series Editor

INDIGENOUS DISPOSSESSION, ANTI-IMMIGRATION, AND THE PUBLIC PEDAGOGY OF US EMPIRE

Leah Perry

THE OHIO STATE UNIVERSITY PRESS
COLUMBUS

Copyright © 2024 by The Ohio State University.
All rights reserved.

Library of Congress Cataloging-in-Publication data available online at https://catalog.loc.gov
LCCN: 2024009546
Identifiers: ISBN 978-0-8142-1520-3 (hardback); ISBN 978-0-8142-5913-9 (paperback); ISBN 978-0-8142-8359-2 (ebook)

Cover design by adam bohannon
Text composition by Stuart Rodriguez
Type set in Minion Pro

♾ The paper used in this publication meets the minimum requirements of the American National Standard for Information Sciences—Permanence of Paper for Printed Library Materials. ANSI Z39.48-1992.

For my teachers

CONTENTS

Acknowledgments   ix

INTRODUCTION	The Public Pedagogy of US Empire	1
CHAPTER 1	Proximal Public Pedagogies: Native American Law, Immigration Law, and Media	33
CHAPTER 2	"Entitlement" Warfare: Welfare and Remapping National (B)orders	71
CHAPTER 3	US Culture Is Always-Already Rape Culture	108
CHAPTER 4	Food, Farming, Fat, and National(ist) Dyspepsia: Revolting Indigenous and Immigrant Foodways	145
CONCLUSION	Queer Empire and the Public Pedagogy of Decoloniality	193

Bibliography   223

Index   243

ACKNOWLEDGMENTS

This book was written with the help of many. Any errors contained within are entirely my own.

At the American Studies Association (ASA) conference held days after Trump's 2016 election, a panel of Indigenous scholars doing critical Indigenous studies work implored the visibly disturbed non-Natives in the packed session to join them to fight for necessarily decolonial social justice. As they pointed out, our ostensibly progressive antiracist, feminist, queer research, teaching, and activism often erased Indigenous peoples and replicated Indigenous dispossession. I heard the call. I have since worked to not only consider but to center Indigeneity, settler colonialism, and decolonization in my thinking, research, teaching, and action. I am deeply indebted to many Indigenous scholars, activists, and creators. As I continue to learn, I am changed by their work and, I hope, accountable to it and to Indigenous peoples.

I am very grateful to The Ohio State University Press Editorial Director Kristen Elias Rowley and Race and Mediated Cultures series editors Camilla Fojas and Mary Beltrán for their enthusiastic support for and meticulous attention to all aspects of this project. The thoughtful, thorough feedback from my two anonymous reviewers was invaluable, making this a much stronger and more ethical project.

I express my deepest gratitude to Rachel Ida Buff for her vital feedback on the beginning stages of this project and for engaging me and my work over the years. Her generosity and commitment to social justice via scholarship, teaching, and activism continue to shape my work. I also thank Rachel for connecting me with Joe Genetin-Pilawa, whose early commentary helped me to center Indigeneity and settler colonialism. Juliana Hu Pegues's feedback at ASA on what has become chapter 3 was crucial. I thank Scott Manning Stevens (Akwesasne Mohawk) for his comments at the Hungarian ASA. Karen Adams's perusal of my first draft made this project stronger and clearer. She is missed.

A previous version of chapter 2 appeared in the anthology *Migration, Identity, and Belonging: Defining Borders and Boundaries of the Homeland*. I thank editors Kumarini Silva and Margaret Franz for their insights, which helped me to clarify my thinking on the topic.

I thank Kris Erikson, Fan Yang, Katy Razzano, Allison Lakomski, Sean Johnson Andrews, and Jaafar Aksikas for thoughtful commentary on portions of this project (and the other big ones that came before) and for continuing to be a part of my intellectual community.

I could not have written this book, or the previous one, without the mentorship of a number of scholars over the years. Matt Jacobson continues to model the kind of ethical, rigorous, generous scholar and teacher I strive to be. I hope I am paying it forward. As a doctoral student in George Mason University's Cultural Studies program, all that Paul Smith, Alison Landsberg, Larry Levine, Scott Trafton, Roger Lancaster, and Suzanne Scott taught me about scholarly rigor and pedagogy continues to be deeply influential.

My students show me again and again that boundaries between scholarship, teaching, and social justice are imaginary. *Mulțumesc* especially to the University of Bucharest American Studies students in my 2022–23 Fulbright classes for giving me life in the shadow of the pandemic. In the class US Foodways, Gender, and Race, students' creative, impressive scholarship (and our always wildin' discussions) sharpened and expanded my thinking about foodways and social justice. I am better for having met all my UniBuc students.

SUNY Empire State University provided generous research funding for this book. I especially thank Dean Nicola Allain. My appreciation for the support of Dana Gliserman-Kopans, my department chair, work wife, and dear friend, is immeasurable.

My gratitude to my emotional support humans outside of academia: Rachel Page, Courtney Wahl, Heather McDonald, Marvin White, Mirza Molberg, Malou Kurpick, Andreea Ciobanu, and Dana Nazzaro Palmieri.

Finally, I thank my parents, Al and Camille Perry, for their lifelong support and enthusiasm for my dream of a scholarly life. As my first teachers, they taught me to love learning . . . and, as usual, I took things to the extreme. And I am so grateful for Stellina, my pandemic puppy/BFF, who makes every day meaningful and fun. I am honored to be her guardian and caregiver.

INTRODUCTION

The Public Pedagogy of US Empire

The film *Fort Apache, The Bronx* (1981) is one of a handful of popular mainstream media texts that illustrates the gendered, sexualized entanglement of Indigenous dispossession and settler colonialism, white supremacy, and anti-immigration key to the establishment, expansion, and ongoing exertion of US empire. The popular Daniel Petrie–directed crime drama,[1] set in a mostly Puerto Rican and Black impoverished South Bronx neighborhood filled with burned and bombed-out buildings and resembling a war zone, was inspired by white police officers' experiences working at the 41st precinct in the Bronx in the late twentieth century. The precinct was nicknamed Fort Apache after the nineteenth-century Fort Apache military outpost, located in the western frontier when "savage Indians" threatened the manifesting destiny of US empire. The plot is driven by the notion that protecting white heteropatriarchy—coded as law and order and morality—is nearly impossible in the face of Latinx and Black—and "Indian"—criminality in the abject urban frontier. Like nineteenth-century settlers, the police officers in the film, Irish American Murphy (Paul Newman) and Italian American Corelli (Ken Wahl), are at war in a "foreign territory," battling crime, anarchy, and corruption, endangered and under attack from the Latinx and Black residents, many of whom are drug dealers, addicts, gang bangers, and sex workers and many of whom speak

---

1. "Fort Apache, The Bronx," The Numbers, updated 2023, http://www.the-numbers.com/movies/1981/0FABR.php.

Spanish while most officers do not. Antagonists such as a murderous, drug-addicted Black sex worker (Pam Grier) and the doomed romance between Murphy and a Latinx nurse who dies by drug overdose (Rachel Ticotin) drive home the message that gender, sexuality, and race render these people—peoples—alien and "forever foreign"[2] to the film's white, male, heterosexual emblems of US American morality and law and order.

Along with the sensationalistic content of the film, formal aspects bombard spectators with the message that white heteropatriarchal civilization is under siege from rebellious colonized, racialized, queer(ed) populations, and to avoid a return to savagery, modern-day criminal aliens must be contained, excluded, or eliminated. The tagline proclaims, "No Cowboys, No Indians, No Cavalry to the Rescue, Only a Cop." A defensive opening intertitle states that because the film portrays "the lives of two policemen working out of a precinct in the South Bronx" it depicts only criminals rather than "law abiding members of the community" and "individuals and groups who are struggling to turn the Bronx around." Not surprisingly and perhaps inspiring the intertitle, the film's characterization of the Latinx and Black neighborhood as a foreign warzone led some critics to pan it as an over-the-top portrayal. Residents of the South Bronx where the film was shot on location also threatened to sue the filmmakers for the racist depiction of their home.[3] According to Richard Slotkin, *Fort Apache, The Bronx* treats violence in low-income, urban Black and Latinx neighborhoods "in terms of the standard cavalry/Indian paradigm" of the Western film genre but inverts the "myth of the frontier," an ideology of westward expansion justifying and glorifying US imperialism from the nineteenth century. The "borders [these] heroes confront are impermeable to the forces of progress and civilized enlightenment [. . .] with the civilized world threatened with subjugation to or colonization by the forces of darkness."[4] The film, which inspired the long-running crime drama *Hill Street Blues* (1981–87), is part of a collection of late twentieth-century popular media that, as part of a neoliberal backlash against multiculturalism, proclaimed and perpetuated notions of a crime crisis coded in gendered, sexualized terms as Black and Latinx and, with regard to the latter, immigrant and often "illegal," regardless of the alleged alien's citizenship status.

---

2. Tuan, *Forever Foreigners or Honorary Whites?*

3. Variety Staff, "Fort Apache, The Bronx," *Variety*, December 31, 1980, http://www.variety.com/review/VE1117791034/; and Roger Ebert, "Fort Apache, The Bronx," *Chicago Sun Times*, January 1, 1981, http://rogerebert.suntimes.com/apps/pbcs.dll/article?AID=/19810101/REVIEWS/101010327/1023.

4. Slotkin, *Gunfighter Nation*, 635.

But more than that, *Fort Apache, The Bronx* is an explicit case of art or at least media imitating life within the long durée of US empire. Audra Simpson (Kahnawake Mohawk) observes that the threat of Indigenous sovereignty overlaps with racialized border control with the "seemingly newer threat to settler sovereignty and security—the illegal alien, the always possible terrorist—rendering perhaps all bodies with color as border transgressors with the presumed attempt to harm."[5] For instance, in the aftermath of the nineteenth-century Modoc War, white settlers' framing of the Modoc as the instigators of violence in systems, institutions, procedures, social relations, and arenas of trade rationalized violence against Indigenous peoples in a host of US territorial and imperial projects, helping to lay the legal foundation for defining twentieth- and twenty-first-century racialized threats and "terrorists."[6] Indeed, assemblages of Indigenous dispossession, white supremacy, and heteropatriarchy—what Aileen Moreton-Robinson (Goenpul) calls "white possessive logics"—are the heart of settler nations such as the United States.[7] In inherently gendered, sexualized ways, the imperative of settler colonialism, to procure and protect white property interests, applies to various racialized groups in distinct but always interconnected ways in the US. In this racial project of accumulation, Indigenous genocide, removal, and dispossession intersects with the landed, spatialized, racialized violences necessary to capitalism. The latter is emblematized in the dispossession of Black peoples' lands and bodies through enslavement, anti-Black fungibility, and the exclusion and/or exploitation of differentially racialized migrants. Gendered, sexualized entanglements of Indigenous dispossession and the uneven racialization of populations of color to further white accumulation (of land, resources, and other forms of property) continue to underpin US empire as neoliberalism both polices territorial boundaries and enables the deterritorialization of capital and the mobility of bodies, data, and cultural practices under conditions of global and local structures of inequality and dehumanization. This book argues that as part of a colonial throughline, what I call the "public pedagogy of US empire" crystalizes in the gendered, sexualized entanglement of Indigenous genocide and dispossession and differentially racialized anti-immigration, both historically and into the neoliberal context. I define "public pedagogy" as policy and mainstream media discourses that provide powerful teachings and lessons to those within and outside of US borders about Indigenous peoples and racialized immigrants / those racialized as aliens, all as part and parcel of the white possessive logics of US empire. Historically specific public pedagogies both

---

5. Simpson, *Mohawk Interruptus*, 12.

6. Cothran, *Remembering the Modoc War*.

7. Moreton-Robinson, *White Possessive*, xix.

4 • INTRODUCTION

justify and do the work of dispossessing Indigenous peoples and containing im/migrant populations of color to accumulate and protect white property interests, creating and recreating the colonial and racial violences structuring US empire.

Fort Apache, the Bronx, a sensationalistic, moderately successful film from the 1980s, is also an emblematic example of the public pedagogy of US empire because the spaces it references and represents are sites of settler colonial and racial violence. First a US military outpost in what is now Arizona during the so-called Apache Wars (1861–86), Fort Apache remained a military post until 1922, becoming the site of the Theodore Roosevelt Indian School in 1923.[8] As I will discuss, the systematic removal of Indigenous children from their communities and the rape of Indigenous women are potent tools of US empire-building. The Fort Apache Indian Reservation, home to the White Mountain Apache Tribe, is extant in northeastern Arizona.

Similarly, the Bronx, one of the five boroughs of New York City, has also always been a site of settler coloniality and racialized violence. The Wiechquaesgecks, Siwanoy, and Lenape who inhabited the land that became known as the Bronx[9] were dispossessed by the first colonial settlement in the area, established by Jonas Bronx in 1639.[10] The Bronx was home to mostly Irish, Italian, and Eastern European immigrants at the turn of the twentieth century as the development of the subway system urbanized the area. Immigrants from the Caribbean, migrants from Puerto Rico, and Black migrants from the Southern US followed.[11] Puerto Rican people are not immigrants, though they, along with other Latinxs, are often coded as such. The Puerto Rican barrio in the Bronx formed in response to migration and displacement engendered by US agrarian capitalism following colonization of the island in 1898, the island's industrialization program, and US migration programs.[12] By 1960 a neoliberalizing federal economy and, in the Bronx, racial population shifts, housing deterioration and shortages, suburbanization, federal highway construction, and urban renewal programs "coincided with an outbreak of drug-related street crime, leading to abandoned and burned buildings, and white flight."[13] By the 1970s as New York City itself verged on bankruptcy, the

---

8. "Fort Apache Historical District," National Park Service, accessed March 8, 2021, https://www.nps.gov/nr/travel/amsw/sw11.htm.

9. Burrows and Wallace, *Gotham*.

10. "Jonas Bronx," Bronx Historical Society, updated 2008, https://web.archive.org/web/20080509163707/http:/www.bronxhistoricalsociety.org/notebx.html.

11. Gonzalez, *The Bronx*.

12. Perez, Guridy, and Burgos Jr., introduction to *Beyond El Barrio*, 3.

13. Gonzalez, *The Bronx*, 5.

THE PUBLIC PEDAGOGY OF US EMPIRE · 5

Bronx and especially the South Bronx were impoverished with high rates of violent crime, experiencing intensive urban decay into the 1980s that was in policy, policing, and media coded as Black and Latinx. Some redevelopment and gentrification began in the 1990s.[14] Like New York City itself, the Bronx remains a site of gendered, racialized inequality and often unchecked police violence against Black and Latinx people, that is, a site of the persistent afterlives of a nation built on, expanded through, and designed to protect white possession.

The Fort Apache nickname for the 41st precinct therefore pointed to the colonial history of the original military outpost and the Bronx, as well as the enduring ways that pedagogies of empire target Indigenous peoples and populations of color. As one South Bronx resident put it, the nickname is a racial slur that "evokes images of savage people, uncontrollable people, people society gives up on." Moreover, before the release of the film, police personnel renicknamed the precinct "Little House on the Prairie" after two-thirds of the neighborhood's predominantly Puerto Rican and Black residents fled.[15] The *Little House on the Prairie* television series (1974–83) adapted from Laura Ingalls Wilder's autobiographical "Little House" book series, focused on the adventures of a white, heteropatriarchal settler family living in the West in the late nineteenth century. The new nickname suggested that with two-thirds of the "savages" gone, the neighborhood could be properly settled and "civilized" according to white, heteropatriarchal metrics.

In sum, the film built upon the histories of the lands it referenced and was filmed on, working in tandem with actual, on-the-ground violences caused by settler colonialism and racial capitalism to render the barrio and its residents—groups with distinct histories and current experiences of violence at the hands of the US in pursuit of empire—inherently alien and dangerous to white people, property, and posterity. Jodi A. Byrd (a citizen of the Chickasaw Nation of Oklahoma) avers, "In the United States, the Indian is the original enemy combatant who cannot be grieved."[16] Like the real-world nickname(s) police personnel gave the 41st precinct, in explicitly gendered, sexualized terms the film dehumanized Black and Latinx people by drawing an analogy between, on the one hand, the mythologized nationalist narrative of nineteenth-century US frontier military battles with "primitive," "savage" Indigenous peoples blocking progress and civilization and capitalist expansion

---

14. Denton Tarver, "The New Bronx: A Quick History of the Iconic Borough," *Cooperator News New York*, April 2007, https://cooperatornews.com/article/the-new-bronx/full#cut.

15. Ian Fischer, "Pulling Out of Fort Apache, the Bronx: New 41st Precinct Station House Leaves Behind Symbol of Community's Past Troubles," *New York Times*, June 23, 1993.

16. Byrd, *Transit of Empire*, xviii.

6 · INTRODUCTION

in a "wild" landscape and, on the other, modern policing of Black and Latinx criminals in impoverished urban areas. In linking and capitalizing on settler colonial and racist stereotypes and infusing peoples, places, and certain kinds of commodification/marketplaces (illegal economies such as narcotics sales and sex work) with danger, degeneration, and alienness in contrast to white heteropatriarchal possession and carcerality, *Fort Apache, the Bronx* exemplifies how and why entanglements of Indigenous dispossession, race and racism, and anti-immigration comprise the public pedagogy of US empire.

To be clear, Indigenous dispossession and Indigenous peoples are more than the palimpsests upon which US empire was and continues to be mapped. The settler colonial structure, established to dispossess Indigenous people, continues to necessitate dispossession and protect white property from groups differentially racialized as nonwhite. Indigenous dispossession is thus the basis for and fundamentally entangled with the multiple gendered, sexualized, and racialized violences, exclusions, and selective incorporations forming the literal and ideological ground of the United States and its various means of continental and global conquest, including the notion of the US as a neoliberal multicultural democracy. Importantly, while Indigenous peoples are often erased and sometimes only selectively included in national and nationalist narratives, immigration, immigrants, migration, migrants, and those coded as such are often centered. Various iterations of a racialized "immigration emergency" have long operated alongside the notion of the US as the exceptionally increasingly inclusive and democratic "nation of immigrants." The discordant combination of explicitly gendered and racialized border policing/exclusion and welcoming/inclusion—the pairing engendered in late twentieth-century policy and media—was, as I have argued elsewhere, critical to rebranding the US as a multicultural neoliberal democracy[17] and the ongoing exertion of US empire in that image. Policy and mainstream media discourses provided powerful teachings and lessons—public pedagogy—to people within and outside of US borders about gender and racial inclusion and capitalism, democratic progress, and justice, as well as about the need to also safeguard US citizens and resources from undocumented im/migrants, gendered and racialized as "illegal aliens," and from those gendered and racialized as "alien" within. Unseen in this ascensionist version of US history is the Indigenous genocide and dispossession providing the preconditions for gendered, sexualized, and racialized capitalism founded on and persisting in Black fungibility;[18]

---

17. Perry, *Cultural Politics of U.S. Immigration.*

18. Some anti-Blackness scholars argue that "Black fungibility—rather than labor—defines and organizes Black value within relations of conquest" (King, *Black Shoals,* 23; see also Hartman, *Scenes of Subjection*). As I will discuss, a distinct but connected interchangeability defines and organizes the relationship between settlers and racialized im/migrants.

the repetition of the frontier myths of battling Native "savages" and "civilizing"/incorporating them that regimes of racialized immigrant exclusion and inclusion expand upon; and pedagogies of empire that persistently dispossess Indigenous peoples and manage differentially racialized groups to protect and advance white possession. As the editors of a special issue of *Social Text* on "economies of dispossession" argue, "Racialization—manifesting in systemic and everyday forms of devaluation, exploitation, and expendability, as well as the violence of racial terror and carceral regimes—and ongoing colonial modes of settlement, occupation, governmentality, and jurisprudence work in tandem with more capacious forms of US global militarism and empire."[19] Colonialism and racial capitalism "have been historically co-constitutive and are of necessity together confronted by Indigenous peoples and the racially subordinated."[20] Moreover, unraveling the racial relations of colonialism and capitalism[21] is necessary to understanding decolonization and abolition.[22]

Examining policy and media from colonization into the early twenty-first century in understudied areas and foregrounding Indigenous dispossession and racialized anti-immigration as it relates to and intersects with it, I argue that via various forms of public pedagogy, both gendered, sexualized coloniality and racialized anti-immigration underpin the foundation and development, the mapping and remapping, of US empire, including the redrawing of the US as a neoliberal multicultural democracy. I analyze significant policy for Indigenous peoples and im/migrants and media (including novels, plays, film, television, music videos, news media, and emergent media) produced in the shadow of policy, uncovering, tracing, and connecting the historical throughline of pedagogies of empire. Debates over Indigencity and immigration occurred not only on the battlefield, on the congressional floor, in the courtroom, and at territorial borders (of reservations; of urban, rural, and suburban areas; of the nation-state and its noncontinental colonies) but also in US American culture, providing powerful, accessible public pedagogy about gender, sexuality, race, democracy, and justice to citizens, denizens, and "aliens." These debates appear in early colonists' diaries and into the nineteenth and early twentieth centuries in captivity narratives; dime novels; Buffalo Bill's Wild West Show; plays about immigrant assimilation like *The Melting Pot*; silent films like *S— Man*,[23] *Birth of a Nation,* and *Broken Blossoms*; and sensationalistic news media. Debates

---

19. Byrd et al., "Predatory Value," 1.

20. Byrd et al., "Predatory Value," 2.

21. Gilmore and Lambert, "Making Abolition Geography," 14–19.

22. Day, "Racial Capitalism," 1033–46.

23. Here and throughout, I elide the full title of Cecil B. DeMille's 1914 film, which contains an offensive epithet for Indigenous women. See chapter 2 for an in-depth discussion of the epithet and film, which profoundly influenced the development of US cinema and was remade twice.

continue to surface in various media. Over time, developments have always occurred proximally, the imperatives of settler colonialism applied to Indigenous peoples and people of color in different but always entangled ways to support white possessive empire. With relational frameworks and analytics that synthesize the gendered, sexualized relationship of Indigenous dispossession and the differential racialization of multiple groups of immigrants, this book builds on scholarship that examines the co-constitution of colonialism and racial capitalism to intervene in critical immigration and race studies and critical Indigenous studies (CIS). I aim to illuminate how and why, in the ascendant neoliberal conjecture as historically, Indigenous peoples and differentially racialized immigrants were at the center of major policy changes and media that formed and furthered US empire.

ON TERMINOLOGY

The question of terminology used to describe identities is vexing given that all identities are dynamic and fluid, and the terms for racial, ethnic, gender, and sexual identities are often polemical within the communities they describe. The terms I use reflect self-determination and what is respectful within the communities in question at the time of writing. At points I unpack terms to clarify what is obscured.

I use "Indigenous," "Native American," and "Native" interchangeably to refer to Indigenous peoples residing within the land currently occupied by the United States. "First Nations," a term often used by Indigenous peoples residing within the land currently occupied by Canada, is also used where appropriate. Specific Indigenous nations are named wherever possible given that Indigenous peoples are not a monolith and given that in addition to federal Native American policy, tribal-nations often also have specific relationships with the US government and different positions on various issues. Moreover, many tribal-nations' traditional lands cross settler colonial nation-state borders. "Indian" is often viewed as offensive term when used by non-Natives because it is the term European colonizers of the Americas used to describe the peoples they encountered, believing they were in India. As a non-Native, I use the term "Indian" only as used in policy, media texts, and direct quotations, or framed in quotation marks to illuminate when it is weaponized as a stereotype.

The terms "Black" and "Black Americans" are used to describe Black US Americans. I do not use the term "African American" unless describing voluntary migrants or immigrants from Africa, as the US "American" modifier connotes voluntary migration and could consequently occlude the history of the enslavement of Black people and ongoing anti-Blackness in the US.

I use the term "Latinx" when referring to people from Latin America or nations with histories of Spanish colonization. Although the term "Hispanic" is often used interchangeably with "Latina/o" and "Latinx," it refers to people from Spain and Spanish-speaking nations in the Americas. In the 1970s and 1980s, the US government created the "Hispanic" category to conglomerate a new voting bloc. It was quickly taken up by corporations as a marketing demographic. It erases or obviates important differences among people of Latin American descent such as race, Indigenous heritage, and nationality.[24] While "Latina/o" also has the potential to homogenize people of Latin American descent[25] and the adoption of "Latinx" is debated, the former is often preferred as a matter of self-determination, and the latter arose to respond to feminist concerns about gendered language and to include people of all gender identities.[26] In connection with the civil rights movement in the 1960s, Mexican Americans began using the term "Chicana/o" as a matter of self-determination. I use the term "Chicanx," like "Latinx," to include all genders, and I use these terms contingently and as descriptive categories, making more fine-grained distinctions where necessary for clarification.

I use the term "Asian American" to describe Americans of Asian descent. Although the term, like "Latinx," may conglomerate important differences among "Asian Americans," it was coined during the Yellow Power movement of the 1960s as a corrective to the term "Oriental," viewed as offensive, and has allowed for collective antiracist action.[27] Using the term "Asian" to describe people of "Filipino/a" or "Filipinx" descent as a racial group is complex given that the Philippines is populated by Indigenous peoples, people with Spanish and East Asian ancestries, and of course people of mixed heritage. I also use the terms "Asian" and "Filipinx" contingently and as descriptive categories, again making more fine-grained distinctions where necessary for clarification.[28]

Whiteness, a category generally understood to refer to light-skinned people descended primarily from Europe, has always been inconstant. For instance, Irish and Eastern and Southern European immigrants were considered "lesser"

---

24. Alonso and Koreck, "Silences," 111.

25. Valdivia, "Is Penelope to J. Lo as Culture Is to Nature?," 132; and Davila, *Latinos Inc.*

26. Lopez, "Notes on Terminology," x.

27. Spiritu, *Asian American Panethnicity.*

28. For an overview of the field of Asian American studies and terminology, see Schuland-Vials, Vo, and Wong, *Keywords.*

white races at the turn of the twentieth century.[29] The term and identity "white ethnic," coined during the civil rights movement to distinguish these groups and their descendants from white Northern Europeans and their privileges, became part of the multicultural politics of recognition and inclusion that upheld or deepened white supremacy.[30] I use the lowercase "white" and "white ethnic" while using capitalized terms for groups racialized as nonwhite to center marginalized groups.

Numerous identities fall under the umbrella of categories like queer, lesbian, bisexual, transgender, intersex, and Two-Spirit, as none of the terms fully encompass the intricacies of gender and sexual identity. Generally, I use the term "queer" as an individual identity category and synonym for LGBTQ+ people and also as an analytic rubric that illuminates the intersectional workings of power and fluidity and instability of all identity categories. I follow the editors of *Queer Indigenous Studies: Critical Interventions in Theory, Politics, and Literature* in my use of "queer" provisionally when referring to Indigenous LGBTQ+ and Two-Spirit people (LGBTQ2S or LGBTQTS) because the term critiques heteronormativity and is linked to the ambiguity and fluidity of gender and sexuality and all identity categories.[31] I use "Two-Spirit" in accordance with specific history, meaning, and politics of identification among Indigenous people. When possible, I use Indigenous nations' specific terms for gender diverse identities. I use the terms "gender and sexual variance" and "gender and sexual diversity" interchangeably.

I use the terms "immigrant" and "migrant," at times "im/migrant," to refer to people who have crossed an international border as defined by non-Native nation-states. State-sanctioned legal statuses "reflect not 'types' of migrants but the workings of power and knowledge that seek to differentiate among migrants; delimit rights and protections that they will be granted or denied; and shape forms of surveillance, discipline, normalization, and dispossession to which they are subjected."[32] While some recent scholarship uses the term migrant to avoid recirculating pernicious state-generated categories, I use both immigrant and migrant to show how those categories operate in specific instances as public pedagogy about settler coloniality and anti-immigration.

Finally, I use the term "US empire" to refer to the United States' domestic and international efforts for political, economic, military, and cultural conquest and dominance. My use of the term encompasses and illuminates what Manu Karuka calls "continental imperialism" in tracing how Native peoples

---

29. Jacobson, *Whiteness of a Different Color.*
30. Jacobson, *Roots Too.*
31. Driskill et al., introduction to *Queer Indigenous Studies*, 3.
32. Chávez and Luibhéid, introduction to *Queer and Trans Migrations*, 8.

and Chinese migrant laborers were subjected to interconnected forms of violence to further US empire: the differentiated modes of capitalism dispossess some and exploit others via racialized labor. Karuka's term illuminates that there is no "national" territory of the US but rather only colonized territories. Moreover, there is no "national" US political economy but only an imperial one maintained "not through the rule of law, contract, or competition, but through the renewal of colonial occupation" that is domestic as well as international.[33] My use of "US empire" names unending US continental and global imperial expansion, and when relevant I distinguish between the two intertwined modes of empire.

NEOLIBERALISM AND SETTLER COLONIALISM

Joanne Barker (Lenape, a citizen of the Delaware Tribe of Indians) writes that "the normalization of Indigenous erasure from an analysis of the US empire reinscribes the imperial and racist relations and conditions through which that erasure is cast as fait accompli."[34] Neoliberal governmentality is rooted in entrepreneurial values; deregulation of the economy, trade liberalization, and privatization of state services; and the theory that consumerist free trade will bring unprecedented prosperity to the whole world.[35] Neoliberal economic and political practices enact US empire, for they are "predicated on a disavowal of older modes of racial and settler colonial violence, through multiple but linked formations of erasure."[36] Moreover, "claiming that racial and settler colonial dispossession and violence are entirely of the past is exactly the ideological structure through which settler colonialism replicates itself in the present."[37] This section outlines how the obfuscation of ongoing Indigenous dispossession and racialized anti-immigration is key to US neoliberal empire.

To clarify what neoliberalism means in the context of this project, the constellation of policies and ideologies that comprise neoliberalism in the US developed after World War II as a critique of statism, social engineering, and the welfare state, with liberation of the market from governments posited as the solution to totalitarianism and persons' dependency on the state. Although white accumulation in the US hinges on gendered, sexualized ongoing Indigenous dispossession, chattel slavery and the afterlives of anti-Blackness, the

---

33. Karuka, *Empire's Tracks*, xii.
34. Barker, "Territory as Analytic," 25.
35. Steger and Roy, *Neoliberalism*, 11–14, 55; and Harvey, *Brief History of Neoliberalism*, 2–5.
36. Hong, "Speculative Surplus," 111.
37. Hong, "Speculative Surplus," 112.

exclusion and/or exploitation of differentially racialized immigrants, and the unpaid and/or exploited labor of women, dependency has long been demonized and/or met with racialized paternalism in policy and the culture at large. Proto-neoliberal critiques of state dependency gained traction after President Lyndon Johnson expanded New Deal welfare programs with his War on Poverty. "Liberalism" and Franklin Delano Roosevelt's New Deal social welfare policies were linked to dangerous, antidemocratic state reliance[38] that was often not so thinly gendered and racialized, just as civil rights, feminist, LGBTQ+, and Indigenous movements made unprecedented legal and ideological gains in struggles for justice. Neoliberalism, advanced by subsequent administrations on both sides of the aisle, negotiated this changing socioeconomic landscape to continue to support white heteropatriarchal possession.

Regarding the colonial and racial violences structuring and sustaining neoliberalism as it crystalized in the later decades of the twentieth century, Indigenous "dispossession as a present mode of imperialism, as the mode by which imperialism is operationalized,"[39] grounds what Grace Hong calls neoliberalism's structures of disavowal. To disavow the older structures of settler colonial and racial violence underpinning US empire, neoliberalism selectively ingests and regurgitates aspects of progressive movements, such as multiculturalism, feminism, LGBTQ+ rights, and Indigenous struggles for justice, alongside more overt backlash against them that is cast as necessary. This allows neoliberal ideology to claim "that protected life is available to all and that premature death comes only to those whose criminal actions and poor choices make them deserve it."[40] By the 1970s, neoliberalism was "an ascendant framework that thoroughly depended on, yet denied the relevance of, institutionalized racism, (hetero)sexism, capitalist exploitation, and empire."[41] This occurred in two ways. On one hand, neoliberalism extracts surplus value from gendered, sexualized, racialized bodies with universalized discourses of value detached from race ("colorblind"), gender, and sexuality, moving beyond the notion of equal opportunity for all to the notion of the market itself as the conduit of equality. On the other hand, multicultural and feminist rhetoric is mobilized "as the key to a post-racist world of freedom and opportunity."[42] The selective incorporation of racial and gender difference "compose an assimilative multicultural order that makes US global hegemony appear just and fair."[43] The latter, the neoliberal multicultural politics

---

38. Aksikas and Andrews, "Neoliberalism, Law and Culture," 745.
39. Barker, "Territory as Analytic," 31.
40. Hong, *Death beyond Disavowal*, 17.
41. Luibhéid, "'Treated neither with Respect nor with Dignity,'" 21.
42. Melamed, "Reading Tehran in *Lolita*," 78.
43. Melamed, "Reading Tehran in *Lolita*," 82; and Melamed, *Represent and Destroy*.

of recognition, reduce racial, gendered, and sexual "difference" to individual identities to be recognized by or included in the settler colonial polity, thereby denying ongoing structural violence, marginalization, and poverty. Exclusion from and selective inclusion/incorporation into white possession is thereby framed as a matter of "personal responsibility" and having "choices" on an increasingly level market / playing field that, as in the former neoliberal discourse, is itself a conduit of inequality. For Indigenous peoples, the multicultural politics of recognition are especially pernicious, reframing Native Americans as one racial group among many seeking individualized rights and incorporation into settler colonial systems. While colonialism is a racial project of white accumulation binding race and land, and Indigenous people are racialized (categorized and marginalized according to race), the legal framing of Indigenous peoples as a racial group erases their unique status as a political group, obstructing Indigenous sovereignty and efforts for decolonization.

Furthermore, the late twentieth-century disavowal of Indigenous dispossession and living Indigenous peoples, as neoliberalism was becoming hegemonic, is especially significant not only because settler colonialism is the framework through which neoliberalism is operationalized but because the late 1960s and 1970s brought an unprecedented period of Indigenous activism and media visibility that threatened the extant public pedagogy of US empire. The concept of Indigenous self-determination (self-rule, economic self-sufficiency, and cultural survival) was formulated through collective Indigenous resistance to termination (ending all federal support and treaties, with the intent of assimilation) via organizations like the National Congress of American Indians (NCAI) and American Indian Movement (AIM).[44] In the Self-Determination Era (1970s–present) of US national policy for Native nations, multiple laws passed in response to Indigenous activism and wider awareness generated by media coverage of high profile actions, such as the occupation of Alcatraz (1969–71), the "Trail of Broken Treaties" march and occupation of the Bureau of Indian Affairs (BIA) in Washington, DC (1972), the occupation of Wounded Knee (1973), and Sacheen Littlefeathers's refusal to accept Marlon Brando's Oscar for *Godfather* at the 1973 Academy Awards to raise awareness of Indigenous struggles for self-determination and in solidarity with Wounded Knee protestors. Less visible but also powerful challenges to pedagogies of empire included Indigenous feminist and queer activism and knowledge production that emphasized the intimacies between land and Indigenous peoples and illuminated how undoing heteropatriarchy was necessary to decolonial projects.[45]

---

44. Deloria and Lytle, *Nations Within*, 216.

45. Driskill et al., *Queer Indigenous Studies*; Barker, *Critically Sovereign*; and Lee-Oliver et al., "Imperialism, Settler Colonialism, and Indigeneity," 226–56.

14 • INTRODUCTION

Struggles for sovereignty underscored US federal legislation such as the Indian Self-Determination and Education Assistance Act (1975), Indian Religious Freedom Act (1978), and Indian Child Welfare Act (ICWA; 1978), designed to remedy the ongoing systemic removal of Native children from their communities by granting tribal governments jurisdiction in custody, foster care, and adoption cases. While these much-celebrated[46] laws increased tribal authority, US law defined and adjudicated it, and state authority fundamentally conflicts with Indigenous epistemologies emphasizing reciprocal, nonviolent relationships with land and the natural world.[47] Moreover, empire powerfully extends itself through the "intimate domains—sex, sentiment, domestic arrangement, and child rearing."[48] The US government has long used Indigenous children to attack tribal sovereignty, for a tribe without children will cease to exist. Forcing Native Americans into heteropatriarchal kinship arrangements in connection with individualized commodification of land was also a tool of conquest.[49] As neoliberalism calcified, these policies and Supreme Court cases such as *Oliphant v. Suquamish Indian Tribe* (1978), which denied tribal courts jurisdiction over non-Natives who commit crimes on tribal lands, recognized Indigenous peoples as a racial rather than political group.

Moreover, directly eliminative settler colonial efforts persisted in the Nixon administration's appropriation of Indigenous self-determination with ongoing gendered, heterosexualized juridical dispossession[50] as part of Republican "New Federalism," which removed federal barriers to the fiscal autonomy of local communities—often by reducing federal aid. While Nixon declared an end to termination policy, it persisted through financialization and austerity. Continuing the Johnson administration's War on Poverty, which identified overpopulation as a cause of impoverishment, under the Nixon administration's generously funded "family planning" policies, sterilization abuse against Indigenous women at the hands of the Indian Health Service (IHS) was rampant. Indigenous women were targeted for sterilization, often in connection with welfare receipt, and labeled with long-standing stereotypes about Indigenous women's fecundity and poor parenting as proof of Natives' inferiority to white settlers.[51]

---

46. Fletcher, Singel, and Fort, *Indian Child Welfare Act at 30*.

47. Barker, "For Whom Sovereignty Matters," 19.

48. Stoler, "Tense and Tender Ties," 829. Feminist scholars have well-theorized the "intimacies of empire." See McClintock, *Imperial Leather*; McClintock, "No Longer"; and Stoler, *Race and the Education of Desire*.

49. Piatote, *Domestic Subjects*; Deer, *Beginning and End of Rape*; and Smith, *Conquest*.

50. Williams, *Like a Loaded Weapon*; and Rifkin, "Around 1978," 169–206.

51. Torpy, "Native American Women and Coerced Sterilization."

THE PUBLIC PEDAGOGY OF US EMPIRE · 15

Meanwhile, white liberal counterculture fetishized supposed Indigenous mysticism, environmentalism, and unity, updating the "noble savage" stereotype for the civil rights era[52] in ways that registered in mainstream popular culture—for example, in the "Crying Indian" antipollution public service announcement commercial[53] and a spate of revisionist Westerns and other films that sympathized with Indigenous peoples or instrumentalized them to critique social ills such as racism and the Vietnam War. Broadly, gendered, (hetero)sexualized, pan-Indigenous dress, arts, and culture supplanted a "costumed affiliation" with Indigeneity for legal claims and rights to governance, territories, and cultures.[54] Indigenous decolonial struggles were reduced to inclusion or visibility in the new multiculture at large as baldly necropolitical austerity policies continued to dispossess living Indigenous peoples.

Then Reagan's brand of "New Federalism" included pioneering (pun intended) a "termination by accountants,"[55] that in its co-optation of Indigenous self-determination and sovereignty with more financialization and austerity was a testing site and paradigm for quintessentially neoliberal policies and rhetoric that targeted racialized immigrant women and women of color. To enduring consequence, what we might call Reagan's frontier ethic of development was offered up as the means to restore US pride and prosperity following the Vietnam War and stagflation. Reaganite "personal responsibility" politics functioned as backlash against the excesses of 1960s and 1970s social movements and any lingering social safety net, casting dependency as crippling to individuals, groups, and society. Policies furthered antifederalism via deregulation, privatization, liberalization and integration of global markets, consumerism, and increased defense spending.[56] Federal funding for programs for Native people, including healthcare, water, sanitary facilities, education—the things that quite literally made life livable when reservations and Indigenous people living in urban areas were already disproportionately impoverished—was decimated. Despite Indigenous peoples' distinct relationship to the welfare state (a complex matter of treaty obligations owed to Indigenous people, see chapter 2), Reagan framed this iteration of termination as personal or individualized self-determination: Native people would be liberated from federal dependence with austerity, private sector development, and

---

52. P. Deloria, *Playing Indian*, 159–61; and Kilpatrick, *Celluloid Indians*, 67.

53. The "Crying Indian" actor, Iron Eyes Cody, identified as Native American but was the son of Italian immigrants. This points to the complex connections between the representational politics of Indigeneity and immigration.

54. Barker, "Introduction: Critically Sovereign," 2–3.

55. Morris, "Termination by Accountants," 63–69.

56. Rowland and Jones, *Reagan at Westminster*.

development of tribal natural resources.[57] In a dizzying radio interview, James Watt, Reagan's Secretary of the Interior, did not bother with subtlety. Watts framed all federal support for Indigenous peoples as oppression that caused "overwhelming social problems, including drug abuse, alcoholism, unemployment, divorce and venereal disease." He also linked "liberating" Indigenous peoples with austerity to anti-Blackness.[58] The Reagan administration's neoliberal assault on welfare, which baldly targeted women of color, crystalizing the enduring "welfare queen" stereotype, and racialized immigrants, intersected with slashing federal funding for programs for Native people and casting Native people as welfare dependents. In gendered, sexualized terms, settler colonialism was thereby authorized in neoliberal policy and media: "freeing" Native peoples from welfare was the lynchpin of their ongoing dispossession, while casting people of color as lazy cheats undeserving of welfare was the lynchpin of their ongoing containment. Together these public pedagogies protected and furthered white possession in a new phase of empire.

Indigenous nations that succeeded within the neoliberal framework also experienced the gendered, racialized, settler colonial limits of the multicultural politics of recognition, taking their personal responsibility too far for white possessive logics. While the dispossession and exploitation of Indigenous lands at the hands of the federal government and various industries was nothing new as the literal basis of US empire, "the 1980s saw an unprecedented wave of private industry hit the reservations" with extractive capitalism that was devastating for many nations.[59] Some nations responded by developing gaming industries. Gaming, successful for only some nations and controversial among both Indigenous peoples and non-Natives, engendered a new twist on the "savage" stereotype: the wealthy, often criminal Native gamer who takes taxpayers' money.[60] These two public pedagogies, underscoring federal budget cuts and surfacing in media, are connected to earlier settler fears of Indigenous sovereignty, wealth, and militarism but became prevalent from the 1980s as part of neoliberalization, that is, Indigenous peoples apparently threatened white possession as *both* uncivilized welfare dependents and shrewd, thieving gamers.

---

57. Reagan, "State of the Union Address," February 4, 1986, transcript, http://www.reagan.utexas.edu/archives/speeches/1986/20486a.htm. See also Hertzberg, "Reaganomics on the Reservation," *New Republic,* November 2, 1982, 15–18.

58. Robert Sangeorge, "Interior Secretary James Watt Called Reservations 'an Example of the Failure of Socialism,'" *United Press International,* January 18, 1983, https://www.upi.com/Archives/1983/01/18/Interior-Secretary-James-Watt-Tuesday-called-Indian-reservations-an/2653411714000/.

59. Kilpatrick, *Celluloid Indians,* 102.

60. Kilpatrick, *Celluloid Indians,* 103; and Dunbar-Ortiz and Gilio-Whitaker, *"All the Real Indians Died Off,"* 117–22.

On the heels of highly visible Indigenous struggles for sovereignty and decolonization, ostensibly more progressive US policy for Indigenous peoples, the popularity of countercultural and mainstream "costumed affiliations" with Indigeneity, and in the midst of inaugural neoliberal policy and rhetoric targeting Indigenous peoples, they were largely absent—or *absented*—from the most public of the public pedagogies calcifying US neoliberal empire in the 1980s. Differentially racialized im/migrants were centered in ways that, like *Fort Apache, the Bronx* but much less obviously, were inseparable from Indigenous dispossession and settler colonialism. As mentioned, disavowal of ongoing colonialism and systemic racial violence is necessary for the overtly negative as well as "positive" aspects of neoliberal multiculturalism: selective gendered, sexualized, racialized inclusion in the settler colonial state—in other words, incorporation into what Scott Lauria Morgensen calls "settler citizenship."[61] As in the past, white possession overdetermined the neoliberal "immigration emergency." This began in the nineteenth century. As frontier battles ended and federal policy for Native people was formulated, the US federal immigration system (and overseas imperial projects) cohered, producing the nation and citizenship as sites of inequality within a dual system that legally favors immigrants who serve white, heteropatriarchal, middle-class interests. Other im/migrants were criminalized and/or rendered disposable. Early twentieth-century policies and practices codified the two immigration tracks:

> one for admission and settlement by primarily migrants from Northern and Western Europe, structured around a heteronuclear family with a male breadwinner; and another track that built on the history of exclusion of Chinese and other Asian migrants while making migrants from Mexico, Central and South America, and the Caribbean primarily temporary, exploitable labor that could be summoned when needed then dismissed.[62]

In the ascendant neoliberal context, exclusion of racialized aliens at national borders and containment within them occurred alongside and as a complement to the economic and political imperatives of the day: Multicultural inclusivity was mitigated in the name of "safety" in the Nixon administration's extension of the War on Poverty and anti-immigrant xenophobia. Then the Reagan administration passed the Immigration Reform and Control Act (IRCA), which was quintessentially neoliberal immigration legislation that fused the multicultural politics of recognition and labor exploitation (amnesty provisions granted disproportionately to undocumented Mexican men) with

---

61. Morgensen, *Spaces between Us,* 91. See also 17–20; 44–49.
62. Luibhéid, "'Treated neither with Respect nor with Dignity,'" 20–21.

increasing racialized, gendered illegalization, deportation, and border militarization that targeted Latinx and especially Mexican migrants and set the stage for subsequent immigration legislation. Additionally, the contemporaneous Reaganite "War on Drugs" was followed by the "War on Terror." The latter dominated national politics until the Trump administration attempted to "make America great again" (incidentally Reagan's campaign slogan for his second successful run for president was "Let's Make America Great Again") by recentering overt heteropatriarchal white supremacy in policy, policing, and rhetoric and inciting domestic racial terror.

As historically, mediated public pedagogy about Indigenous peoples and immigrants elaborated on the white possessive archive. As media studies scholar Douglas Kellner states, media does the work of "educating us on how to behave and what to think, feel, believe, fear, and desire—and what not to."[63] Media swung between and across lessons about elimination, exclusion, and selective incorporation, often drawing from and elaborating upon originary colonial stereotypes of Indigenous peoples as living Indigenous peoples disappeared in mainstream media. The "vanishing Indian" myth, or notion that Indigenous people are nearly extinct, arose at the turn of the twentieth century when Indigenous peoples' wars of resistance ended, and colonial victory was clear. As Jean M. O'Brien (Ojibwe) argues, this was a local as well as national process. New England settlers established their modernity in contrast to Indigenous peoples' lack of it: through the written word, pageants, commemorations, monument building, and lecture hall performances, "the colonial regime is constructed to be the 'first' to bring 'civilization' and authentic history to the region." New England settlers also thereby relegated Indigenous peoples to the past, asserting their extinction. This denial of Indigenous modernity and a narrative of extinction extended nationally.[64] Indigenous populations had indeed been diminished by slavery, disease, war, and Christianization/assimilation. However, the extinction narrative justified ongoing attempts to seize Indigenous lands and resources[65] and preserved the mythology of the US as an inclusive liberal, then multicultural *neoliberal*, democracy despite such attempts. Film and television have long frozen Natives—usually presented as a monolithic, generic racial group—in a pre-1900 and therefore "vanishing" context. For instance, this is evident in classic Westerns such as *Stagecoach* (1939), more "sympathetic" 1970s revisionist Westerns that critiqued aspects of US empire by instrumentalizing "Native" stories, and blockbusters *Dances With Wolves* (1990) and *The Last*

---

63. Kellner, "Cultural Studies, Multiculturalism, and Media Culture," 6.

64. O'Brien, *Firsting and Lasting*, xv.

65. Dunbar-Ortiz and Gilio-Whitaker, *"All the Real Indians Died Off,"* 9–10.

of the Mohicans (1992). In these later, ostensibly "sympathetic" films, Indigenous peoples are still effectively/affectively relegated to the past, represented as essentially extinct, or appropriately dying out when confronted by superior white Euro-American civilization. In connection with the turn to multiculturalism in the 1990s, mainstream representations increasingly employed Indigenous actors (rather than white actors in "Red face") and paid more attention to Indigenous nations' distinctions and linguistic accuracy (rather than depicting a pan-"Indianness" and including dialogue with made-up or woefully inaccurate Indigenous languages). A few more nuanced mainstream representations of present-day Indigenous peoples, such as the award-winning television show *Northern Exposure* (1990–95), were also produced. But these were exceptions and by no means unproblematic, and, of course, mainstream media capitalized on the trendy multiculturalism of the day. In a host of cultural texts, the "vanishing Indian" is also referenced in an "untamed," "wild," available landscape[66] awaiting a white US American cowboy like Reagan—or the right kind of immigrant or corporation—to develop it.

Simultaneously, mediated immigration public pedagogy was ubiquitous. On one hand, news media, films, and TV shows about Latinx drug dealers and gang bangers like *Scarface* (1983), *Colors* (1988), and *Miami Vice* (1984–90) and films about unfit, criminal Latina mothers like *Mi Vida Loca* (1993) proliferated, warning the public in by now all-too-familiar terms that the "immigration emergency" was gendered and racialized and that border control was imperative. As in *Ft. Apache, the Bronx,* in these and other representations of racialized aliens, Indigenous peoples were referenced as the original ungrievable, "savage" enemies of US empire.

On the other hand, there was "multiculturalism[, which] collapses difference into smooth trajectories of inclusion and asylum that have depended upon narratives of 'vanishing natives' and indigenous dispossession."[67] The "nation of immigrants" mediated thread of neoliberalism included popular 1980s films and TV shows like *Moscow on the Hudson* (1984), *Perfect Strangers* (1986–93), and *Golden Girls* (1985–92) that featured lovable, increasingly affluent and assimilating, and of course self-supporting, patriotic white ethnic immigrants. News media magazines such as *Newsweek* and *Time* celebrated this national imaginary and announced that Asian immigrants and Asian Americans had transitioned from excludable aliens to "model minorities," who with their increasing affluence and assimilation provided an example to other people of color. (The "model minority" thesis has since been mobilized

---

66. Rifkin, *Settler Common Sense.*
67. Byrd, "Arriving on a Different Shore," 175.

again and again to argue against affirmative action and to minimize anti-Asian violence). The profligate 1986 Statue of Liberty Centennial celebration and Ellis Island Museum also naturalized this national mythology of a fair system that welcomed the personally responsible immigrant of any race and invited them, if they played by white heteropatriarchal rules, to settle on stolen Indigenous land that was invisible as such because Indigenous people had vanished. Multicultural immigrant incorporation narratives in media therefore also worked assiduously to support white possession.

Occasionally the co-constitution of settler colonialism and racialized anti-immigration underpinning US neoliberal empire has been clear if not transparent in public pedagogy. The post-9/11 War on Terror included a regime of detention without trial or charges, deportation, torture, and US military codes describing Osama Bin Laden as "Geronimo" and the use of "tomahawk" missiles in overseas military strikes. The neoliberal militarization of US borders and immigration enforcement has also "deepened the experience of violent occupation" for Indigenous peoples. For example, the land of the Tohono O'odham nation spans the US–Mexico border. They are frequently harassed by Border Patrol agents on their own land, and the walling, checkpoints, and presence of helicopters and drones has "harmed the earth and plants, disrupted traditional ways of life, and reflects ongoing abrogation of the nation's sovereignty."[68] More often than not, however, some measure of multiculturalism is hegemonic on the left and right, even after Trumpism brought flagrant white supremacy and heteropatriarchy back out of the closet.

At the time of writing, settler coloniality and racialized anti-immigration under the Biden administration continue to propel the white possessive US neoliberal empire-building. During the 2020 election, the Biden-Harris campaign proposed a plan to "uphold[ ] the US's trust responsibility to tribal nations, strengthening the Nation-to-Nation relationship between the United States and Indian tribes, and working to empower tribal nations to govern their own communities and make their own decisions,"[69] and the administration's COVID-19 relief bill provided more federal funds to Indigenous peoples than ever before. But at the same time, Biden, a key player in neoliberal policy and rhetoric first as a senator and as then as vice president to Barak Obama, undermined Indigenous sovereignty by likening tribal-nations to states in his relief speech. The historic appointment of Rep. Deb Haaland (Pueblo of Laguna and Jemez Pueblo heritage; D-New Mexico), the first Indigenous person nominated and confirmed to serve in the cabinet as secretary

---

68. Luibhéid, "'Treated neither with Respect nor with Dignity,'" 28.

69. "Biden-Harris Plan for Tribal Nations," joebiden.com, accessed March 22, 2021, https://joebiden.com/tribalnations/.

of the interior, emblematizes the multicultural politics of recognition in/by a settler colonial structure. Protecting Native children according to white possessive logics also remains a lynchpin of Indigenous dispossession. In 2022 in *Oklahoma v. Castro-Huerta,* the Supreme Court ruled in favor of the state of Oklahoma, allowing the state to prosecute a non-Native man convicted of child neglect against a Native child on Cherokee land. The court dramatically increased states' power over Indigenous tribal nations and lands, as such cases were previously under the jurisdiction of tribal courts or the federal government. The far right has also repeatedly used court cases against ICWA—often consolidating custody battles over white families seeking to adopt Indigenous children—to attack tribal sovereignty and civil rights writ large. The systemic removal of Indigenous children continues to be excessive, yet such cases, one of which reached the Supreme Court, claim ICWA racially discriminates against non-Native adoptive parents and Native children alike.[70] While the Supreme Court upheld ICWA in 2023, challenges to ICWA illuminate how the multicultural politics of recognition continue to be weaponized to serve white possession.

In terms of im/migration, the Biden administration promised progressive immigration reform that it has not delivered. The draconian neoliberal system in place before the Trump administration that exacerbated gendered, sexualized, racialized violences and cruelties remains as the Biden administration seeks to undo some of the most overtly problematic aspects of it while upholding others. For instance, Deferred Action for Childhood Arrivals (DACA), which allows undocumented children brought into the US a path to legalization, was renewed. The policy has provided meaningful difference to recipients, who are disproportionately Latinx. However, it allows the US to extract value from recipients without giving them the social benefits of legal status and doubles down on the multicultural politics of recognition with rigorous requirements demanding respectability according to white possessive metrics. Accordingly, respectable DACA recipients are celebrated as assets to the US in the media.[71] At the time of writing, the Biden administration proposed an asylum ban similar to the Trump administration policies that were blocked by federal courts. As in the past, the destiny of neoliberal US empire continues to manifest via entanglement of Indigenous dispossession and anti-immigration.

•

---

70. See Nagle, *This Land* podcast.

71. Luibhéid, "'Treated neither with Respect nor with Dignity,'" 27.

This brief parallel(ed) history of policy and media about Native Americans and im/migrants, elaborated upon throughout this book, points to how ongoing Indigenous dispossession works in tandem with differentially racialized immigration discourses to comprise the public pedagogy of US empire historically and into the neoliberal context. To protect and further white possession, the land must continue to be emptied of Indigenous peoples (cast as hostile savages or at least uncivilized, primitive "savages," both appropriately vanishing in the face of a superior race and/or "civilization") and the state must continue to contain racialized immigrants. Additionally, the past and present violences of colonization and racial capitalism must be disavowed for the multicultural politics of recognition, which incorporates some Indigenous people and im/migrants who serve white possessive logics into the settler state, to have gravitas.

CONTEXT: SETTLER COLONIALISM AND RACIAL CAPITALISM

The relationship between Indigenous peoples and immigrants in the US is part of a long, fraught history beginning with conquest and colonization and shaped by racialized, gendered, sexualized distinctions between forced, coerced, and voluntary migration in connection with labor to serve white accumulation. In parsing out the public pedagogy of US empire, my work is most closely aligned with and builds on recent scholarship on the co-constitution of Indigenous dispossession and racial capitalism and how the settler colonial logics of elimination (of Indigenous peoples), exploitation and exclusion (of populations of color), and the selective inclusion of both groups as a mechanism of settler coloniality "operate on a moving spectrum of biopolitical violence."[72] However, because the relation between im/migrants, people of color, and settler colonialism is debated among scholars, activists, and the people(s) in question, the following section outlines the contours of the debate.

Broadly, CIS scholars emphasize that "land establishes the relationship Indigenous peoples have with the colonizer"[73] and that "Indigenous relationship-to-place" is unique and critical to the survival of Indigenous peoples.[74] Indigenous feminist and queer frameworks emphasize intimacy between Indigenous peoples and land that preceded colonization and is key

---

72. Day, *Alien Capital,* 25; and Wolfe, *Traces of History.*
73. Day, *Alien Capital,* 26.
74. Deloria and Wildcat, *Power and Place.*

THE PUBLIC PEDAGOGY OF US EMPIRE · 23

to decolonization[75] given that US imperialism is "predicated on gendered, sexist, and homophobic discrimination and violence" connecting land and bodies as the sites of trauma.[76] Generally Indigenous worldviews and epistemologies—which are not a monolith—view land in terms of kinship, mutuality, and responsibility, not property/rights,[77] and as "the social and political order of Indigenous governance and society."[78] Settler colonialism is an ongoing structure of genocide, spatial removal, and biological and cultural assimilation to eliminate the Native as Native[79] or contain Indigeneity, to commodify land as and for white property. It is, as Glen Coulthard (Yellowknives Dene) states, "territorially acquisitive in perpetuity."[80] Maintaining intimacy with and responsibilities to land and their interconnected geopolitical systems, including various structures of collective subjectivity that are "unintelligible within the terms of US law and Indian policy,"[81] puts Indigenous peoples fundamentally at odds with settler colonial authority, making them perpetually vulnerable to "surveillance and violence because, in practice, [land] places Indigenous bodies between settlers and their money."[82]

The white possessive logics of US empire, rooted in Indigenous dispossession, also target racialized groups within and attempting to enter US borders. The status of Black US Americans and racialized im/migrants is, however, debated among Indigenous activists and CIS scholars. Because im/migrants, regardless of race, settle on Indigenous lands, some, such as Haunani-Kay Trask (Kanaka Maoli), argue that "immigrant" is "a particularly celebrated American gloss for 'settler,'"[83] as acquiring Indigenous land "has been the central factor that has shaped the relationships between Indigenous peoples and immigrant[s]."[84] The status of nonwhite immigrants as settlers is about their relationship to Indigenous people in a settler state and not their political power (or lack of it). For instance, Native Hawaiians experience a doubled history of colonization: first "discovery" and settlement by European and US businessmen and missionaries followed by the descendants of Japanese, Chinese, and

---

75. Goeman and Denetdale, "Native Feminisms," special issue, *Wicazo Sa Review*.

76. Barker, "Introduction: Critically Sovereign," 15; Goeman and Denetdale, "Guest Editor's Introduction," 9–13; and Deer, *Beginning and End of Rape*.

77. V. Deloria, *God Is Red*; and Corntassel, "Toward Sustainable Self-Determination," 105–32.

78. Nichols, "Theft Is Property!," 3–28.

79. Wolfe, "Settler Colonialism and the Elimination of the Native," 388.

80. Coulthard, *Red Skin, White Masks*, 152.

81. Rifkin, "Erotics of Sovereignty," 175.

82. Simpson, "Land as Pedagogy," 9.

83. Trask, "Settlers of Color and 'Immigrant' Hegemony," 46.

84. Dunbar-Ortiz and Gilio-Whitaker, *"All the Real Indians Died Off,"* 7.

24 · INTRODUCTION

Filipino plantation workers rising to dominance in the islands.[85] While the Hawaiian context is unique, other scholars likewise argue that immigrating (to the US mainland, to other settler colonies) is part of "a colonizing fantasy, where 'progress' was supposedly available to everyone in European societies" and immigrants of color often participate in the "colonizing fantasy" despite their intended exclusion from it.[86] Therefore people and im/migrants of color are subject to specific structures of racism *and* also structurally located as settlers: "there are no good settlers; there are no good colonizers."[87]

Other scholars distinguish between white settlers and Black people and migrants of color given histories of forced and coerced migration, exclusion and exploitation, and ongoing white supremacist violence. Although US racial discourse is often organized around a Black–white binary that erases Native people, some anti-Blackness scholars have powerfully addressed the connections between pedagogies of empire that dehumanize Black and Indigenous people. Cheryl Harris's seminal work showed that whiteness is the full property of US citizenship derived in colonial uses of the law, legally defining persons as free or slave, conferring tangible economic benefits. Whiteness is a possession that operates proprietarily in law through the appropriation of Indigenous lands and the enslavement of Africans.[88] Jack D. Forbes (Powhatan-Renape) was one of the first Black studies scholars to focus on Black and Native relations in *Africans and Native Americans: The Language of Race and the Evolution of Black-Red Peoples* (1993). Subsequent scholarship such as the anthology edited by Tiya Miles and Sharon P. Holland, *Crossing Waters, Crossing Worlds: The African Diaspora in Indian Country* (2006), examined slavery among the Five Civilized Tribes. Both Angela Davis and Ruthie Wilson Gilmore have worked extensively on carcerality as a key feature of settler colonialism and racial capitalism.[89] Recently Tiffany Lethabo King, drawing from and expanding on Black and African diaspora scholarship that challenges Black and Indigenous dehumanization in Western thought and practice, such as Sylvia Wynter's work, interrogated how anti-Blackness and Indigenous genocide structure white supremacy and the enduring "quotidian spectacle of death as conquest."[90]

---

85. Fujikane, "Introduction: Asian Settler Colonialism in the US Colony of Hawai'i," 9–11.

86. Snelgrove, Dhamoon, and Corntassel, "Unsettling Settler Colonialism," 6.

87. Snelgrove, Dhamoon, and Corntassel, "Unsettling Settler Colonialism," 4. See also Wolfe, "Recuperating Binarism," 263.

88. Harris, "Whiteness as Property," 1707–91.

89. See Davis, *Freedom Is a Constant Struggle*; and Gilmore, *Abolition Geography*.

90. King, *Black Shoals*, 11. See also King, "Labor's Aphasia"; and King, "Racial Ecologies."

THE PUBLIC PEDAGOGY OF US EMPIRE • 25

Regarding racialized im/migrants, Evelyn Nakano Glenn described "the settler colonial mobilization of race and gender to manage 'exogenous others'" as including and moving between the poles of 'elimination' and coercive 'exploitation'" of Indigenous peoples, Black people, and other people of color.[91] Daniel Kanstroom explored the interchange between dispossessive Native American Law and deportation law, arguing, "Indians were, from the earliest days of European settlement, treated like aliens."[92] Anthologies such as *Transnational Crossroads: Remapping the Americas and the Pacific* (2012), edited by Camilla Fojas and Rudy P. Guevarra, and *Militarized Currents: Toward a Decolonized Future in Asia and the Pacific* (2010), edited by Setsu Shigematsu and Keith L. Camacho, interrogate the "intimacies between empires": the "complicated legacies of overlapping colonialisms on gendered, racialized subjects in the Americas, Asia, and the Pacific Islands."[93] In *Alien Capital: Asian Racialization and the Logic of Settler Colonialism* (2016), Iyko Day examined the "triangulation of Native, alien, and settler." Day traces the

> widely divergent conditions of voluntary and forced migration that are central features of the United States' specific configuration as a settler colony. In the contemporary context, the racialized vulnerability to deportation of undocumented, guest-worker, or other provisional migrant populations similarly exceed the conceptual boundaries that attend "the immigrant." Our awareness of these distinctions does not absolve any of these groups from being willing or unwitting participants in a settler colonial structure that is driven to eliminate Indigenous people. However, folding them into a generalized settler position through voluntaristic assumptions constrains our ability to understand how their racialized vulnerability and disposability supports a settler colonial project.[94]

Jodi A. Byrd, Alyosha Goldstein, Jodi Melamed, and Chandan Reddy, editors of the 2018 *Social Text* special issue, "Economies of Dispossession: Indigeneity, Race, Capitalism," theorized Indigenous dispossession and racial capitalism as fundamentally co-constitutive. The anthology *Colonial Racial Capitalism* (2022), edited by Jodi A. Byrd, Lisa Marie Cacho, Brian Jordan Jefferson, and Susan Koshy, explores the entanglements of anti-Blackness, Indigenous dispossession, racialized anti-immigration, and colonialism throughout the

---

91. Glenn, "Settler Colonialism as Structure," 60.

92. Kanstroom, *Deportation Nation*, 64.

93. Lew, "Intimacies between Empires," 189.

94. Day, *Alien Capital*, 20–21. See also Patel, "Nationalist Narratives, Immigration and Coloniality."

globe. Elsewhere Byrd used the term "arrivant" to describe racialized people forced into the Americas by Euro-American colonialism and imperialism.[95] Byrd explains that "the colonization of indigenous lands and peoples by the United States functions not so much as a binary between settlers and natives but through a series of recognitions and misrecognitions that coerce settlers, *arrivants,* and natives into service as proxies, agents, and at times beneficiaries, however undesired and unwanted, of the processes that have stripped land, lives, and nations away from the indigenous peoples who have always been here."[96] Some other texts that broadly explore settler colonialism and racialization include Patrick Wolfe's magisterial *Traces of History: Elementary Structures of Race* (2016) and Brenna Bhandar's *On Colonial Lives of Property: Law, Land, and Racial Regimes of Ownership* (2018), which argues that colonial property law is the basis for Indigenous dispossession and the establishment of whiteness as human, tying subjectivity to land and making "rights" (property rights) dependent upon Indigenous dispossession. Important in-depth considerations of one racialized migrant group in the triangulation of Native, alien, and settler include Monisha Das Gupta's work on how settler colonialism mediates immigration regulation for Mexican migrants in Hawai'i,[97] Day's *Alien Capital* (Asian North Americans), Manu Karuka's *Empire's Tracks: Indigenous Nations, Chinese Workers, and the Transcontinental Railroad* (2019; Chinese migrants), and Quynh Nhu Le's *Unsettled Solidarities: Asian and Indigenous Cross-Representations in the Américas* (2019). The concluding chapter of *Queer and Trans Migrations: Dynamics of Illegalization, Detention, and Deportation* (2020), edited by Karma R. Chávez and Eithne Luibhéid, puts CIS and im/migration studies scholars in dialogue to illuminate how "US citizenship stems from and reproduces settler colonialist, racializing, heterogendering, and anti-poor logics. Immigration controls including illegalization, detention, and deportation support this form of US citizenship."[98]

My interrogation of the public pedagogy of US empire builds on scholarship on the co-constitution of settler colonialism and racial violence. To expand upon my previous work on anti-immigration by reconsidering it as indivisibly entangled with Indigenous dispossession, here I foreground CIS methodologies and Indigenous dispossession. While my central intervention is the argument that US empire was founded and furthered via entangled public pedagogies about Indigenous peoples and racialized im/migrants, as Leece

---

95. Byrd, *Transit of Empire.*

96. Byrd, "Arriving on a Different Shore," 175.

97. Das Gupta and Haglund, "Mexican Migration to Hawai'i," 455–80.

98. Luibhéid, "'Treated neither with Respect nor with Dignity,'" 32; and Lee-Oliver et al., "Imperialism, Settler Colonialism, and Indigeneity," 226–56.

Lee-Oliver (Blackfeet/Choctaw/Cherokee/Wyandot) argues, settler colonialism and coracialization of Indigenous peoples

> are at the root of imperial militarization, domestic policing, violence against those viewed as marginalized—aka dependent—and gender nonconforming peoples. In the United States, Native America is ground zero. The technologies of oppression were tested, practiced, sophisticated, and refined into a network of interlocking laws and institutions—ideologies, with assigned arbiters and practitioners, from vigilantes to homemakers, who operate and mutually produce the nation-state by performing nativist belonging in a variety of ways.[99]

Indigenous gender, sexuality, and feminist studies scholarship, activism, and knowledge production also deeply informs and anchors my project. Devon Abbot Mihesuah (Choctaw) reminds us, "There is no one voice among Natives because there is no such thing as the culturally and racially monolithic Native woman."[100] Reducing Indigenous peoples to a monolith is a settler tactic, and some Indigenous women reject the label of "feminist" for various reasons. Therefore, my methodology is influenced by and strives to honor the fine-grained, often Indigenous nation-specific, landed analyses of how "gender conceptions continue to underpin and affirm the US nation-state and its global imperialism."[101] This is exemplified in texts such as the *Wicazo Sa Review* issue, "Native Feminisms: Legacies, Interventions, and Indigenous Sovereignties" (2009), edited by Mishuana Goeman (Tonawanda Band of Seneca) and Jennifer Nez Denetdale (Diné/Navajo), and the anthology *Critically Sovereign: Indigenous Gender, Sexuality, and Feminist Studies* (2017), edited by Barker, and other pathbreaking and current Indigenous feminist, gender, and sexuality studies scholarship, activism, and knowledge production.[102] Goeman points out that addressing "history at the level of the materiality of the body" and theories of the flesh like those articulated by Cherrie Moraga and other Chicana feminists in the groundbreaking *This Bridge Called My Back: Writings by Radical Women of Color* (1981), is also critical for Native women given that "the body feels the brute force of colonization."[103] Queer Indigenous and Two

---

99. Lee-Oliver et al., "Imperialism, Settler Colonialism, and Indigeneity," 232.

100. Mihesuah, *Indigenous American Women*, 7.

101. Goeman and Denetdale, "Guest Editor's Introduction," 10. See also Barker, "Introduction: Critically Sovereign," 1–44.

102. For example, Moreton-Robinson, *Talkin' Up to the White Woman*; and Green, *White Possessive*.

103. Goeman, "Ongoing Storms and Struggles," 111.

28 · INTRODUCTION

Spirit activism and theorizing that was inspired by and markedly expanded queer women of color theorizing,[104] connecting land- and body-based epistemologies, also underpins my analysis of pedagogies of empire.

I also build on immigration scholarship that grapples with the intersections of race, gender, sexuality, and migration,[105] Latinx studies,[106] scholarship on Indigenous Latinxs and the intersections of Indigenous and Latinx identities and experiences in relation to coloniality,[107] Asian American studies,[108] and whiteness/white ethnic studies.[109] Broadly, im/migration studies focuses on social inequality, particularly through the lens of race and class and, more frequently now, gender and sexuality, and how various groups of im/migrants have assimilated and/or struggled for justice in the US. In scholarship and among activists, im/migrant "rights"/inclusion are often (but by no means always) presented as the solution to histories of forced and coerced migration, labor exploitation, and socioeconomic and political exclusion. And as Trump administration immigration policies aggressively reminded us, the need for im/migrant rights and protection from the US government and its various actors remains urgent. Yet im/migrant activism and im/migration studies often leave out or at best only tangentially address Indigenous peoples and settler colonialism. Indigenous peoples are often only legible in terms of their mobility or migrations within the US, if at all. The "rights" and inclusion model of justice centered in multiculturalism and mainstream antiracist and feminist movements also reproduces Indigenous dispossession, obviating Indigenous sovereignty and geopoliticality and the centrality of land in Indigenous struggles for justice. US empire—US imperial globalization—has certainly "forced the world to move."[110] But while the points of US empire for Indigenous peoples and racialized immigrants are contrapuntal, necessitating comparative methodologies and connected struggles for justice, Indigenous

---

104. Morgensen, "Unsettling Queer Politics," 136–40.

105. For example, Luibhéid, *Entry Denied*; Luibhéid and Cantú, *Queer Migrations*; Cantú, *Sexuality of Migration*; Cacho, *Social Death*; Ngai, *Impossible Subjects*; Buff, *Deportation Terror*; and Chávez and Luibhéid, *Queer and Trans Migrations*.

106. For example, Rodriguez, *Sexual Futures, Queer Gestures*; Gutiérrez, *Fertile Matters*; Chavez, *Latino Threat*; Fregoso, *MeXicana Encounters*; Camacho, *Migrant Imaginaries*; Valdivia, *Latina in the Land of Hollywood*; Santa Ana, *Brown Tide Rising*; Molina-Guzman, *Dangerous Curves*; Molina-Guzman, *Latinas and Latinos on TV*; and Mendible, *From Bananas to Buttocks*.

107. For example, Castellanos, Nájera, and Aldama, *Comparative Indigeneities of the Américas*; Ramirez, *Standing Up to Colonial Power*; and Saldaña-Portillo, *Indian Given*.

108. For example, Hong, *Death beyond Disavowal*; E. Lee, *At America's Gates*; Kim, *Ends of Empire*; Jun, *Race for Citizenship*; and Ku, Manalansan, and Mannur, *Eating Asian America*.

109. For example, Jacobson, *Roots Too*; Jacobson, *Whiteness of a Different Color*; Roediger, *Working toward Whiteness*; Duffy, *Who's Your Paddy?*; and Sadowski-Smith, *New Immigrant Whiteness*.

110. Byrd, "Arriving on a Different Shore," 177.

THE PUBLIC PEDAGOGY OF US EMPIRE • 29

peoples' experiences of oppression are distinct from those of other groups: again, equivalency is a tool of colonialism.[111] To understand the US as an imperial and settler colonial framework, migration scholars (and activists) must understand Indigenous peoples as geopolitical entities rather than a racial group; Indigenous peoples must be legible beyond consideration of their mobility; and distinctions between the genocide and dispossession of Indigenous peoples, which points to specific issues of land rights, and displacement of migrants, who may or may not be Indigenous, must be parsed.[112] For instance, Indigenous women migrants, including lesbians, transgender, and cisgender women, are hypervulnerable to various structural violences, often without rights at every step of their journey.[113]

It bears repeating that the history of settler colonialism and consequent diasporas in the US depend upon vertical interactions "at the site of governmentality, the juridical, and legal recognition, on one hand, and the horizontal at the site of inclusion, affinity, and multicultural neoliberalism on the other"[114] that cannot be understood without grounding in the specificity of Indigenous materials, responses, and spaces. To unpack the entanglements of Indigenous dispossession and anti-immigration structuring the public pedagogy of US empire, this book centers CIS methodologies and especially Indigenous feminist and queer knowledge production, while also traversing across the boundaries and borders of critical race and ethnic studies, im/migration studies, and gender and sexuality studies, relocating the history of immigrant racialization within the development of settler colonialism and in relation to the ongoing Indigenous dispossession upon which it depends and with which it overlaps. Additionally, historically US empire has operated unevenly and asymmetrically to achieve its aims. Under neoliberalism

> local alliances, cultural projects, nationalist agendas, and economic policies work together, unevenly and often unpredictably, rife with conflict and contradiction, to redistribute the world's resources upward—money, security, healthcare, and mobility; knowledge and access to communication technologies; leisure, recreation, and pleasure; freedom—to procreate or not, to be sexually expressive or not, to work or not; political power—participatory access to democratic public life, and more . . . in short, resources of all kinds.[115]

---

111. Byrd, "Arriving on a Different Shore," 177–78.
112. Lee-Oliver et al., "Imperialism, Settler Colonialism, and Indigeneity," 243.
113. Speed, "States of Violence," 282.
114. Byrd, "Arriving on a Different Shore," 176–77.
115. Duggan, *Twilight of Equality*, 70–71.

This interrogation of pedagogies of empire is accordingly uneven and asymmetrical. Although my project cannot do justice to the staggering extent of US violence against Indigenous peoples and im/migrants of color and focuses on the machinations of empire rather than on modes of resistance to it (though some examples of resistance are touched on), I aim to expose and thereby help to dismantle the ongoing public pedagogy of US empire. The dynamics of US refugee policy, though clearly linked with processes of displacement, migration, and settlement,[116] are beyond the scope of this analysis. While in-depth exploration of anti-Blackness is also beyond the scope of this book, at points I discuss connections and continuities.

Chapters focus on how, to further white possession, the imperatives of US empire apply in distinct but entangled ways to Indigenous peoples and differentially racialized im/migrants in often unexamined or understudied spheres: welfare, rape, foodways, and sexuality. I attempt to answer the following questions: How does US empire as a project of white possession cohere, calcify, and carry on through entangled public pedagogy about Indigenous peoples and differentially racialized groups of immigrants? How and why over time are policy and media discourses about welfare, rape, foodways, and sexuality key tools of empire-building in relation to Indigenous peoples and racialized immigrants, respectively? Finally, what might Indigenous decolonial coalitional epistemologies and praxis teach us about resisting the always-already white possessive logics underpinning the public pedagogy of US empire, as well as reimagining and remapping nations, nationalisms, and borders?

The first chapter chronicles how developments in policy for and media about Indigenous peoples and im/migrants have, from first settlement, occurred proximately, if not exactly contemporaneously, to triangulate Native, racialized immigrant alien, and settler to support white possessive empire-building. With a comparative review of policy and media for and about Native Americans and immigrants, this chapter is designed as a primer for the major policies and the broad strokes of concurrent media discourses that will allow readers to contextualize the specific topics and relevant policy and media examined in subsequent chapters. I focus on the most significant (in the book's terms) policies, laws, Supreme Court rulings, and mainstream media as a basis for the following chapters, where I expand on key pedagogies of empire.

Subsequent chapters begin with a media example providing entry into the topic as a tool of US empire-building. Chapter 2 examines welfare as a lynchpin of Indigenous dispossession and anti-immigration in three key instances: the late nineteenth- and early twentieth-century eugenics movement, sterilization

---

116. Le, *Unsettled Solidarities.*

abuse in the 1970s, and neoliberal personal responsibility politics / multicultural politics of recognition that rationalized devastating cuts of federal aid to Native peoples and general welfare in the 1980s and 1990s. I argue that historical and neoliberal gendered public pedagogies about Indigenous peoples and racialized immigrants in relation to welfare are crucial to protecting and advancing the white heteropatriarchal property interests underpinning US empire.

In chapter 3, I argue that the culture of the US is foundationally and fundamentally a racialized rape culture: entangled public pedagogy that renders Indigenous women and racialized immigrant women rapeable is a key tool of US empire. As Indigenous feminist scholars have shown, rape is and has historically been a tool of colonialism. Indigenous women experience the highest rates of rape and sexual violence in the US, a direct result of the US government's attacks on Indigenous peoples' sovereignty over their bodies, lands, and powers to adjudicate crime. The US has also long demanded the "willing subservience (and gratitude) of migrant bodies."[117] Im/migrant women of color also experience disproportionately high levels of rape and sexual violence, a direct result of US policy that has historically sexually pathologized them and continues to render them hypervulnerable to exploitation and abuse at the hands of immigration agents, government officials, and their employers. US rape law, an offshoot of colonial property law, has also always been racialized as well as gendered. Meanwhile, media casts Indigenous women's and racialized immigrant women's sexuality as deviant, excessive, and "savage," rendering them "unrapable." I trace how pedagogies of empire co-constitute the un/rapeability of Indigenous and racialized immigrant women in similar but distinct, entangled ways.

Chapter 4 examines Indigenous and immigrant foodways as significant targets of coloniality and anti-immigration and also as powerful sites of decolonization and revolt, as in current Indigenous and global peasant food sovereignty movements. Historically the US government used starvation to subdue Indigenous peoples and erased the complex and varied geopolitical sustenance systems of Indigenous nations to rationalize dispossession and the forcing of Euro-American farming, dietary, and heteropatriarchal kinship models upon Native peoples. Proximally, gendered, racialized policy has channeled immigrants into indentured agricultural labor and work in the food industries, dispossessed Chicanx and Asian American farmers, and demanded immigrants' dietary assimilation, including banning certain foods. Neoliberal food systems also cause economic and environmental devastation that necessitate migration, and food insecurity and food deserts are disproportionately prevalent

---

117. Rodríguez, *Sexual Futures*, 148.

on reservations and within impoverished communities of color, as are health disparities created by a lack of access to healthy food that is culturally and environmentally appropriate. Meanwhile, extant mainstream nutritional and health metrics are rooted in colonial, white supremacist ideology and aims. Indigenous women and women of color are targeted by stereotypes about fatness and excess as personal failures, often in connection with mothering and poverty. All the while, appropriating Indigenous and immigrant foodways has always been critical to establishing and exerting US empire. This chapter shows how, as part of a colonial throughline, the public pedagogy of US empire—and revolt against it—crystalizes in the entanglement of Indigenous and immigrant foodways.

The conclusion explores how public pedagogy about "American" sexuality functions as a tool of US empire, including when it is ostensibly queer and multicultural, and how, in turn, the decolonization of sexuality—and decolonization writ large—necessitates reterritorialization and horizontal solidarities exemplified by Indigenous community-based resistance. I end the book with examples of Indigenous-led decolonial coalitional praxis that migrate (pun intended) beyond the public pedagogy US empire.

This book traces the throughline of gendered, sexualized Indigenous dispossession and differentially racialized anti-immigration constituting the public pedagogy of US empire. This historical project also aims to help readers contextualize current debates over Indigeneity, Indigenous dispossession, and anti-immigration, from the hyperaggressive, heteropatriarchal, overt, white-supremacist, anti-immigrant xenophobia of the Trump administration and the efforts of white nationalists to dismantle rather than co-opt extant economic, legal, educational, and political institutions, to the Biden administration's pursuit of an ostensibly more progressive, inclusive, and democratic return to modern US American normalcy (the multicultural and sometimes queer politics of recognition), as well as the indelible connections and continuities between these threads of US empire as a global pandemic has deepened existing inequalities. In illuminating pedagogies of empire historically and into the neoliberal context, I hope to help unsettle the white possessive curriculum of coloniality and anti-immigration.

CHAPTER 1

Proximal Public Pedagogies

Native American Law, Immigration Law, and Media

This chapter surveys the entangled public pedagogies that established and maintained the Indigenous dispossession and anti-immigration constituent to US empire from the early colonial period through the early neoliberal context. While policies for and about Indigenous peoples were foundational to the formation of gendered, sexualized, and racialized borders and regimes of belonging in the US, developments in Native American policy and immigration policy and conventions of mainstream media representation of both groups have from first settlement occurred proximately, if not exactly contemporaneously. Here I outline that four-hundred-year history, providing a broad overview of the most significant (in the book's terms) policies and conventions of media representation (and scholarship about each) as a basis and point of reference for subsequent chapters.

ORIGINAL ALIENS:
CONQUEST TO THE EIGHTEENTH CENTURY

Colonialism has always been legally and culturally authorized. Pointing to Indigenous dispossession as the material and ideological lynchpin of settler nationalism and its regimes of racism and racialization, Maria Josefina Saldaña-Portillo argues that shifting colonial ways of perceiving "Indianness"—the

34 • CHAPTER 1

nomadic, ignoble, brutish "savage" (and its complementary converse, the "noble savage," who is inferior but amenable to white settlers); the "vanishing Indian"; and the Indigenous subject capable of freely alienating land—are the conditions of possibility for the emergence of the US and Mexico. They function heterotemporally as ongoing historical and geographical processes in the (b)ordering of national space and belonging; national racial geographies are "Indian given."[1] And Karen A. Kosasa draws on Edward Said to remind us that geographical conquest "is not only about physical violence, but also about ideas, forms, about images and imaginings."[2] Consequently, "Indian policy," as it sometimes still is called in federal documents, immigration policy, and media, has long rendered both groups "alien," foreign, or part of another nation[3] to serve "white possession" (the white heteropatriarchal property interests underpinning settler colonialism).[4] While Indigenous peoples are uniquely structurally positioned by settler colonialism because genocide, spatial removal, and biological and cultural assimilation aim to eliminate the native *as native* from the land,[5] racialized alienation in US law and culture began with Indigenous people, who were "from the earliest days of European settlement, treated like aliens."[6]

In the Americas, settler colonialism was first legally authorized through the Doctrine of Discovery (1492–1600). The policy granted power to the government sponsoring the "discovery" of lands and provided the bedrock of British and US Native American policy by canonizing a gendered, sexualized notion of Indigenous savagery. The doctrine, formulated in response to the conquering of the Americas by the Spanish Catholic philosopher Francisco de Vitoria, rationalized the assertion of European sovereignty over the lands and peoples of the "New World": the inhabitants of the Indies that Columbus encountered were viewed as rational beings who chose to forsake the *jus gentium* (law of nations) in favor of incest, homosexuality, sodomy, bestiality,

---

1. Saldaña-Portillo, *Indian Given*, 8–11.

2. Kosasa, "Sites of Erasure," 196.

3. Iyko Day's important scholarship on the US settler colonial triangulation of Native, settler, and heterogeneously racialized alien employs the Marxist definition of alienation as the exploited status of workers in a capitalist economy because of their separation from the products of their labor. Day thereby asserts that enslaved Black people were the original aliens (*Alien Capital*, 28). I diverge from Day, employing the broader, standard definition of *alien* as a foreigner, a person who belongs to a foreign nation or is perceived as such, and *alienation* as the processes of ascribing and sustaining foreignness. I thus argue Indigenous peoples are the original racialized aliens and that processes of alienation are heterogeneously extended to people of color often though not exclusively in relation to labor.

4. Moreton-Robinson, *White Possessive*.

5. Wolfe, "Settler Colonialism and the Elimination of the Native," 388.

6. Kanstroom, *Deportation Nation*, 64.

PROXIMAL PUBLIC PEDAGOGIES · 35

and human sacrifice and were therefore inferior—and alien—to Europeans/ Christians. Consequently, Natives' right to occupy land was inferior to the sovereign's property rights (and by extension the sovereign's subjects, Europeans).[7] Natives were "savage," a word that originated in the twelfth century from the French "sauvage," which means "wild, savage, untamed, strange, pagan." Non-Christians were thus inherently savages[8] who could only occupy land, while the civilized sovereign and their subjects (and later the federal government and its citizens) had property rights.

Continuing to nurture the imagination of empires in what became the US, the "bedrock themes of Enlightenment thinking—taxonomy/fixity versus mutability/improvement—equipped race with a strategic versatility that enabled subject populations to be differentially racialized,"[9] developing the proto-white possessive logics of the Doctrine of Discovery to render Indigenous peoples alien in a dizzying array of ways. In the context of the US American Revolution, early US Americans embraced Enlightenment binaries and heteropatriarchal ideals of freedom, democracy, and individualism. Massacres, removals, and the denial of political rights were justified given Natives' inherent savagery.[10] Simultaneously, policy treated Natives as rational enough to freely cede their land for "the expansion of democracy as individual property, the expression of the expansion of democracy as individual property, the expression of (white) property as liberty."[11] The view of Natives as "primitive" and "innocent" "noble savages," improvable and assimilable in gendered, sexualized terms, also made them worthy targets for missionaries and reformers.[12] Additionally, Philip Deloria (Dakota) has shown that "playing Indian" was, dating from the Boston Tea Party (1773), crucial to the formation of US nationalism.[13] In this canonical origin story of US American character, white male protestors distinguished themselves from British colonists by costuming themselves as Mohawk Indians. Coded as freedom, "wild Indianness" or "noble savagery" critiqued aspects of Western society.[14]

---

7. Wolfe, *Traces of History*, 141–43.

8. Dunbar-Ortiz and Gilio-Whitaker, *"All the Real Indians Died Off,"* 38–39.

9. Wolfe, *Traces of History*, 9.

10. Wolfe, *Traces of History*, 9.

11. Saldaña-Portillo, *Indian Given*, 63. Saldaña-Portillo builds on Cheryl Harris's pathbreaking argument that whiteness is the full property of US citizenship derived in colonial uses of the law, legally defining persons as free or slave, conferring tangible economic benefits. Whiteness is a possession that operates proprietarily in law through the appropriation of Indigenous lands and enslavement of Black Africans (Harris, "Whiteness as Property," 1726).

12. Kilpatrick, *Celluloid Indians*, xvii.

13. P. Deloria, *Playing Indian*, 2.

14. P. Deloria, *Playing Indian*, 3–4.

36 • CHAPTER 1

These figures of "Indians" underpinned what legal scholar Robert A. Williams (Lumbee Tribe) calls a system of "racial apartheid" delineated in foundational US documents, laws, and treaties.[15] The explicit language of violent "Indian savagery" is featured verbatim in the inaugural legal document of US empire, the Declaration of Independence (1776). Charges against the king of Great Britain include bringing upon "the inhabitants of our frontiers the merciless Indian Savages, whose known rule of warfare, is an undistinguished destruction of all ages, sexes, and conditions."[16] The Continental Congress adopted George Washington's so-called "Savage as the Wolf" border policy, which in 1783 recommended that Indigenous peoples "should be kept apart from the civilized population of the United States, behind a boundary line drawn to facilitate the gradual and planned colonial expansion on the country's frontier" until the "backward race" vanished in the face of a superior civilization.[17] And in 1787, the Constitution granted the US government "the exclusive sovereign capacity of buying and selling all the lands held by Indian tribes,"[18] shifting from state-oriented policy to a federal centralization of "Indian" affairs, reminiscent of British-style centralized policy. This included establishing a standing army to address the Indigenous threat.[19] Therefore, even as treaties such as the Treaty of Fort Pitt (1778), the first federally ratified treaty with an Indigenous nation, the Lenape, which granted Washington's army "free passage through their country,"[20] seemed to recognize tribal nations as sovereign foreign nations, as a matter of inaugural federal policy, Native peoples were aliens against whom borders must be drawn.

While the scope or "mass" part of mass media required innovations in publishing, broadcasting, literacy, and public education that came later, beginning in the seventeenth century, captivity narratives in which white women were taken captive by Natives were the forerunner of mass cultural texts that also constituted the inaugural public pedagogy of US empire.[21] Colonizing expansion produced the phenomenon of captivity from the seventeenth century into the nineteenth century; as a "nonfiction" genre, the captivity

---

15. Williams, *Like a Loaded Weapon*, 45.

16. Jefferson, "Declaration of Independence: A Transcription," *America's Founding Documents*, US National Archives and Records Administration, last modified June 8, 2022, https://www.archives.gov/founding-docs/declaration-transcript.

17. Williams, *Like a Loaded Weapon*, 40–43.

18. Williams, *Like a Loaded Weapon*, 40–43; 45.

19. Wolfe, *Traces of History*, 147.

20. "Treaty with the Delawares, 1778."

21. Many scholars have examined the centrality of the novel to European colonialism and empire. See Said's definitive *Culture and Imperialism*. More recently Bhandar analyzed the novel as colonial tool in relation to property and property ownership (*Colonial Lives of Property*). Benedict Anderson importantly demonstrated that (print) media is crucial to the formation and reproduction of nationalism (*Imagined Communities*).

narrative both fanned and allayed white settlers' fears about race, gender, sexuality, land, and inchoate borders, often by emphasizing the vulnerability of white Christian womanhood to the corruption or pollution of male "Indian savagery," as in the emblematic example of the biography of Mary Rowlandson, *A True History* (1682).

Simultaneously, early colonists also, as Deloria argued, became US American by "playing Indian" in explicitly gendered, sexualized ways in a host of media. In print media, representing the colonies as an Indian Princess evoked fertility and was a symbol of liberty that justified rebellion or rendered the colonies as vulnerable, abused, violated, and enslaved by England.[22] This depiction is ironic, to put it mildly, given settlers' use of rape as a tool of colonization (chapter 3). In accordance with Enlightenment ideas of environmentalism that included the notion that one is literally what one eats, in (white) men's clubs and societies, laudatory plays and songs about the mythic "Tammany" (based on Tamenend, the Delaware leader who granted William Penn access to lands that would become Pennsylvania and surrounding areas),[23] also celebrated the abundance of wildlife in the "New World" and freedom from English laws that permitted only elites to hunt, allowing "every man to imagine himself a patriarch in a gentry of egalitarianism."[24] These complementary figures of "Indianness," built into foundational colonial and national policy, documents, and nationalist mythology that lives on in popular culture, overdetermined what a nation rooted in white possessive logics would—and could—be.

Gender, sexuality, race, property, and inaugural immigration law also underscored the establishment and expansion of US empire: the aims of colonization and immigration in settler colonial nations are indivisible. While in Canada the naming of the Department of Immigration and Colonization from 1917 to 1936 made this explicit, in the US some unpacking is needed. In 1790, the same year the Indian Intercourse Act held that no sale of lands made by Indigenous peoples was valid unless made by public treaty "held under the authority of the United States," the Naturalization Act or Free White Persons Act (1790) declared that "any alien, being a free white person" residing in the US for two years, may become a citizen if "he is a person of good character."[25] In practice Native Americans, indentured servants, enslaved people, free Black people, most women, and soon Asians were ineligible, making whiteness an official precondition for citizenship (and later provoking debate around immigrant whiteness).[26] This immigration law, along with its successors, reveals

---

22. P. Deloria, *Playing Indian*, 30–31.
23. P. Deloria, *Playing Indian*, 13–14.
24. P. Deloria, *Playing Indian*, 19–20.
25. Naturalization Act of 1790, Pub. L. No. 1-3, 1 Stat. 103 (1790).
26. See Haney Lopez, *White by Law*.

38 • CHAPTER 1

the disavowal of Indigenous sovereignty upon which rest the "inextricable connections between white possessive logics, race, and the founding of nation-states."[27] Property and citizenship was non-Native, white, male, and not queer, and the gendered, sexualized, and racialized legal distinctions that followed in immigration law were predicated upon Indigenous dispossession, even when ostensible democratic progress was made with the inclusion of once excluded groups. Soon the first federal immigration law, the 1819 Steerage Act, limited incoming ship passengers to curtail the entrance of impoverished European immigrants, who usually came through unskilled labor migration networks. In this moment when Black Africans were preferred for enslavement and national democratic ideology fetishized the freedom of nonenslaved people to work for wages, the law initiated the differential racialization of nonelite immigrants with a "spiral of illegality."[28] At this early point in US history, media representations of Natives were more prevalent than those of immigrants racialized as nonwhite. This is not surprising given the significance that Indigenous peoples and lands had for every aspect of nation-building and given that most early settlers, the first immigrants, were white.

Thus, in policy and media, various gendered, sexualized, racialized discourses about Indigenous and im/migrant aliens, respectively, legally and culturally authorized white possessive US empire-building. As I will elaborate on in subsequent chapters, public pedagogy that made and remade white possession had distinct material consequences for Natives, the original aliens already within nascent national borders; others rendered alien, such as enslaved Black people; and im/migrant aliens attempting to enter national borders. Also, to be clear, although white nonelite immigrants were structurally disadvantaged, they were certainly not property, as enslaved Black people were, and unlike migrants racialized as nonwhite, they could become citizens and propriate Indigenous lands. As became ever more evident in the nineteenth century, Asian immigrants and Mexicans were, like others deemed alien, not only denied those privileges but also subject to often extreme state-sanctioned violence.

ENTANGLEMENTS OF EMPIRE:
THE NINETEENTH CENTURY

In the nineteenth century the gendered, sexualized, racialized interplay of Indigenous dispossession and anti-immigration constituting the public pedagogy of US empire, which in this period also began to include global as well as

---

27. Moreton-Robinson, *White Possessive*, xiii.
28. Sadowski-Smith, "Unskilled Labor Migration and the Illegality Spiral," 783.

continental imperialism, became explicit. The mythologization of the frontier was key to this phase of empire-building and became ensconced in US culture. Richard Slotkin defines the "Frontier Myth" as "the conception of America as a wide-open land of unlimited opportunity for the strong, ambitious, self-reliant individual to thrust his way to the top."[29] According to the myth, a "magical growth of American wealth, power, and virtue" will result from the linking of "bonanza economics" (amassing resources without commensurate labor and investment) and political and moral "regeneration" through "savage war" (war against "savages").[30] The ideology of Manifest Destiny, a term coined in 1845 naming the widely held (though not uncontested) cultural belief that the United States was destined by God to expand throughout and develop the lands of North America, rationalized violence against Indigenous peoples and populations of color to advance white possession. When Indigenous wars of resistance ended and Indigenous peoples were incarcerated on reservations, the "Frontier Thesis," posited by historian Frederick Jackson Turner in 1893, asserted that the US was ending its first, formative "epoch, whose triumphs of democracy and economic power he associated with the development of the agrarian frontier,"[31] and thus experiencing an ideological crisis. The Frontier Myth, Manifest Destiny and the Frontier Thesis, which built upon the former in a more secular, ostensibly academic way, continued to frame white possession—in policy, media, and indeed US historiography—as an exceptional and just national mission.

The legal authorization of the explicitly white possessive empire-building of the day began with the Marshall Trilogy, landmark Supreme Court decisions (1823–32) that formed the basis of federal Native American law and *some immigration law*. The first ruling, *Johnson v. M'Intosh* (1823), a land dispute between two men, used the Doctrine of Discovery to render Indigenous land state property so that "the taking of Indian land based upon racial, cultural, and religious superiority of Europeans was justified; and language was codified that would justify future federal incursions into Indian lives and resources."[32]

Federal institutions and policy also expanded the discourse and means of Indigenous dispossession delineated in inaugural US legal documents. The Bureau of Indian Affairs (BIA), which continues to oversee and administer relations with Indigenous nations to this day, was formed within the War Department in 1824,[33] as some tribal nations continued to pose a military

---

29. Slotkin, *Regeneration through Violence*, 5.

30. Slotkin, *Gunfighter Nation*, 645.

31. Slotkin, *Gunfighter Nation*, 29.

32. Dunbar-Ortiz and Gilio-Whitaker, *"All the Real Indians Died Off,"* 56.

33. "What Is the BIA's History?," Indian Affairs, US Department of the Interior, last modified January 12, 2021, https://www.bia.gov/faqs/what-bias-history.

40 • CHAPTER 1

threat to US empire-building. The BIA was transferred to the Interior Department in 1849, when colonial victory was clear.[34] Perception of Natives as enemies or aliens threatening nation-building from within would underpin the next two eras of Native American policy: the so-called Indian Removal Era (1830–50) and the Reservation Era (1850–80s).

The Indian Removal Act (1830), which authorized the federal government to forcibly relocate Indigenous peoples to lands west of the Mississippi, openly structured nation-building as a white possessive project. This genocidal effort began under President Andrew Jackson, who as an army general proudly fought Indigenous peoples and made no secret of his contempt for them. While the IRA required tribal consent for removal, when tribal nations resisted, they were subjected to extreme state violence, as with the death of at least 4,000 Cherokees on the Trail of Tears (1838–39), which is only the most well-known of numerous removal marches. While the violent or brute "savage" was evoked to justify warfare, Jackson also paternalistically claimed that removal, segregation, and government "protection" would allow Indigenous peoples to "cast off their savage habits and become an interesting, civilized, and Christian community."[35] Indigenous peoples, again racialized in various ways, were thus also the first alien deportees.[36] In taking and settling Indigenous territories, "the United States would be able to establish densely populated cities, strengthen its borders from invasion, and most important, increase the wealth of the nation."[37]

The remaining Marshall Trilogy rulings and subsequent adjudication and policy continued to unequivocally cast Indigenous peoples as aliens to advance US empire as a fundamentally white possessive project. *Cherokee Nation v. Georgia* (1831) made Indigenous tribal nations "domestic dependent nations" rather than sovereign foreign nations. Marshall stated, "They are in a state of pupilage. Their relation to the United States resembles that of a ward to his guardian."[38] With this paternalistic infantilization, Indigenous nations lost the right to petition the Supreme Court when states interfered with their ability to govern their own people within their own land.[39]

---

34. "What Is the BIA's History?"

35. Andrew Jackson, *A Compilation of the Messages and Papers of the President*, vol. 3., 1897, 1083, quoted in Kanstroom, *Deportation Nation*, 67.

36. Commissary General of Subsistence, *Correspondence on the Subject of the Emigration of Indians*.

37. Byrd, "'Variations under Domestication,'" 123.

38. Cherokee Nation v. Georgia, 30 U.S. 1 (1831).

39. Byrd, "'Variations under Domestication,'" 124; and Cacho, "Civil Rights, Commerce, and US Colonialism," 67.

Finally, in *Worcester v. Georgia* (1832), the Marshall Court held that although Indigenous tribes were sovereign and self-governing, they were ultimately subject to federal law. Only the federal government—not states—could negotiate with tribes, and the government could terminate Indigenous nations' land claims. Marshall's federalist agenda in this case, which might seem to conflict with the previous ruling, likewise furthered US empire: "Dispossession was consummated by Indian sovereignty" to legitimate the basis of the United States' acquiring of territory: via treaties, sovereign Indigenous nations would consent to the termination of their land rights.[40] As Jodi A. Byrd (a citizen of the Chickasaw Nation of Oklahoma) observes of these two cases, "So began the alchemy of settler statecraft that produced autonomy and sovereignty as the adjudicative modes for the dialectical processes of possession and dispossession. State, tribe, and individual all collapse into the recognitive affirmations of consent, while the disavowal of refusal is remaindered to the uncivil, the resentful, and the retrograde."[41] Incidentally, *Dred Scott* (1857) referenced the foreign status of Native Americans—their alienage—to justify denying Black citizenship,[42] providing another example of the intertwinement of colonialism and anti-Blackness explicitly underpinning US empire-building.

When colonial victory was evident, US institutions shifted from baldly genocidal efforts to assimilation as the primary means of Indigenous dispossession.[43] This change was punctuated by the massacre at Wounded Knee (1890) when the US army murdered between 250 and 300 Lakota, many of whom were unarmed women and children, on the Lakota Pine Ridge Reservation. Public pedagogies that framed Natives as the "savage" instigators of violence persisted to rationalize such violence. And the consequence and correlate of the US successfully manifesting its destiny, the myth of the "vanishing Indian" alongside and in connection with Turner's Frontier Thesis, also reached its apex in the late nineteenth century. The Indigenous population was diminished by slavery, disease, war, Christianization, and assimilation, but according to the "vanishing Indian" myth, and in accordance with social Darwinian "survival of the fittest" and white possessive logics, Indigenous peoples, confronted by a superior civilization, were becoming extinct. These intertwined myths conveniently occluded ongoing attempts to seize Indigenous lands and resources.

---

40. Wolfe, *Traces of History,* 159.
41. Byrd, "'Variations under Domestication,'" 125.
42. Kanstroom, *Deportation Nation,* 68.
43. Wolfe, *Traces of History,* 164.

In the Era of Allotment and Assimilation (1887–1930), to advance US empire-building, treaty rights and other special statuses were phased out, and allotment was the primary tactic of Indigenous dispossession. The Dawes Act (1887) divided communally held Indigenous lands into individual allotments that rewarded heteropatriarchal nuclear households with larger allotments (heads of household were given 160 acres; 60 for single individuals; 40 for individuals under 18). The title of individual allotments was held by the federal government for twenty-five years, and at the conclusion of the trust period, Natives received the title and became US citizens. If a member of a tribe sold their allotment, it became "surplus" land, available to white settlers and railroad companies.[44] As Vine Deloria Jr. (Standing Rock Sioux) and Clifford Lytle note, "Not only did the allotment act breach numerous treaty provisions, but also Indian agents, under orders from Washington, refused to issue rations and other annuities to Indians unwilling to work their allotments, making the policy especially onerous to plains tribes, who viewed farming with distaste."[45] Furthermore, an 1891 amendment allowed the secretary of the interior free rein to lease the lands of any allottee who the secretary believed "by reason of age or other disability" could not improve their allotment according to Euro-American metrics.[46] Allotment devastated Indigenous peoples: landholdings were reduced from 138 million acres in 1887 to 48 million in 1934, and almost 20 million of those remaining acres were desert or semiarid land that was unusable for farming.[47] Native children were also removed from their families to attend compulsory boarding schools. Heteropatriarchal curriculum, designed to obliterate Indigenous ways of knowing, social relations, religions, foodways, and customs and to prepare children for labor, was taught, and physical and sexual abuse was rampant.

Differentially racialized "blood" as a metric of entitlement to some property anticipated the increasing exertion of US empire in connection with eugenics, the pseudoscience of controlling reproduction and the selection of desired heritable characteristics to improve future generations. Blood quantum requirements biologized Indigenous dispossession by attempting to "breed" Indigeneity—and thus Indigenous land claims or rights to property—out of the US. Previously intermarriage between whites and Natives was weaponized to acquire Indigenous land and, during times of military conflict with European powers and other Indigenous tribes, secure allegiances.

---

44. Glenn, "Settler Colonialism as Structure," 57.

45. Deloria and Lytle, *American Indians, American Justice*, ch. 1. Citations of this text are from the Kindle version.

46. Deloria and Lytle, *American Indians, American Justice*, ch. 1.

47. Deloria and Lytle, *American Indians, American Justice*, ch. 1.

From the seventeenth into the nineteenth century, early colonial then state and federal policies offered financial incentives to white citizens who married Natives.[48] Notably the infamous stereotype of the exotic, sexually available, assimilable Native princess was established with the mythologization of John Rolfe's marriage to Pocahontas, the twelve-year-old daughter of Powhatan, the leader of the Powhatan confederacy, in 1614.[49] Allegedly Pocahontas assimilated so thoroughly—marrying a white man, taking a white name, and converting to Christianity—that their children were considered white under law[50] and could therefore inherit land. Although blood quantum requirements were not widely federally used prior to the Indian Reorganization Act (1934), to advance white property interests, colonies, states, and the federal government selectively applied them earlier. To be recognized by a settler governing authority as a member of a tribal nation and therefore access the federal resources provided to that tribal nation, a person had to have a certain "amount" of "Indian" blood, as measured by the blood of one's parents, grandparents, and so on. For instance, the child of one Sioux parent and one white parent would be half Indigenous. References in treaties to "half-breeds" and "quarter bloods" can be traced to 1817.[51] Thus blood quanta criteria, which overrode Indigenous ways of defining their own communities, also legally made Indigenous peoples a racial rather than political group[52] as "a biogenetic extension of the frontier homicide."[53] Not coincidentally, the "one drop rule" of Black racial identity contemporaneously doubled down on racial capitalism. Prior to the Civil War, the value of Black people as labor had to be secured (given the ubiquity of white men raping enslaved Black women), so that miscegenation would not negate slave status. Post emancipation and in connection with Jim Crow and lynching, the rule that "one drop" of Black blood or any Black ancestry made a person Black cemented racial status to legally authorize anti-Blackness and protect white property interests and whiteness itself as a kind of property or currency.

Nineteenth-century media was another powerful vehicle for pedagogies of empire. The development of free public education, libraries, and technological advances that allowed for faster printing, cheaper paper, and railroads to disperse new commodities made reading more accessible and made books properly "mass" culture. This also increased the capitalist and soon corporate

---

48. Kaplan, "Historical Efforts," 126–32.
49. Mihesuah, *American Indians*, 11; 61.
50. Berger, "After Pocahontas."
51. Spruhan, "Legal History of Blood Quantum," 10.
52. TallBear, *Native American DNA*.
53. Wolfe, *Traces of History*, 4.

44 • CHAPTER 1

interests that shaped media. In the shadow of removal when most settlers learned about Indigenous peoples exclusively from media, captivity narratives, novels, and especially Western dime novels[54] nurtured the imagination of US empire with the Frontier Myth.

For example, James Fennimore Cooper's novels codified representations of the frontier that had appeared in various genres, from the personal narrative to history to sermon, among others. With his attempt to ideologically justify the Indigenous genocide and dispossession endemic to US history, Cooper provided generations of authors, filmmakers, and other creators with a blueprint of racial stereotypes.[55] *Last of the Mohicans* (1826), a novel adapted for Hollywood films five times, used the landscape and its original occupants as a background for a changing national imaginary that spoke to the settler-postfrontier ideological angst Turner would name. Cooper's idealized frontiersman protagonist, Hawkeye, is a white man raised by Delaware Indians. He and two Indigenous men assist in transporting the daughters of a US colonel during the French and Indian wars. While "savage" Natives continued to menace the advancement of white possessive empire-building, justifying violence against them, "noble" Natives, helpful to settlers and amenable to assimilation, are the last of their kind (hence the book's title), vanishing and leaving Indigenous lands open to white settlers. Moreover, "Cooper's creation of the 'manly' and Indianized white intermediary and hero of the new American mythology would later become a buttress of the film industry"[56] as well as "the model for future versions of the frontier hero in the writings of antebellum historians, journalists, and politicians interested in the important questions of Indian policy, emigration, and westward expansion."[57]

In nineteenth-century captivity narratives "there is less emphasis on the American Indians' paganism and more on their role as hindrances to the advance of Euro-American 'progress' and 'civilization,' which of course included Christianity."[58] Returned captives were "presented as parables of moral, religious, and, for women, feminine correctness."[59] Some examples of transculturation, that is, blending Indigenous cultures with white "civilized" culture, were published, such as the story of returned captive and popular author and public speaker Olive Oatman, a Mormon woman adopted by the Mohave and given traditional facial tattoos to signal her tribal membership.

---

54. Bold, *Selling the Wild West.*
55. Slotkin, *Gunfighter Nation*, 13–14.
56. Kilpatrick, *Celluloid Indians*, 4.
57. Slotkin, *Gunfighter Nation*, 16.
58. Derounian-Stodola, "Indian Captivity Narratives," 40–41.
59. Mifflin, *Blue Tattoo*, 147.

Although such examples complicate consent and "captivity,"[60] by the mid-nineteenth century, the captivity narrative was "an exploitative political vehicle to facilitate genocide."[61]

Dime novels, born in 1860, generally depicted Native peoples as primitive, bellicose foils to white male heroes who slaughtered them quickly, often to protect white women. While most of these "lurid" dime novels were written and marketed to male readers, women's dime novels, many of which were written by white women, were also popular and are considered the precursor to the romance genre.

Buffalo Bill's Wild West traveling show also widely circulated the Frontier Myth. A popular dime novel hero, Buffalo Bill Cody, who had been an army scout, Pony Express rider, and theater star, ran his traveling theater/rodeo show from 1882 to 1913.[62] In dime novels and Buffalo Bill's show (and later films), the linking of cowboys and Indians—and rendering of US American heroism as synonymous with white men fighting and killing Natives—continued to become a Western staple and nationalist trope. In short, nineteenth-century media codified and systematized the Frontier Myth, providing public pedagogy that justified and often romanticized white possessive empire-building.

•

Simultaneously, the legal system, established to dispossess Indigenous peoples and authorize empire, differentially racialized, gendered, and sexualized immigrants to advance white possession. Anti-immigrant discourse was also becoming increasingly biologized and entangled with eugenics. The Marshall Trilogy and Native American policy solidified the gendered, sexualized racist ideologies of immigrant removal—via the "right of conquest," the conflation of whiteness and "civilization," and what would become known as plenary power—underscoring the Chinese Exclusion Act (1882) and Supreme Court cases upholding its legality.[63] The law prohibited naturalization for all Chinese and the entry of Chinese laborers, considered "a menace to our civilization."[64] It followed the Page Law (1875), which banned convicts, involuntary Chinese migrant laborers, and Chinese women suspected of sex work. In fact, with the Transcontinental Railway nearing completion, Chinese laborers threatened

---

60. Stratton, *Captivity of the Oatman Girls*. See also Mifflin, *Blue Tattoo*; and Derounian-Stodola, "Captive and Her Editor," 2.

61. Derounian-Stodola, "Indian Captivity Narratives," 44.

62. Kilpatrick, *Celluloid Indians*, 12–13.

63. Kanstroom, *Deportation Nation*, 63–64.

64. Chae Chan Ping v. U.S. (Chinese Exclusion Case), 130 U.S. 581 (1889).

46 • CHAPTER 1

white settlers in the post–Civil War economy.[65] Day asserts that the recruitment of Chinese indentured and "free" labor added provisionality, excludability, and deportability to the idea of alien-ness. Consequently, "the heterogeneously racialized alien is a unique innovation of settler colonialism."[66]

Explicit entanglements of state violence against Indigenous peoples and immigrants of color to advance always-already white possessive US empire continued with the turn of the twentieth century, especially through plenary power. *United States v. Kagama* (1886), which unilaterally imposed federal criminal law on Indigenous nations, established the plenary power doctrine. In the unanimous decision, the US Supreme Court evoked the wardship language of *Cherokee Nation v. Georgia*: "Because they were 'dependent on the United States—dependent largely for their daily food; dependent for their political rights'—these 'remnants of a race once powerful, now weak and diminished in numbers' were under the plenary authority of Congress."[67] The court then reiterated plenary power to support the Chinese Exclusion Act in *Chae Chan Ping v. United States* (1889) and *Fong Yue Ting* (1893). Reemphasizing the power of Congress over Indigenous peoples, in *Lone Wolf v. Hitchcock* (1903), also known as "the Indian Dred Scot case," the court maintained the Allotment Act against challenges based on treaty violations and due process grounds and cited the Chinese Exclusion Act: "The national government was seen to have "'inherent and plenary power' not only over immigrants, but also 'over foreign nationals already in the midst of a colonial country—unassimilated, tribal, non-citizen indigenous peoples.'"[68] Legal and extralegal tactics used to dispossess and eliminate Indigenous people were also used against Chinese people: segregation, terrorism, destroying Chinese settlements, and expelling Chinese with "roundups" from 1850 to about 1900. Local and state laws also barred Chinese from owning land and businesses.[69] Chinese (or "Mongolian," according to the racial taxonomy of the day) "blood" was, like Black "blood," also considered a pollutant to the white race.[70]

Gendered, racialized restrictions against certain European immigrants also increased, though they rarely experienced the extent of state-sanctioned and often administrative violence nonwhite immigrants and people of color were subject to. Never barred from citizenship, they could also ostensibly pursue the white possession at the core of the Frontier Myth. At the turn of the

---

65. Norton, *Story of California*, 283–96.
66. Day, *Alien Capital*, 24.
67. Williams, *Like a Loaded Weapon*, xx.
68. Kanstroom, *Deportation Nation*, 64.
69. Glenn, "Settler Colonialism as Structure," 65.
70. Jacobson, *Whiteness of a Different Color*, 161.

nineteenth century, influxes of "new immigrants" from Eastern and Southern Europe, who often worked for low wages and under poor conditions, were the largest labor pool following Chinese restriction. Nativists and eugenicists viewed these often Jewish or Catholic and "darker-skinned, more visibly ethnic"[71] immigrants as biological and cultural threats who were inclined toward crime, laziness, fecundity, and unethical behavior. A surge of immigration of mostly Catholic and destitute Irish due to the Irish famines of the 1840s provoked similarly racialized xenophobia.[72] Unlike the mostly white Northern European Protestant citizenry, "white ethnic" immigrants were considered unfit to populate the nation.[73] The Immigration Act, also passed in 1882, established a head tax on all entering through seaports and deemed excludable immigrants "Likely to Become a Public Charge" (LPC), that is, those who authorities believed might need welfare because of a mental or physical disability.[74] Diseases, felony convictions, crimes involving a vaguely defined "moral turpitude," polygamy, and failure to pay for one's own ticket were grounds for exclusion or deportation. LPC provisions were initially used to restrict white ethnic women, often employed as factory laborers and domestic servants, whom nativists and eugenicists viewed as racially inferior, fecund potential burdens on the state. The moral turpitude clause was also used to bar women who engaged in pre- or extramarital sex or who were suspected of sex work. Men were rarely, if ever, subjected to the same kind of policing.[75] Additionally, in 1891 immigrants suffering from disease, those convicted of a crime of moral turpitude, and polygamists were barred from entry, and Congress established the Office of the Superintendent of Immigration in the Treasury Department. Controlling sex work among European immigrant women was one of the tasks of this new agency. This was one of many instances in which the Marshall Trilogy's characterization of Indigenous nations as "domestic dependent nations"—the United States' first burden—infused policy enacting border militarization, interior enforcement, illegalization, detainment, and deportation.[76]

Immigrants, differentially racialized in media as in policy, were often depicted as gendered pollutants and threats to white US American society. Robert Lee described how popular songs and minstrelsy represented the

---

71. Landsberg, *Prosthetic Memory*, 52.

72. See Ignatiev, *How the Irish Became White*.

73. Gardener, *Qualities of a Citizen*, 165–66; 169; Jacobson, *Whiteness of a Different Color*; and Roediger, *Working toward Whiteness*.

74. Hutchinson, *Legislative History of Immigration Policy, 1798–1965*.

75. Moloney, "Women's Sexual Morality," 100.

76. Lee-Oliver et al., "Imperialism, Settler Colonialism, and Indigeneity," 236.

Chinese immigrant as an economic and social contaminant. On stage, white actors performed in yellow-face and, as with Indigenous representations, often spoke in caricatured languages or ate animals Euro-Americans considered pets or vermin.[77] Continuing a British tradition of representing the "wild Irish" as cannibals, murderers, and sodomites to rationalize the twelfth-century invasion and colonization of Ireland, in US cartoons and periodicals Irish immigrants were rendered as simian to convey that they were still too "wild"—drunk, intractable, fecund—for citizenship.[78] An infamous 1876 cover of *Harper's Weekly,* then tellingly subtitled *Journal of Civilization,* depicts a Black man and an Irish man seated upon two separate scales weighing the same and thus equally problematic to Southern and Northern "civilization," respectively.[79] However, the relative privilege of white ethnic immigrants as eligible for citizenship—potential US Americans, potential agents and beneficiaries of empire—in comparison to Indigenous peoples, Black people, Chinese immigrants, and other people of color is illustrated in spectatorship as well as policy, if not yet media. Buffalo Bill's Wild West shows were popular with factory workers and white ethnic immigrants (often one and the same) in the eastern US.[80]

Before policy turned Mexicans into "immigrants"—the contemporary quintessential "criminal aliens"—they too were legally and culturally cast as aliens and managed in ways that intersected with Indigenous dispossession and immigration control to advance and protect white property interests. (And many Mexicans are Indigenous. The conquest of North America engendered a division between "'white' rulers from subjugated 'nonwhites,' and 'civilized' Europeans from 'savage' Indians and 'mongrelized' Mexicans"[81] who in the US were considered a "degraded race" of Indigenous, European, and African ancestry.[82]) Because in the US, Mexicans were not initially "immigrants" under the law and have distinct experiences under a racist class structure that is not equivalent to settler colonialism,[83] I discuss people of Mexican origin separately until policy rendered them "immigrants" in the early twentieth century.

---

77. R. Lee, *Orientals,* 36–38.

78. Duffy, *Who's Your Paddy?,* 51–63.

79. Nast, "The Ignorant Vote—Honors are Easy" (Cartoon), *Harper's Weekly,* 20.1041, New York, December 9, 1876, last updated 2023, https://glc.yale.edu/ignorant-vote-honors-are-easy-cartoon.

80. Kilpatrick, *Celluloid Indians,* 13.

81. Jacobson, *Whiteness of a Different Color,* 141.

82. Fregoso, *MeXicana Encounters,* 127.

83. Sánchez and Pita, "Rethinking Settler Colonialism," 1043.

With the Treaty of Guadalupe Hidalgo (1848), Mexican territory in what is now California and Texas was annexed, and Mexicans were granted US citizenship. Familiar legal and extralegal tactics including taxation, border control, privatizing communal grazing lands, and changes in the economy were used to dispossess Mexicans' land, and Mexicans were conceived of as feminized and backward—"savage" and alien—to justify violence against them and their exclusion from white possession. As in Native American schools, in schools for Mexican children assimilation was coerced via gendered curriculum designed to erase language and culture and prepare children for a future as laborers: girls were taught sewing while boys were taught carpentry, shoe repair, basketry, haircutting, and blacksmithing. Mexican men were also forced into migratory labor as sheepshearers and vaqueros and later into railroad construction, mining, and agriculture, while women remained in the home in villages, tending to domestic production and subsistence agriculture.[84]

Policing also reflected and reinforced the idea of a wild border area near Mexico—not unlike or entirely distinct from the shaping of the frontier and its Indigenous inhabitants as "savage," "wild," and in need of taming.[85] Under California's anti-vagrancy Greaser Act (1855), any suspected vagabond, or "a person identified by the term 'Greaser' and, generally, all people of Spanish or Indian blood," could be terrorized, have their property confiscated, and be lynched by police and local militias. The name of the law itself is a racial slur: US troops during the Mexican–American War pejoratively referred to men who greased mule cart axels, an occupation typically held by Mexicans, as "greasers."[86] Moreover, Indigenous peoples and Mexicans were conflated in debates during the Forty-Fourth Congress (1875–77) as lawmakers attempted to address security along the Mexican border.[87]

Like Native Americans, in media Mexicans were represented as "savage," inherently alien foils to white heroes and threats to white women, or "good" insofar as they assisted whites and assimilated. They were not, however, "vanishing," which was part of the problem (and has continued to trouble white supremacists and nativists). The bandito/greaser trope of Mexican criminality first appeared in dime Westerns in the 1820s and later in films such as *Licking the Greasers* (1910). While in this genre the male Mexican bandit often threatened white women with violence and rape, in some early films white US

---

84. Sánchez and Pita, "Rethinking Settler Colonialism," 61–63.

85. Rifkin, *Settler Common Sense*.

86. "Early US Race Laws Designed to Protect White Employment," May 13, 1950, Voltaire Network, last updated May 13, 2005, http://www.voltairenet.org/article30264.html.

87. Jacobson, *Whiteness of a Different Color*, 157.

50 • CHAPTER 1

American heroes had "greaser" wives, and some included a "noble greaser" who protected white US Americans from other "greasers."[88]

Nineteenth-century white possessive logics and alienage that would be increasingly biologized underpinned US global as well as continental imperialism. In the context of industrialization and its changing labor markets at home and abroad and the ideological crisis of the closing frontier, the US took up overseas colonizing, beginning with the Philippines, then Hawaii, Puerto Rico, and Guam. While to an extent international colonialism resolved the identity crisis provoked by the closing of the western frontier, it provoked a new one in that new colonies were not "united" or even voluntary states. Consequently, as US empire globalized, public pedagogy racialized colonized populations as "savage," and media such as broadcasted presidential speeches and patriotic songs rebranded the nation as "America," obfuscating overseas colonial and imperial projects.[89]

By the end of the nineteenth century, "legal Indian removal was a well-accepted and well-understood conceptual model" for the exclusion and removal of racialized immigrants.[90] And again, gendered and sexualized mediated representations of Indigenous peoples and differentially racialized immigrants and/or aliens justified and amplified the unabashedly white possessive logics of the empire-building of the day. In policies, legal decisions, institutions, and media that justified and advanced white heteropatriarchal property interests, the public pedagogy of newly globalizing "American" empire crystalized.

CITIZENSHIP, BORDER PATROL, AND BIOPOWER: THE EARLY TWENTIETH CENTURY

Still explicitly white possessive US empire-building persisted through entangled public pedagogies in connection with citizenship, border policing, and eugenics. Foucault theorized that modern nation-states control subjects through biopower,[91] "technologies of power that construct populations as political problems to be managed at the level of the embodied and the biological."[92] Conjuring the "vanishing Indian" stereotype, prominent eugenicist Paul Popeno averred that natural selection rather than genocide was

---

88. Noriega, "Citizen Chicano," 92.
89. Immerwahr, *How to Hide an Empire.*
90. Kanstroom, *Deportation Nation,* 64.
91. See Foucault, *History of Sexuality.*
92. Byrd, "'Variations under Domestication,'" 126.

"appropriately leading to the extinction of decadent races such as the American Indian." To expedite natural selection among populations of color and other groups deemed "a burden to the race," such as the mentally disabled, he called for compulsory sterilization.[93] In 1907, Indiana became the first state to establish a compulsory sterilization law; within twenty years, twenty-six states followed suit.[94] State antimiscegenation laws also continued to safeguard biologized white possession alongside federal and state efforts to "breed" Native peoples—and their land claims and rights—out of existence.

Eugenicists' calls for immigration restriction to protect white possession also quickly manifested in policy. The Naturalization Act (1906) standardized naturalization processes, made some knowledge of English a requirement, and established the Bureau of Immigration and Naturalization within the Commerce Department to oversee federal immigration policy. (Recall that the BIA was initially housed within the War Department, indicating that settler colonial institutions frame and manage Indigenous and immigrant alienage in different ways.) Then in its 1911 report, the Dillingham Commission, a bipartisan congressional committee formed in 1907 to examine changing immigration patterns, found that the increased immigration of allegedly fecund white ethnics threatened US racial equilibrium as white Northern European birthrates and immigration declined.[95]

The policy response, the 1924 Johnson–Reed Act, was a benchmark in terms of protecting white possession with differential racialization. National quota ceilings for immigrants were based on the mostly white Northern European citizen population in 1890, creating a hierarchy of "white races" to maintain a white Northern European Protestant majority. On the heels of the *Ozawa* and *Thind* cases (both 1922) in which the Supreme Court ruled that persons of various Asian descent were not white,[96] under Johnson–Reed, Asians and other groups considered nonwhite remained "aliens ineligible for citizenship." While immigration from the Western Hemisphere was still unrestricted, undocumented immigration became a federal crime, creating "illegal immigrants" (conflating undocumented status with crime), and the Border Patrol, modeled on the Texas Rangers, was formed. While the first wave of inspectors on the Mexican and Canadian borders were tasked primarily with keeping Chinese and white ethnic would-be immigrants out, the Border Patrol was designed to appease both eugenicist and southwestern agricultural interests (that feared alleged Mexican fecundity and wanted to ban

---

93. Stern, *Eugenic Nation*, 50–52.
94. Torpy, "Native American Women and Coerced Sterilization."
95. Gardener, *Qualities of a Citizen*, 165–66.
96. Haney Lopez, *White by Law*, 79; 90.

52 • CHAPTER 1

Mexican immigration or utilize Mexicans for cheap seasonal labor, respectively) and therefore focused on Mexicans.[97] An expansion of border policing also seemed necessary as criminologists, building on extant stereotypes of Indigenous peoples and Mexicans, claimed that hereditarily low intelligence made Mexicans prone to criminality.[98]

While the colonial throughline in border policing is quite clear, Johnson–Reed and its differential racialization of immigrants cannot be understood apart from the Indian Citizenship Act, also passed in 1924. Citizenship was granted to all Indigenous peoples born in the US while not "impair[ing] or otherwise affect[ing] the right of any Indian to tribal or other property."[99] While progressive policy makers and activists framed the law as inclusive, it was controversial among Indigenous peoples as it certainly did not provide Natives with agency, let alone true sovereignty. Also, until 1948 some states refused to abide by the new law.[100] Beth Piatote (Nez Perce, enrolled with Colville Confederated Tribes) argues that Indigenous peoples continued to be systemically classified and paternalistically treated as "domestic dependent nations" under the law. She uses the term "domestic subjects" to name Natives' legal status during the Assimilation Era as one in opposition to US citizenship and to illuminate how individuals' personal and kinship relationships shape and are shaped by political rights to produce the national. Moreover, Piatote asserts that Indigenous "domestic subjects" are the precursor to and condition of possibility for what immigration scholar Mai Ngai calls "impossible subjects,"[101] that is, Asian and Mexican im/migrant laborers cast as "illegal aliens" whose "inclusion in the nation was at once a social reality and a legal impossibility."[102] As Piatote contends, the two 1924 citizenship laws are coextensive: the "illegal alien replaced the domestic subject and [. . .] some form of impossible subjectivity has been a feature of US citizenship from the origins of the nation."[103] Citizenship is a mechanism of marginalization for both Indigenous peoples and immigrants racialized as nonwhite; however, for Indigenous peoples, citizenship is inherently dispossessive. "Rights" granted from a settler colonial government literally depend upon the persistence of Indigenous dispossession. For immigrants of color, exclusion from citizenship was the mechanism of their exploitation as a labor pool. Therefore both

---

97. Stern, *Eugenic Nation*, 73–74.
98. Stern, *Eugenic Nation*, 99.
99. Indian Citizenship Act of 1924, Pub. L. No. 68-175, 43 Stat. 253 (1924).
100. Bruyneel, "Challenging American Boundaries," 30–43.
101. Piatote, *Domestic Subjects*, 8–9; 172.
102. Ngai, *Impossible Subjects*, 8–9; 13; 57.
103. Piatote, *Domestic Subjects*, 9.

"domestic" and "impossible" subjectivity advance white possession in distinct but co-constitutive ways.

The entanglement of Indigenous dispossession and racialized anti-immigration structuring US empire was also evident in citizenship ceremonies. From 1916 Indian agents staged heteropatriarchal citizenship ceremonies on reservations to imagine the transition from Native to citizen. Indigenous men would shoot a "final arrow," indicating the end of their resistance to the US and then put their hands on a plow and vow to become farmers. The Secretary of the Interior also gave men purses to represent thrift. Women received small sewing kits and pins.[104] These rituals inspired the immigrant naturalization ceremony and corporations' graduation ceremonies held for immigrant workers, such as that of the Ford Motor Company English School during World War I.[105]

In terms of popular culture that circulated white possessive logics, "motion pictures became the main format for the creation of a national audience and the popular articulation of a national narrative."[106] "Indians" were literally central to the development of US cinema. The first short films, created by Thomas Edison, focused on often fictionalized Indigenous peoples, such as *Sioux Ghost Dance* (1894). Public peep show projections of film that began in 1896 were followed by moving pictures of the US West featuring a mix of non-Native and Native actors playing Indigenous people. Each year from 1910 to 1913, over one hundred films were made about Native Americans and almost as many in each of the remaining years of the silent film era,[107] until 1929.

Representations of Indigenous people in this period established the paradigm for the celluloid Native, with Westerns doing the lion's share of nurturing the imagination of US empire via the Frontier Myth. Like dime Western novels, silent Western films highlighted the bloodthirsty "savage." For example, Buffalo Bill Cody's production company dramatized battles Cody had fought in. Films such as *The Indian Wars* (1914) presented military conflicts with Indigenous peoples, including the massacre at Wounded Knee, as justified and heroic on the part of the US. Moreover, the government sent troops to film and forced Pine Ridge Sioux to film on their reservation (despite their protests, especially given the film's historical inaccuracies and placement of battle scenes atop Indigenous peoples' graves). The impact of the film as public pedagogy cannot be overestimated given that it was shown to cabinet members,

---

104. Piatote, *Domestic Subjects,* 113–14.

105. McDonnell, *Dispossession of the American Indian,* 96.

106. R. Lee, *Orientals,* 119. See also May, *Screening Out the Past*; Sklar, *Movie-Made America*; and Rollins, *Columbia Companion to American History on Film.*

107. Kilpatrick, *Celluloid Indians,* 22.

congressmen, and dignitaries; became an official government record that the War Department used to encourage recruits; and was very popular with spectators.[108] Another influential text was Zane Grey's novel, the *Vanishing American* (first published as a serial in *Ladies Home Journal,* 1922–23), and a film of the same name (1925), which is about the extinction of the "noble savage" in the face of a "stronger race," as one Native in the film puts it, exemplifying the impact of eugenicist logics in media.

Film scholar Angela Aliess chronicled how an exoticization of Indigenous peoples underpinned both the "sympathetic" and hostile strains of representation of "the white man's Indian." In all cases, adorned clothing and costumes, usually based on Plains tribes; often fictional rituals, blending or outright misrepresenting different tribes' traditions; camera angles; body language; and off-screen music—usually produced by theater pianists, such as the tom-tom beat that conveyed to spectators that "Indians are on the warpath"—highlighted Natives' differences from and incompatibility with white possessive logics.[109] Indigenous characters were generic/monolithic, most actors were white or non-Native playing "red face," and male "Hollywood Indians" usually stood flat-footed with their arms crossed over their chests. Women were presented as meek, adorned in buckskin with fringe and beads,[110] often as princesses, or as "s—s,"[111] dark, quiet beasts of burden who worked while Indigenous men were off fighting or being lazy.[112]

In silent films, im/migrants were heterogeneously racialized as alien to white possession in gendered, sexualized terms. Mexicans were stereotyped as the bandito/greaser, the dark lady/seductress, and the buffoon. Mexican women were portrayed as degenerate and sexually threatening subjects through "exotic costuming, flamboyant gestures, and immoral behavior." In *Red Girl* (1908), a "Mexican Jezebel" (as she is called in the film's intertitles) steals a white woman's gold and the husband of the Indigenous woman who helped her hide from the white woman.[113] The Mexican woman's sexuality is aberrant and depraved in its disrespect for the marital bond and racial boundaries; she is the enemy of *all* women, white property, and law and order. Her betrayal of the Indigenous and white women also suggests that Indigenous peoples should ally themselves with whites, not Mexicans (a false division, given that some Mexicans are Indigenous).

---

108. Kilpatrick, *Celluloid Indians,* 19–22.

109. Aliess, *Making the White Man's Indian,* 1–5.

110. Aliess, *Making the White Man's Indian,* 33–34.

111. See chapter 2 for in-depth discussion of the offensive and harmful public pedagogy that the "s—" stereotype of Indigenous women generates.

112. Dunbar-Ortiz and Gilio-Whitaker, *"All the Real Indians Died Off,"* 137–44.

113. Fregoso, *MeXicana Encounters,* 133.

The diabolical Chinese villain Fu Manchu also provided widespread public pedagogy about the Yellow Peril to US Americans over many years. Sax Rohmer's *The Insidious Dr. Fu Manchu* (1913), *The Return of Fu Manchu* (1916), and *The Hand of Fu Manchu* (1917) set the tone for the book series and films, radio and television shows, and comics that followed about the first "universally recognized Oriental" who "became the archetype of villainy," explicitly representing the "Asiatic" threat of racial annihilation.[114] Writer Earl Derr Biggers created the benevolent detective Charlie Chan as a direct alternative to Fu Manchu in novels, beginning with *A House without a Key* (1925), and then in film and other media. But again, the measure of the racialized alien's worth was their allegiance and subordination to white people, laws, and heteropatriarchal norms.

Because white ethnic immigrants were at the time racialized Others *within* whiteness, eligible if not desired for citizenship, their representation is perhaps especially polysemous. Grotesque, vaudevillian style make-up created pronounced "ethnic" features, such as a big nose to denote a Jew or dark swarthiness to denote an Italian, in silent films. The trope of the greedy, miserly, scheming Jew as a threat to white Anglo-Saxon Protestant society was common in films such as *Cohen's Advertising Scheme* (1904) and *Cohen's Fire Sale* (1907). Yet the notion of the US as a crucible that melted down difference to incorporate all races and creeds, the precursor to the "nation of immigrants" imaginary that would also hinge on white ethnic immigrants, was popularized by Israel Zangwill's play, *The Melting Pot* (1908). The protagonist, Russian Jewish immigrant David Quixano, viewed the US as "God's Crucible, the great Melting-Pot where all the races of Europe are melting and re-forming" and therefore gaining access to new opportunity and freedom.[115] Jewish immigrants and their descendants also shaped US cinema as the founders and heads of many major Hollywood production companies. This also made them targets of anti-Semitism.[116]

In these ways, assemblages of citizenship, border policing, and eugenics continued to propel explicitly white possessive US empire-building in the new century. While Indigenous peoples were no longer considered military threats, Indigenous dispossession via citizenship policy continued to advance white property interests, as policy that differentially racialized and policed immigrants helped to biologize whiteness as property. Media, meanwhile, continued to justify white possessive logics by elaborating upon extant racialized stereotypes of Indigenous peoples and Mexican, Chinese, and white ethnic

---

114. R. Lee, *Orientals*, 114.

115. Zangwill, *Melting Pot*. Incidentally Zangwill was British, the son of Russian Jewish immigrants.

116. Gabler, *Empire of Their Own*.

immigrants, respectively. Moreover, with technological developments, media representations of Indigenous peoples and differentially racialized immigrants became more ubiquitous as entertainment, information (the first films were shown on the same screens and in the same sitting as news films, blurring the lines between the two for audiences), and socialization. Soon public pedagogy shifted to fully incorporate white ethnics into white possessive logics, and voice—sound—was given to Indigenous dispossession and anti-immigration in "talkies."

ONGOING ALIENAGE IN PEACETIME AND WAR: THE MID-TWENTIETH CENTURY

White possessive logics, rebranded as benevolent and sometimes progressive and/or necessary to national security, structured midcentury pedagogies of US empire. With the establishment of the Immigration and Naturalization Service (INS) in 1933, an ideal of heteropatriarchal benevolence that complemented ongoing eugenicist efforts to control immigration to "guarantee the proper racial boundaries of the nation and the intactness of the white American family" supplanted the cowboys vs. "savage Indians" model of border patrolling.[117] Simultaneously, "the deportation terror"[118] was underway. During the Great Depression 400,000 Mexicans were repatriated regardless of citizenship status given fears of labor competition and beliefs that Mexican women were excessively reproducing at public expense.[119] "Benevolent" heteropatriarchal white possessive logics also underscored the Indian Reorganization Act (IRA; 1934), the policy centerpiece of the Indian Reorganization Era (1930s–45), which ended allotment and returned to a measure of Indigenous self-governance and the reservation system in response to widespread criticism of the government's handling of Indigenous affairs.

Although the IRA initiated opportunities for Indigenous revitalization, it failed to undo the damage of allotment and contributed to the ongoing erosion of Indigenous customs and traditions,[120] extending Indigenous dispossession and white possession. Meant to minimize federal discretion and power over tribal governments and promote tribal nations' self-sufficiency via various forms of economic development, in practice, new tribal constitutions

---

117. Stern, *Eugenic Nation*, 78.

118. Buff, *Deportation Terror*.

119. Lortimer, "The Mexican Conquest," *Saturday Evening Post*, June 2, 1929, 26; and Hoffman, *Unwanted Mexican Americans in the Great Depression*, 86–87.

120. Deloria and Lytle, *American Indians, American Justice*, ch. 1.

and bylaws were standardized according to Euro-American systems,[121] and tribal nations were reorganized as corporations, dependent on development funds that could enter and manage contracts with corporations, states, and federal offices. The IRA and other New Deal reforms exacerbated Indigenous economic indebtedness as a form of colonization that persists today[122] and continued to structure Indigenous lives into white heteropatriarchal forms and institutions.[123]

Meanwhile, some immigrants benefited massively from New Deal policies and especially the differential racialization of welfare. White ethnic difference began to systemically "melt" with the establishment of what David Roediger calls "interimmigrant unities" in trade unions like the Congress of Industrial Organizations (CIO) and given New Deal mass politics and government aid programs such as welfare, Social Security, and a two-tier housing aid policy that served the working poor according to Jim Crow practices.[124]

During World War II and its immediate aftermath, Indigenous regeneration ended, and immigrants continued to be differentially racialized to extend and defend US empire. As Nazi admiration of US eugenic race policies became known, scientific racism was repackaged,[125] with sexual conformism, population control, and family planning replacing explicit efforts to eliminate degeneracy.[126] Discourses of "security," especially to protect the "safety" of white heteropatriarchal families and their property, became prevalent public pedagogy.

The Bracero Program (1942–64) provided the prototype for the Mexican and broadly Latinx labor importation/deportation—as well as the stereotype of the "wetback"/undocumented worker, a criminal alien by definition—that would be a key part of subsequent iterations of US empire. Program recruitment of unskilled male Mexican laborers hired on a short-term basis precipitated an increase in undocumented immigration as employers often resorted to illegal means to secure the cheapest labor. An enduring policy model of "imported colonialism"—that is, the recruitment of laborers of color denied the protections and privileges of citizenship and thus, like colonial subjects, displaced by a colonizing nation's domination of the resources, labor, and market of a colonized territory—was established with this creation of a

---

121. Deloria and Lytle, *American Indians, American Justice,* ch. 1.
122. Barker, "Territory as Analytic," 30.
123. Rifkin, *When Did Indians Become Straight?,* 40–41.
124. Roediger, *Working toward Whiteness,* 200–225.
125. Kuhl, *Nazi Connection.*
126. Stern, *Eugenic Nation,* 10.

58 · CHAPTER 1

migratory agricultural proletariat of Mexicans who were excluded from the polity[127] and expelled when no longer needed. The pattern was repeated following the Korean War with the mass deportation of Mexicans under Operation Wetback (1954).[128]

The differential racialization of internal aliens as part and parcel of US empire is also emblematized in the World War II internment of nearly 120,000 Japanese Americans—"both alien and non-alien"—from 1942 to 1946.[129] Roosevelt's Executive Order 9066 attempted to protect white possession from racialized aliens by building on the conceptual model established with Indigenous dispossession and removal and furthered with Chinese exclusion and removal. Likewise in accordance with white possessive wartime logics, the Chinese Exclusion Act was repealed in 1943 as the Chinese became allies against the Japanese.

The technological innovations of sound in film and accessibility of television changed how people received and experienced information, expanding the circulation of pedagogies of empire. Occasionally mass-produced texts offered spectators alternative, nuanced, or more realistic media representations, but familiar stereotypes of Indigenous peoples and racialized immigrants dominated. The definitive portrayal of Indigenous peoples as tropes of white possessive logics cohered in sound Westerns. As seen in *The Plainsman* (1937), films froze Native Americans in a pre-1900 context and elaborated on Turner's Frontier Thesis. (When the popularity of Westerns briefly waned in the early 1930s, a spate of pre–Hayes Code[130] films that attempted to portray Natives more sympathetically were produced, but consumers preferred the "Hollywood Indian."[131]) Similar to silent Westerns, those with sound defined white settlers and Natives in binary opposition, and noble/ignoble "savage" Natives were portrayed as vanishing, given the westward march of superior white settler "civilization." As with stage performances, talkies featured "Indian" language coded as uncivilized with the dropping of articles and slow delivery, and a "tom-tom" beat of drums continued to signal the appearance of Indigenous people.[132] The iconic white, male, "all American" hero, the cowboy, continued to be defined in contrast to Hollywood Natives. John Ford's

---

127. Ngai, *Impossible Subjects*, 13.

128. Camacho, *Migrant Imaginaries*, 109.

129. Daniels, *Prisoners without Trial*; and R. Lee, *Orientals*, 146–47.

130. From 1934 to 1969, the Hayes or Motion Picture Code was used to safeguard morality in films. Sex and violence, for instance, were heavily regulated and censored by the Production Code Administration (PCA), though racial violence was certainly not.

131. Aliess, *Making the White Man's Indian*, 45.

132. Kilpatrick, *Celluloid Indian*, 36–38.

PROXIMAL PUBLIC PEDAGOGIES · 59

Stagecoach (1939) made John Wayne, who starred in eighty-three Westerns, a star. The classic film, which follows a group of white settlers traveling through "dangerous" Apache territory in the nineteenth century (of course) and features predictable portrayals of "savage Indian" attacks and white male heroics, has been remade many times. Subsequent Westerns featured similar themes.

A handful of Westerns that framed the federal government and/or white settlers as protectors of and friends to Indigenous peoples and framed "noble savages" as loyal allies to whites and colonial governmentality also bolstered white possessive logics. The *Lone Ranger* film serial (1938) solidified the white/ Native brotherhood trope via the Lone Ranger and his loyal Indigenous sidekick, Tonto. Played by Victor Daniels / Chief Thundercloud, who controversially claimed various tribal memberships, Tonto's defining characteristic was his loyalty to the Lone Ranger and therefore US governmentality.

In the pre–Hayes Code period, tropes of immigrant criminality also drew audiences with spectacles of violence. The stereotype of the Italian mobster, a dark and swarthy villain, became common following the trials of Al Capone and other Mafiosi. Mafia plots and themes became their own Hollywood genre. Notable examples include *Little Ceaser* (1931) and the original *Scarface* (1932), based on the life of Capone. Paul Muni, a Jewish immigrant, played the mobster. Mexican and Latinx criminality continued in sound Westerns and in films that framed Mexicans as "social problems," often in connection to violence against white women. From 1935 to 1965, these were the only feature-length films about Mexicans or Chicanx until the first Chicanx-produced films in the 1970s.[133] Moreover, films such as *Bordertown* (1935)—which also starred Paul Muni as the Mexican American protagonist, pointing to "ethnic" interchangeability—also portrayed the border or the urban barrio as a wild, abject space where crime and violence are naturalized, overlapping at times explicitly with the US American tradition of portraying the "wild" frontier as a stand-in for "Indian" savagery. Developing from the Mexican dark lady / seductress villainess of silent cinema, the sexy, "hot-blooded," and "exotic" Latina "spitfire" stereotype was embodied by actress Lupe Velez in the 1930s and Carmen Miranda in the 1940s and 1950s.[134]

Gendered, sexualized Asian alienness likewise carried into the talkies of the 1930s and into the 1950s. In *Daughter of the Dragon* (1931), Chinese American actress Anna May Wong cemented the stereotype of the "Dragon Lady," a deceitful, mysterious, and conniving Asian woman. The Fu Manchu and Charlie Chan franchises grew, extending stereotypes of "bad" and "good" Asian

---

133. Noriega, "Citizen Chicano," 91–96.
134. Mendible, *From Bananas to Buttocks.*

60 · CHAPTER 1

men. Thus, in sound film, the differentially racialized Hollywood immigrant, like the Hollywood Native, was fundamentally alien to white possessive logics, even when overtly supporting them as with Tonto and Charlie Chan.

•

Following World War II and into the early decades of the Cold War, the exertion of US empire via proximal Native American and immigration policy was once again overhauled to reflect changing political and social norms. While the latter appeared to be more inclusive, in the Era of Termination and Relocation (1945–61) the US government viciously attempted to end remaining obligations to Indigenous peoples and fully assimilate them.

From 1947 a conservative Republican Congress sought ways to reduce New Deal expenditures, making the trust relationship with Natives—and policies and programs that might resemble socialism or communism—a focal point. President Eisenhower, Congress, the BIA, and mainstream media framed termination as a means of modernization, progress, and freedom for Indigenous peoples. In 1953 the House Concurrent Resolution 108 declared the intent of Congress to terminate its responsibilities to Indigenous peoples, and Public Law 280 executed it. Indigenous peoples were to be "freed from Federal supervision and control and all disabilities specifically applicable to Indians."[135] Federal support or existing treaty agreements were terminated for over a hundred tribes, and the government subsidized the relocation of Indigenous peoples from reservations to urban areas, thereby granting Indigenous peoples all of the same "privileges and responsibilities" as other US citizens.[136] While some liberals and Christian groups called for increased Indigenous civil rights to remedy racist exclusions,[137] this latest extension of US citizenship and civil rights further imposed state legislative and juridical authority upon Indigenous peoples; ramped up land dispossession, with over a million acres of land removed from trust status by 1970;[138] and made Natives' incomes subject to federal taxes as federal resources were taken away from them. These impoverishing policies also continued to imperil Indigenous people's cultural, political, and social systems.[139]

---

135. H.R. Res. 108, 83rd Cong. (1953); and Pub. L. 83-280, 67 Stat. 588 (1953).

136. H.R. Res. 108, 83rd Cong. (1953).

137. Deloria and Lytle, *American Indians, American Justice*, ch. 1.

138. "Termination Era, the 1950s, Public Law 280," Federal Indian Law for Alaska Tribes, University of Alaska Fairbanks, accessed December 12, 2020, https://www.uaf.edu/tribal/112/unit_2/terminationerathe1950spubliclaw280.php#:~:text=Over%20100%20tribes%20were%20terminated,the%20Menominee%20Tribe%20in%20Wisconsin.

139. Deloria and Lytle, *American Indians, American Justice*, ch. 1.

Conflicting demands for labor and racial and ethnic purity also underscored the next major immigration legislation, the 1952 McCarran–Walter Act, also known as the Immigration and Nationality Act. Due to backlash against eugenics and racism following World War II, formal racial barriers were removed from immigration law. Nonetheless, the policy entrenched white possession: while the Western Hemisphere remained exempt from quotas, under an annual limit of 270,000 immigrants, Johnson–Reed quotas favoring nations with predominately white Northern European citizens remained and were bolstered by a new preference system: highly skilled immigrants and their spouses, then immigrants seeking family reunification, then general immigrants. As many Jews sought asylum, refugees were the final category. Responding to mounting Cold War tensions, immigrants deemed subversive could be deported, and subversive visitors denied entry. LGBTQ+ immigrants were also excluded (see the conclusion).

While President Harry Truman vetoed the McCarran–Walter Act as a perpetuation of the racist quota system,[140] cosponsor McCarran (D-Nevada) insisted in a congressional debate in 1953, the same year that termination began, that the law would protect the US from

> hard core indigestible blocs who have not become integrated into the American way of life but which, on the contrary, are its deadly enemies. Today as never before untold millions are storming our gates for admission and those states are cracking under the strain. The solution of the problems of Europe and Asia will not come through a transplanting of those problems to the United States.[141]

His racialized rhetoric of security, with antecedents in colonial fears of "Indian savagery" and the recent World War II rationalization for imprisoning Japanese Americans, complemented Cold War imperatives to protect white US Americans from external threats that could easily become internal. To that end, the preference system also safeguarded heteropatriarchy: most categories of work that women disproportionately did were considered unskilled, even when women did the same work as men.[142]

Moreover, in response to the civil rights movement's exposure of systemic white supremacy with landmark cases such as *Brown v. Board of Education* (1954), which removed all formal legal segregation from US law and recognized the equal rights of Black Americans, the notion of "colorblindness" or

---

140. Quoted in Jacobson, *Rights across Borders*, 49–50.

141. 83rd Cong. Rec. 1518 (1953) (statement of S. McCarran).

142. Gardener, *Qualities of a Citizen*, 213.

62 · CHAPTER 1

race-neutrality and a new multicultural national imaginary coalesced to perpetuate white possession. Racism was severed from systemic, material conditions and reframed as a problem between individuals, and antiracism was accordingly rearticulated as individual rights.[143] Additionally, Matthew Frye Jacobson has shown how the notion of a hierarchy of "white races" ensconced in immigration policy and popular culture was replaced with the singular category "Caucasian." Domestic civil rights politics eclipsed divisions among whites: a black/white dyad of racial politics and the concept of ethnicity was adopted to describe difference that was "cultural" rather than racial and "scientific," and "the 'ethnic' experience of European immigrant assimilation and mobility [. . .] became the standard against which Blacks were measured—and found wanting."[144] Indigenous peoples and people of color were too found wanting. Simultaneously, during the Cold War the notion of a uniquely ethnically diverse nation, especially in connection to immigration, was increasingly embraced as evidence of the exceptional superiority of the US's capitalist democratic system. As the midcentury closed, the multicultural politics of recognition as a new pedagogy of empire began to cohere in policy and media.

During World War II and into the Cold War, media continued to reflect the shifting geography and imagination of US empire. Portrayals of Indigenous peoples and racialized immigrants diversified to an extent, given the wartime recruitment and heroism of Indigenous peoples[145] and people of color; Allies' commitments to antiracism, antifascism, and decolonization; and the increasing momentum of civil rights and Black Power movements. Television also became widely available in the 1950s, with color broadcasting introduced in the 1960s, and it became a dominant medium influencing public opinion.[146] Mostly familiar stereotypes of Indigenous and racialized immigrant aliens prevailed, with only white ethnic representation substantially shifting.

Alongside hackneyed images of Native savagery in Western films and popular television shows such as *Death Valley Days* (1952–70), which Ronald Reagan hosted and acted in from 1963 until 1966, a spate of wartime Western films and TV shows lauded the noble Indigenous warrior who forged political alliances with whites. In *Buffalo Bill* (1944) Cody was reframed as a friend to

---

143. See Bell, *And We Are Not Saved*; Delgado and Stefanic, *Derrick Bell Reader*; Bell, "Racial Realism"; Delgado, "Imperial Scholar"; and Delgado and Stefanic, *Critical Race Theory*.

144. Jacobson, *Whiteness of a Different Color*, 110–11.

145. Twenty-five thousand Indigenous people served in the armed forces during World War II. The heroism of Diné code talkers and Ira Hayes, a Pima Indian and one of the six soldiers photographed raising the US flag on Iwo Jima, was celebrated in mainstream US culture.

146. Kellner, *Media Culture*, 1.

and protector of Natives in the West rather than their conqueror, and Indigenous assimilation into a welcoming US proto-multiculture became a common Western story line. The various figures of Hollywood Natives continued to be visually and often culturally monolithic or just incorrect, with costume designers' interpretations of Plains tribes' clothing continuing to dominate: Native men wore headdresses, breech cloths, and moccasins, and carried a weapon, often a tomahawk (even though the tomahawk as a symbol of Indigenous violence is a white settler invention),[147] and women were Native princesses, clothed in long, beaded and fringed dresses made of buckskin and often beaded headbands with a lone upright feather in the back. These Natives often lived in tipis and hunted buffalo.[148] While the more sympathetic Westerns seemed to improve upon those that centered on conquest, these early iterations of multiculturalism were produced in the shadow of termination policy, occluding the violent realities of historical and ongoing Indigenous dispossession, and in connection with wartime politics in which the US was depicted as heroic rather than as the instigator of Indigenous genocide and racialized violence.

Gendered, racialized binaries of "good" and "bad" immigrants also persisted in film and TV. Social problem films about Mexicans fell into three subgenres: romantic melodrama, courtroom drama / juvenile delinquent, and boxing.[149] Fu Manchu and Charlie Chan were translated to the small screen, with white actor Glen Gordon playing Dr. Fu Manchu, continuing the Hollywood practice of yellow face. Simultaneously, as the Soviet Union cited the US's racial tensions as evidence of its/capitalism's failures, Asian immigrant women were represented as submissive and therefore ideal candidates for assimilation in the increasingly, exceptionally multicultural US. *Sayonara* (1957) starred Marlon Brando as an Air Force pilot during the Korean War and Miiko Taka as a Japanese dancer, his love interest. Lee, drawing a parallel to the Pocahontas-style popular mythology in which a woman of color becomes the mother of the nation through ethnic assimilation, observes that "the Oriental woman is assimilated through the domestication of her exotic (racialized) sexuality" in marriage to a white US American man.[150] The double suicide of another serviceman and his Japanese-born wife, who the military tried to separate, also portrays anti-Asian racism as ugly, deadly, and profoundly un-American.

---

147. Stevens, "Tomahawk," 475–511.
148. Kilpatrick, *Celluloid Indian*, 51.
149. Noriega, "Citizen Chicano."
150. R. Lee, *Orientals*, 179.

64 • CHAPTER 1

Senator John F. Kennedy's best-selling book *A Nation of Immigrants* (1958) was a tipping point in terms of white ethnics' full incorporation into white possession and the crystallization of multiculturalism as a new pedagogy of empire. The book popularized a new multicultural idea of the United States as an exceptionally democratic nation defined by the ethnic diversity of its immigrants, not coincidentally introduced as he was (successfully) aspiring to become the first president born of immigrants and the first Catholic president. But Irish American Kennedy's national imaginary idealized *white* ethnic diversity and hinged on erasure of Indigenous genocide and dispossession and chattel slavery, even going so far as to reframe Indigenous peoples and enslaved Africans as kinds of immigrants.[151]

In a variety of media, the stereotypes of the stingy Jew, the Italian mafia criminal, and the Italian buffoon, anchored in popular TV comedies such as *The Jimmy Durante Show* (1954–56) and *The Abbott and Costello Show* (1952–54), were balanced by alternative representations of hardworking, upwardly mobile white ethnic immigrants. Protagonists of the radio shows *The Goldbergs* (1929–46), about an upwardly mobile Jewish family, and the sitcom *Life with Luigi* (1948–53), about a hardworking Italian immigrant, exemplified the new "nation of immigrants" imagination of empire. The Italian Latin lover stereotype, emblematized by Rudolph Valentino in 1920s silent film, included singers and national sex symbols such as Frank Sinatra and Dean Martin (born Dino Paul Crocetti). Cold War activism in Hollywood, historically known as McCarthyism, targeted the industry and its Jewish leaders, adding a layer of complexity to white ethnic media representation. Thus, as part of the rise of multiculturalism as a new pedagogy of empire, white ethnics shifted to the "settler" position in media as well as policy, while the gendered, sexualized alien statuses of Indigenous peoples and immigrants of color persisted.

MULTICULTURAL MYTH-MAKING: THE 1960S AND 1970S

In reaction to a period of unprecedented activism and visibility for Indigenous peoples and people of color, seemingly progressive policies and official multiculturalism perpetuated white possessive empire-building in more surreptitious ways. Here I elaborate on major Native American and immigration policies and mediascapes in the context of inaugural US neoliberal empire. Subsequent chapters analyze specific late twentieth-century public pedagogies in depth.

---

151. Dunbar-Ortiz, *Not a Nation of Immigrants,* xiii–xiv.

As watershed antiracist laws such as the Civil Rights Act (1964), the Immigration and Nationality Act (INA; 1965), and the American Indian Civil Rights Act (1968) passed, President Lyndon Johnson's War on Poverty reflected a fear that US resources were insufficient for the future population. Antiracist, multiculturalist pedagogies of empire protected and furthered white possession, mitigating that fear, among others.

Following postwar ostensible commitments to antiracism, antifascism, and decolonization, and the increasing movements for civil rights, a series of multiculturalism(s) reframed white supremacy.[152] Carrying on with Kennedy's vision of a multicultural "nation of immigrants," INA lawmakers and Johnson himself "intended to redress the grievances of European ethnic groups and to give more than token representation to Asians."[153] INA equalized quota limits for all nations (including the Western Hemisphere) and privileged family reunification; it was anticipated that heterosexual white ethnic immigrants would fill most new slots. LGBTQ+ immigrants were more explicitly excluded. Building on the group identity politics of the civil rights movement, the so-called "ethnic revival" politics underpinning INA and other policy initiatives cast white ethnics as the victims rather than perpetrators/beneficiaries of racism. By allegedly overcoming poverty and discrimination with nothing but hard work and tenacity (a narrative that erases the federal welfare given to white ethnics with the New Deal and in post–World War II policies such as the GI Bill), white ethnic immigrants and their descendants were rendered models of assimilation, self-sufficient upward mobility, and gendered, sexualized respectability in the newly officially multicultural "nation of immigrants."[154]

The model minority thesis, part of the "nation of immigrants"/multiculturalism myth, likewise ostensibly proved that US capitalist democracy was inclusive. Sociologist William Petersen coined the term "model minority" in the 1966 New York Times Magazine article "Success Story: Japanese American Style." The model minority is defined by self-sufficient economic success and a strong family ethic that enabled Japanese Americans to avoid becoming a "problem minority" despite discrimination.[155] Gendered "Asian" racial difference was redefined as individual enterprise and self-regulation, with education and parenting cast as the most important investments.[156] Like the rhetoric of "colorblindness," the new multicultural "nation of immigrants" and model

---

152. Melamed, *Represent and Destroy*.

153. Daniels, *Guarding the Golden Door*, 139; and Johnson, "Remarks at the Signing of the Immigration Bill, Liberty Island, New York, October 3, 1965," 1038.

154. Jacobson, *Roots Too*.

155. Petersen, "Success Story, Japanese-American Style," *New York Times Magazine*, January 9, 1966.

156. Jun, *Race for Citizenship*, 130–32; and Day, *Alien Capital*, 5.

minority imaginaries erased or rationalized the entanglements of Indigenous dispossession and racism structuring US empire.

After all, as historically, immigrants were differentially racialized in policy to safeguard the newly "ethnic" white property interests underpinning US empire. By the 1970s, poverty in immigrant-sending nations (often due to US austerity policies), INA's expansion of family reunification when the backlog for white ethnics was mostly resolved and immigration from Europe had declined, and demand for a pool of cheap immigrant labor made Mexican, Latin American, Caribbean, and Asian immigrants the most prevalent groups, and more women were migrating. Mexico was the top source of documented and undocumented immigration.[157] Although the *volume* of immigrants had not changed much, Nixon's Commissioner of Immigration, Leonard F. Chapman, declared an undocumented immigration crisis,[158] emphatically racialized as Mexican and to an extent Latinx, gendered, and sexualized. Simultaneously, free market economists such as then-governor of California Ronald Reagan wanted cheap Mexican immigrant labor. The two distinct imaginings of immigration and the nation—the "nation of immigrants" and "immigration emergency"—began to circulate in the late 1960s and 1970s, reaching national prominence in policy and media in the 1980s and into the early 2000s, providing a crucial ingredient in the formation of the neoliberal idea of democracy.[159] Thus amid and also through the new multicultural myth, the settler colonial government, established to dispossess Indigenous peoples, differentially racialized immigrants (as white ethnic idealized citizens, "Asian" model minorities, and Mexican and Latinx criminals and/or "illegal aliens") to continue to advance white possession.

In the Self-Determination Era (1970s–present) of Native American policy, multiple laws were passed, often the result of Indigenous activism, that, also connected to the new multicultural national narrative, ultimately continued to dispossess Indigenous peoples. Despite Nixon's responsive 1970 declaration of an era of "self-determination without termination,"[160] his administration quickly appropriated Indigenous self-determination with "New Federalism"—austerity framed as liberation in true neoliberal form—in the context of the ongoing War on Poverty ideology of a scarcity of resources (though the scarcity of politicians' willingness to share resources was the real problem). Chapter 2 examines sterilization abuse against Indigenous and racialized immigrant women in connection with welfare receipt under Nixonian War on

---

157. Zolberg, *Nation by Design*, 340.
158. Daniels, *Guarding the Golden Door*, 119–220; and Zolberg, *Nation by Design*, 340.
159. Perry, *Cultural Politics of US Immigration*.
160. Nixon, "Special Message to the Congress on Indian Affairs."

Poverty "family planning" efforts as part of the throughline of white possessive reproductive policies and politics.

While the Indian Self-Determination and Education Assistance Act (1975), as well as the Indian Religious Freedom Act and Indian Child Welfare Act (ICWA; both 1978), improved Indigenous peoples' lives in some regards, ICWA and *Oliphant v. Suquamish Indian Tribe* (1978) also made "Native sovereignty dependent upon biological difference and a heteronormative logic of reproduction."[161] Through an ongoing legacy of boarding schools, state agencies removed one-quarter to one-third of Indigenous children from their families; the rate of Native children's adoption by non-Natives was twenty times higher than the national average.[162] ICWA remedied this with federal standards for the removal of Indigenous children and granted tribal courts jurisdiction over the care of Indigenous children, prioritizing placement "in homes which will reflect the unique values of Indian culture."[163] However, while settler colonialism is organized by racialization, legally defining Indigenous peoples as a racial rather than political group is dispossessive, complicating if not negating Indigenous people's unique relationship with the federal government. The first item of ICWA also (re)stated Congress' plenary power over Indigenous affairs.[164] In *Oliphant* the Supreme Court ruled that tribal courts have no jurisdiction over non-Natives who commit crimes on their lands. In addition to defining Indigenous peoples as a race, the ruling, written by then associate justice William Rehnquist (who became Chief Justice and issued many racist decisions), cited and quoted over a dozen nineteenth-century Supreme Court precedents, policy statements, acts of Congress, and reports, all of which stereotyped Natives as "lawless, uncivilized, unsophisticated, hostile, or warlike savages."[165] Part of a colonial throughline, early Self-Determination Era legislation thus continued to circumscribe Indigenous sovereignty along gendered, sexualized, racialized, variously biologized lines.

In these ways and others that I will explore, in the ascendant neoliberal context, US empire continued to be exerted via proximal policy for Indigenous peoples and differentially racialized immigrants. The public pedagogies of US neoliberal empire would continue to rebrand white possessive logics in connection with civil rights, multiculturalism, and self-determination.

---

161. Rifkin, "Around 1978," 171.

162. Strong, "What Is an Indian Family?," 205–31.

163. "Indian Child Welfare Act," US Department of the Interior: Indian Affairs, accessed July 28, 2023, https://www.bia.gov/bia/ois/dhs/icwa.

164. Indian Child Welfare Act of 1978, Pub. L. 95-608 (1978).

165. Williams, *Like a Loaded Weapon*, xxiii.

68 • CHAPTER 1

Jacobson notes that the culture industries began to lavish attention on ethnicity in the 1970s,[166] when the multicultural politics of recognition / multiculturalism as *the* imagination of a new phase of US empire began to chart. While differentially racialized immigrants and their descendants were once again portrayed according to gendered, sexualized "good" and "bad" poles, drawing from older tropes and the bedrock of figures of Indigenous alienness and savagery, white liberal counterculture and some mainstream texts appropriated and instrumentalized Indigeneity. Again, in the end, white possessive empire-building was the same, but the settler colonial means of positioning Indigenous peoples and differentially racialized groups of immigrants differed.

Popular media about white ethnics and Asian model minorities, often in comparison to "problematic" racial groups, built on JFK's multicultural "nation of immigrants" ideal. Nathan Glazer and Daniel Patrick Moynihan's definitive *Beyond the Melting Pot: The Negroes, Puerto Ricans, Jews, Italians, and Irish of New York City* (1963) asserted that ethnic groups such as Black people and Puerto Ricans could achieve equal standing through organization and self-help because white ethnic European immigrants had, despite their failure to fully assimilate or "melt." As a sociologist, a soldier in Johnson's "War on Poverty," and eventually a senator (D-New York) elected in 1982, 1988, and 1994, Moynihan powerfully shaped policy with his views. In another instance that explicitly illuminates the entanglements of settler colonialism and racial capitalism, he also prepared *The Negro Family: The Case for National Action,* also known as *The Moynihan Report* (1965), a document for the Department of Labor in which he claimed that Black women heading families caused persistent poverty among Black people, despite civil rights gains.[167] He argued for eliminating Black people's dependence on state assistance by reinstating (coercing) traditional gender norms and marriage because white Italian American and Jewish nuclear families had far higher rates of "married-spouse present" homes than their Black counterparts and were not impoverished.[168]

On the big screen, the Oscar-winning *Rocky* (1976), directed by John Avildsen and written by and starring Italian American actor Sylvester Stallone as boxer Rocky Balboa, visualized ideas of gendered white (ethnic) settler grievance and anti-Blackness for eager spectators. The uneducated, hardworking Rocky cannot become the world heavyweight boxing champion because he is beaten by Black boxer Apollo Creed (Carl Weathers). Popular representations of the model minority stereotype did similar multicultural work to support white possessive logics. For instance, *Flower Drum Song* (1960), like

---

166. Jacobson, *Whiteness of a Different Color,* 9.
167. Thaggert, "Marriage, Moynihan, Mahogany," 721.
168. Moynihan, *Negro Family.*

Sayonara, held up submissive, subservient Chinese American women as the ideals and conduits of ethnic assimilation.

Anticipating the 1980s, when a fundamentally Mexican/Latinx "immigrant emergency" and criminality became ubiquitous in media (what Leo Chavez calls the Latino Threat),[169] and in contrast to white ethnic and Asian men, Latinx men were most frequently represented as criminals on the big and small screen, and Latinx women were increasingly hypersexualized. *West Side Story* (1961), the first major film and play about Puerto Ricans in the US, combined a stereotype of Puerto Rican males as violent gang members[170] with a "nation of immigrants" imaginary of the mainland US as filled with opportunities for upward mobility. In the shadow of the Puerto Rican independence movement, films such as *Badge 373* (1973) marked a shift in representations of Puerto Ricans from an inferior group of aliens in need of civilization/assimilation (a by now very familiar refrain) to criminal aliens who needed to be contained.[171]

Simultaneously, white liberal counterculture fetishized supposed Indigenous mysticism, closeness to nature, and unity, updating the "noble savage" stereotype for the civil rights era with the "groovy injun," or environmental "Indian."[172] White antiestablishment sentiment also embraced an anti-imperial version of the "noble savage": "nineteenth-century native resistance provided a homegrown model for opposition to the American military imperialism that protestors saw in Vietnam."[173] Additionally, many 1960s and early 1970s films used Native Americans or Indigenous identity as metaphors for oppressed groups, building on *Broken Arrow* (1950), one of the first "sympathetic" Westerns, with revisionist Westerns such as *Cheyenne Autumn* (1964). As in the past, many films featured inaccurate and homogenized Indigenous cultures and cast non-Natives in Native roles.

---

169. Chavez, *Latino Threat.*

170. Perez, "From Assimilation to Annihilation," 142–63.

171. It bears repeating that Puerto Rico is a US colony. Puerto Ricans became US citizens under the 1917 Jones Act but continue to be treated like aliens. US projects such as the Chardon Plan, the Chicago Plan, and Operation Bootstraps shaped Puerto Rican migration to/from the continental US. For instance, in the 1950s, Operation Bootstraps courted Puerto Ricans as migrant workers, factory workers, and domestic workers. When their numbers increased and Puerto Ricans became more politically active in the 1970s, they were linked to Blackness, poverty, and crime and thus cast as threats to US stability. Perez, *Near Northwest Side Story*; and Molina-Guzman, *Dangerous Curves,* 85. Therefore, Puerto Ricans share commonalities with other Latinx people and Latinx im/migrants but are uniquely structurally positioned given their status as US citizens and *technically* former colonial subjects.

172. P. Deloria, *Playing Indian,* 159–61; Kilpatrick, *Celluloid Indians,* 67; and Dunbar-Ortiz and Gilio-Whitaker, *"All the Real Indians Died Off,"* 4.

173. P. Deloria, *Playing Indian,* 159.

70 • CHAPTER 1

Broadly, the popularity among usually white non-Natives of a gendered, mostly (hetero)sexualized, homogenized pan-Indigenous dress, arts, and culture required "Indigenous people to fit within the heteronormative archetypes of an Indigeneity that was authentic in the past but is culturally and legally vacated in the present." This settler imagining of Native "authenticity" supplanted a "costumed affiliation" with Indigeneity for Indigenous legal claims and rights to governance, territories, and cultures.[174] In queer countercultures, Indigenous gender variance was appropriated to make a case for non-Native LGBTQ+ people's inclusion or belonging in the settler state.[175] In what was becoming quintessentially neoliberal form, decolonization was reduced to inclusion in the multicultural milieu and the marketability of ostensibly Indigenous commodities, hetero- and homonormative appropriation of Indigeneity, and sympathy for Indigenous peoples.

In accordance with much Self-Determination Era policy, mainstream media representations of Indigeneity perpetuated white possessive logics as they seemed to challenge them, entrenching multiculturalism as a key pedagogy of US neoliberal empire. What Byrd calls the "originary trauma" of colonization had to be erased or relegated to the past for the ascensionist imagination of the US as a multicultural liberal and then neoliberal democracy to exist, embracing some racialized immigrants and citizens while exploiting/excluding others. The "myth of the multiculture" replaced the myth of the frontier.

In sum, entanglements of Indigenous dispossession and anti-immigration in proximal public pedagogies founded and furthered US continental and global empire. White possessive geographies, imaginaries, and myths would continue to underpin US neoliberal empire.

---

174. Barker, "Introduction: Critically Sovereign," 2–3.
175. Morgensen, "Settler Homonationalism," 105–6.

CHAPTER 2

"Entitlement" Warfare

Welfare and Remapping National (B)orders

The first feature film, Cecil B. DeMille's *S— Man* (1914, remade in 1918 and 1931), provided audiences with an enduring education about Indigenous women and especially mothers as obstacles to US empire, for the films influenced the development of early cinema.[1] The plot is based on the eponymous play (1904) and novel (1906) by Edwin Milton Royle. Accused of a crime he did not commit, a wealthy, educated white Englishman flees to the West, which along with its Indigenous inhabitants is cast via undeveloped, "wild" landscape, costuming, and intertitles as primitive and abject in contrast to the white wealth and refinery of England and to an extent the eastern US. A Native woman, Nat-U-Ritch, daughter of the Ute chief, kills a white villain to save the Englishman from him, and they marry and have a child. But other settlers pejoratively view him as a "s— man" given their interracial union, and a sheriff pursues Nat-U-Ritch for murder. When the Englishman is exonerated and free to return East, because Nat-U-Ritch cannot or will not assimilate into white society, he decides to remain with her and, without her consent, send their child to England to be educated and raised as a white man by a white woman. Hunted by law enforcement and devastated to be separated from her child, the Indigenous woman completes suicide. In the final scene of the original film, which featured Lillian St. Cyr (Winnebago Tribe), the only

---

1. Merskin, "The S-Word," 356.

72 • CHAPTER 2

Indigenous actor to play Nat-U-Ritch, the Englishman holds the Indigenous woman's body as their child's new white mother shields his eyes from the tragedy. A crowd of white townspeople and a few elaborately costumed Natives look on.

Colonial power is imprinted on bodies in gendered, sexualized ways, and protecting the white heteropatriarchal property interests underpinning it necessitates controlling the reproduction of Indigenous peoples and people of color. At the turn of the twentieth century, the public pedagogy of US empire was forcefully exerted though the "intimate domains" of sex, domestic arrangement, and parenting,[2] as well as in connection to welfare. Regarding Native American policy, allotment under the Dawes Act, which forced Indigenous peoples into heteropatriarchal kinship arrangements and rendered communal Indigenous lands private property, and the removal multitudes of Indigenous children from their communities to be educated in Christian schools with heteropatriarchal curricula was underway. The settler colonial state also solidified its view of its financial relationship to Indigenous peoples as part of fiduciary duty to an infantilized, dependent racialized group rather than a form of payment owed to a subject population.

And in media, through the abject body of the Indigenous woman, Hollywood's first feature film "underscores the belief that white civilization has no room for American Indians. Its message is bold: society rejects Native Americans and simultaneously destroys their kinship."[3] The *S— Man* films, which adhered to the same basic plot (with differences in the casting and character of Nat-U-Ritch and the final scene), established what M. Elise Marubbio calls the "Celluloid Indian Maiden," a Native woman allied with a white male hero as a lover and/or helper who must die so that US empire can thrive. The mixed-race child's "heritage and 'savage' environment remain latent threats that must be erased through proper education, separation from his mother, and removal to a superior and more civilized space. [. . .] The woman's sacrifice ensures her son's future as a civilized American."[4] Similar themes followed in Progressive Era films, the Indigenous woman representing "the colonial relationship between Native America and the American nation."[5]

Furthermore, the archetypal Celluloid Indian Maiden, an embodied justification of genocide to advance white heteropatriarchal property interests, or "white possession,"[6] was actually a sanitized version of the s— stereotype,

---

2. Stoler, "Tense and Tender Ties," 829.

3. Aleiss, *Making the White Man's Indian*, 21.

4. Marubbio, *Killing the Indian Maiden*, 44.

5. Marubbio, *Killing the Indian Maiden*, 60.

6. Moreton-Robinson, *White Possessive*.

which has had a pernicious impact upon the quality of life of, perceptions of, and opportunities for Indigenous women for over four hundred years.[7] Continuing Euro-American settlers' racialization of Indigenous peoples as marked by gender and sexual perversity, their bodies equated with dirt and pollution and therefore violable for the sake of civilization, from the seventeenth century on, Euro-American writers and commentators persistently described Indigenous women as dark, dirty drudges, fecund mothers, and abused beasts of burden who were forced to do all of the work within Indigenous communities (because men were savagely waging warfare or lazy) and/or as wanton and sexually depraved.[8] Likely an English and French appropriation of an Eastern Algonquian word, the term s— first appeared in print around 1634. According to some Indigenous scholars and activists, in the Algonquian and Mohawk languages the word means vagina or female genitalia.[9] Others aver it means "the totality of being female," and the Algonquin *esqua, squa, skwa* does not translate to a woman's female anatomy.[10] What is not debated is that white settlers used the term as a racial slur[11] to reduce Indigenous women to things to be violated and discarded or, at best, to render them "uncivilized," inferior, and therefore inevitably doomed, as in the *S— Man* films. From the nineteenth century, the stereotype persisted in captivity narratives, dime novels, film, television, and advertisements. For instance, a 1885 Procter & Gamble advertisement for Ivory Soap framed uncleanliness as a symptom of savagery: a male "Indian" proclaimed that Ivory Soap "civilized my s— and me / And made us clean and fair to see."[12] Branded foods such as S— sifted peas and Siwash S— apples also capitalized on the stereotype's linking of land and gendered labor.[13] Therefore, in the shadow of Progressive Era policy that attacked Indigenous sovereignty and survival through the intimate domains, the mediated reification of Indigenous women as s—s, princesses, or some combination of the two grafted inferiority, savagery, dirtiness, and even danger onto their bodies. This public pedagogy cemented Indigenous women's violability and

---

7. Merskin, "The S-Word," 345. The s— is often the often older, heavier, darker converse to the Native princess. Both representations of Native women insinuate white Euro-American superiority and Indigenous women's bodily availability—Indigenous women's conquerability—to settlers and the settler state. See chapter 3 for in-depth discussion of the Native princess stereotype. Dunbar-Ortiz and Gilio-Whitaker, *"All the Real Indians Died Off,"* 138; and Marubbio, *Killing the Native Maiden.*

8. Smits, "S— Drudge," 27–49.

9. Merskin, "The S-Word," 348.

10. Vincent Shilling, "The S-Word: Offensive or Not?," *Indian Country Today,* September 23, 2018, https://ictnews.org/archive/the-word-squaw-offensive-or-not.

11. Piatote, *Domestic Subjects.*

12. Smith, *Conquest.*

13. Smits, "S— Drudge," 27–49.

74 • CHAPTER 2

made it clear that preventing or controlling the birth of the next generation of Natives was critical to the future of white possessive US empire-building.

While elements of the s— stereotype persisted in the treatment of racialized immigrant women, the imperatives of settler colonialism were applied through Progressive Era policy and programs to immigrant women distinctly. Differentially racialized immigrant women were cast as dirty and sexually depraved, inferior mothers, and/or excessively fecund burdens on the US welfare state to justify their exclusion from the US. Chinese women, viewed as lascivious sex workers, were excluded under the Page Law (1875) and more comprehensive Chinese Exclusion Act (1882). Although only a small number of Chinese women were sex workers, and many were coercively brought to the US, "Chinese" sex work as a racial and moral pollutant galvanized advocates of the Chinese Exclusion Act. Mostly invisible in popular entertainment, the sensationalized Chinese and sometimes Japanese female sex worker was a prevalent figure in late nineteenth-century newspapers, magazines, and official studies about new cities in the West.[14] On the East Coast, from 1882, white ethnic women, eligible for citizenship yet perceived as racially inferior to white people of Northern European descent and alarmingly fecund,[15] were excluded under "Likely to Become a Public Charge" (LPC) provisions and restricted via nation-based quotas under the Johnson–Reed Act (1924). Newspapers and magazines such as the *Saturday Evening Post* also frequently fretted over white ethnic women's potential to pollute the national stock and overwhelm the welfare state. While Western Hemisphere immigration was exempt from the quota system and Mexicans and Mexican women were likewise a matter of racial concern to eugenicists and lawmakers, cinematic representations of Mexican women as hypersexual and promiscuous were prevalent. Notably Lupe Velez, characterized later in her career as the "Mexican spitfire," played a hypersexualized Nat-U-Ritch in the 1931 *S— Man*. White possession was also advanced via Progressive Era policies, programs, and discourse aiming to assimilate and "uplift" Indigenous peoples and racialized immigrants—and especially women and mothers—through education, improving home and health conditions, and domestic work.[16]

In a throughline from the Progressive Era expansion of white possessive logics of US empire via intimate domains, the onset of neoliberal personal responsibility politics calcified in mid- to late twentieth-century public pedagogy about Indigenous peoples and racialized immigrants, especially mothers, in relation to welfare. Personal responsibility politics aver through "circuits

---

14. R. Lee, *Orientals,* 90–91.

15. Moloney, "Women's Sexual Morality," 95–122.

16. Hunziker, "Playing Indian, Playing Filipino," 432.

of cultural disavowal"[17] that inclusion and belonging in the settler state is available to all hard working, self-sufficient persons on a level playing field, blaming marginalized groups for the "premature death"[18] they are subject to precisely because of colonialism, white supremacy, and other systemic violences. Building on earlier pathologizations of Native and immigrant women such as the s— stereotype and racialization of immigrant women as immoral, hyperfertile, and/or likely to need public assistance, Nixon administration "family planning" policies, advancing Johnson's War on Poverty, resulted in widespread sterilization abuse that targeted Indigenous and immigrant and citizen women of color in connection with welfare. Sterilization abuse is defined as "the misinformed, coerced, or unknowing termination of the reproductive capacity of women and men." As Elena Gutierrez has noted, the history of sterilization abuse in the US "has demonstrated that practitioners of coercive sterilization have targeted their subjects according to race, class, and gender."[19] Although use of the s— racial slur diminished with the rise of multiculturalism, the stereotype is immortalized in media, continues to be used in numerous place names (although Indigenous activists continue to challenge its use),[20] and its afterlives continue to underpin state interventions in Indigenous women's reproductive autonomy, bodily sovereignty, and sovereignty writ large. Latina immigrants and citizens, stereotyped as impoverished, fecund, sexually depraved, and criminal, were likewise subject to sterilization abuse in connection with welfare. In short, sterilization is a genocidal tactic aimed at Indigenous peoples and racialized groups, especially women, to protect white possession. A "termination by accountants"[21] under the Reagan administration followed, advancing the Nixonian New Federalist appropriation of Indigenous self-determination to cast austerity as "liberation." Federal Native American programs, including healthcare, water, sanitary facilities, and education were decimated. A slashing of "entitlements," or the basic social services that make life livable such as healthcare and prenatal care, for immigrant and citizen women followed, rationalized by accusations that Black and undocumented Latinx immigrant "welfare queens" abused and thereby endangered the welfare state and future generations of (white) US citizens and needed to be liberated from the shackles of state dependency.

Lenape scholar Joanne Barker states "there is no postcolonial."[22] This chapter traces public pedagogy about welfare as a key tool of historical and

---

17. Day, "Racial Capitalism," 1043.
18. Hong, *Death beyond Disavowal*, 7.
19. Gutierrez, *Fertile Matters*, 36–37.
20. Merskin, "The S-Word," 345–66.
21. Morris, "Termination by Accountants," 63–69.
22. Barker, "Introduction: Critically Sovereign," 23.

ongoing US empire-building. I argue that the entanglement of gendered, sexualized welfare discourse about Indigenous peoples and racialized immigrants crystallized the premature death that, in connection with personal responsibility politics, provided the public pedagogy necessary to make US neoliberal empire thrive. I begin with the history of welfare in the US, which in connection with healthcare was foundational to US empire. I then explore eugenics in connection to welfare and its crescendos in sterilization abuse in the early twentieth century and into the 1970s. Next, I detail how Reaganite and late twentieth-century welfare discourse built on those policies and politics to continue to protect white property interests. I conclude with a return to the question of premature death and the ultimate cost of remapping US neoliberal empire via public pedagogy about welfare.

WELFARE AS BIOPOLITICAL WARFARE

The gendered organization of the US economy and government around Indigenous genocide and dispossession, the enslavement of Black people, and the expropriation of Mexicans guided the formation of the welfare state beginning in the seventeenth century,[23] and not coincidentally welfare and other governmentally created payments do not legally count as legitimate property. Welfare recipients—who are often disproportionately Indigenous peoples and people of color—are therefore further distanced from white property and whiteness itself as a property that bestows legal and economic benefits.[24] While he did not address settler colonialism, Michel Foucault theorized that modern nation-states control subjects through biopower, "an explosion of numerous and diverse techniques for achieving the subjugations of bodies and the control of populations."[25] Welfare has long been a nexus of white possessive biopower in a nation that centers propertied individualism in its political culture and policies, but welfare has also been a sphere of women's and especially Black women's resistance. Moreover, Indigenous peoples have a unique relationship to the welfare state; they were arguably the first welfare recipients given the colonial state's fiduciary duty to them. Through treaty agreements and later policy, the federal government has an obligation to deliver services such as healthcare, education, and other structural supports, as well as other forms of compensation, to Indigenous nations. Moreover, this "trust

---

23. Mink, "Lady and the Tramp," 92–122.
24. Harris, "Whiteness as Property," 1726–27.
25. Foucault, *History of Sexuality*, 140.

responsibility" obligates Congress to address Indigenous affairs in ways that benefit Indigenous people.[26]

Federal funds dispersed to Indigenous peoples may be fulfillment of treaty commitments, compensation for land ceded (often by force) to the US government, lease income on property held in trust by the federal government, or payment for the extraction of natural resources (a per capita percentage dispersed among tribal members).[27] The colonial state's fiduciary duty to Native peoples is therefore markedly distinct from general need-based welfare that all citizens are eligible for, and it is also distinct from federal programs such as New Deal housing loans or the GI Bill, both driven by different logics. (The New Deal focused on providing relief for the unemployed and the poor, as well as recovering and reforming the economy. Like other New Deal programs, loans and other governmental support were disproportionately given to whites. Through the latter the government paid or rewarded World War II veterans.) Both forms of governmental financial support that Indigenous peoples are eligible to receive and discourse about them have been critical to mapping and remapping the white possessive pedagogies of US empire. Therefore, the history of welfare begins with Indigenous peoples.

The Bureau of Indian Affairs (BIA) was created to manage federal relations with and obligations to Indigenous peoples. The BIA offers a range of programs for Native Americans allegedly comparable to state and local government programs, "e.g., education, social services, law enforcement, courts, real estate services, agriculture and range management, and resource protection."[28] The Indian Health Service (IHS), part of the US Department of Health and Human Services (HHS), serves Indigenous peoples. According to the IHS website,

> The provision of health services to members of federally-recognized tribes grew out of the special government-to-government relationship between the federal government and Indian tribes. This relationship, established in 1787, is based on Article I, Section 8 of the Constitution, and has been given form and substance by numerous treaties, laws, Supreme Court decisions, and Executive Orders. The IHS is the principal federal health care provider and health advocate for Indian people, and its goal is to raise their health status to the highest possible level.[29]

---

26. Dunbar-Ortiz and Gilio-Whitaker, *"All the Real Indians Died Off,"* 87–91.

27. "Frequently Asked Questions," Native American Rights Fund, last updated 2023, https://www.narf.org/frequently-asked-questions/; and Mihesuah, *American Indians,* 89.

28. "Benefits and Services," Tribes, US Department of the Interior, accessed July 31, 2023, https://www.doi.gov/tribes/benefits.

29. "About IHS," Indian Health Service, accessed on July 31, 2023, https://www.ihs.gov/aboutihs/.

78 · CHAPTER 2

Some other federal programs, such as the Administration for Native Americans, support tribal governments and social and economic development on reservations. Like all US citizens, all Native Americans, regardless of whether they are members of federally recognized tribes, are eligible for state welfare services.[30]

From the start of colonization in what became the US, welfare/healthcare was deployed as a biopolitical tool of conquest, beginning with British commander Lord Jeffrey Amherst's desire to send smallpox-infected blankets to Indigenous people as an act of warfare.[31] From 1775, the newly formed United States governed "Indian affairs" through the Continental Congress, transferring responsibility to the War Department upon its formation in 1789. Secretary of War John C. Calhoun established the BIA within his department in 1824.[32] The US government therefore first addressed Indigenous peoples' healthcare through the War Department: vaccines and other procedures were used on Indigenous people in proximity to military outposts and soldiers to prevent infectious diseases. An 1832 treaty between the Winnebago and US government was the first to include medical services.[33] In 1849, when colonial victory was clear, the BIA was transferred to the new Interior Department.[34] By 1875, half of the federal Native American agencies had doctors, and the first federal hospital was built in Oklahoma in the 1880s. In the early twentieth century, the BIA created a distinct health division with programs to prevent diseases and provide health education classes. Under the Indian Citizenship or Snyder Act (1921), Congress granted the BIA authorization to provide Indigenous healthcare. In 1955 Congress moved that responsibility to the Public Health Service, a division of the Department of Health, Education, and Welfare (HEW). This agency was renamed IHS in 1958. Subsequently, Congress appropriated more money for healthcare. Although IHS doctors increased from the 1960s and the Indian Healthcare Improvement Act (IHCIA) passed in 1976, a low ratio of medical professionals to Indigenous people continued into the 1980s, and IHS has always been severely underfunded.[35] Significantly, from 1831, these developments in Indigenous welfare/healthcare occurred in the shadow of *Cherokee Nation v. Georgia,* the first Marshall Trilogy case. The Supreme Court ruling infantilized Indigenous peoples as "domestic dependent nations" as opposed

---

30. "Benefits and Services."
31. Deloria and Lytle, *American Indians, American Justice,* ch. 9.
32. "What Is the BIA's History?" Indian Affairs, US Department of the Interior, last modified January 12, 2021, https://www.bia.gov/faqs/what-bias-history.
33. Lawrence, "Indian Health Service," 400.
34. "What Is the BIA's History?"
35. Lawrence, "Indian Health Service," 400.

"ENTITLEMENT" WARFARE · 79

to sovereign foreign nations, rendering them the US's first burden. Moreover, that inaugural language of Indigenous dependency has been and continues to be evoked or elaborated upon to justify border militarization, interior enforcement, and the illegalization, detainment, and deportation of im/migrants.[36] As this brief history indicates, Indigenous welfare/healthcare and the racialized discourse of dependency around it was built into US empire.

BETTER BREEDING AND BORDER CONTROL

To further early white possessive empire-building, genocidal projects targeted Indigenous women and children as the reproducers and next generations of Indigenous peoples, while enslaved Black women were forced to reproduce to provide the next generation of free laborers.[37] At the turn of the twentieth century when US colonial victory was apparent and slavery had been abolished, alongside Allotment Era and Progressive "uplift" policies and programs focused on intimate domains, controlling women's reproduction through scientific racism, in connection with welfare and discourses of dependency, became an important facet of the biologized violence endemic to US empire-building.

Although eugenics, the pseudoscience of improving the human race via "better breeding,"[38] has transformed over time, it has always been weaponized to support white possession. Sir Francis Galton, a British statistician and cousin of Charles Darwin, coined the term "eugenics" in 1883. He described it as "the science which deals with all the influences that improve the inborn qualities of a race; also with those that develop them to the utmost advantage."[39] Eugenic science spread quickly through Europe in the late nineteenth and early twentieth centuries and was popularized in the US when scientists began to focus on human heredity.[40] Initially, US-based eugenics was "positive" in that white Anglo-Saxon Protestants, already considered biologically superior according to phrenology and other spurious science, were encouraged to have more children. The "unfit"—Indigenous peoples, Black people and other people of color, racialized immigrants, and the poor and disabled—were considered biologically inferior, potential pollutants of the white race. To protect white property (and whiteness as a property), a subsequent

---

36. Lee-Oliver et al., "Imperialism, Settler Colonialism, and Indigeneity," 236.
37. Volscho, "Sterilization Racism," 18.
38. Stern, *Eugenic Nation*.
39. Galton quoted in Stern, *Eugenic Nation*, 10–11.
40. Ordover, *American Eugenics*, 126–30.

wave of "negative eugenics" focused on preventing the reproduction of the "unfit" with sterilization or excluding them from the nation.

In the first wave of US "negative eugenics" (which inspired Hitler), empire-expansion through entangled public pedagogies about Indigenous peoples, racialized immigrants, and welfare was sometimes explicit. In his speech at the Second National Conference on Race Betterment (SNCRB) in (1913), prominent eugenicist Paul Popeno noted that natural selection was "appropriately leading to the extinction of decadent races such as the American Indian." To bolster it and race improvement, he and his colleagues advocated for expanded compulsory sterilization policies and medical inspection of immigrants to keep the "unfit" out.[41] Margaret Sanger, who coined the term "birth control," opened the first birth control clinic in the US and founded the organizations that became Planned Parenthood. Sanger also "courted eugenicist support, championed economically coerced sterilization of those deemed 'unfit,' endorsed medical experimentation on poor women," established sterilization programs throughout the US and especially in Black communities, and wrote eugenicist and explicitly racist works.[42]

A range of policies enacted these "scientific" measures to protect ableist white property. In 1907, Indiana was the first state to establish a compulsory sterilization law for institutionalized persons deemed "unimprovable."[43] In the 1927 *Buck vs. Bell* case, about the sterilization of a Black woman considered hereditarily mentally disabled, the Supreme Court upheld a state's right to intervene in an institutionalized mentally disabled person's reproductive autonomy. Within twenty years, twenty-six more states passed compulsory sterilization laws for persons deemed a burden to the state. Yet in 1911, the first general welfare program, the Mothers' Pension program, was designed for white widows. Similar state programs proliferated, eventually declining with the Great Depression.[44] According to the logics of these roughly contemporary policies, white mothers (who were presumably improvable) deserved or were owed financial support from the government, while the disabled and women of color—and especially disabled women of color—were undeserving of bodily autonomy. Welfare, dependency, and disability were therefore racially coded in policy, and state-sponsored sterilization was a genocidal tactic aimed at "the unfit" to protect white possession. This was not the last time the colonial state coded dependency and/or welfare receipt among people of color as grounds for compulsory sterilization.

---

41. Stern, *Eugenic Nation*, 50–52.
42. Ordover, *American Eugenics*, 126–30.
43. Indiana General Assembly, *1907 Laws of the Indiana General Assembly*, 377–78.
44. Chang, *Disposable Domestics*, 70–71.

"ENTITLEMENT" WARFARE · 81

Immigration restriction, another white possessive eugenicist tactic, obviated a later "need" for sterilization at the expense of the state. As noted, explicitly gendered, racialized Progressive Era immigration policies and border policing that also attempted to regulate intimate domains, sometimes explicitly in connection to welfare receipt, included the Page Law (1875), the Chinese Exclusion Act (1882), the targeting of white ethnic immigrant women under LPC provisions (1882), and the national quota system introduced by the Johnson–Reed Act (1924).

Eugenicists also targeted Puerto Rican people, who though granted US citizenship in 1917 continue to be treated like both colonized peoples and immigrant aliens. Puerto Rico, originally home to the Taino, was colonized by Spain in 1493 and acquired (colonized) by the US in 1898. From 1928, eugenicists within the birth control movement lobbied for population control in Puerto Rico as a palliative for poverty that US colonization had created by devaluing the peso and dispossessing Puerto Rican ranchers and farmers, rendering 70 percent of the population landless by 1925. With Sanger's consultation, President Franklin Delano Roosevelt's Puerto Rican Reconstruction Administration established birth control clinics that James Gamble (of the Procter & Gamble company that advertised Ivory soap as a cure to gendered Native savagery) used as recruitment centers for sterilization and pharmaceutical product testing. The then highly experimental drug that became the birth control pill was tested on impoverished Puerto Rican women. Women with multiple children were also targeted for sterilization at certain hospitals and refused admittance if they refused to "consent" to sterilization.[45] Abuse of medical power, essentially absolute in Puerto Rico,[46] was part and parcel of US empire.

Overt US state-sponsored eugenics fell out of favor as the Nazi horrors became evident to the world but did not disappear as a tool of always-already white possessive empire-building. In March 1945, months before the Japanese surrendered, Representative Jed Johnson (D-Oklahoma) proposed an initiative to sterilize interned Japanese Americans whose land and property had been seized by the state. Some female internees reported being sterilized without their knowledge.[47] Eliminating racial degeneracy was then reinvented as the aggressive heterosexual conformism of the 1950s, and social Darwinism was repackaged as population control and family planning to combat poverty,[48] combining extant ideologies of gender, race, and class with

---

45. Ordover, *American Eugenics*, 150–51.
46. Ordover, *American Eugenics*, 150–51.
47. Ordover, *American Eugenics*, 160.
48. Stern, *Eugenic Nation*, 10.

82 • CHAPTER 2

increasing concerns about overpopulation and welfare expenses.[49] The Population Council, formed by John D. Rockefeller III in 1952 and comprised of wealthy, elite white men, many of whom were associated with eugenics and some of whom were Nazi supporters, advocated fertility control for the impoverished and people of color.[50] The group funded "contraceptive technology" and provided "technical assistance on family planning" and public education on "population matters."[51] The range of biopolitical violence used to protect the white possessive logics of US empire in the early to mid-twentieth century, which cast race, disability, and dependency as biological properties that could be bred out or excluded at the borders, bled into the 1960s and 1970s, when "policy makers, physicians, and self-proclaimed experts commenced a targeted plan for compulsory reproductive control on those deemed undesirable economic and social burdens."[52]

WELFARE AS BIOPOLITICAL WARFARE 2.0

Late twentieth-century public pedagogy about Indigenous peoples, differentially racialized immigrants, and welfare was critical to US neoliberal empire-building, with sterilization resurfacing as a genocidal white possessive tactic. As multiculturalism was becoming official with watershed legislation such as the Civil Rights Act (1964) and the Immigration and Nationality Act (INA; 1965) and as mainstream "second wave" feminism, dominated by white, middle- to upper-class women, focused on reproductive autonomy as a right to *not* have children, the Johnson administration's War on Poverty reflected fear that US resources were insufficient for the future population. Sterilization of poor women, who were disproportionately Indigenous and people of color due to centuries of settler colonial racial capitalism, reemerged as a solution to poverty and overpopulation.

Several factors led to the crystallization of what would become neoliberal personal responsibility politics in sterilization abuse against Indigenous women and women of color. First, public pedagogies about Indigenous women as impoverished, fecund, bad mothers, especially on reservations,[53] continued to underscore Native American policy. The Council on Indian Affairs successfully petitioned for inclusion in the War on Poverty and the Economic Oppor-

---

49. O'Sullivan, "Informing Red Power," 967.
50. Ralstin-Lewis, "Continuing Struggle against Genocide," 75.
51. O'Sullivan, "Informing Red Power," 967.
52. O'Sullivan, "Informing Red Power," 967.
53. Lawrence, "Indian Health Service," 405.

tunity Act. Participation, separate from treaties as well as healthcare and other benefits specifically for Indigenous peoples, included Indigenous peoples in a federal program for all US Americans. Over thirty tribes received War on Poverty benefits by 1965. The Office on Economic Opportunity (OEO) provided Native nations with direct funding for educational and economic development as well as health and legal centers. Some healthcare funding went into "family planning," which, I will show, under the Nixon administration was funding for sterilization abuse. Additionally, the Indian Child Welfare Act (ICWA; 1978) was enacted to strengthen Indigenous families and the survival of Indigenous nations given the persistently excessive removal of Indigenous children from their communities.[54] Though not unproblematic given its framing of Indigenous peoples as a reprosexual racial group rather than political group, its passing shows that even the federal government was pressed to address extant white possessive attacks on Indigenous peoples via children and parenting.

Second, the afterlives of public pedagogy about women, mothers, and families of color in connection to poverty and welfare co-constitutively served neoliberalizing white property interests. In the aftermath of slavery, welfare policy and administration continued to exploit Black women's labor while punishing Black women for reproduction that ceased to be the source of a new generation of free labor. Racialized mothers' pension programs reemerged as the prototype for the 1935 Social Security Act's Aid to Families with Dependent Children (AFDC) program.[55] Southern congressmen, in accordance with business interests, successfully lobbied for state administration of programs, and under some states' "employable mother" rules, such as those enacted in Louisiana in 1943, AFDC families with children ages seven and older were denied assistance if the mother was deemed to be employable in agriculture. Black women, disproportionately employed in agriculture, were de facto excluded.[56] Thus early welfare policy and administration cast white women as fit mothers and Black women as appropriate for low-wage labor and inappropriate for motherhood. The Moynihan Report (1965), commissioned for the War on Poverty, which infamously pathologized Black families and especially Black mothers as the cause of persistent poverty among Black Americans in explicit comparison to white ethnics,[57] updated this pedagogy of empire for the ascendant neoliberal multicultural context. Despite the massive

---

54. Strong, "What Is an Indian Family?," 205–31; and Bual, "Native American Rights & Adoption."

55. Leff, "Consensus for Reform," 397–417.

56. Amott, "Black Women and AFDC," 288; and Abramovitz, *Regulating the Lives of Women,* 317.

57. Moynihan, *Negro Family,* 1965.

84 • CHAPTER 2

federal welfare that white ethnics received under New Deal and World War II programs, and then via redlining and other discriminatory practices that allowed them to fully transition to and partake of the property of whiteness,[58] "nation of immigrants" multiculturalism idealized white ethnics for their self-sufficient, "personally responsible" pursuit of a better life for future generations in the face of discrimination. People of color were found wanting in comparison.[59] In the early 1960s, anthropologist Oscar Lewis pathologized Mexican and Puerto Rican families along similar lines.[60] Additionally, some Asian immigrants and citizens were, via gendered discourses of "good" parenting and upward mobility in the face of discrimination, recast as "model minorities."

Third, gendered, racialized discourses about immigrants similarly pathologized immigrants / those racialized as aliens as threats to white possession, and such thinking became tangible in 1980s immigration reform. The Nixon administration claimed the country was experiencing an undocumented immigration and population crisis though the volume of immigration had not substantially increased.[61] Rather, INA's liberalization of quota restrictions and prioritization of family reunification, poverty in sending nations, and demand for a pool of cheap immigrant labor made Latinxs and Asians the largest im/migrant groups. Mexico was the largest sending nation,[62] and more Mexican, Latinx, and Asian women, viewed as excessively fertile burdens on the welfare state, were migrating.

Fourth, Sanger's legacy persisted in mainstream "second wave" feminist struggles for reproductive freedom, narrowly defined as the right to not have children. Several Supreme Court rulings in the 1960s and early 1970s liberalized birth control restrictions. Sterilization was one method of birth control the court defended if "informed consent" (i.e., a doctor must inform the patient of the nature of the procedure, risks involved, and alternative treatments and be sure the patient understands the procedures and its consequences) was given.

This collective set the stage for the next crescendo of sterilization abuse and the entrenchment of personal responsibility politics in connection with welfare as a key tool of US neoliberal multicultural empire. In 1968 President Lyndon B. Johnson's Committee on Population Control and Family Planning proposed voluntary and incentivized birth control programs and involuntary

---

58. Sadowski-Smith, *New Immigrant Whiteness*, 13.
59. Jacobson, *Roots Too*.
60. Lewis, *Children of Sanchez*; and Lewis, *La Vida*.
61. Daniels, *Guarding the Golden Door*, 119–220.
62. Zolberg, *Nation by Design*, 340.

governmental fertility controls to address the population and poverty crisis.[63] Subsequently, states passed legislation that discouraged or even punished the birth of illegitimate and impoverished children, and federal legislation established funding for sterilization.[64]

Building on Johnson's efforts to combat overpopulation and poverty, Nixon created the Commission on Public Growth and the American Future in 1970. With the Family Planning Act (1970), the Nixon administration generously funded through HEW most annual sterilization costs for impoverished people. Before 1969, the government did not allow federally supported family planning services to subsidize sterilization and abortion services. This new policy made sterilization funding accessible. Medicaid covered 90 percent of the cost.[65] In a period marked by a reduction of healthcare services, HEW family planning funding increased from $51 million to $250 million, with the OEO funding clinics that offered sterilization, incentivizing them to perform the procedures.[66] Simultaneously, technical advances in tubal ligation surgery and more relaxed requirements for procedures made sterilization the most popular form of birth control.[67] Sterilization for women increased 300 percent between 1970 and 1977, from 192,000 to 548,000 sterilizations each year (to get an idea of the massive increase, between 1907 and 1964 only 63,000 sterilizations overall were done in the US).[68] Moreover, although the Hyde Amendment (1976) cut almost all federal funding to hospitals and doctors for abortions (except to save a woman's life or if the pregnancy was the result of incest or rape), profoundly impacting women on Medicaid, it maintained 90 percent reimbursement for sterilization.[69] While "informed consent" was required, consent protocol varied wildly, and forms were often available only in English.

Consequently, and with the support of federal legislation and funding, medical professionals and social service workers forced or pressured scores of Indigenous and immigrant and citizen women of color, deemed problematic

---

63. "United States: Report of the President's Committee on Population and Family Planning," 1–4.

64. Contemporary sterilization is performed by hysterectomy, removal of the uterus, or by tubal ligation. The latter can be performed under general or local anesthesia and immediately after vaginal or caesarian birth. A hysterectomy cannot be reversed and reversing tubal ligation, while technically possible, depends upon the extent of the damage to the fallopian tubes. Both sterilization procedures can and have been performed without women's knowledge (Carpio, "Lost Generation," 967).

65. Gutierrez, *Fertile Matters*, 37.

66. O'Sullivan, "Informing Red Power," 967–68.

67. Gutierrez, *Fertile Matters*, 37.

68. O'Sullivan, "Informing Red Power," 967–68.

69. Torpy, "Native American Women and Coerced Sterilization."

in terms of poverty, dependency, and overpopulation rather than biologized race as in the early twentieth century, to agree to sterilization procedures, or sterilized them without their consent or even their knowledge, and did so with impunity. No documented cases reported sterilization abuses against white women.[70] Building on previous public pedagogies about welfare, ascendant neoliberal personal responsibility politics rationalized the biological and territorial genocidal white possessive warfare that sterilization abuse enacted against Indigenous women and women of color.

On multiple occasions the government and courts acknowledged extensive gendered, racialized sterilization abuse under the auspices of family planning and the role of welfare receipt in that abuse without making any meaningful change in practice. As early as 1973, revised regulations specified by HEW, published in the *Federal Register,* included a moratorium on sterilizations of anyone under age twenty-one and anyone considered mentally incompetent. Informed consent, a signed consent form, and a seventy-two-hour waiting period between the granting of consent and the procedure were required. Then in *Relf v. Weinberger* (1974) Federal District Court Judge Gerhard Gesell ruled in favor of two mentally disabled Black sisters, ages twelve and fourteen, who were sterilized without consent. The family lived in public housing and received state health benefits. Their mother, who was illiterate, signed a form that she thought granted permission for the girls to be given birth control shots but actually "consented" to their sterilization.[71] Gesell stated that "the dividing line between family planning and eugenics is murky" given that those sterilized were usually impoverished people of color and many had been "coerced into accepting a sterilization operation under the threat that variously supported welfare benefits would be withdrawn unless they submitted."[72] Regulations were revised again, updating the definition of informed consent and including a statement "that the individual is free to withhold or withdraw his or her consent to the procedure at any time prior to the sterilization without prejudicing his or her future care and without loss of other project or program benefits to which the patient might otherwise be entitled." All consent forms also had to state clearly at the top of the form "*NOTICE: Your decision at any time not to be sterilized will not result in the withdrawal or withholding of any benefits provided by programs or projects.*" And Medical professionals were also required to tell patients verbally that welfare benefits would not be denied if they refused sterilization.[73]

---

70. Gutierrez, *Fertile Matters,* 39.

71. "Relf v. Weinberger," Sterilization Abuse, The Southern Poverty Law Center, accessed July 31, 2023, https://www.splcenter.org/seeking-justice/case-docket/relf-v-weinberger.

72. Stern, *Eugenic Nation,* 202.

73. Lawrence, "Indian Health Service," 406.

But sterilization abuse against Indigenous women and women of color in connection to welfare receipt persisted, and Indigenous peoples were uniquely vulnerable to and harmed by it. The United Nations recognizes prevention of births in a target population as a form of genocide, with the policy of the global organization illuminating in this case specifically that "the sterilization and birth control campaign was significantly more than an attack on women in general: it was a systematic program aimed at reducing the Native population, or genocide."[74]

As Nixon declared an end to termination, welfare was the lynchpin of this ascendant neoliberal form of genocidal warfare against Indigenous peoples to protect the white heteropatriarchal property interests underpinning US empire. Centuries of paternalistic policies rendered Indigenous peoples dependent upon the federal government for services such as healthcare, placing them "at a greater risk than other minority groups for abuses by the medical profession."[75] HEW already barely regulated chronically underfunded IHS and affiliated contract facilities, and under the Nixon administration's family planning policies, sterilization was profitable: tubal ligations earned IHS hospitals and affiliates $250 and hysterectomies $750.[76] Additionally, policymakers, administrators, and healthcare providers misunderstood differences between treaty rights and War on Poverty program benefits and often viewed Native women through the lens of the afterlife of the s— stereotype as dirty, fecund, poor, and incapable of the same emotions as white women and consequently neglectful of their children,[77] casting them as ideal candidates for sterilization. For instance, in 1974 HEW circulated pamphlets in Indigenous territories and communities praising the benefits of sterilization. One, titled "Plan Your Family," featured a rudimentary cartoon in which the "before" sterilization Natives are unhappy, frowning with numerous children and just one horse, while the "after" are happy, smiling with just one child and many horses. The paternalistic message, that sterilization relieves the poverty and unhappiness engendered by having many children, is quite clear.[78]

In truth, sterilization abuse devastated Indigenous women and communities. While Native communities define membership variously, reproduction is considered by many tribal nations as necessary for their survival. Sterilization abuse, activists and tribal leaders emphasized, curtailed the birth of the next generation of Natives in an attempt to eliminate Indigenous peoples once and

---

74. Ralstin-Lewis, "Continuing Struggle against Genocide," 72.

75. Ralstin-Lewis, "Continuing Struggle against Genocide," 77.

76. O'Sullivan, "Informing Red Power," 969.

77. Volscho, "Sterilization Racism," 19; Mihesuah, *American Indians*, 61; Green, "Pocahontas Perplex," 698–714; and Bird, "Gendered Construction," 61–83.

78. Ralstin-Lewis, "Continuing Struggle against Genocide," 78.

88 • CHAPTER 2

for all and appropriate their remaining land and natural resources.[79] According to the 1970 census, the "average" Indigenous woman had 3.79 children in comparison to a 1.79 child median for all other groups. In her survey of census data from 1970 and 1980, Jane Lawrence found that for Indigenous women of various nations, the average number of children declined to 1.99 over that decade. Sterilization was a significant factor in this decline.[80] Therefore, an entire generation of Indigenous children "who may have learned and passed down tribal traditions, ceremonies, and language, and continued the fight for cultural and political self-determination" are missing.[81] Moreover, in numerous Indigenous communities in which biological women are viewed as the backbone and keepers of life, for many Indigenous women and their families, the loss of reproductive capability was personally shattering.[82] Sterilization also impacted participation in ceremonial practices. In Pueblo tribes, for example, women participate in religious ceremonies, and a "woman" is defined as one who has children.[83]

That most sterilizations of Indigenous women were coerced or nonconsensual, and that numerous Indigenous women were pressured by physicians and healthcare professionals to agree to sterilization under the threat of losing their welfare benefits and/or custody of their children, is a matter of extensive record. In 1972, Dr. Constance Pinkerton-Uri, a Choctaw/Cherokee physician with the IHS in Oklahoma, was galvanized by her patients' reports of coerced and nonconsensual sterilizations. Numerous other instances of sterilization abuse were reported throughout Indian Country,[84] including reports of women who were unknowingly sterilized or had no recollection of "consenting" to sterilization because they were medicated after having just given birth. Others were told the procedures were reversible.[85] Pinkerton-Uri attended law school to help her combat sterilization abuse and founded Women United for Justice, a Los Angeles–based organization dedicated to legal action for Indigenous women.[86] The group lobbied Senator James Abourezk (D-South Dakota), an ally to Native Americans and author of ICWA, to help end government-funded sterilization abuse against Indigenous women and peoples. The government's response, the Government Accounting Office (GAO)

---

79. Ralstin-Lewis, "Continuing Struggle against Genocide," 83.
80. Lawrence, "Indian Health Service," 405.
81. Carpio, "Lost Generation," 51.
82. Ralstin-Lewis, "Continuing Struggle against Genocide," 71; 84.
83. Carpio, "Lost Generation," 50.
84. Lawrence, "Indian Health Service," 400.
85. Carpio, "Lost Generation."
86. O'Sullivan, "Informing Red Power," 971.

report, *Investigations of Allegations Concerning Indian Health Services* (1976), was woefully inadequate but nonetheless found that Indigenous women were pressured by physicians and healthcare professionals to agree to sterilization *under the threat of losing their welfare benefits or custody of their children or were targeted for sterilization because of their welfare receipt.*[87]

The GAO report, covering fiscal years 1973–76, confirmed sterilization abuse against Indigenous women, but the scale of abuse was significantly larger. IHS, under the umbrella of HEW, sterilized over 3,400 Indigenous women in the Aberdeen, Albuquerque, Oklahoma City, and Phoenix areas. Of the 3,406 sterilizations, 3,001 were performed on women of childbearing age, and 1,024 were performed at IHS contract facilities.[88] Importantly, these are only four of the twelve IHS areas, and the GAO study did not include sterilizations contracted out to non-IHS facilities. Therefore, the GAO report count of sterilizations, which given the small size of the Indigenous population at the time would be equivalent to sterilizing 452,000 non-Native American women in the same time span, was a gross underestimate.[89]

Though inadequately small, GAO's study also revealed the clear patterns underpinning systemic sterilization abuse. For example, HEW failed to ensure that IHS facilities adhered to regulations. The GAO report found thirty-six moratorium violations from 1973 to 1976, twenty-three of which occurred after the moratorium but prior to area directors being informed of the new HEW sterilization regulations,[90] and in instructions for caregivers HEW had flat out "omitted the requirement 'that individuals seeking sterilization be orally informed at the outset that no Federal benefits can be withdrawn because of failure to accept sterilization.'"[91] Medical records show that many forms were dated the same day a woman gave birth, often by Cesarean section, and therefore the women were under the influence of medication when they gave "consent." Some consent forms were signed the day *after* the sterilization.[92] Additionally, GAO did not interview patients to determine if they were adequately informed before consenting to sterilization procedures because "we believe such an effort would not be productive because recently published research noted a high level of inaccuracy in the recollection of patients 4 to 6 months after giving consent."[93] The stakes—Indigenous women's bodily

---

87. Comptroller of the United States, *Investigations of Allegations.*
88. Comptroller of the United States, *Investigations of Allegations,* 3–4.
89. Wagner, "Lo the Poor and Sterilized Indian," 75.
90. Comptroller of the United States, *Investigations of Allegations,* 21.
91. Comptroller of the United States, *Investigations of Allegations,* 4.
92. Lawrence, "Indian Health Service," 407–8.
93. Comptroller of the United States, *Investigations of Allegations,* 3–4.

90 · CHAPTER 2

autonomy, reproductive freedom, and the survival of Indigenous communities—were unbelievably high, yet GAO could not be bothered to evaluate sterilization abuse in all of Indian Country or to even speak with women who had been violated.

Indigenous peoples' independent and nongovernmental studies more accurately illustrate the staggering breadth of sterilization abuse in connection with welfare receipt and neoliberal personal responsibility politics. Pinkerton-Uri found that from 1970 to 1976 IHS doctors sterilized at least 25 percent of Indigenous women between the ages of fourteen and forty-four. Her study also revealed that IHS facilities singled out full-blooded Indigenous women for sterilization, and that women agreed to sterilization only when threatened with the loss of their children or welfare benefits. Moreover, most "consented" while sedated during or immediately after a Cesarean-section birth, or while in labor. Some also did not understand consent forms, which were available exclusively in English.[94] Cheyenne tribal judge Marie Sanchez found that twenty-six of fifty Cheyenne women she interviewed were sterilized without consent. Mary Ann Bear Comes Out, of the Northern Cheyenne nation, found on the Northern Cheyenne Reservation and Labre Mission that IHS sterilized 56 of 126 total women between the ages of thirty and forty-four. Overall, nongovernmental studies found that from 1970 to 1976, 20 to 50 percent of Indigenous women of childbearing age were sterilized without consent.[95] Other studies show that from the mid-1960s through 1976, out of only 100,000 to 150,000 Native women of childbearing age, 3,400 to 70,000 were subject to sterilization abuse via tubal ligation or hysterectomy.[96] Moreover, between 1970 and 1980, the birthrate for Indigenous women declined at a rate seven times higher than that of white women.[97]

Independent research also confirmed that welfare was a causal cornerstone for sterilization abuse against Indigenous women to protect white possession. The Indigenous women who were interviewed reported that public and private agencies and agents threatened to terminate their benefits if they had additional children or to remove their children from the home if they did not agree to sterilization. The threat of removing children was surely an especially powerful coercion technique given the long history and contemporaneous practice of the US government attacking Indigenous peoples' survival and sovereignty through child removal. Other 1970s studies revealed that most doctors who performed the sterilizations were white men who, in accordance

---

94. Lawrence, "Indian Health Service," 412.

95. Stern, *Eugenic Nation*, 202; Gutierrez, *Fertile Matters*, 39; and Lawrence, "Indian Health Service," 410.

96. Ralstin-Lewis, "Continuing Struggle against Genocide," 71–72.

97. Ralstin-Lewis, "Continuing Struggle against Genocide," 72.

"ENTITLEMENT" WARFARE • 91

with the white possessive praxis of the War on Poverty, felt they were helping society by limiting births among low-income Indigenous families. Doctors also believed they were helping the government reduce funding for Medicaid and welfare and so decreasing their taxes accordingly.[98] Doctors at urban hospitals likewise cited welfare receipt as a rationale for sterilization abuse; fecundity and welfare receipt, these doctors claimed, was a legitimate reason to control the reproductive autonomy of impoverished women who were disproportionately Indigenous and nonwhite.[99] Furthermore, a 1972 study found that only 6 percent of doctors recommended sterilization as permanent birth control for white patients whereas 14 percent of doctors recommended sterilization for poor and minority patients on public assistance. Ninety-seven percent of doctors recommended or preferred sterilization for welfare mothers with three or more children.[100]

Simultaneously, despite generous federal funding for sterilization, Native healthcare was grossly underfunded and inadequate (including after the passing of the IHCIA), and this too was a tool of white possessive neoliberal empire-building. A 1977 study by the American Indian Policy Review Commission for Congress "found the system antiquated and lacking in adequate policy, funding, delivery of services, state and local agencies' responsiveness toward Indians," and "oversight and accountability at all levels of Indian Health Service." IHS hospitals and healthcare centers, often located miles from major hospitals and from Indigenous communities, were far below accreditation standards, were understaffed (with one doctor for every 1,700 reservation residents in 1975), and had insufficient supplementary funds for contract facilities and doctors.[101]

The consequences of insufficient healthcare are also arguably genocidal. In 1977 the life expectancy for a Native American was 47 years versus 70.8 years for the general population. On reservations, the infant mortality was three times the national average, the tuberculosis rate eight times the national average. In 1976 the approximate Indigenous population was 800,000. Subpar healthcare or sterilization abuse alone threatened Indigenous survival; together, the two were literally eliminative, as the Native American Solidarity Committee pointed out.[102] Senator Abourezk noted that the Nixon administration's impounding of funds for Indigenous healthcare "literally is forcing

---

98. Lawrence, "Indian Health Service," 410.

99. O'Sullivan, "Informing Red Power," 970.

100. Ralstin-Lewis, "Continuing Struggle against Genocide," 76.

101. Torpy, "Native American Women and Coerced Sterilization."

102. Native American Solidarity Committee in coordination with the American Indian Treaty Council Information Center, "Documentation of Current (20th Century) Genocidal Policy: Sterilization Abuse," June 1977.

IHS to play Russian roulette with the lives of Indian people." By the administration's actions, thousands of people requiring medical attention went without help,[103] while sterilization was lavishly funded. Thus, to protect the white possessive logics underpinning US empire historically and into the neoliberalizing context, the federal government continued to wage biopolitical war against Indigenous peoples via sterilization abuse and healthcare writ large in connection to various forms of welfare.

Indigenous women, however, combatted sterilization abuse on multiple fronts. Some fought through the courts. For instance, Norma Jean Serena (Creek and Shawnee) filed a civil suit, the first of its kind, to address sterilization abuse as a civil rights issue. In 1970 in Apollo, Pennsylvania, social service workers took Serena's two children shortly before she gave birth to her third child; she signed sterilization consent forms after her newborn son was also taken from her. In the first part of her case, the all-white jury determined that social workers had placed her children in foster homes under false pretenses, and she received $17,000 of the $20,000 she sought in damages from the Department of Public Welfare. Her children were not, however, returned to her until 1974. In the second part of her case, which took place in 1979 and focused on the blatant abuse of her reproductive rights, the jury decided that Serena had consented to sterilization and acquitted the doctors and social worker involved.[104] Three Northern Cheyenne women also filed a class action suit against HEW in 1977, which was directed against the hospital physicians who coerced them into "consenting" to sterilization by threatening the loss of welfare benefits, claiming that the surgery was necessary, or that the surgery could be reversed in the future. Each woman accepted a cash settlement from the defendant's lawyers with the condition that the terms of the agreement and the women's names would be sealed.[105]

Women of All Red Nations (WARN), established in 1978 to address the need for more independent investigations into sterilization abuse and Indigenous women's concerns in general, explicitly connected women's bodily and tribal geopolitical sovereignty. Red Power, a resistance movement comprised of many different nations, formed following a 1967 meeting of the National Congress of American Indians (NCAI) with the goal of self-determination. Although Red Power did not specifically address sterilization abuse, Indigenous women drew on their policies of self-determination to connect bodily and tribal sovereignty. Organizations such as United Native Americans and the International Indian Treaty Council (IITC) launched campaigns against

---

103. Torpy, "Native American Women and Coerced Sterilization."
104. Torpy, "Native American Women and Coerced Sterilization."
105. Torpy, "Native American Women and Coerced Sterilization."

"ENTITLEMENT" WARFARE • 93

the IHS and other government institutions; WARN and other women's organizations mobilized to demand reproductive justice when their concerns were excluded from or insufficiently addressed in both mainstream feminist reproductive rights efforts and Indigenous sovereignty efforts.[106] Kitsi of WARN put it succinctly: "The real issue behind sterilization is how we are losing our sovereignty."[107] Indigenous women understood sterilization abuse as part of the long durée of settler colonial warfare against Indigenous peoples and its gendered imprint on bodies. Viewing fertility as a human right and a civil right guaranteed to members of sovereign, self-governing nations, Indigenous women organized, educated, and lobbied to end sterilization abuse and in so doing expanded both mainstream feminist understandings of reproductive freedom and the Indigenous sovereignty movement.[108]

•

While the US settler colonial system positions Indigenous peoples and people of color in distinct but intertwined ways to advance its white possessive logics, US neoliberal empire was exerted and expanded via sterilization abuse as a genocidal tactic against both Indigenous and Latinx women in connection with welfare. For Latinx immigrant women and citizens subject to sterilization abuse, bodily autonomy, survival as people of color within the US, and exclusion or deportation, which became more prevalent in the 1980s and 1990s, was at stake. The sterilization abuse Latinas were subjected to was likewise supported by federal agencies that dispersed funds as part of War on Poverty family planning efforts[109] and was underscored by proto-personal responsibility politics along with stereotypes of Mexican and Latinx women as "hyper-fertile baby machines" and a simultaneous uproar about undocumented immigrants illegally receiving welfare. Demographic studies undertaken in the 1970s that claimed that Latinas had excessive fertility rates were prevalent in the medical community, as with demographer Donald Bogue's 1971 paper at the Annual American College of Obstetrics and Gynecology in which he claimed that the "Spanish-speaking population" and other "high fertility" groups were responsible for national population growth.[110] Californians especially feared that Mexican women crossed the border to have babies and "illegally" exploit welfare benefits (though a Los Angeles study revealed that

---

106. O'Sullivan, "Informing Red Power," 965–66.
107. Lawrence, "Indian Health Service," 410.
108. O'Sullivan, "Informing Red Power," 976.
109. Stern, *Eugenic Nation*, 200–203.
110. Gutierrez, *Fertile Matters*, 51.

94 • CHAPTER 2

the number of undocumented immigrants receiving welfare was negligible and that actually state welfare agencies often discriminated against Spanish-speaking California residents). Meanwhile media exposés warned the public about "pregnant pilgrims."[111] In the entertainment industries, the trope of the hypersexual Latina that had taught spectators and consumers about Latinxs, from the silent film *Red Girl*'s depiction of a Mexican woman as the enemy of all women, sexual morality, and white property, to the sexy Latina spit-fire emblematized by Lupe Velez in the 1930s and Carmen Miranda in the 1940s and 1950s, was extant with celebrities such as Charo.[112] These public pedagogies about Latinas and immigration, citizenship, hypersexuality, hyper-fertility, and welfare abuse crystalized in sterilization abuse as medical profes-sionals pressured Latinas into sterilization, or performed it without consent. Some women were threatened with deportation if they refused to agree to sterilization.[113]

Many Chicana activists from grassroots, professional, advocacy, and health organizations also emphasized the existential threat that sterilization abuse posed to Mexican American communities, and some, Gutierrez notes, "referred to the sterilization abuse of women of Mexican origin as genocide, and some accused the state outright of being complicit in this genocide of the Chicano community."[114] Latinas also organized and resisted sterilization abuse through the courts and activism, their fight against the colonial state for reproductive rights and civil rights distinct from but interconnected with Indigenous women's fight against the colonial state for reproductive justice as a matter of bodily as well as tribal sovereignty. In *Madrigal v. Quilligan* (1978) working-class, Mexican-origin women, many of whom were immigrants and, incidentally, none of whom were receiving public assistance, sued the Wom-en's Hospital at the University of Southern California / Los Angeles County General Hospital in California for nonconsensual sterilizations performed to allegedly protect public health. The judge ruled in favor of the defendants, the doctors who perpetrated the sterilization abuse.[115]

Sterilization abuse against Puerto Ricans could also be considered geno-cidal. HEW reported in 1976 that 37.4 percent of women of childbearing age in Puerto Rico were sterilized.[116] Puerto Rican women living in the mainland

---

111. Gutierrez, *Fertile Matters*, 53.

112. See Mendible, *From Bananas to Buttocks*.

113. Gutierrez, *Fertile Matters*, 39–44.

114. Gutierrez, *Fertile Matters*, 105.

115. Stern, "Sterilized in the Name of Public Health," 1128–38; and Camacho, *Migrant Imagi-naries*, 177–78.

116. Ordover, *American Eugenics*, 151.

US suffered similar rates of sterilization abuse.[117] Like Indigenous and Chicanx women, Puerto Rican women organized. Responding to claims of sterilization abuse made by Puerto Rican women in New York City, Dr. Helen Rodríguez Trías founded the Committee to End Sterilization Abuse in 1975.[118]

In 1978, in response to the assiduous, multivalent activism of Indigenous women and women of color (and often despite opposition from mainstream feminist organizations such as the National Organization for Women [NOW], which feared a restriction of women's reproductive right to not have children), Congressional hearings engendered new HEW regulations to combat sterilization abuse, which, Congress acknowledged, disproportionately impacted women who because of "educational [. . .] linguistic [. . .] or cultural barriers did not comprehend the terms of sterilization as presented to them by medical professionals." Obtaining consent while medicated or during labor and childbirth was also censured and prohibited, and the new consent form stated, "Your decision at any time not to be sterilized will not result in the withdrawal or withholding of any benefits provided by programs or projects receiving federal funds."[119] Reports of sterilization abuse consequently diminished. Like Indigenous women's efforts, Latinas' resistance influenced policy changes, and in some cases Indigenous women, women of color, and white women formed coalitions to end sterilization abuse as with the National Women's Health Network (NWHN), also founded by Dr. Rodríguez Trías. By 1979 the group, comprised of numerous other organizations, including the Mexican American Women's National Association (MANA), the California Coalition for the Medical Rights of Women, and Indian Women United for Justice, focused on ending sterilization abuse. Three Indigenous women, Pinkerton-Uri, Marie Sanchez, and Rayna Green, served on its board. The group distributed a publication explaining HEW's new regulations, addressed the difficulties in monitoring those regulations, provided ways for groups to monitor healthcare providers, and supported sterilized women with legal action.[120]

While reports of sterilization abuse diminished given Indigenous and racialized women's struggles for justice, this recent form of white possessive biopolitical and territorial warfare laid the groundwork for the Reaganite calcification of US neoliberal multicultural empire in welfare reform and personal responsibility politics. The Reagan administration enacted massive cuts to general programs for Indigenous peoples, making their lives

---

117. Gutierrez, *Fertile Matters*, 3; and Lopez, "Agency and Constraint," 155–71.

118. Stern, *Eugenic Nation*, 200–203.

119. O'Sullivan, "Informing Red Power," 976; and "Policies of General Applicability: Provision of Sterilization in Federally Assisted Programs of the Public Health Service."

120. O'Sullivan, "Informing Red Power," 976–77.

96 · CHAPTER 2

more precarious, and established a paradigm for welfare cuts that made the lives of nonwhite citizen and immigrant welfare recipients more precarious. Moreover, welfare restrictions were used to exclude and potentially deport undocumented immigrants, and the legacy of controlling women of color's reproduction in connection with welfare to protect white possession aggressively continued in 1990s policy.

REAGAN'S WILD WEST WELFARE

The extractive and racial project of white accumulation underpinning settler colonialism received a neoliberal update in Reaganite policy and contemporaneous media, particularly in relation to welfare. To return to a national consensus on domestic and foreign issues given the malaise engendered in the 1970s by defeat in Vietnam, an economic crisis, and a crisis of leadership (Nixon was disgraced and discredited; Gerald Ford and Jimmy Carter were unpopular), the so-called Reagan Revolution revised the nineteenth-century idea of the frontier as the preordained site of US expansion via the twinning of "bonanza economics" and "savage war." In the postindustrial revision of the "Frontier Myth," rather than agrarian commodities and industrial expansion, supply-side economics, or what would come to be known as "trickle-down" Reaganomics, would release a "bonanza" of new capital via tax cuts and deregulation that favored business and the wealthy. Simultaneously, "more vigorous prosecution of Cold War (against Russia as 'evil empire') and savage war (against enemies like Ghadafy [*sic*] of Libya, Maurice Bishop of Grenada, and the Sandinista regime in Nicaragua)" would ostensibly regenerate the nation's spirit and exceptionalism in the world.[121] As president, Ronald Reagan, "an apostle of the marketplace whose premise had always been that the US economic pie should be enlarged, not that everyone should receive an equal slice,"[122] proffered two brands of national identity that, connected with frontier mythology, indexed the remapping of US neoliberal empire through welfare public pedagogy: America was (1) the homeland of the cowboy, the emblematically free, independent, industrious, westward-expanding individual and (2) the "nation of immigrants," a land of opportunity and abundance for the hardworking individual (that was also negotiating an "immigration emergency"). He fetishized a sense of himself as the former. Reagan, the first Hollywood actor elected president, frequently conflated the movies and reality

---

121. Slotkin, *Gunfighter Nation*, 645–46.
122. Cannon, *President Reagan*, 454.

to, as Michael Rogin observed, "make himself the hero of American cultural myths."[123] As an actor he repeatedly pleaded with Warner Brothers for Western roles.[124] He left the studio to choose his own roles, subsequently starring in Westerns such as *The Last Outpost* (1951), *Cattle Queen of Montana* (1954), and *Law and Order* (1953).[125] He also hosted and acted in the television Western, *Death Valley Days,* from 1963 until 1966, when he won the California governorship, for which he campaigned in cowboy attire on horseback. As president, he quoted popular film dialogue from Western actors such as Clint Eastwood, claiming it was easier to solve a problem when he had a "horse between his knees." Reagan's Secret Service codename was "Rawhide,"[126] and he spent 345 days of his presidency at Rancho del Cielo (one of four ranches he owned in his lifetime).[127] In a 1981 meeting with aides after the US shot down Libyan jets, Reagan evoked his Western lawman persona, miming a cowboy firing six-shooters.[128]

Reagan's revised Frontier Myth was central to his presidential politics, which were extractive and racialized in ways that became quintessential to US neoliberal empire-building. This was visually immortalized in posters for his successful 1980 "Let's Make America Great Again" presidential campaign. Behind a photograph of him in a Stetson cowboy hat are four faded drawings of US landscapes: Washington, DC, and Mount Rushmore; the Alamo; a barn and church; and the Statue of Liberty in New York City. Red, white, and blue text proclaims: "AMERICA: REAGAN COUNTRY."[129] The poster, casting him as a government outsider in touch with the common man, offered Reagan Country voters the national imaginary of a frontier awaiting development, that is, the fiscal if not land-based opportunity to extend colonial settlement. The ostensibly race-neutral campaign poster points to Reagan's frontier ethic of development as the means to restore US pride and prosperity through policies of deregulation, privatization, liberalization, integration of global markets, and increased defense spending.[130] Another poster "Bedtime for Brezhnev," designed to look like an advertisement for a Western film, highlights the "savage war" aspect of the Reaganite Frontier Myth. In the forefront, "star" Reagan, clad in cowboy attire, grabs the Russian politician roughly by

---

123. Rogin, *Ronald Reagan,* 3, 7.

124. Cannon, *President Reagan,* 464.

125. Rogin, *Ronald Reagan,* 38.

126. Schaller, *Reckoning with Reagan,* viii; 4.

127. Cannon, *President Reagan,* 464.

128. Rogin, *Ronald Reagan,* 38–39.

129. Kathryn Henderson, "10 Iconic Political Posters," *Complex,* November 5, 2012, accessed May 18, 2018, http://www.complex.com/style/2012/11/10-iconic-political-posters/.

130. Rowland and Jones, *Reagan at Westminster.*

the lapels. The poster also features images of Reagan's "co-stars," US politicians such as George H. W. Bush and other "villains" such as Castro and Khadafy [*sic*]. The "original concept" of the film is attributed to overt white supremacist Barry Goldwater. Reagan was not the first president to allude to the Frontier Myth to cast himself as a hero; as Richard Slotkin has noted, Theodore Roosevelt was elected as "The Rough Rider" and "Cowboy President." Roosevelt, however, had been a stockman, sheriff, and Rough Rider, whereas Reagan's cowboy claims were entirely fictional, performed only in films and television shows. Yet this did not hinder Reagan's two successful presidential campaigns or his deployment of the Frontier Myth as an organizing principle for policymaking[131] that implemented a range of white possessive neoliberal strategies. At the heart of Reaganite ideology was the notion that the reasonable and capable individual rather than the government was the path to prosperity and the locus of social responsibility; thus, the racialized and feminized welfare state was anathema to the US exceptionalism and individualized financial accumulation that his white male cowboy ideal epitomized.

Both Reaganite national mythologies, like the nation itself, relied on multiple racial disavowals and especially the foundational disavowal of historical and ongoing Indigenous dispossession. In the 1980s context, Indigenous struggles for self-determination ceased to be headline news, though they had not abated; the fetishization of Indigenous clothing and culture was supplanted by Reaganite consumerism as patriotism: in the context of ascendant neoliberal multiculturalism, Reagan balanced neoconservative heteropatriarchal "family values" with "modern" ideas of celebrity culture and consumption. Consumerism cultivated a sense of national unity, as atomizing individualism, personal responsibility / self-sufficiency, and a "wild West" (deregulated) market became the new normal. And as his landscape campaign poster suggested, the frontiers of the US in the 1980s, evacuated of Indigeneity, awaited an entrepreneurial cow*boy*—or perhaps the right kind of immigrant—to develop/exploit them.

Indigenous dispossession, necessarily the foundation of Reagan's brand of white possessive US Americanism, also persisted in the culture at large. Although *Broken Rainbow,* a film about the forced removal of Diné/Navajo people in the Southwest so that their land could be strip-mined, won the Oscar for Best Documentary in 1985, and sympathy for Native Americans and multiculturalism was normalized in the 1960s and 1970s, most mainstream media representations of Indigenous peoples—few and far between in the 1980s—circulated hackneyed stereotypes and paternalism that also ultimately

---

131. Slotkin, *Gunfighter Nation,* 644.

"ENTITLEMENT" WARFARE • 99

disavowed ongoing Indigenous dispossession. A remake of *Stagecoach* (1986) was patronizing; *The Emerald Forest* (1985) fetishized Native Americans as natural ecologists, an offshoot of the noble savage stereotype; "sympathetic" 1990s box office hits *Dances with Wolves* (1990) and *The Last of the Mohicans* (1990) reinvigorated the "vanishing Indian."[132] A conglomerated New Age "pan-Indianness," often disconnected from Indigenous cultures and people, was also deployed as a prop for white quests for individual "authenticity," perhaps in response to Reaganite consumerism.

Furthermore, despite neoliberalism's (and Reagan's campaign poster's) imagination of a borderless frontier, neoliberal pedagogies of empire often centered on immigration issues, which almost as a rule erase Indigeneity. Protecting white property interests continued to necessitate a range of strategies in the context of neoliberalizing empire. On one hand, in contrast to the specter of what Reagan christened the "evil empire" of the USSR and communism, Reaganite immigration discourse powerfully reframed the US as an exceptional multicultural neoliberal democracy. Discourses that extended the ethnic revival's "nation of immigrants" trope to selectively include gendered, racialized immigrants cast Reagan's US as an ever-increasingly equal, democratic multiculture for hardworking, entrepreneurial, personally responsible individuals. On the other hand, complementary discourses about another specter, namely, gendered, racialized crime and dependency, rebranded as individuals' failure to take personal responsibility on that increasingly level multicultural field, cast the increased im/migration of Latinx and Asian people and especially women as an "immigration emergency," an invasion demanding decisive action. The policy centerpiece of this iteration of white possession, which would become the model for subsequent neoliberal immigration policy, was the Immigration Reform and Control Act of 1986 (IRCA). IRCA included amnesty that, framed as multicultural, democratic progress on the congressional floor and in the news media, captured a pool of cheap Mexican male laborers. Other IRCA provisions included welfare restrictions disproportionately used to exclude Latina mothers, sanctions for employers of undocumented immigrants designed and implemented to protect employers, and border militarization. The law thereby appeared to be racially inclusive of some (hardworking) immigrants and punitive only toward those who broke the law, but as I discuss elsewhere, from congressional debates to the language of the law itself to its implementation and impact on im/migrants, protecting white property interests, including Reagan's own investments in agriculture, underpinned the seemingly dissonant provisions of the law. Moreover,

---

132. Kilpatrick, *Celluloid Indians,* 101–3; and *Reel Injun.*

popular films and TV shows echoed the ostensible availability of the Reaganite multicultural US American Dream to deserving (that is, personally responsible) immigrants, who, as Neil Diamond declared in his Centennial performance of "Coming to America," his 1981 pop song, were invited and enticed to come from "everywhere around the world [. . .] every time the flag unfurls." Simultaneously Latinx immigrants were targeted in Reagan's "War on Drugs," and in policy and media discourse Latinx drug dealers and gang bangers and hyperfertile, unfit, criminal Latina mothers loomed large.[133]

Welfare calcified as a lynchpin of US neoliberal empire in the Reagan administration's weaponization of personal responsibility politics against Indigenous peoples and immigrants of color. Reagan campaigned on welfare cuts first during his 1970 bid to be reelected governor of California; in his 1976 presidential campaign he relentlessly told the story of Linda Taylor, a Black woman arrested for welfare fraud. Taylor was the basis for the "welfare queen" stereotype, "the symbolic embodiment of welfare fraud for legislative conservatives who were trying to reduce welfare costs"[134] following the progressive welfare reform driven by Black women in the 1970s.[135] Reagan's obsession with welfare, coded as Black and female, carried into his presidency and was coded as Indigenous and Latina as well in distinctive but interconnected ways. His administration's drastic cuts first to federal welfare programs for Native peoples—unique as federal obligations to tribal nations—then immigrant welfare, then general welfare inaugurated a gendered, racialized neoliberal welfare regime that, with its siren song of personal responsibility rationalizing austerity, justified and did the work of white possessive neoliberal empire-building.

Under Nixon, to advance white possessive empire-building, termination continued in sterilization abuse, inadequate healthcare, and drawing rhetorical connections between self-determination and New Federalist cost-cutting. Reagan elaborated upon the latter tactic: his "termination by accountants" hinged on his rhetorical invitation to Native Americans to participate in consumer nationalism. Reagan's neoliberal coupling of self-determination and termination centered on "freeing" Indigenous people from federal dependence by helping them develop or rather extract their natural resources. This was not as overtly genocidal as sterilization abuse but rather a more subtle limitation or denial of all forms of welfare that make life livable, and which were already underfunded and inadequate: healthcare, water and sanitation services on reservations, and educational and employment support. He centered Indigenous personal responsibility in his brand of New Federalism, which served as a

133. Perry, *Cultural Politics of U.S. Immigration*.
134. Cannon, *President Reagan*, 456–57.
135. Amott, "Black Women and AFDC," 288–89.

precursor to subsequent administrative welfare cuts.[136] In a special issue of *Social Text*, titled "Dispossession: Indigeneity, Race, Capitalism," the editors state:

> When we perceive financialization as always already predisposed and config-
> ured by settler colonialism and empire, today's austerity becomes legible as
> a new civilizing discourse, another iteration of propriation, a civilizationism
> redux for neoliberal times. [. . .] Austerity discourse recycles and modifies
> repertoires of racialization, heteropatriarchy, and colonialism by articulating
> them in registers of economic necessity.[137]

Reagan's 1982 budget proposal called for massive cuts to Native American programs: decreasing IHS funding by $136.9 million, decreasing BIA funding by $72.9 million, terminating funding for constructing reservation water and sanitary facilities, phasing out Housing and Urban Development (HUD) funding by 1983, slashing the Business Enterprise Fund from $2.4 million to $1.3 million, and ending funding for employment training programs. Funding for the public-service employment pieces of the Comprehensive Employment and Training Act (CETA) and similar programs would end. It was estimated that if discontinued, approximately 10,000 Indigenous people living on reservations would be unemployed. Education funding would be reduced from $285 million to $217 million. In turn, the BIA closed numerous schools, sometimes without warning.[138] When Congress blocked some cuts, the Reagan administration implemented internal BIA changes hindering access to (remaining) Indigenous programs with increasingly strict blood quantum requirements[139] and demands for federally recognized tribal affiliation.[140] To receive federal aid, Indigenous peoples also had to live on or near reservations,[141] which also hindered access for many.

Reagan's Native American Policy statement on January 24, 1983, reiterated the connection between austerity and/as neoliberal coloniality. Opening by diminishing Indigenous sovereignty by likening Indigenous governments to state and local governments that should have their "responsibilities and resources" restored, he outlined a plan to reduce self-determination to a matter of private sector development:

---

136. Cook, "Reagan's Indian Policy in Retrospect," 13, 15.
137. Byrd et al., "Predatory Value," 9.
138. Cook, "Reagan's Indian Policy in Retrospect," 14–16.
139. TallBear, *Native American DNA*.
140. Cook, "Reagan's Indian Policy in Retrospect," 14–16.
141. Mihesuah, *American Indians*, 89.

102 • CHAPTER 2

Instead of fostering and encouraging self-government, federal policies have by and large inhibited the political and economic development of the tribes. Excessive regulation and self-perpetuating bureaucracy have stifled local decision-making, thwarted Indian control of Indian resources, and promoted dependency rather than self-sufficiency.

This administration intends to reverse this trend by removing the obstacles to self-government and by creating a more favorable environment for the development of healthy reservation economies.[142]

As Reagan called on Congress to officially repudiate termination, his administration decimated Native American programs, excluding Indigenous peoples—except for kindred spirits who favored austerity like his Assistant Secretary on Indian Affairs appointee, Kenneth L. Smith, member of the Wascoe tribe—from decision-making processes, destroying and usurping natural resources, and failing to support even his own financialized spin on self-determination. For example, the government acquired $10 million in seed money for reservation economic projects. Many nations lacked resources to develop, and with over 283 federally recognized nations in 1983, $10 million was massively insufficient. Reagan also established the Presidential Commission on Indian Reservation Economies (PCIRE) to identify barriers to economic development and recommend changes and ways to encourage private sector involvement. PCIRE, comprised of six Indigenous and three non-Indigenous members, found that differences among nations' and reservations' impoverishment was due not to centuries of genocidal and dispossessive US policy, but rather tribal nations' emphasis on the group rather than the individual, fast turnover of tribal governments leading to businesses' instability, and tribal governments' poor business management.[143] "Indian savagery" was thus reframed in financial terms, and the solution offered was austerity in the image of the deregulated US government and economy.

While no substantial changes in Native American policy followed the PCIRE report or Reagan's statement, neoliberalized white property interests were quite literally advanced as proposed budget cuts were implemented and waves of private industry invaded reservations, usually to extract nations' natural resources rather than help develop them. The BIA budget was cut from $1.5 billion in 1983 to $923 million in 1987. The IHS budget was reduced by $88 million in 1986, and by an additional $85 million in 1987. By 1986 the NCAI

---

142. Ronald Reagan, "Statement on Indian Policy," January 24, 1983, Ronald Reagan Presidential Library & Museum, National Archives, https://www.reaganlibrary.gov/archives/speech/statement-indian-policy.

143. Cook, "Reagan's Indian Policy in Retrospect," 17–18.

was cut.[144] In 1977, IHS facilities included fifty-one hospitals, eighty-six health centers, and other health facilities. By 1984 the number of hospitals and health centers dropped to forty-eight and seventy-nine, respectively.[145] Again, IHS was already massively underfunded, with facilities lacking personnel, equipment, and accessibility. Due to employment program cuts implemented from 1980 to 1982, unemployment on reservations rose from 40 to 80 percent.[146] Neoliberal logic updated the "implacable logic of the white man's burden," for both speak the "language of delay, of the need for people cut off from circuits of capital accumulation to develop their capacities, to adjust to the standards of the more advanced world, to reform their backward ways. In this way, through the alibis of debt and scarcity, austerity regimes produce commensurability for dispossession."[147]

After gutting Indigenous programs, the Reagan administration decimated immigrant and general welfare, extending austerity to people of color. Combining the stereotypes of Latinas as "hot" and hypersexual seductresses and as pure virginal Catholic girls / married obedient wives and mothers, in the 1980s and 1990s, the "Latina Threat" discourse perpetuated the stereotype of Latinas as hyperfertile baby machines clamoring to cross the border to exploit social services,[148] warranting draconian welfare cuts. To mitigate fears that amnesty—explicitly designed to address undocumented Mexican im/migration—would burden the already beleaguered welfare state,[149] under IRCA's welfare provisions newly legalized aliens were disqualified for five years from need-based federal programs. Food stamps, some Medicaid, and programs that aided families with dependent children were cut. Immigrants remained eligible for emergency and prenatal services.[150] LPC provisions were also expanded to examine immigrants' pasts and demonstration of current self-sufficiency.[151] INS also used welfare restrictions to exclude Latinas from amnesty. *Zambrano vs. INS* (1988), in which Latina immigrants with dependents argued that implementation of welfare restrictions targeted undocumented mothers, was dismissed in 1998, but the legitimacy of their claim is

---

144. Executive Office of the President, Report, cited in Cook, "Ronald Reagan's Indian Policy," 18–19.

145. Torpy, "Native American Women and Coerced Sterilization."

146. Cook, "Ronald Reagan's Indian Policy," 14–16.

147. Byrd et al., "Predatory Value," 10.

148. Chavez, *Latino Threat*.

149. Immigration Reform and Control Act of 1982: Hearing before the Subcommittee on Immigration, Refugees, and International Law and Subcommittee on Immigration and Refugee Policy, 97th Cong., 2nd sess. (1982) (Joint hearing).

150. The Immigration Reform and Control Act of 1986, Pub. L. No. 99-60, 100 Stat. 3445 (1986).

151. Wheeler and Zachovic, "Public Charge Ground," 35; and Gerken, *Model Immigrants*.

104 · CHAPTER 2

clear: 70 percent of amnesty recipients were Mexican, over 20 percent Central American and Caribbean, but over 68 percent were male.[152] To advance neoliberal empire, as Native American policy and budget cuts to Native American programs continued to dispossess Indigenous peoples, execution of IRCA continued to fill the historical role of the state in using immigration and welfare policies to maintain women of color as a super-exploitable, low-wage labor force. Under threat of exclusion, policy and its implementation coerced racialized immigrant women into the secondary labor force, private household work, and institutional service work.[153] Contemporaneously, films such as *Lonestar, Mi Familia,* and *Real Women Have Curves* and abundant news media panics over "anchor babies" amplified the criminalization of Latinxs in connection with the "immigration emergency" and continued to pathologize Latina immigrant and citizen mothering.

Finally, all forms of welfare were cut. With the Family Support Act (1988) developed by none other than Moynihan, poverty aid programs such as AFDC, school lunch programs, and Medicaid were turned over to states, and "entitlement" programs such as Social Security and Medicare were subject to market values. Eligibility requirements were multiplied, and work incentives and requirements added.[154]

In the 1990s, public pedagogy about immigrants, welfare, and personal responsibility politics built on these precedents, continuing to serve white possession as neoliberal empire-building rendered borders more permeable for goods and labor. Elaborating on the IRCA paradigm, in the 1990s neoliberalism brought increased militarization of the US–Mexico border and increased criminalization of immigration with policies such as the 1996 Illegal Immigration Reform and Immigrant Responsibility Act (IIRIRA), which expanded illegalization, detention, and deportation logics, processes, and institutions.[155] At the risk of stating the obvious, deportable migrants are extremely vulnerable to labor exploitation and other forms of abuse. Attempts to control the reproduction of women of color also resurfaced first in California's Proposition 187 (1994), which barred undocumented immigrants from all medical services, including prenatal care, and explicitly targeted Latina immigrant mothers.[156] Then a federal version, the Personal Responsibility and Work Opportunity Reconciliation Act (PRWORA) (1996) severely limited welfare for documented immigrants, unwed teenage mothers, and children born to mothers on welfare. Temporary Assistance to Needy Families (TANF) replaced AFDC,

---

152. Daniels, *Guarding the Golden Door,* 229.
153. Chang, *Disposable Domestics,* 55–92.
154. Steger and Roy, *Neoliberalism,* 34–35.
155. Luibhéid, "'Treated neither with Respect nor with Dignity,'" 28.
156. Jacobson, *New Nativism;* and Luibhéid, *Entry Denied.*

giving states more control over welfare, capping lifetime receipt to five years, and requiring most adult recipients to work after two years.[157] The transition to "workfare" and calcification of personal responsibility politics as a pedagogy of empire was complete. Moreover, it came with the reincentivization of sterilization and controlling the reproduction of poor women who continued to be disproportionality nonwhite: family caps, illegitimacy bonuses for states that lowered nonmarital births without increasing abortion rates, and birth control and sterilization incentives for the poor were included in the policy.[158] Congress allocated $250 million for states with "abstinence only" public school programs.[159] State and local governments were barred from providing all services except emergency care to undocumented immigrants, including prenatal care. Half of the $54 billion in savings the law accrued came from denying aid to undocumented immigrants and restricting food stamps and supplemental security income (SSI) for documented immigrants.[160] Dorothy Roberts observed that policies that target immigrant women function eugenically, harming "not only the immigrants themselves, but also their descendants."[161] In short, Reaganite public pedagogy about Indigenous peoples and racialized immigrants that, in connection with personal responsibility politics, rendered both groups multivalently precarious was critical to US neoliberal empire.

CONCLUSION

Characterizing the government's fiduciary duty to Indigenous peoples as "abusive," James Watt, Reagan's secretary of the interior, claimed in a 1983 radio interview that "socialistic government policies on Indian reservations" exacerbated rampant "drug abuse, alcoholism, unemployment, divorce and venereal disease." "Indians" were, he said,

> trained through 100 years of government oppression to look to the government as the creator, as the provider, as the supplier, and have not been trained to use the initiative to integrate into the American system. [. . .] If

---

157. The Personal Responsibility and Work Opportunity Reconciliation Act of 1996, Pub. L. No. 104-93, 110 Stat. 2105 (1996).

158. Acs, "Does Welfare Promote Out-of-Wedlock Childbearing?," 3.

159. Chang, *Disposable Domestics*, xv.

160. Chang, *Disposable Domestics*, 8.

161. Roberts, "Who May Give Birth to Citizens?," 205.

we had treated the black in America like we're now treating the Indians [. . .] there would be a social revolution that would tear the country up.[162]

In his attempt to cast racialized austerity as just, Watt linked ending all forms of federal welfare for Indigenous peoples, including the reservation system, and the anti-Blackness underpinning the "welfare queen" stereotype as well as welfare public pedagogy in general. An anti-environmentalist who supported unlimited development of public—and Indigenous—lands, a hardline assimilationist, and an overt racist, Watt encouraged Reagan to veto bills that might have supported actual self-determination, conserved natural resources, and provided tribal nations with clean water.[163] Watt also aggressively advocated neoliberalized termination: welfare recipients of any sort, whether Indigenous (and thus receiving federal support under treaty obligations and/or as general welfare), Black, or Latinx, were characterized as lazy and feckless threats to the state, their own children, and themselves. While Watt's spokesperson, Douglas Baldwin, claimed Watt did not advocate abolishing reservations, Watt's intent to terminate—and gaslight the targets of white supremacy—shone through. And true to Reaganite form, personal responsibility was presented as the cure to welfare dependence of any sort.

As noted, Indigenous peoples, arguably the first welfare recipients in the US, have a unique relationship to the federal government, which is obligated through treaty agreements and other policies to provide various financial supports and services to Indigenous nations. Again, this is distinct from need-based welfare programs all US citizens are eligible for. Nonetheless, many non-Natives, like Watt and the medical professionals who abused sterilization in the 1970s, viewed Indigenous peoples as lazy, greedy, welfare takers getting a "free ride" from the federal government. Thus, Watt attacked and dismissed Indigenous sovereignty, the baseline of federal duty to Indigenous peoples, while erasing historical and ongoing systemic violence against Natives, Black people, and immigrants of color to support white possession. NCAI revoked their support of Reagan, demanding an apology and Watt's resignation. Watt did both in October 1983, but this had more to do with his polemical environmental policies than accountability for his racist attacks against Indigenous peoples.[164]

---

162. Robert Sangeorge, "Interior Secretary James Watt Called Reservations 'an Example of the Failure of Socialism,'" UPI Archives, United Press International, January 18, 1983, accessed July 31, 2023, https://www.upi.com/Archives/1983/01/18/Interior-Secretary-James-Watt-Tuesday-called-Indian-reservations-an/2653411714000/.

163. Cook, "Ronald Reagan's Indian Policy," 16.

164. Cook, "Ronald Reagan's Indian Policy," 16.

Furthermore, the Reagan administration's intent to dispossess Indigenous peoples to advance white possession was clear with and without Watt. Reagan announced his plans to cut Native American programs just days after Watt's interview, and his administration began implementing those cuts. The Reagan administration also ended numerous federally funded studies that uncovered evidence of federal treaty violations. The BIA came under scrutiny in the late 1980s and legislation proposed by some Indigenous leaders that granted a measure of self-determination passed (for instance, the Tribal Self-Governance Demonstration Project, under the 1988 Self-Determination Amendments, granted twenty nations block grants for planning and enacting programs previously administered by the federal government). Many nations also established gaming industries on reservations to mitigate the ongoing incursion of private and federal industry on their lands, and some were very successful (engendering the new stereotype of the rich Native who does not pay taxes, which further rationalized cutting Indigenous programs). Yet the federal budget cuts to Native American programs were an estimated ten times greater than those affecting other groups.[165] As such, Reagan administration cuts to Indigenous programs, discursively framed as liberatory and undertaken as Reagan revised the Frontier Myth and cultivated an image of himself as a "wild West" cowboy hero, built on sterilization abuse against Indigenous, racialized women in connection to welfare and provided a template for welfare and personal responsibility politics as a lynchpin of white possessive neoliberal empire-building in the multicultural "nation of immigrants."

I have argued that historically and into the neoliberal context, settler colonial power, necessarily imprinted on bodies in gendered, sexualized ways, has been powerfully exerted and expanded through entangled public pedagogies about Indigenous and racialized peoples in connection to welfare. Ruthie Gilmore named racism as "the state-sanctioned or extra-legal production and exploitation of group-differentiated vulnerability to premature death."[166] Reagan-era policy, praxis, and discourse about Indigenous peoples and racialized immigrants and groups, welfare, and personal responsibility politics—the direct legacy of advancing white heteropatriarchal property interests through Progressive Era regulation of "intimate domains," eugenics, and sterilization abuse—biologically and territorially remapped US neoliberal empire. These death-dealing pedagogies of empire live on in the gendered, sexualized precaritization of the lives of Indigenous peoples and people of color via welfare austerity.

---

165. Kilpatrick, *Celluloid Indians*, 103.
166. Gilmore, *Golden Gulag*, 28.

CHAPTER 3

US Culture Is Always-Already Rape Culture

Although it might seem unfair to say white US American singer Gwen Stefani has made a career out of the kind of gendered, sexualized coloniality and racism that makes US culture a foundationally and fundamentally racialized rape culture,[1] she has certainly profited from cultural appropriation and the exploitation of public pedagogies about Indigenous women and women of color that render them more vulnerable to rape as an enduring tool of US empire. Two examples of Stefani's work, read together, illuminate how, to advance the "white possessive logics" of settler colonialism,[2] US culture is always-already

---

1. I use the word "rape" to refer to actions defined by forced sex, sexual violation, and the abuse of sexual power against either adults or children, including isolated incidents and ongoing abuse. Defining "rape" to mean only forced intercourse or penetration by a penis or other object diminishes the significance of nonpenetrative forced sex, sexual violations, and sexual abuse and erases nonpenetrative sex as sex, for instance, sex between women without penetration. Clinical terms such as sexual assault, sexual abuse, sexual violence, and nonconsensual sex also downplay the violence and domination inherent to rape. This reflects state efforts to deny the existence of "rape culture," a culture in which rape is common and rape against women is normalized in and excused by social and political institutions. Therefore, I use the terms "rape," "rapeability," and "un/rapeability" to highlight the inherent violence and pervasiveness of rape. The term "sexual violence" is used as it appears in sources. The origins of the concept and term "rape culture" are explored later in the chapter. While same-sex rape and rape against men is certainly part of rape culture and sex trafficking is a related form of violence, these topics are beyond the scope of my analysis.

2. Moreton-Robinson, *White Possessive*, xix.

rape culture. In 2012 US rock band No Doubt released the video for "Looking Hot," the final single from their sixth studio album, *Push and Shove*. The video featured a "cowboys and Indians" theme and pan-Indigenous imagery and symbols such as tipis, fire and smoke signals, and feathers, some of which have spiritual significance to living Indigenous peoples. White, blonde lead vocalist Stefani plays a hypersexualized and seductively imperiled Native woman. In one notable scene, Stefani, scantily clad in all white "traditional" Indigenous clothing, including a headdress and crop top, dances and writhes suggestively with her hands bound above her head as a white male cowboy, clad in all black, points a gun at her; her innocence and vulnerability to his aggression and power is overtly sexualized. Meanwhile, the song lyrics are a tongue-in-cheek reflection about Stefani being perceived as an attractive female performer—"looking hot"—into her forties within the entertainment industry, which often discards or dismisses women as they age. To make a case for a white woman's empowerment, in addition to "playing Indian" with hackneyed stereotypes and imagery long used to cast Indigenous peoples as "savage" to justify violence against them,[3] the video and Stefani eroticize the rape and murder of Indigenous women endemic to nineteenth-century US westward empire expansion.

Responding to a wave of social media criticism of the video as profoundly offensive to Indigenous people, No Doubt pulled it from YouTube and issued a tepid apology on their website that, with its litany of neoliberal buzzwords and a bald lie, continued to illuminate how the rapeability of Indigenous women is entangled with the production of the white subject or beneficiary of settler colonialism: "As a multi-racial band our foundation is built upon both diversity and consideration for other cultures. Our intention with our new video was never to offend, hurt or trivialize Native American people, their culture or their history." This typically neoliberal brandishing of multiculturalism in evoking a token (bassist Tony Kanal is of Indian descent) and declaring the band's commitment to considering diversity and "other cultures" in the production of their commodities was followed by the claim that the band had "consulted with Native American experts in the University of California system."[4] In an open letter to No Doubt, Angela R. Riley (citizen of the Potawatomi Nation of Oklahoma), then director of the American Indian Studies Center at the University of California Los Angeles (UCLA), stated that no consultation had occurred, and that the video was not only offensive to

---

3. P. Deloria, *Playing Indian*.

4. Spin staff, "No Doubt Pull 'Looking Hot' Video, Apologize to Native American Community," *Spin*, November 3, 2012, https://www.spin.com/2012/11/no-doubt-looking-hot-video-apologize-native-americans/.

Native Americans but endangered them, and especially Native women. Riley emphasized that Native women in the United States were "in a state of crisis," given the disproportionate and epidemic rates of intraracial rape and violence against them, and that

> the video is rife with imagery that glorifies aggression against Indian people, and, most disturbingly, denigrates and objectifies Native women through scenes of sexualized violence. Much like the nineteenth century paintings advancing the ethos of manifest destiny [. . .] the video draws on familiar tropes of the conquest of the continent and, concomitantly, the ravage of the Native female.[5]

Joanne Barker (Lenape, a citizen of the Delaware Tribe of Indians) also points to Stefani's obviation of accountability for her wearing of a headdress and buckskin while "engaging in sexual torture in the music video *Looking Hot*," as one of many instances of the "costumed occupations" of gendered, sexualized Indigeneity in the public spaces of fashion, film, music, and politics that "reenact the social terms and conditions of US and Canadian dominance over Indigenous peoples."[6] Stefani and No Doubt created, circulated, and planned to profit from gendered, sexualized pedagogies of neoliberal empire that, as historically, made Indigenous women exceptionally vulnerable to rape and violence to advance white possession.

Stefani has also been criticized for appropriating Black, Latinx, and Asian cultures.[7] During her Harajuku Girls era, she pointedly reenacted white domination over racialized immigrant women and profited immensely from it, fortifying white female racial authority and "one-way globalization" maintained in the neoliberal market through cultural and economic imperialism and simultaneous strategies of homogenization and localization reliant upon racialized and gendered categories.[8] The Harajuku Girls are the four women Japanese backup dancers / entourage Stefani began using when she launched a solo career in 2004. She also created lucrative clothing and perfume lines based on the Harajuku Girls theme and executive produced *Ku Ku Harajuku,*

---

5. Angela R. Riley, "An Open Letter to No Doubt, Supersonic Public Relations and Interscope Records in Response to No Doubt's Video, 'Looking Hot,'" American Indian Studies Center, UCLA, November 5, 2012, accessed August 1, 2023, https://main.aisc.ucla.edu/2012/11/05/an-open-letter-to-no-doubt-supersonic-public-relations-and-interscope-records-in-response-to-no-doubts-video-looking-hot/.

6. Barker, "Introduction: Critically Sovereign," 3–4.

7. Jesa Marie Calaor, "Gwen Stefani: 'I Said, My God, I'm Japanese,'" Interview, *Allure*, January 10, 2023, https://www.allure.com/story/gwen-stefani-japanese-harajuku-lovers-interview.

8. Rowe, "Reading 'Reading Lolita in Tehran' in Idaho," 258.

an animated series for Nickelodeon in 2016, which ran for three seasons. Although Stefani claims that the Harajuku Girls are intended to be a "fun art project" inspired by and meant to pay homage to the subversive, often home-made fashions of the women of Japan's Harajuku district,[9] she required her employees to perform long-standing racist stereotypes of Asian immigrant women as passive, docile, infantilized, mysterious, inscrutable ornaments or props, hypersexualized in and through their subservience to whiteness. She renamed Maya Chino, Jennifer Kita, Rino Nakasone Razalan, and Mayuko Kitayama as Love, Angel, Music, and Baby and contractually required them to speak only Japanese in public though one performer is US American and the others speak English fluently; in fact, they rarely spoke but often giggled in interviews.[10] Additionally, in public appearances, promotional materials, and live performances, the Harajuku Girls, all of whom are of shorter stature than Stefani, surrounded and bowed down to her, often while clad in school-girl outfits. Not surprisingly, Stefani was accused of racism and cultural appropriation. For instance, Korean American comedian and actor Margaret Cho said that to her "a Japanese schoolgirl uniform is kind of like blackface."[11] Mihi Ahn memorably noted in *Salon* that Stefani "swallowed a subversive youth culture in Japan and barfed up another image of submissive giggling Asian women" so that her "big kiss to the East ends up feeling more like a big Pacific Rim job."[12] Stefani, who is of Italian and Irish American descent, has continued to insist that the Harajuku Girls were about her admiration of Japanese culture and not appropriation,[13] and she actually claimed in a 2023 *Allure* interview that she *is* Japanese. Accusations of cultural appropriation continue to surround her work.[14] As we shall see, sexual stereotypes of im/migrant women of color have long justified immigration restriction and rationalized rape in connection with and *as* border control in service of white possessive empire; therefore, as with Indigenous women, a white woman perpetuating racist stereotypes of immigrant women in mainstream media is no small matter.

---

9. Clark Collins, "Holla Back," *Entertainment Weekly* 909, November 22, 2006.

10. Mihi Ahn, "Gwenihana," *Salon,* April 9, 2005, https://www.salon.com/2005/04/09/geisha_2/.

11. Margaret Cho, "Harajuku Girls," *Margaret Cho* (blog), October 31, 2005, http://margaretcho.com/2005/10/31/harajuku-girls/.

12. Ahn, "Gwenihana."

13. Chelsea Ritschel, "Gwen Stefani Addresses Accusations of Cultural Appropriation over Harajuku Girls: 'I Thought They Were My People,'" *Independent,* November 20, 2019, https://www.independent.co.uk/arts-entertainment/music/news/gwen-stefani-harajuku-girls-cultural-appropriation-japan-fashion-a9210941.html.

14. Calaor, "Gwen Stefani."

112 • CHAPTER 3

Stefani's eroticization of the rape of Indigenous women and hypersexualization of women of color for profit exemplifies how the white subject of US empire is produced and reproduced. Her appropriation of gendered, sexualized Indigenous and Japanese stereotypes and cultures emblematizes neoliberal multiculturalism and feminism, for she has long claimed feminist identity grounded in white privilege and centered on individual empowerment rather than systemic change.[15] She is also part of a long tradition of white feminists taking from or at the very least excluding Indigenous women and women of color in ways that perpetuated or exacerbated their vulnerability to rape as a tool of coloniality and racial capitalism. In short, Stefani has unapologetically embraced, profited enormously from (in 2019 she had an estimated net worth of over $100 million, a chunk of which is from Stefani's Harajuku Lovers brand "empire"),[16] and popularized the kinds of gendered, sexualized stereotypes of Indigenous women and racialized immigrant women that make US culture rape culture.

This chapter argues that the culture of the United States is foundationally and fundamentally a racialized rape culture because entangled public pedagogies about the un/rapeability of Indigenous women and racialized immigrant women have historically and into the neoliberal context been key to establishing and expanding US empire. As Indigenous feminist scholars and activists have shown, rape is a tool of colonialism. Indigenous women experience the highest rates of rape in the US, a direct result of the US government's attacks on Indigenous peoples' sovereignty over their land, powers to adjudicate crime, and bodies. To protect and further white possession, the US has also long demanded the "willing subservience (and gratitude) of migrant bodies."[17] Im/migrant women of color also experience disproportionately high levels of rape, a direct result of policy that has historically sexually pathologized them and continues to render them hypervulnerable to exploitation and abuse at the hands of immigration agents, government officials, and their employers. Undocumented women's vulnerability to violence is obviously exacerbated.

The gendered, racialized assignation of sexual deviance and availability to Indigenous women and immigrant women of color through pedagogies

---

15. On the reshaping of feminism as an individualistic discourse that reestablishes traditional ideas about femininity, see McRobbie, *Aftermath of Feminism*. On "postfeminism," which is arguably synonymous or at least significantly overlaps with neoliberal feminism, see Vered and Humphreys, "Postfeminist Inflections in Television Studies," 155–63; and Rottenberg, "Rise of Neoliberal Feminism," 418–37. On Stefani's brand of feminism, see Wald, "Just a Girl?," 588.

16. Alyssa Choiniere, "Gwen Stefani Net Worth 2019: 5 Fast Facts You Need to Know," Heavy, last updated April 17, 2023, https://heavy.com/entertainment/2019/11/gwen-stefani-net-worth-2019/.

17. Rodríguez, *Sexual Futures*, 148.

of empire likewise renders both groups un/rapeable, that is, inherently in/violable because violation is systemically and ideologically illegible; they are illegible as victims of rape. For Indigenous peoples, that un/violability extends to their lands and resources; for racialized immigrants (and enslaved Black people), their labor. Casting racialized women as unrapeable, or inviolable, obviates the violence of the physical act of rape and justifies the racialized forms of violence—colonization, dispossession, exclusion, and labor exploitation—inherent to US empire-building and nationalism, producing and reproducing the circular "logic" of white heteropatriarchal possession[18] in which rape and racialized un/rapeability rationalize each other. I trace the throughline of public pedagogies that have established, maintained, and routinized the un/rapeability of Indigenous and immigrant women of color as one of the most powerful machinations of US empire.

COLONIZATION AND/AS RAPE

The entanglements of Indigenous dispossession and racialized alienation necessary to/for white possession are strong foundations upon which rape and other forms of gendered, sexualized violence occur and are rationalized. Moreover, Sarah Deer, a citizen of the Muscogee (Creek) Nation of Oklahoma, has chronicled how in precolonial Indigenous cultures, rape against women was rare[19] "because of the immediate and severe consequences for disrupting balance in society,"[20] and many Indigenous societies abhorred sexual violence, including in the context of warfare.[21] In fact in travel writings, diaries, and histories, early Euro-American colonists marveled over the rarity of rape within Indigenous societies.[22] Paula Gunn Allen (Laguna Pueblo) argued in her pathbreaking work on rape and colonization that "the oppression and abuse of women is indistinguishable from fundamental Western concepts of social order."[23] Imposing heteropatriarchy, in no small part through rape, upon Native communities was therefore "essential to establishing

---

18. Moreton-Robinson, *White Possessive*.

19. Deer, "Toward an Indigenous Jurisprudence," 121. See also Leanne Betasamosake Simpson, "Not Murdered, Not Missing: Rebelling against Colonial Gender Violence," *Leannesimpson.ca*, March 8, 2017, accessed August 31, 2018, https://www.leannesimpson.ca/writings/not-murdered-not-missing-rebelling-gainst-colonial-gender-violence; and Block, *Rape and Sexual Power*, 225–29.

20. Deer, *Beginning and End of Rape*, 22.

21. Deer, *Beginning and End of Rape*, 20–21.

22. Block, *Rape and Sexual Power*, 225–29.

23. Allen, *Off the Reservation*, 66. See also Allen, *Sacred Hoop*, 194–208.

114 • CHAPTER 3

colonial rule, because patriarchy naturalizes social hierarchy."[24] Furthermore, heteropatriarchy is "the building block of the nation-state form of governance, which is based on domination and control."[25]

In the Americas, the use of rape and an expansive if not totalized notion of racialized un/rapeability as a tool of colonization/conquest began with Columbus and his cohorts and inaugural colonial policy[26] that formed the bedrock of British and then US Native American policy. As noted previously, the Doctrine of Discovery (1492–1600) gave power to the government by whose subjects or authority "discovery" of land was made by casting non-Christians as savages because, ironically, of their nonheteropatriarchal kinship and political structures and behaviors.[27] The sovereign and their subjects (and later the federal government and its citizens) thereby framed the violation of sinful, degraded Indigenous bodies, lands, and resources as righteous and/or illegible as violation. That logic is embedded in policy that continues to impact Indigenous peoples.

Christian moralization in other early colonial policies and practices—Spanish Catholic and Puritan, respectively—also rendered Indigenous women un/rapeable in distinct ways that continued to serve white heteropatriarchal property interests. First, early colonial Spanish missions exposed Indigenous women to a spectrum of violence. Albert Hurtado describes how "spiritual, military, and sexual conquest went hand in glove on the California frontier."[28] Catholic missionaries, aiming to incorporate Natives into Spanish society as part of Native and *mestizo* (mixed) families where sanctioned marital conjugal relations could occur, heavily policed Indigenous women's sexuality at missions. Yet Spanish missions also allowed sex work, uncommon prior to colonization, to thrive in California: demand among soldiers plus the economic ravages of colonization and displacement resulted in the ubiquity of sex work among Indigenous women.[29] Spanish soldiers also frequently raped Native women, which concerned missionaries even as they helped to create and sustain a rape culture by dispossessing Native lands, deliberately disrupting Indigenous economies and social structures by sexually surveilling and disciplining Natives and especially Native women and necessitating the presence of soldiers to protect priests and mission property. Colonists' inculcation of heteropatriarchy by casting Indigenous women as unrapeable, lascivious

---

24. Smith and Kauanui, "Introduction: Native Feminisms Engage American Studies," 241.
25. Smith and Kauanui, "Introduction: Native Feminisms Engage American Studies," 247.
26. Deer, *Beginning and End of Rape*, 32–33; and Wolfe, *Traces of History*, 141–43.
27. Wolfe, *Traces of History*, 141–43.
28. Hurtado, "When Strangers Met," 60.
29. Hurtado, "When Strangers Met," 59.

bodies to be Christianized and/or available to be taken, purchased, and used also had tangible consequences within Indigenous nations. In New Mexico in the eighteenth century some Indigenous nations adopted the Spanish colonial practice of enslaving and raping Indigenous female captives, at times in ritualized public spectacles.[30]

Second, Puritans were, like Spanish missionaries, horrified and fascinated by the sexual freedom and socioeconomic power Indigenous women had and queer sexualities and kinship arrangements within some societies. This too embedded the un/rapeability of Indigenous women in the settlement of what became the US.[31] Puritans likened Natives to biblical Canaanites, destroyed by God because of their sexual acts of perversion in Sodom. This turned Indigenous bodies "into a pollution of which the colonial body must constantly purify itself." And "because Indian bodies are 'dirty,' they are considered sexually violable and 'rapeable,' and the rape of bodies that are considered inherently impure or dirty simply does not count."[32] In travel narratives, early Euro-American colonists remarked on the sexual availability of Indigenous women, describing them as exotic, wild, and easy to love and leave because they were unbound by the "civilized" bonds of marriage and commitment.[33] Descriptions of "unrelenting sexual overtures from Native women" were also common in men's travel writing.[34]

Fur traders throughout North America also helped build the un/rapeability of Indigenous women into the budding colonial, capitalist economies of the US and Canada. While intermarriage among Indigenous women and white men created mixed families central to trade and frontier society along the Great Lakes and the Canadian frontier, fur traders misunderstood Indigenous ceremonial sexual relations, which were usually reciprocal and consensual, as commodity exchanges. In turn, fur traders created and perpetuated a market for enslaved Native women whom they purchased for sexual pleasure, companionship, and domestic servitude. For instance, in Mandan and other slave markets fur traders purchased Native women captives from enemy nations, often Shoshone, Sioux, and Arikara. Significantly, the Shoshone woman Sacagawea, who assisted the Lewis and Clark expedition as an interpreter (and who became the emblematic, fabled feminized "noble savage" "helper," explored more below), was with another woman purchased from Hidatsa

---

30. Blackhawk, *Violence over the Land*, 148.
31. Rifkin, *When Did Indians Become Straight?*
32. Smith, *Conquest*, 3.
33. Berger, "After Pocahontas," 26.
34. Block, *Rape and Sexual Power*, 227.

116 • CHAPTER 3

traders between 1800 and 1804 by Toussaint Charbonneau. He married both women, which we can speculate was nonconsensual.[35]

Additionally, as discussed in chapter 2, in every representational sphere, the common thread of stereotypes of Indigenous women—princess, "s—," or a combination of the two—is availability to white male settlers/civilization, justifying the conquest, genocide, and assimilation of Indigenous peoples.[36] Pocahontas is the prototype of the exotic, desirable, available (to white men) and amenable (to white heteropatriarchal assimilation) Native princess that endures in policy and as a pop culture icon today. Yet rape is a part of Pocahontas's story, and her marriage allowed European colonists to establish a foothold in Virginia and the South.[37] While the details of her life are known only through English reports, some facts are well supported. Matoaka (Pocahontas), a member of the Powhatan Confederacy, met and possibly rescued Captain John Smith in 1608 when she was twelve years old. She was then kidnapped and raped by the English.[38] She was sent to Jamestown, converted to Christianity in 1613, married John Rolfe in 1614, gave birth to Thomas Rolfe in 1615, went to England with her husband and child in 1616, and became a celebrity as an exemplary "civilized" "savage." She died in 1617.[39] Because her voice is absent from the historical record, we do not know how Pocahontas or her community experienced these events, including her marriage, and US settlers have repeatedly seized and propagandized her narrative. In the pre- and early Revolutionary period, her story was politically compelling as uniquely US American. From the eighteenth century as violent continental US empire-building was underway, public pedagogy about her marriage and assimilation reframed the conquest of Indigenous peoples as a consensual process that need not be violent. In saving Smith and fully assimilating, she exemplified Indigenous allegiance to white possession. These pedagogies of empire allowed Euro-Americans to pursue the nation's manifest destiny while assuaging guilt or misgivings about Indigenous genocide and dispossession, which always included rape, as its precondition.

Public pedagogy about Pocahontas's ostensible alacrity to avail herself to white possession and the illegibility of the rape of Native women as endemic to settler coloniality also underscored the codification of white supremacy in US law for generations to come. Jodi Byrd (citizen of the Chickasaw Nation

---

35. Hurtado, "When Strangers Met," 60–61.

36. Marubbio, *Killing the Indian Maiden*, 3–4.

37. Berger, "After Pocahontas," 51.

38. Berger, "After Pocahontas," 26; 51; and Kilpatrick, *Celluloid Indians*, 151–52.

39. Marubbio, *Killing the Indian Maiden*, 14. For an in-depth history of Pocahontas, see Kupperman, *Pocahontas and the English Boys*.

of Oklahoma) describes how the so-called "Pocahontas Exception" in the Virginia Racial Integrity Act of 1924 allowed the "first families" of Virginia "to preserve their whiteness through a claim to a hyperdescent Indianness." This resolved the racial complexity of their New World origin story by claiming descent from Thomas Rolfe, son of Pocahontas and John Rolfe, and by refusing possible Black ancestry for Indigenous peoples living in the state. By law, a white person could only marry another white person, or "a person with no other admixture of blood than white and American Indian."[40] While eugenicists were casting Indigenous peoples as decadent, inferior civilizations that were consequently dying out and could be bred out, a biologized "Indianness" simultaneously preserved white possession, much of which was likely a product of rape, as a matter of policy. Moreover, Euro-American reframing of Pocahontas's father's community status as a "king" and hers as "princess" granted her descendants an "aristocratic" genealogy. Vine Deloria (Standing Rock Sioux) describes the popular "Indian grandmother complex that plagues certain whites" (the idea that white people have a long-lost Native grandmother): while a male Native ancestor would be too "savage," a "young Indian princess" was "royalty for the taking. Somehow a white was lined with a noble house of gentility and culture if his grandmother ran away with an intrepid pioneer."[41] This extant appropriation of Indigeneity, which erases the violence and rape inherent to US empire-building, also renders contemporary Indigeneity "an inconsequential ethnicity in the racial topographies of US liberal multiculturalism in which many now claim an Indian great-great-grandmother."[42] In sum, early colonial policies and popular discourses that stereotyped Native women as princesses (and/or "s—s") made "consent" to white possessive logics the defining characteristic of Indigenous womanhood, rendering Indigenous women un/rapeable as a central tool of colonialism.

Early colonial sexual regulation policies and rulings about rape and un/rapeability also helped to establish and protect the white possessive logics of US empire.[43] US rape law, based on the common law of England, treated all women as chattel: rape was a property crime against white men given that women were viewed as the property of husbands and fathers. But it did so within a racialized and class-based hierarchy[44] so that the "Americanization

---

40. Byrd, "*Loving* Unbecoming," 224; and "Virginia Health Bulletin: The New Virginia Law to Preserve Racial Integrity, March 1924," *Document Bank of Virginia*, accessed August 1, 2023, https://edu.lva.virginia.gov/dbva/items/show/226.

41. V. Deloria, *Custer Died for Your Sins*, 3.

42. Byrd, "*Loving* Unbecoming," 224–25.

43. Block, *Rape and Sexual Power*, 10.

44. Deer, *Beginning and End of Rape*, 23.

118 • CHAPTER 3

of British law was the racialization of rape."[45] In the eighteenth century, as the criminal justice systems of British colonies became more formalized and Puritan religious ideologies gave way to an emphasis on the secular and social costs of sexual misconduct, rape—defined as an attack by a man on a woman who was not his wife, with the archetypal rape being an isolated attack by a stranger—was viewed as an outgrowth of men's natural sexual needs or "passions." Women were also perceived as unreliable and often as uncontrolled temptresses and, into the early nineteenth century when the norms of white femininity changed, expected to regulate men's sexual behavior. A gendered double standard thus made women responsible for sexual acts and their consequences, and consent, coercion, violence, and sex often overlapped.[46] Meanwhile, men's racial and class identities determined whether they could rape and coerce sex with impunity, and women's identities determined the extent of their vulnerability to men's violence. Not surprisingly, elite white men often avoided prosecution and punishment for rape and shaped coercion into consent. While women could not be judges, sit on juries, or even testify, for white women and especially elite white women, heteropatriarchy held some possibility of providing protection from rape or punishment for an assailant. Yet Indigenous women, viewed as tainted by "savage," primitive sexuality that obviated the "need" to rape them, were excluded from the status of rape victim and were not permitted to testify in courts until the late nineteenth century.[47] Rape of enslaved Black women was also inherent to chattel slavery: Black women's reproduction was desired as the source of more free laborers, and enslaved women had no legal recourse for rape at the hands of white enslavers.[48] Enslaved Native women were also subject to extreme sexual and physical violence that was illegible as such. In the early colonial justice system, rape was therefore a "tool of colonization [. . .] that marked a woman's gendered and racial inferiority."[49]

Throughout the eighteenth and early nineteenth centuries, lawmakers also punished Black men convicted or even accused of raping white women much more harshly than white men, and statutes linked rape and other rebellious behavior among enslaved Black people, inaugurating the now hackneyed myth of the Black rapist as part of colonies' and later states' efforts to control

---

45. Block, *Rape and Sexual Power*, 152.

46. Block, *Rape and Sexual Power*, 16–52.

47. Deer, "Decolonizing Rape Law," 149–67.

48. Block, *Rape and Sexual Power*, 4; 227. As Black feminist scholars have argued, raping enslaved women was inherent to racial capitalism. The myth of the Black male rapist targeting white women has also justified extreme anti-Black violence into the present day. See Davis, *Women, Race, Class*; and Painter, "Soul Murder and Slavery."

49. Block, *Rape and Sexual Power*, 84.

enslaved and then free Black men. Indigenous men were also cast as sexual threats to white women.[50] As Angela Davis has stated, "in the history of the United States, the fraudulent rape charge is one of the most formidable artifices invented by racism"[51] that to this day justifies the criminalization of men of color and extreme state and extrajuridical violence against them. Despite the abundance of evidence that white male settlers frequently and with impunity raped Indigenous and Black women, persons' racial and class identities, rather than the quality of a sexual interaction, defined rape. As Susan Block argues, "The very absence of recorded categorization of such acts as rape was crucial to early American systems of sexual and social power."[52] In sum, early colonial public pedagogy that rendered Indigenous women—and by extension all Indigenous peoples, lands, and resources—and women of color un/rapeable was a foundational tool of colonization in the Americas because it advanced and protected white heteropatriarchal property interests and produced whiteness as property, or the subject of settler colonialism and racial capitalism.

CODIFYING US RAPE CULTURE

In the nineteenth century when, along with Indigenous peoples, influxes of differentially racialized immigrants threatened white possessive hegemony, entangled pedagogies of empire cast Indigenous and racialized immigrant women as un/rapeable. In numerous ways, the un/rapeability of Native and racialized women was further embedded into the economy and geography of the US as a key part of what Manu Karuka calls "continental imperialism" in his study of the co-constitution of Indigenous dispossession and Chinese migrant laborers' exploitation in nineteenth-century US empire-building. Karuka shows that there is no "national" territory of the United States but rather only colonized territories, and no "national" political economy but rather only an imperial one maintained "not through the rule of law, contract, or competition, but through the renewal of colonial occupation."[53] First, rape was a tactic of warfare until colonial victory was clear. In fact, many Indigenous-initiated conflicts were a response to the kidnapping, rape, and sexual abuse of women and the federal government's complicity in that violence, as with the 1862 US–Dakota War or "Sioux Uprising."[54]

---

50. Block, *Rape and Sexual Power*, 148–49.
51. Davis, "Rape, Racism, and the Capitalist Setting," 130.
52. Block, *Rape and Sexual Power*, 3.
53. Karuka, *Empire's Tracks*, xii.
54. Deer, *Beginning and End of Rape*, 34.

120 • CHAPTER 3

Second, rape was common on forced migrations during removal and on newly formed reservations. Incarcerated on reservations, Indigenous people depended upon the military and local traders for food, clothing, and shelter. Soldiers and other male settlers exploited that for sexual favors, and sex work continued to be a means of survival for some Indigenous women within new colonial borders.[55]

Third, the rape of Indigenous women decimated Indigenous geopolitical systems, bolstering the imperial US economy by forcing Indigenous peoples to participate in it in various ways. Among the Paiute, for instance, women ceased to be the primary food gatherers because of widespread rape.[56] The California Gold Rush (1848–59) provoked mass westward migration from within the US and abroad and reinvigorated the US economy. Just before it began, white male settlers organized hunting parties that systematically attacked Indigenous communities and especially targeted Indigenous women.[57] Then with the influx of white settlers seeking fortune, the abduction, murder, sale, and sexual enslavement of Natives increased.[58] Mining districts became "an arena for assaults on women that further debilitated a population already in decline and suffering from a variety of infectious diseases." Indigenous women, whose sexual lives were shaped by "colonial warfare, starvation, and the frequency of sexual assault," were some of the first sex workers in the new market for sex work that mining engendered.[59] So common was the rape of Indigenous women by white male settlers during the Gold Rush that newspapers such as the San Francisco *Bulletin* and *Sacramento Union* often reported on it as a cause of Indigenous uprisings.[60]

Fourth, Progressive Era policy and projects undertaken by humanitarian organizations such as Friends of the Indian that focused on assimilating Indigenous peoples by controlling what Beth Piatote (Nez Perce, enrolled with Colville Confederated Tribes) calls the "intimate domestic" furthered continental coloniality[61] by continuing to cast Indigenous women as inviolable. Lest there is any confusion about the heteropatriarchal impetus of allotment, which rewarded heteropatriarchal nuclear households with larger segments of private property, and gendered, racialized Indigenous dispossession as the foundation of US political/property rights, Supreme Court Justice William

---

55. Deer, *Beginning and End of Rape*, 65.
56. Deer, *Beginning and End of Rape*, 50.
57. Karuka, *Empire's Tracks*, 84.
58. Deer, *Beginning and End of Rape*, 67–68.
59. Hurtado, "When Strangers Met," 64–66.
60. Hurtado, "When Strangers Met," n. 64, 73.
61. Piatote, *Domestic Subjects*, 2.

Strong was transparent: he opposed allotting land to married Native women because "civilizing" Natives necessitated a male head of family and patriarchal descent of property.[62] Indigenous women's "ig/noble savage" sexuality also excluded them from the Jacksonian emergence of the cult of true white womanhood and its centering of piety, chastity, and domesticity.[63] Moreover, the goal of Indigenous girls' education at compulsory boarding schools was to force "patriarchal norms into Native communities so that women would lose their place of leadership in Native communities."[64] Overcrowded schools lacked adequate food and medical care; death from starvation and disease was common as was sexual, physical, and emotional abuse. Into the 1980s the US government refused to address or even investigate accusations.[65]

Through nineteenth-century marriage law, white men also gained the right to Indigenous women's land without becoming citizens of her nation, another policy that furthered white possessive continental empire expansion by rendering the widespread rape and murder of Indigenous women illegible. Often marrying settler men to survive, Indigenous wives were frequently discarded or mistreated once a white husband had access to their land/wealth,[66] a practice supported by the legal doctrine of "divorce by abandonment," based on white male judges' view of informal divorce in some Indigenous societies as an offshoot of Indigenous women's sexual depravity.[67] The violence of gendered, sexualized commodification was also taken to its logical conclusion: in the early twentieth century in Oklahoma, so many Osage women were murdered for their land that the Federal Bureau of Investigation initiated one of its earliest serial murder investigations.[68]

---

62. Berger, "After Pocahontas," 17.

63. Berger, "After Pocahontas," 8.

64. Smith, *Conquest,* 37; 39; and Glenn, "Settler Colonialism as Structure," 57.

65. Smith, *Conquest,* 39. As Smith describes, despite the devastating, multigenerational trauma the boarding school system caused, the BIA did not address the ubiquitous reporting of sexual abuse until 1987 or issue policy to strengthen background checks of instructors until 1989. In 1990 the Indian Child Protection Act established a sex offender registry in Indigenous territories, created a reporting system, and provided BIA and IHS guidelines for employee background checks and guidelines for recognizing sexual abuse for parents, school employees, and law enforcement. Unsurprisingly the law was not sufficiently funded or implemented, and rates of rape in Indigenous territories have increased since it passed. Many class action suits against the US government on behalf of all persons who were sexually, physically, or mentally abused at boarding schools from 1890 to the present have been filed with varying results (36–49).

66. Deer, *Beginning and End of Rape,* 66–67.

67. Berger, "After Pocahontas," 39.

68. Deer, *Beginning and End of Rape,* 66–67.

Crucially, the Major Crimes Act (MCA; 1885) made it nearly impossible for Indigenous peoples to address and adjudicate rape and sexual assault, continuing to provide a strong foundation upon which rape and sexual violence against Indigenous women could and did continue to support white possessive empire-building. MCA placed jurisdiction of "major" crimes such as murder and rape under federal rather than Indigenous nations' jurisdiction, according to the paternalistic logic that Indigenous justice systems cannot properly address serious crimes. Most of what MCA considers "major crimes" are acts of violence against the body, such as murder and rape. Here colonial governing cast Natives as "savage" not because they were viewed as sexually sinful or even as racial pollutants as in earlier periods but rather because of their inability to protect *their own* bodies by sufficiently punishing violent crimes. MCA initiated a series of laws and court rulings that calcified the rapeability of Indigenous women as a key tool of colonial empire-building into the neoliberal context.

Thus, in nineteenth-century policy, as Mishuana Goeman (Tonawanda Band of Seneca) writes:

> The training of the perceived "savage" body became a main objective of colonization, from missionizing Indians to enforcing boarding schools. It is the settler imaginary of Native savagery that legitimates conditions through which bodies were and are continually disciplined. This move in the structures of colonialism, however, is read as "civilizing" or, in today's language, as helping to "develop" Native nations so they can "share" in progress. The traces of this history linger and fester and manifest themselves on the bodies of Native women.[69]

Film, the new media of the day, simultaneously served white possessive empire-building by rendering Indigenous women inviolable, portraying them as either depraved "savages" or eager to assimilate. As discussed previously, the Celluloid Maiden is a Native princess who is a lover of or helper to white men; she longs for the white male hero or Euro-American culture and often sacrifices herself, either by completing suicide or being killed in the midst of her efforts to protect white possession.[70] Consequently, "her gender makes her a target for rape, while her death ensures the end of a generation."[71] Representative lover films include the first and second *S— Man*. Along similar lines, emblematic "helpers" such as Sacagawea and other women scouts have

---

69. Goeman, "Ongoing Storms and Struggles," 114.
70. Marubbio, *Killing the Indian Maiden*, 29.
71. Marubbio, *Killing the Indian Maiden*, 3–4.

been "portrayed as compliant and helpful to US government spies, such as Lewis and Clark, and fur traders and explorers."[72] Examples of helper films include shorts like *Red Wing's Gratitude* (1909), D. W. Griffith's *The Broken Doll* (1910) and *Iola's Promise* (1912), and the feature-length *The Vanishing American* (1925). This first set of "Celluloid Maiden" films highlighted Indigenous peoples' alacrity to assimilate but ultimate incompatibility with "civilization" through the ostensibly willing—and thus un/rapeable—Native woman's body. They were produced and popular in the shadow of ubiquitous anxieties about shifting gender norms, industrialization, the closing of the frontier, and a connected Progressive-Era fixation on "preservation" of the natural environment and the "primitive" artifacts of the "vanishing Indian" if not actual Indigenous human beings.

Nineteenth-century pedagogies of empire proximally rendered differentially racialized im/migrant women, who, like Indigenous peoples, could not or would not assimilate into English-speaking, white Anglo-Saxon Protestant society, as un/rapeable. As discussed earlier, Chinese and other East Asian women were cast as sexually depraved in periodicals and in the Page Law (1875), which banned Chinese women suspected of sex work from entry.[73] Meanwhile, as the "Likely to Become a Public Charge" (LPC; 1882) provisions pathologized white ethnic immigrant women as fecund burdens on the US welfare state, the Bureau of Immigration focused on controlling sex work among European immigrant women, "viewed as future citizens" and the mothers of future citizens.[74] Periodicals fretted alongside policymakers and social reformers over white ethnic women's potential to pollute the national stock, overwhelm the welfare state, and fail to assimilate. While sex work among Mexican women along the border was not a major concern for the Bureau of Immigration given the view that sexually satisfied migrant male Mexican laborers would not bring their wives and families across the border to settle,[75] un/rapeability has always been a part of controlling the border of what became Mexico and the US. Continuing with colonial Spanish efforts in Mexico to combat "hostile" Indios, the Texas Rangers, the model for the Border Patrol, formed in 1873 to push Apaches and Comanches back into Mexico or onto reservations. Composed of white men, the Rangers' vigilantism and aggression included lynching Mexicans and Chicanx[76] and raping and abusing

---

72. Dunbar-Ortiz and Gilio-Whitaker, *"All the Real Indians Died Off,"* 138.
73. R. Lee, *Orientals*, 90–91.
74. Moloney, "Women's Sexual Morality," 105.
75. Moloney, "Women's Sexual Morality," 105.
76. Hong, *Ruptures of American Capital*, 136.

124 · CHAPTER 3

women. The Border Patrol, created in 1924, has continued to perpetrate rape.[77] The extant stereotype of Mexican women's sexual depravity was also prevalent in film (see chapters 1 and 2).

Nineteenth- and early twentieth-century US rape law, which continued to treat women like property and was underpinned by the idea of true (white) womanhood, further embedded public pedagogy about the un/rapeability of Native and racialized women in US culture. Rape laws continued to define rape as forced intercourse with a woman who was not a man's wife, and the act was perceived as an unusual occurrence, though now borne of men's "natural," more animalistic sexuality. Rape law thus codified the paradigm of rape as a stranger attacking a woman, which does not address the experience of most women. The burden of proving rape continued to fall on victims, a problem that victims of other crimes do not have to contend with. A victim had to establish that she resisted her attacker (in accordance with the Jacksonian cult of true womanhood, women needed to be convinced to have sex, making consent obsolete by making coercion part of normative heteropatriarchal relations), report the rape immediately, and corroborate her testimony with evidence. Juries were told to meet testimony with suspicion. Despite the frequency of marital rape, husbands who raped their wives were exempt from prosecution because a man could not violate property that was legally his. Beginning in the 1970s, marital rape was recognized as a crime in some states, but only in 1993 did it become a crime in all fifty states. Some states still have forms of marital rape exemptions.[78] Meanwhile, rape against Indigenous women, Black women, and other women of color remained almost entirely illegible, rarely prosecuted, and punished to a lesser degree than the rape of white women, if punished at all. For instance, in a 1909 Congressional debate over punishment for the perpetrators of sexual assault against Indigenous women, Rep. George W. Norris (R-Nebraska) stated to the House that "the morals of Indian women are not always as high as those of a white woman and consequently the punishment should be lighter against her."[79]

•

Entangled pedagogies of empire about the un/rapeability of Indigenous and racialized immigrant women persisted into the 1930s and 1940s. Recall that the Indian Citizenship Act (1924), the Indian Reorganization Act (IRA; 1934), and FDR's inclusion of Native Americans in Depression recovery recognized

---

77. Montejano, *Anglos and Mexicans*, 117–20; and Stern, *Eugenic Nation*, 73–74.

78. Shaw and Lee, "Sexual Assault and Rape," 552.

79. Quoted in Deer, *Beginning and End of Rape*, 24.

Indigenous rights only in connection to ongoing assimilation, which for Indigenous women and girls continued to center on correcting their ostensible un/violability in the intimate domestic realm.

Simultaneously, the hypersexualization of Indigenous and racialized women in film continued to calcify both groups' un/rapeability as a profitable feature of US popular culture. With the lifting of some censorship codes, which allowed for more lascivious characters, what Marubbio calls the "sexualized maiden" version of the Celluloid Native Maiden supplanted the Native princess. The sexualized maiden emblematized the danger of miscegenation and colonization gone awry; she is an "ignoble savage." The sexualized maiden was often played by Latina actors, and the character was sometimes both Indigenous and Latina, pointing to the white possessive intertwinement of Indigenous dispossession and racialized alienation. For instance, Mexican actor Lupe Velez, who played a wanton version of the Indigenous princess in the 1931 S— Man, played a more explicitly wanton Indigenous woman, Slim Girl, in *Laughing Boy* (1934). Velez, often typecast as a sexual object for a white male lead, came to personify the "hot-blooded" hypersexual Latina temptress.[80] While the combination of racial exoticism, sexual promiscuity, and physical threat to the white hero / white possession overlaps with the femme fatale trope of the 1940s, underscored by fears of sexually aggressive women, the sexualized maiden is presented as "tainted" by her "bad blood" (she is often of mixed heritage), which causes or justifies her death and returns order to the (white) community.[81] The sexualized maiden stereotype is most prevalent in 1940s "prestige pictures," that is, high-end Westerns and nation-building epics by well-known producers and directors such as *Northwest Mounted Police* (1940), *My Darling Clementine* (1946), *Duel in the Sun* (1946), and *Colorado Territory* (1949). She surfaces in a handful of 1950s and 1960s Westerns.[82] Notably sadism against a sexualized maiden Native and Mexican character, Chihuahua (played by white actor Linda Darnell), is featured in John Ford's *My Darling Clementine,* rated a top ten film of the year by the National Board of Reviews and considered a classic Western.

Meanwhile, against the backdrop of still uncapped Western Hemisphere immigration and ongoing perceptions of Mexicans and by extension Latinxs as biological and territorial threats to the white heteropatriarchal property interests underpinning US empire, the Hollywood Good Neighbor films produced between 1939 and 1947 reflected the FDR administration's "Good Neighbor" foreign policy of nonintervention in Latin America. In these films, Latina stars

---

80. Lopez, "Are All Latins from Manhattan?," 404–24.

81. Marubbio, *Killing the Indian Maiden,* 8.

82. Marubbio, *Killing the Indian Maiden,* 93.

126 · CHAPTER 3

such as Velez, Carmen Miranda, and Dolores del Rio were, through a framing of their sexuality as innate or more potent than that of white women, cast as nonthreatening but not quite assimilable. This allowed for the marketing of these films to white US and Latin American audiences.[83] Additionally, to support an increasingly multicultural imagining of US empire during and just after World War II, the Production Code Administration carefully monitored representations of Latinas, and Native men were linked to white men to promote a vision of "racial cooperation." The industry did not, however, censor or regulate racial stereotyping of or violence against Indigenous women[84] or Japanese people, for that matter.

In these myriad ways, nineteenth- and early twentieth-century pedagogies of empire rendered Indigenous and differentially racialized immigrant women un/rapeable. While Native women were uniquely subject to unabashed, systematic un/rapeability as part of the establishment of the US and the nation's perhaps most overt phase of continental and global imperialism, the nineteenth- and early twentieth-century entanglement and often taxonomizing of Indigenous and racialized immigrant women's un/rapeability in policy, border policing, and media further calcified the production of the white subject of US empire and US culture as rape culture.

RAPE, A NEOLIBERAL ECONOMY OF DISPOSSESSION

Understanding the current epidemic of rape against Indigenous women as "a fundamental result of colonialism, a history of violence reaching back centuries,"[85] Deer emphasizes that "alienation from one's homeland provides a strong foundation upon which sexual violence can take place."[86] To support the white possessive project of US empire, racialized im/migrant women are alienated in distinct but related ways by economic policies that necessitate migration and immigration policies that exacerbate their vulnerability to rape and labor exploitation. US rape law and mainstream discourse has also continued to be inadequate for all women and to marginalize if not erase Indigenous women and women of color as victims and as agents in their own sexual lives. To further white possession, the colonial state and then the modern corporation attempt to control where and how gendered, racialized bodies

---

83. Lopez, "Are All Latins from Manhattan?"
84. Marubbio, *Killing the Indian Maiden*, 112.
85. Deer, *Beginning and End of Rape*, x.
86. Deer, *Beginning and End of Rape*, xv.

move.[87] This section focuses on entangled pedagogies of US neoliberal empire that render Indigenous and racialized immigrant women un/rapeable.

US law continued to make Indigenous women incredibly vulnerable to rape as a tool of neoliberal coloniality. MCA catalyzed a series of laws and court decisions that forced heteropatriarchal Euro-American models of justice upon Indigenous people and impeded the development of Indigenous justice systems, ensuring that Indigenous women's un/rapeability would continue to be a potent part of Indigenous dispossession writ large. Prior to IRA most Native communities used an oral tradition for legal systems that, unconfined to institutions and not requiring "experts" or capital to navigate, was open and accessible to all. Most Indigenous justice systems were also victim-centered. Rehabilitation rather than punishment was standard, though in cases of rape and sexual assault, traditional punishments were swift and harsh.[88] In contrast, the Euro-American system, designed to protect white heteropatriarchal property interests, is regimented, formal, and requires experts (lawyers) and capital (fees) to navigate it. The adversarial system also gives defendants rights with very little regard for victim's rights, that is, the defendant has the right to remain silent, but victims are often required to testify. Incarceration is the standard of punishment.

Public Law 280 (PL 280), passed in 1953 in the Termination Era, further eroded Indigenous sovereignty and justice systems, and in so doing increased Indigenous women's un/rapeability as a tool of settler colonialism. PL 280 gave states criminal and some civil jurisdiction over Indigenous nations and territories. Neither states nor Indigenous nations consented to this, and neither were given funding. Consequently, many reservations lacked a consistent criminal justice system and the means to develop one. State governments were also ill-suited to provide justice to Indigenous peoples because states and Indigenous nations are often at odds over natural resources, taxes, gaming, and child welfare. While neither MCA or PL 280 fully divested Indigenous sovereignty, both exacerbated Indigenous women's vulnerability to rape and other forms of violence.[89]

Relocation under termination also increased Native women's vulnerability to rape and sexual exploitation. Although the government and BIA recruitment framed relocation to urban areas from reservations as a generous opportunity for young people, recruits were given only a small travel stipend and no help upon arrival. By 1969 the average per capita income for Indigenous

---

87. Karuka, *Empire's Tracks*, xiii.

88. Banishment and the death penalty were some traditional punishments used for sex offenders (Deer, "Decolonizing Rape Law," 154; 158).

89. Deer, *Beginning and End of Rape*, 38.

people was below half the national poverty level. Unemployment was almost ten times the national average. As in the past, US policy rendered Natives vulnerable to economic exploitation; Indigenous women were especially vulnerable to trafficking and being coerced into sex work as a means of survival.[90]

In the shadow of Termination policy, mediated pedagogies of empire continued to circulate stereotypes of Indigenous women's un/rapeability. In 1953 Disney's animated *Peter Pan* (1953) (re)taught generations of children that Indigenous peoples were ignorant "savages" along gendered, sexualized lines, particularly via the song "What Makes the Red Man Red?" Along with bellicosity, speaking in halting, broken English, and having literally red skin, according to the song it is sexuality and sexism. Lyrics proclaim that both the "s—" and maiden nonsensically make "the red man red." To further convey their "savagery," the film's Natives force Wendy, the white heroine, to serve them while her brothers and other boys play.[91] Meanwhile Tiger Lily, the Native princess, is hypersexualized and seductive:[92] to express her gratitude to Peter Pan when he rescues her from pirates, she dances suggestively for the white hero and kisses him. He is embarrassed and Wendy is jealous. Thus, in explicitly gendered, sexualized terms, these cartoon Natives are ill-suited for white "civilization" and even the pretend world of Neverland, where white boys have the option to never grow up. Into the mid-twentieth century, Hollywood, through the body of hypersexual/ized, un/rapeable Native woman, continued to present Indigenous peoples as both alacritous and alien to white possession.

As a tool of empire-building, several Self-Determination Era policies and rulings also increased Indigenous women's vulnerability to rape by further divesting Indigenous sovereignty. In 1968 although the Indian Civil Rights Act (ICRA) required Indigenous governments to enforce US legal norms, provisions for Indigenous nations to retrocede from PL 280 with the permission of a given state were also established. Later laws founded concurrent jurisdiction (tribal nation and state). Many Indigenous nations developed justice systems, some retaining BIA-appointed judges, others entirely independent, but other laws continued to limit sentencing, punishments, and the stability of tribal governance systems. Impoverishment also obstructed Indigenous governments' ability to respond to rape: police departments were understaffed, correctional facilities were overcrowded, and funds for anti-rape programs

---

90. Deer, *Beginning and End of Rape*, 73.

91. Mari Ness, "Using Tinker Bell to Shake Magic into Everything: Disney's Peter Pan," tor.com, June 25, 2015, https://www.tor.com/2015/06/25/using-tinker-bell-to-shake-magic-into-everything-disney-peter-pan/.

92. Aliess, *Making the White Man's Indian*, 150.

and strategies were minimal or nonexistent.[93] Then in *Oliphant v. Suquamish* (1978), the Supreme Court divested Native courts of jurisdiction over non-Natives, ensuring that tribal nations could not punish non-Native assailants. As stereotypes about Indigenous women's inviolability continued to be prevalent, Indigenous nations were once again forced to rely on a government designed to dispossess them for justice. Moreover, geographical distance and language and cultural barriers further circumscribed the federal government's capacity to prosecute rapists who target Indigenous women.[94]

In the late twentieth century, Indigenous women's un/rapeability as a lynchpin of US empire reached measurable epidemic proportions. On the bedrock of centuries of colonialism, the combination of federal policy impeding Indigenous justice systems, sterilization abuse at the hands of Indian Health Services (IHS) via the War on Poverty and Nixon-era family planning policies, Reaganite austerity policies that aggressively decimated already underfunded reservation healthcare, education, employment, housing, and law enforcement programs and resources, and a racialized and sometimes explicitly racist feminist anti-rape movement and rape legislation allowed a neoliberal rape culture to thrive in Indian Country.[95]

Since a 1999 Bureau of Justice Statistics report, scores of studies have found that Indigenous women experience the highest rates of rape per capita in the US. A commonly quoted statistic is that "1 in 3 Native women will be raped in her lifetime," a number first published in a 2000 report on the National Violence Against Women Survey.[96] This is double the national average for other racial groups,[97] but the numbers are likely higher. While rape is underreported among all women, it is especially so among Indigenous women because Indigenous nations have been denied the ability and resources to administer justice and Indigenous women may wish to handle trauma in individual or communal ways that are not understood or recognized by non-Natives.[98] So common is rape among Native women that many "talk to their daughters about what

---

93. Deer, *Beginning and End of Rape*, 39–43.

94. Deer, *Beginning and End of Rape*, 24; 42–43.

95. The National Congress of American Indians (NCAI) defines "Indian Country" as "wherever American Indian spirit, pride, and community are found. It resides not only in law books, legislation, and historical treatises but also on ancestral homelands, within our homes, and in the hearts of American Indian and Alaska Native people everywhere" (NCAI, "NCAI Response to the Usage of the Term 'Indian Country,'" National Congress of American Indians, December 29, 2019, 2021, https://www.ncai.org/news/articles/2019/12/27/ncai-response-to-usage-of-the-term-indian-country).

96. Deer, *Beginning and End of Rape*, 2–4.

97. Dunbar-Ortiz and Gilio-Whitaker, *"All the Real Indians Died Off,"* 140–41.

98. Deer, *Beginning and End of Rape*, 13.

130 · CHAPTER 3

to do when they are sexually assaulted, not if they are sexually assaulted, but *when*."[99] Importantly, while most rapes in the US are intraracial, Indigenous women report that most assailants are non-Native: the original 1999 Bureau of Justice Statistics report found that nine in ten Indigenous victims of rape or sexual assault had white or Black assailants. Another report found that over 70 percent of assailants were white.[100] This points to a direct pipeline of interracial rape against Indigenous women from policies such as MCA, PL 280, and *Oliphant*, which were designed to protect US empire and its white subject.

Subsequent data too points to the rape of Indigenous women as an enduring tool of colonialism embedded in policy and discourse devised to dispossess. A 2007 Amnesty International report, *Maze of Injustice: The Failure to Protect Indian Women from Sexual Violence in the USA*, delineated the numerous structural challenges Indigenous women who are the victims of violent crime must contend with when seeking justice.[101] A 2010 Department of Justice survey (published in a 2016 National Institute of Justice Research report) of 2,473 "American Indian and Alaska Native" women found that more than half (56.1 percent) experienced sexual violence in their lifetime; more than one in three women (35 percent) experienced sexual violence with penetration, and almost all Indigenous women (96 percent) experienced sexual violence from an interracial perpetrator. Female victims are three times more likely to have experienced sexual violence from an interracial perpetrator as non-Hispanic white-only female victims (96 percent versus 32 percent).[102] More than four in five Indigenous women (84.3 percent) experienced violence (including sexual violence, physical violence from an intimate partner, stalking, and psychological aggression from an intimate partner) in their lifetime; 66.5 percent of Native women were concerned for their safety. Indigenous women are also 1.2 times more likely to have experienced violence than non-Hispanic white women in their lifetime and are 1.7 times as likely to have experienced violence in the past year. Again, the number of Native women affected by violence is likely much higher, and the infrastructure for women to report and address incidents continues to be underfunded and difficult for Native women to navigate.[103] Moreover, the report, one of the first national reports to include significant research on perpetrators' race, revealed that

---

99. Native American Women's Health Education Research Center, *Indigenous Women's Dialogue: Roundtable Report on the Accessibility of Plan B as an Over the Counter (OTC) within Indian Health Service*, February 2012, quoted in Deer, *Beginning and End of Rape*, 5.

100. Deer, *Beginning and End of Rape*, 6.

101. Amnesty International, *Maze of Injustice*, 27–39.

102. Rosay, "Violence against American Indian," 18–19.

103. Rosay, "Violence against American Indian," 2–3.

US CULTURE IS ALWAYS-ALREADY RAPE CULTURE • 131

most perpetrators were white. Andre Rosay, director of the Justice Center for the University of Alaska and author of the study, said that the most glaring finding was that almost every single victim—man or woman—experienced interracial violence.[104]

The Justice Department report concluded in 2016, the year of publication:

> Past-year estimates for American Indian and Alaska Native people showed that more than 1 in 7 women (14.4 percent) and more than 1 in 11 men (9.9 percent) have experienced sexual violence in the past year. More than 1 in 22 women (4.6 percent) and more than 1 in 44 men (2.3 percent) have experienced sexual violence with penetration. More than 120,000 American Indian and Alaska Native women and men have experienced sexual violence with penetration at least once in the past year. This implies that the annual number of victimizations is at least 120,000.[105]

Into the present, studies confirm the disproportionately high levels of rape and violence against Indigenous women as an enduring part of settler colonialism. Nearly one in three Indigenous women have been raped, more than double the average for white women. As in previous studies, this is likely an undercount.[106] Some studies estimate that Native Americans are 2.5 times more likely to experience sexual assault and rape than any other racial or ethnic group in the US. Rape is often perpetrated on reservations, often with impunity.[107] IHS, which has often hired doctors convicted of sexual assault, is also a frequent perpetrator of rape and impunity for perpetrators.[108] Indigenous men and boys have also become both the perpetrators of rape, and are the victims of rape at rates much higher than men of other races.[109] In May 2022, Amnesty International released another report, *The Never-Ending Maze: Continued Failure to Protect Indigenous Women from Sexual Violence in the USA*, noting that since their first report on the issue in 2007, "rates of violence against Indigenous women have not significantly changed, and the US government continues to fail to adequately prevent and respond to

104. Rosay, "Violence against American Indian."

105. Rosay, "Violence against American Indian," 19.

106. Hallie Golden, "US Indigenous Women Face High Rates of Sexual Violence—with Little Recourse," *The Guardian*, May 17, 2022, https://www.theguardian.com/world/2022/may/17/sexual-violence-against-native-indigenous-women.

107. Lyndsey Gilpin, "Native American Women Still Have the Highest Rates of Rape and Assault," *High Country News*, June 7, 2016, accessed August 1, 2023, https://www.hcn.org/articles/tribal-affairs-why-native-american-women-still-have-the-highest-rates-of-rape-and-assault.

108. Deer, *Beginning and End of Rape*, 53.

109. Deer, *Beginning and End of Rape*, 8.

132 • CHAPTER 3

such violence." Recognizing that US policy designed to dispossess Indigenous peoples has produced epidemic levels of rape among Indigenous women, the report calls for the US to restore tribal jurisdiction on Indigenous lands.[110] The human cost of white possessive US policy is starkly evident in its multigenerational, neoliberal afterlife and renewal in epidemic levels of rape, abuse, and other forms of violence against Indigenous women and within Indigenous communities.

Mediated pedagogies of empire also continue to normalize or trivialize rape and sexual violence against Indigenous women by rendering them un/rapeable through different threads of hypersexualization. Embodying popular countercultural and antiestablishment sentiments and the rise of official multiculturalism, what Marubbio calls a hybrid Celluloid Maiden surfaced in the 1970s revisionist Westerns. Like previous princess figures, this sexually uninhibited Indigenous woman is an exoticized representative of "Native America" who is tied

> to old stereotypes about "primitive cultures" being closer to nature and less restrictive than "civilized" cultures. Unlike her early predecessors, and more in keeping with the dangerous power of the sexualized Maiden, the hybrid character captivates the hero and reinforces his rejection of white civilization and the "progressive" march of civilization.[111]

And yet, like earlier figures, her death is inevitable and "aborts the possibility of the hero's permanently 'going native.'"[112] The hybrid Celluloid Maiden is featured in films such as *A Man Called Horse* (1970), *Little Big Man* (1970), *Jeremiah Johnson* (1972), and *The Man Who Loved Cat Dancing* (1973). While these revisionist Westerns may have aimed to challenge negative stereotypes of Indigenous peoples and colonial narratives, Indigenous women continued to be hypersexualized in the shadow of US policy that continued to render Indigenous women un/rapeable to serve white possession.

In the 1990s as multiculturalism became official and officially lucrative, the Celluloid Maiden was revived and remixed again to support US neoliberal empire. Another handful of revisionist Westerns such as *Thunderheart* (1992), *Silent Tongue* (1993), and *Legends of the Fall* (1994) represented Indigenous women as in possession of a gendered, sexualized primitivism, as "noble savages." Numerous Critical Indigenous Studies (CIS) scholars and film scholars have chronicled how Disney's wildly successful *Pocahontas* (1995) perpetuated

---

110. Amnesty International, *Never-Ending Maze,* 2022.
111. Marubbio, *Killing the Indian Maiden,* 167–68.
112. Slotkin, *Gunfighter Nation,* 631.

stereotypes of Native women and peoples within a plot that erased genocide and the rape endemic to colonial conquest, and indeed part of Pocahontas's actual life. Co-director Eric Goldberg and Disney executives proclaimed Disney's commitment to multiculturalism and political correctness,[113] Indigenous people worked on the film and were hired as consultants,[114] and the film does not gleefully embrace the offensive gendered, sexualized stereotypes that *Peter Pan* did. It does, however, recycle the silent-era Native maiden: the animated Pocahontas is an exotic, beautiful, and alluring ally to the white male hero, and though she does not die, at the end of the film she remains in what would become the US surrounded by animals and nature as her lover sails to England. Her Indigeneity is also physically white-washed and sexualized: she is "'an ethnic blend' of 'softened' features: her convexly curved face was African, her dark slanted eyes Asian, and her body proportions Caucasian."[115] She also has a disproportionately tiny waist atop curvaceous hips and legs and sings to John Smith about her closeness to nature in a short, tight dress. Like so many other films, the cartoon reframed colonial conquest as a multicultural love and adventure story, in this case for children,[116] through the body of a "noble" sexualized "savage" perfectly willing to sacrifice herself and her Indigenous community for the white subject of colonialism.

The hypersexualized Indigenous princess stereotype continues to be a lucrative pedagogy of empire beyond Hollywood and is firmly embedded in US culture. The "Poca-hottie" Halloween costume, usually a skimpy pan-Native dress or two-piece top and skirt made of buckskin (or fabric meant to resemble it) and decorated with feathers and other "traditional" imagery, is extremely popular despite years of criticism and objections from Indigenous people.[117] The "rez girl," a Native woman who is always sexually available, is also a common trope in the pornography industry. The video game *Custer's Revenge,* first released in 1982, does not bother with any pretense of consent: the goal of the game is for the white male Custer character to navigate Native arrows and enact his revenge against Indigenous peoples by raping an Indigenous woman. These images perpetuate a notion of the un/rapeability of Indigenous women; they are—if media from films, including Disney cartoons, to Halloween costumes to porn to video games to music videos are to be

---

113. Betsy Sharkey, "Beyond Teepees and Totem Poles," *New York Times,* June 11, 1995.

114. Kilpatrick, *Celluloid Indians,* 153.

115. Animator Glen Keane described his creation of *Pocahontas* in *Allure* magazine, June 1995, cited in Aleiss, *Making the White Man's Indian,* 150.

116. Berglund, "Pocahontas," 50.

117. For example, see Adrienne Keene, "Open Letter to the Pocahotties: The Annotated Version," *Native Appropriations* (blog), October 9, 2013, https://nativeappropriations.com/2013/10/open-letter-to-the-pocahotties-the-annotated-version.html.

believed—readily available to and for white possession and profit. In the neoliberal context, Indigenous dispossession therefore persists in public pedagogy that casts Native women's bodies as the sites of conquest. As the data plainly illustrates, policy designed to protect white possession and white perpetrators continues to render Indigenous women more vulnerable to rape, while media continues to render Native women illegible as rape victims, together emblematizing how and why US culture is an always-already racialized rape culture.

Late twentieth-century neoliberal pedagogies of empire also sustained racialized im/migrant women's rapeability to further white possession. As noted in the last chapter, Reaganite neoliberal personal responsibility politics, anchored in gendered, racialized criminalization of poverty and dependency, began with the decimation of federal programs for Native Americans and calcified in the gutting of "entitlements" for immigrants and citizens of color, treated like aliens in policy and US culture writ large. Similar thinking about a "Latina Threat," which cast Latinas as hyperfertile baby machines clamoring to cross the border to exploit social services by having "anchor babies,"[118] underscored the use of rape as a tool of neoliberal border control and labor expropriation. For instance, welfare cuts and increased border militarization and criminalization under the Immigration Reform and Control Act (IRCA; 1986) were warranted by the "Latina Threat." In the October 1986 Senate session in which IRCA was passed, lawmakers on both sides of the aisle claimed Mexican im/migrant mothers strained US resources, echoing the concerns of overtly eugenicist anti-immigrant organizations such as the Federation for American Immigration Reform (FAIR) and Zero Population Growth (ZPG). Paul Simon (D-Illinois), an organized labor advocate, warned his fellow senators that "if, by the end of this century, Mexico reaches a status where one female produces one female—I am not trying to be sexist, but that is the way demographers talk about zero population growth—Mexico will taper off with a population of 175 million people."[119] Containing Mexican women and their ostensibly hyperfertile, hypersexual, out-of-control bodies was, explicitly, at the center of this inaugural neoliberal immigration policy.

The real danger is for im/migrant women, who are at an increased risk for rape in every phase of the migration process, which is inseparable from the US (imperial) economy. Increasingly feminized migrations, including internal, regional, and international, "have become a survival strategy and a way to resolve the structural inequalities and labor disruptions created by

---

118. Chavez, *Latino Threat*.

119. The Immigration Reform and Control Act of 1986: Hearings before the Subcommittee on Immigration and Refugee Policy, 99th Cong. (1986) (statement of Paul Simon, senator).

neoliberalism."[120] For many women in the Global South, neoliberal structural adjustment policies that impoverish already struggling communities necessitate migration to work in the global assembly line in maquiladoras, or in other low-wage jobs in the US and other receiving nations.[121] A women's economic status heightens her vulnerability to rape before, during, and after crossing the border. Women and girls, especially those without legal status and traveling in remote areas or trains, are at high risk for sexual assault from gangs, people traffickers (coyotes), other migrants, and immigration officials. Rape is often not reported, nor is medical attention sought afterward because im/migrant women fear those processes will prevent them from reaching the US, result in their deportation, or lead to further abuse in the US.[122] Impoverished, undocumented women are also vulnerable to being forced into sex work to pay a coyote's smuggling fees and to being exposed to sex trafficking once in the US.[123]

Furthermore, the increasing scope of neoliberal border militarization, underpinned by the "Latina Threat," ensured that, as it has been historically, rape would be structurally embedded in border policing. IRCA border militarization included increased funding, personnel increases (from 2,500 to 4,800), the erection of steel fence, more technology to detect and detain undocumented migrants, and large-scale enforcement efforts in the early 1990s such as Operation Blockade / Hold the Line (1993) in El Paso, Texas, and Operation Gate Keeper (1994) in San Diego, California. The Illegal Immigration Reform and Responsibility Act (1996) increased deportable offenses, adding "expedited removal" for the undocumented, and authorized doubling the number of agents from 1997 to 2001.[124] Post-9/11 legislation increased budgets and agents again, making the Immigration and Nationality Service (INS) the largest federal law agency. With the creation of Immigration and Customs Enforcement (ICE) under the Department of Homeland Security (DHS) in 2002—which combined the criminal investigative and intelligence resources of the US Customs Service with the criminal investigative, detention, and deportation resources of INS and the Federal Protective

---

120. Toro-Morn, Guevarra, and Flores-González, "Introduction: Immigrant Women and Labor Disruptions," 3.

121. Toro-Morn, Guevarra, and Flores-González, "Introduction: Immigrant Women and Labor Disruptions," 3–4. For in-depth analyses of the gender, race, and class politics of the murders of migrant women *maquiladora* workers in Ciudad Juarez, Mexico, see Fregoso, *MeXicana Encounters*; and Camacho, *Migrant Imaginaries*.

122. Amnesty International, *Invisible Victims,* 15–16.

123. González-López, *Erotic Journeys,* 203–4.

124. Luibhéid, *Entry Denied,* 119–20.

136 · CHAPTER 3

Service—ever-increasing border militarization from Republican and Democrat administrations followed.

Under IRCA's prototype for neoliberal border militarization, rape culture has continued to thrive, inculcating im/migrant women into internal white possessive hierarchies at territorial borders. All nongovernmental organizations (NGOs) that examine human rights abuses at the US border, such as Amnesty International and Human Rights Watch, report the frequency of the rape and sexual abuse of migrants. Border Patrol agents accused of raping and sexually assaulting women and queer and gender-nonconforming migrants are not held accountable, procedures for receipt and review of complaints are inadequate, and a "code of silence" among law enforcement officers[125] persists. Sexual abuse is also ubiquitous in detention facilities. The ACLU National Prison Project found over two hundred reported cases of sexual abuse in immigration detention facilities between 2007 and 2011.[126] Transgender women are especially at risk.[127] Moreover, overt, unapologetic human rights violations and abuses at the border were endemic to Trump administration immigration policy. According to a 2018 report, rape was especially rampant, systemic, and institutionalized at immigration detention facilities, particularly against LGBTQ+ and trans women.[128] Rape of im/migrant women by Border Patrol agents, immigration officials, and law enforcement personnel at the border and in detention facilities is vastly underreported given women's fears of deportation and further violence.

Additionally, Trump, who as a flagrant white supremacist and accused rapist multiple times over embodies US rape culture, manipulated an oft-cited, misreported statistic from a 2010 Amnesty International report that 60 percent of women are sexually assaulted attempting to cross the border. He claimed that the wall he hoped to build at the Mexican border would protect migrant women from rape by deterring migration.[129] Trump's manipulation of the estimated data from the now dated 2010 report, some of which is based on a 1999 report, obscures that historically and into the neoliberal context, as

125. Luibhéid, *Entry Denied,* 121–22.

126. ACLU, "Sexual Abuse in Immigration Detention Centers," cited in Rodríguez, *Sexual Futures,* 155.

127. Luibhéid, "'Treated neither with Respect nor with Dignity,'" 30; and US Government Accountability Office, "Immigrant Detention: Additional Actions Could Strengthen DHS Efforts to Address Sexual Abuse," published November 2013, publicly released December 6, 2013, https://www.gao.gov/products/gao-14-38#:~:text=GAO%20recommends%20that%20 DHS%20(1,performing%20oversight%20of%20SAAPI%20provisions.

128. Luibhéid, "'Treated neither with Respect nor with Dignity,'" 30.

129. Glenn Kessler, "No, Amnesty International Does Not Say 60 Percent of Migrant Women in Mexico Have Been Raped," Fact Checker, *Washington Post,* February 1, 2019, https://www.washingtonpost.com/politics/2019/02/01/no-amnesty-international-does-not-say-percent-migrant-women-mexico-have-been-raped/.

well as under his administration, US immigration policy, border policing, and political economy, which relies on and profits from migrant labor, precludes migrant women's sexual and bodily safety because that preclusion serves white heteropatriarchal property interests. Moreover, the Trump administration's overt white supremacist immigration policies, building on the history of US coloniality and racialized anti-immigration, included the detainment and separation of children and families and the incarceration of babies and children in cages. While the Biden administration has undone some draconian Trump-era policies, the architecture of US neoliberal immigration policy and border policing remains; rape culture continues to be rampant and largely unchecked. Thus, neoliberal immigration policy and policing places the gendered, racialized "illegal alien," like the still "savage" Indigenous woman, outside the boundaries of "civilized"—that is, "law-abiding"—society because of her hypersexuality and poor choices / failure to take personal responsibility. Punishment is justified; rape and labor exploitation are illegible.

Moreover, the scope of un/rapeability as a neoliberal economy of dispossession persists into the work and home lives of many undocumented women. Undocumented women are often employed in the secondary sector and face highly exploitative working conditions that heighten their vulnerability to rape and other forms of violence. A Coalition for Immigrant and Refugee Rights Services (CIRRS) survey found undocumented women experienced numerous forms of exploitation such as not being paid, being paid lower wages than documented workers, and sexual harassment. A 1991 US Labor Department investigation of the garment industry revealed similar abuses. Most workers were Latinas applying for legalization.[130] Home healthcare, another unregulated industry in which immigrant women of color are concentrated, is also rife with exploitation and violence: immigrant workers report frequent sexual harassment and other abuses from their clients, including threats of deportation and being treated as slaves.[131] Abuse is also prevalent in the intimate domains: multiple studies undertaken in the late 1990s and early 2000s found 30 to 50 percent of the Latina, South Asian, and Korean immigrant women surveyed were sexually or physically assaulted by a male intimate partner.[132] Again, statistics for the rape of im/migrant women within the US are underreported given women's fears of deportation or losing their legal status, especially if the perpetrator has power over them as an immigration or law enforcement official or employer. As with Indigenous women, language and cultural differences provide another barrier to im/migrant women who have been raped and are seeking justice through the US legal system. The

---

130. Surveys cited in Chang, *Disposable Domestics,* 67.

131. Chang, *Disposable Domestics,* 133.

132. Raj and Silverman, "Violence against Immigrant Women," 367.

trafficking of women from the Global South for labor and sex work is another aspect of neoliberal US empire expansion in need of further exploration.

From the 1980s to the present, neoliberal pedagogies of empire in media also rendered Latinas un/rapeable. Juana María Rodríguez describes the "racialized erotics of Latina submission," exemplified on Borderbangers.com, a pornographic subscription site. Website text states that these women are "willing to do anything" to get into the US. When not serving/servicing agents at the border, the Latina characters labor in service and domestic professions. They are portrayed as eager, willing, and grateful to submit sexually—and to their place in the economic underclass—to enter and remain in the US. The site is structured around the eroticization of Latina sexual (and labor) submission as a condition for entry.[133] This idea of women's alacrity to sexually serve their employers or "superiors" is part of a throughline from foundational white possessive pedagogies of empire that cast Indigenous women as perpetually available to white men and enslaved Black women as "naturally" eager to sexually serve their white enslavers. In Revolutionary War–era court rulings and popular culture, for example, the labor a servant provided was conflated with the sexual services such wifely (i.e., domestic) labor implied.[134] Add race and immigration status into the mix, and rape remains illegible to serve white heteropatriarchal property interests, much as it was in the colonial and early nineteenth-century US. In 2014 the pornography giant MindGeek, discarding any pretense of consent, not unlike *Custer's Revenge*, created the web series *Border Patrol Sex*, which glorifies the rape of undocumented Mexican and Central American women: undocumented Latinas are caught trying to cross, arrested, raped, and deported. The market appeal of hypersexualized, un/rapeable Latinx women "lies squarely within the racially eroticized display of power that the US–Mexico border represents"[135] within its proprietary anchor in settler coloniality.

Thus, as neoliberalism made national borders more permeable for labor and goods, the ongoing entanglement of the un/rapeability of Indigenous and racialized im/migrant women in policy enforced and expanded the ideological and territorial borders of white possession. While porn and media are not the source of women's oppression nor is the staged representation of rape and violence equivalent to actual rape and violence, media worked in tandem with "the disciplinary power of the state acting upon the flesh of unwilling human bodies,"[136] generating neoliberal pedagogies of empire that render Indigenous and racialized immigrant women un/rapeable.

---

133. Rodríguez, *Sexual Futures*, 154–55.
134. Block, *Rape and Sexual Power*, 66.
135. Rodríguez, *Sexual Futures*, 157–58.
136. Rodríguez, *Sexual Futures*, 156.

AGAINST WHOSE WILL? COLONIALITY AND RACISM IN THE ANTI-RAPE MOVEMENT

The neoliberalization of pedagogies of empire that cast Indigenous women and women of color as un/rapeable occurred against the backdrop of an ostensible sea-change in US rape policy and discourse. As the anti-rape movement, a cornerstone of US "second wave" feminism, transformed understandings of rape and rape policy, coloniality and racism within the movement perpetuated Indigenous and racialized women's precarity.

In the late 1960s and early 1970s the notion of a "rape culture," a culture in which rape and sexual violence against women is pervasive and normalized, was popularized by two key texts, Susan Brownmiller's best-selling book *Against Our Will: Men, Women and Rape* (1975) and the documentary *Rape Culture* (1975), produced and directed by Margaret Lazarus. The notion of rape as a rare crime of violence usually perpetrated by a stranger continued to shape policy that often put the disproportionately female victims of rape rather than the disproportionately male perpetrators on trial. Mainstream media also continued to normalize the objectification of women and present women as needing to be coerced into sex. Both texts reframed rape as a mechanism of patriarchy, a political crime perpetrated by men against women normalized and sanctioned in all social and political institutions. While the filmmakers take credit for the term "rape culture,"[137] Brownmiller's book popularized the reframing of rape as a common occurrence that was in all instances a tool of patriarchal power, throughout history a manifestation of systemic gender violence legitimated and justified in the wider culture.[138]

Brownmiller's work and the mainstreamed concept of rape culture failed, however, to center how the white possessive logics of US empire necessarily render Indigenous women and women of color more vulnerable to rape, or to grapple seriously with how (often false) accusations of rape from white women have long been used to criminalize, incarcerate, and justify violence against Native men, Black men, and other men of color. Brownmiller essentialized women and men, framing rape "from prehistoric times to the present" as "nothing more or less than a conscious process of intimidation by which *all men* keep *all women* in a state of fear."[139] She acknowledged that during US westward expansion "the rape of a 's—' by white men was not deemed

---

137. Williams, "Rape Culture"; and "Rape Culture," *Cambridge Documentary Films,* last updated February 15, 2021, https://www.cambridgedocumentaryfilms.org/filmsPages/rapeculture.html.

138. For another early and often cited genealogy of the concept see Herman, "Rape Culture," 45–52.

139. Brownmiller, *Against Our Will,* 15.

140 • CHAPTER 3

important" and was surely pervasive though Native women were silenced because their testimonies were not recorded. She also noted the rarity of rape in many precolonial Indigenous societies, referencing early captivity narratives. Yet Brownmiller questions the veracity of those narratives, speculating that former captives did not want to be marked with signs of moral degradation, that is, voluntary or forced sexual relations with Indigenous men. She spends the bulk of the thirteen pages devoted to "Indians" chronicling later captivity narratives and government reports in which white women claimed to have been raped by Indigenous men and instances of white settlers claiming that genocidal campaigns such as the Sand Creek Massacre, in which US cavalry slaughtered and sexually mutilated the bodies of Cheyenne men, women, and children, were retaliation for Indigenous men raping white women.[140] She describes rape in the context of settler colonial expansion without centering rape as a tool of colonialism and theorizes rape as something that men—both white and Indigenous—perpetrated against women in the context of the frontier and military conflicts between Indigenous peoples and settlers as in other contexts. Brownmiller therefore rewrites the rape of Indigenous women and women of color endemic to US empire-building as examples of (all) men's violence against (all) women.

Additionally, Angela Davis observed that racist ideas pervaded Brownmiller's work. Davis argued that sexism, racism, and capitalism create and sustain rape culture in the US, as in the rendering of enslaved Black women un/rapeable as the property of white enslavers and the use of white women's fraudulent rape charges to justify the murder of Black men. Responding to Brownmiller's claim that Black men are disproportionately likely to become rapists, a legacy of casting Indigenous and Black sexuality as "savage" and "primitive" to justify Indigenous genocide, enslavement, and extreme anti-Black violence, Davis contends "recognizing the part played by racism in abetting sexual violence, the anti-rape movement must not only defend women of color, it must also defend growing numbers of victims of false rape charges."[141] Incidentally in 2019 Brownmiller reiterated her essentialist view of women and men and was explicitly dismissive of Davis's criticisms of racism in her work.[142]

Unfortunately, Brownmiller was not an outlier in the mainstream feminist anti-rape movement but rather emblematic of it: as noted in chapter 2, Indigenous feminists and activists pointed out in the 1970s in connection with sterilization abuse that mainstream feminist theories about gender violence overlooked colonialism and gendered violence as a problem of colonial power,

---

140. Brownmiller, *Against Our Will*, 140–53.
141. Davis, "Rape, Racism, and the Capitalist Setting," 129–32.
142. Frank and Gutterman, "Against Our Will," *Sexing History* podcast.

a pernicious, persistent elision of which rape is an inherent part. Moreover, for Native women activists, bodily sovereignty and Indigenous sovereignty are inseparable.[143] The mainstream anti-rape movement also perpetuated the myth of the Black rapist[144] and erased women of color's identification of rape and sexual violence as integral to white supremacy, as well as their pathbreaking organizing to combat it. Elsewhere I have discussed how white feminists' erasure of women of color and their vital work in the anti-rape movement has persisted in more recent anti-rape activism, as within the Riot Grrrl movement and SlutWalk.[145] And in 2017 white actors such as Alyssa Milano and Rose McGowan were credited with starting the #MeToo movement, which was founded by Black civil rights activist Tarana Burke to expose the frequency of rape and sexual violence impacting Black women. The "second wave" feminist anti-rape movement and the legacy of its concepts have also been criticized for a lack of attention to same-sex sexual violence and sexual violence against men, for obviating women's sexuality / sexual pleasure as part of heterosexual as well as queer sex and/or within the context of consensual BDSM (bondage, discipline, sadism, masochism) sexual relations, and for its focus on media and especially pornography as the source of women's oppression.

At the same time, the 1970s anti-rape movement transformed the mainstream conversation about rape and resulted in policy changes that challenged rape culture in unprecedented ways. Before the publication of Brownmiller's book and release of the *Rape Culture* documentary, feminist lawyers, influenced by and/or a part of activist groups such as the New York Radical Feminists, worked to reform the legal system to support survivors and effectively prosecute perpetrators. Beginning in the 1970s some states passed "rape shield" laws, which limit attorneys' ability to introduce evidence about rape victims' past sexual behavior and to cross-examine them in rape cases. Some rape shield laws also prohibit media from publishing the names of alleged rape victims. In 1986 Congress passed the Sexual Abuse Act, which amended federal law to address a series of "graded" sexual offenses such as "aggravated sexual abuse," "sexual abuse," "sexual abuse of a minor or ward," and "abusive sexual conduct."[146] According to an official memorandum to President Reagan from James C. Miller III, then budget director, the law would rectify a vague legal definition of "rape" to cover other forms of sexual offenses under federal rather than state jurisdiction, to include offenses within a "Federal Enclave

---

143. O'Sullivan, "Informing Red Power," 965–82.

144. Davis, "Rape, Racism, and the Capitalist Setting," 132.

145. Perry, "'I Can Sell My Body If I Wanna.'"

146. "Summary: H.R.4745—Sexual Abuse Act of 1986, 99th Congress (1985–1986)," Congress. gov, https://www.congress.gov/bill/99th-congress/house-bill/4745.

142 · CHAPTER 3

(e.g., within the special maritime or territorial jurisdiction of the United States or in Indian country)," and to clarify the meaning of "statutory rape." The new law would, in this order, create a series of offenses graded according to their seriousness; "substitute more modern terminology (e.g., 'sexual abuse') for common law terms (e.g., 'rape' or 'carnal knowledge'); define sexual offenses in gender-neutral terms; define the offenses so that the focus in a trial is on the conduct of the defendant, rather than the conduct or state of a mind of a victim." The granting of federal jurisdiction to prisons and sentencing lengths was also covered in the document. Significantly, Miller's report emphasizes that despite the new law, "federal sexual offenses are not a problem of major proportions."[147] One cannot help but wonder if women and especially Indigenous women and women of color would have agreed. Concepts such as "date rape," "marital rape," and sexual harassment also became part of the national lexicon and were eventually legislated, though unevenly and with varied results that often continued to sustain a racialized rape culture.

The Violence Against Women Act (VAWA; first enacted in 1994 and reauthorized most recently in 2022) was the first federal law designed to protect women against sexual and other forms of physical violence. The inaugural version had vast bipartisan support in Congress. Whom the law protected and how was, not surprisingly given US history, racialized, as the above data about the ongoing un/rapeability of Indigenous and racialized immigrant women illustrates. VAWA granted $1.6 billion for the investigation and prosecution of violent crimes against women, imposed automatic and mandatory restitution on convicted offenders, allowed for civil suits in unprosecuted cases, and created a federal rape shield. The law also created the Office on Violence Against Women within the Department of Justice. From the start, women of color activists and scholars were critical of VAWA: VAWA was ultimately signed into law as part of President Bill Clinton's big crime bill, the Violent Crime Control and Law Enforcement Act (1994). With its "three strikes" provisions, this neoliberal legislation ramped up mass incarceration, targeting people of color and (re)connecting racialized criminalization to capitalization in the mushrooming of for-profit prisons and prisoner fees that followed.[148] And it bears repeating that the police are often the source of, not solution to, violence in communities of color.[149] Moreover, Native women were not protected under

---

147. James C. Miller, "Memorandum for the President: Enrolled Bill H.R. 4745—Sexual Abuse Act of 1986," *Executive Office of the President, Office of Management and Budget,* November 6, 1986, Ronald Reagan Presidential Library Digital Collections, https://www.reaganlibrary.gov/sites/default/files/digitallibrary/smof/publicliaison/anderson/oa17954/40-011-12004881-OA17954-001-2018.pdf.

148. See Alexander, *New Jim Crow.*

149. See Cacho, *Social Death.*

the original VAWA because of extant Native American policy restricting tribal nations' jurisdiction.

Some protections for Indigenous women and other marginalized groups have been incorporated into VAWA reauthorizations. The 2013 reauthorization included, as the result of Indigenous women's activism, a partial *Oliphant* fix that restored Indigenous nations' jurisdiction to prosecute non-Natives for domestic violence. However, Indigenous nations' jurisdiction to prosecute major crimes like sexual assault, child abuse, and rape outside of domestic relationships continued to be circumscribed under *Oliphant,* as Indigenous justice systems continued to lack resources and support from local law enforcement.[150] The Biden administration's 2022 reauthorization includes new economic justice provisions and bolsters access for survivors of all genders by strengthening nondiscrimination laws and creating an LGBTQ services program. The law also restores tribal jurisdiction, allowing tribes to hold non-Native perpetrators accountable, improves existing housing protections and increases access to emergency and short-term housing, and creates dedicated investments in culturally specific service providers to ensure survivors of color are supported.[151]

To reiterate again, as the perpetrator of violence against Indigenous peoples and people of color that advances and protects white heteropatriarchal property interests, the colonial legal system is obviously a problematic solution to it, and the data above clearly show that Indigenous women and racialized im/migrant women have since VAWA's passing and previous reauthorizations continued to be subject to rape and violence at epidemic levels. Nonetheless, Indigenous peoples must engage with the federal government, and avoiding such engagement could result in increasing attacks on Indigenous sovereignty and exacerbate Indigenous women's vulnerability to rape and violence. US citizens and im/migrants, and people of color racialized as aliens, of course, are also subject to US law. Therefore, VAWA moves toward increasing the safety and bodily autonomy of Indigenous and racialized women within the extant settler colonial US justice system. At the time of writing, it is too soon to evaluate the results of the new provisions.

In the US, political institutions have "historically supported men's access to women as sexual property."[152] In the neoliberal context, Indigenous women and immigrant women of color continue to be raped at epidemic rates and face enormous barriers to accessing effective justice when they are raped. This past and present, including the #MeToo movement and the fact that two

---

150. Gilpin, "Native American Women Still Have the Highest Rates of Rape and Assault."

151. "Violence Against Women Act," *National Network to End Domestic Violence,* accessed on August 1, 2023, https://nnedv.org/content/violence-against-women-act/.

152. Shaw and Lee, "Sexual Assault and Rape," 552.

men accused of rape and sexual harassment sit at the time of writing on the Supreme Court and another sat in the Oval Office from 2017 to 2021, indicate that the force of rape as a powerful tool not exclusively of heteropatriarchy but of the intersections of heteropatriarchy, settler colonialism, and white supremacy—the white possessive logics of US empire—is extant.

CONCLUSION

In the neoliberal context, as historically, "Native communities have no boundaries, psychic or physical, that the dominant society is bound to respect."[153] Nor do im/migrant and citizen communities of color. To support white possession, pedagogies of empire cast Indigenous and immigrant women as un/rapeable, structurally positioning them (and by extension the racialized groups they are a part of) as exterior and alien to the territorial, biopolitical, and ideological borders of the United States. While white men have been the predominant perpetrators, enforcers, and beneficiaries of white possession via racialized rape culture, white women, though also systemically vulnerable to rape, have sometimes exacerbated Indigenous and racialized women's vulnerability to rape and the use of rape to oppress, contain, and manage Indigenous men and men of color. The long durée of entangled public pedagogy that renders Indigenous women and im/migrant women of color un/rapeable starkly illuminates how, as a tool of US empire and the making and remaking of its white subject, US culture is always-already rape culture.

---

153. Smith, *Conquest,* 128.

CHAPTER 4

Food, Farming, Fat, and National(ist) Dyspepsia

Revolting Indigenous and Immigrant Foodways

The "First Thanksgiving" is popularly perceived as a 1621 feast solidifying a friendship between the Wampanoag and Pilgrims, who sailed to the "New World" on the *Mayflower* in 1620. This origin narrative of what would become the United States, canonized in a national holiday that revolves around feasting on "traditional" US American foods, works assiduously to erase the Indigenous genocide and dispossession necessary to US empire, much of which has been carried out and sustained through foodways: the cultural, social, and economic practices relating to the production and consumption of food. *A Charlie Brown Thanksgiving*, an Emmy-winning short, animated film based on the wildly popular *Peanuts* comic strip by Charles M. Schultz,[1] debuted on CBS on November 20, 1973. *Peanuts* has long offered multimodal public pedagogy to US consumers, some of which, like the Thanksgiving special and

---

1. Schultz's *Peanuts* syndicated daily comic centers on the adventures of a group of children and the main character Charlie Brown's dog, Snoopy. Adults are rarely seen or heard. The comic, which ran from 1950 to 2000, was published in over 2,600 newspapers in over seventy-five countries and translated into twenty-one languages. It has an estimated readership of 335 million, making it one of the most popular comics of all time. It has inspired numerous Emmy award-winning and -nominated animated television specials, television and web series and films, popular soundtracks and songs, a play, and all manner of merchandise. See Pamela J. Podger, "Saying Goodbye: Friends and Family Eulogize Charles Schultz," *SF Gate*, February 22, 2000, https://www.sfgate.com/bayarea/article/SAYING-GOODBYE-Friends-and-family-eulogize-2774210.php.

FIGURE 1. Promotional still from *A Charlie Brown Thanksgiving,* http://fivecentsplease.org/dpb/; https://en.wikipedia.org/w/index.php?curid=63201068.

This Is America, Charlie Brown television series (1988–89), are explicitly meant to teach children about US history. In accordance with the popular narrative of Thanksgiving celebrations, the now "classic" annual broadcast centers on a large, shared meal and giving thanks for friendship and family. Erudite white male character Linus says "grace" with a prayer referencing the first Thanksgiving feast to which the Pilgrims "invited the great Indian chief Massasoit," who joined the celebration with ninety "Indians" and an abundance of food. The Indigenous presence in the story—and animated film—ends there. Linus then centers "honored" guests at the "first Thanksgiving," such as William Bradford, signatory of the Mayflower Compact and governor of the Plymouth Colony. Linus concludes with a declaration of gratitude to the Christian God for the Pilgrims' homes, food, safety, and the opportunity to "create a new world with freedom and justice."[2] At the meal Snoopy, Charlie Brown's beagle, and his best friend Woodstock, a small yellow bird, are outfitted as male Pilgrims. Indigenous peoples are also not visibly represented. (See figure 1.)

As such, the cartoon is part of an enduring national erasure of the actual history of Thanksgiving that provides entrée into the myriad ways that historically and into the neoliberal context foodways public pedagogies have organized Indigenous peoples and racialized immigrants in entangled ways to accumulate and protect white heteropatriarchal property interests, or "white possession,"[3] creating and re-creating the colonial and racial violences and inequalities structuring US empire.

---

2. *Charlie Brown Thanksgiving.*
3. Moreton-Robinson, *White Possessive.*

FOOD, FARMING, FAT, AND NATIONAL(IST) DYSPEPSIA · 147

In fact, the exclusion of Indigenous peoples from *A Charlie Brown Thanksgiving* is especially problematic given the Indigenous resistance underway when it was first broadcast. In 1970, three years before the special debuted, the United American Indians of England (UAINE) declared the US Thanksgiving holiday a National Day of Mourning, "a reminder of the genocide of millions of Native people, the theft of Native lands, and the relentless assault on Native culture."[4] The multitudes of articles, essays, and social media created by both Native and non-Native people that continue to proliferate around Thanksgiving reiterate these sentiments of Indigenous mourning and revolt against ongoing settler colonialism and racism.[5]

A Charlie Brown Thanksgiving was also released just months after the US government violently responded to Indigenous activists' occupation of Wounded Knee on the Pine Ridge Reservation in South Dakota, which received considerable media attention. Over the course of the seventy-one-day occupation, organized by Oglala Lakota and American Indian Movement (AIM) members to protest a corrupt tribal president and the US government's failure to fulfill treaty obligations, a massive effort including the White House, the Department of Defense (DOD), and the Department of Justice (DOJ) was coordinated to subdue protestors. Officers, deployed from the US Marshals Service (USMS), the Federal Bureau of Investigation (FBI), and the Bureau of Indian Affairs (BIA), used tactics common during colonial warfare, such as prohibiting people carrying ammunition or food to enter the Pine Ridge Reservation. The occupation ended when protestors, faced with diminished food supplies, agreed to "dispossess" the area, and the US government agreed to reconsider treaty rights (without meaningful follow-up).[6] Indigenous struggles for self-determination, decolonization, and public awareness of and sympathy for Indigenous peoples, at a high mark at this moment, were matched with state violence, lies, erasure, and pedagogies of empire—including the cartoon kind—about US Americans' benevolence toward Indigenous peoples in connection with food.

Alyosha Goldstein observed, "In the Americas, settlement, cultivation, and prosperity for some people have entailed the displacement, brutalization, and hunger of others: the taking of lands and removal of Indigenous

---

4. "National Day of Mourning," United American Indians of New England, last updated 2022, http://www.uaine.org/.

5. For example, Tommy Orange, "Thanksgiving Is a Tradition. It's Also a Lie," Op-Ed, *Los Angeles Times*, November 23, 2017, https://www.latimes.com/opinion/op-ed/la-oe-orange-thanksgiving-history-20171123-story.html; and Allen Salway, "Thanksgiving: The National Day of Mourning," *Paper*, November 21, 2018, https://www.papermag.com/thanksgiving-native-american-history#rebelltitem2.

6. Abourezk, *Papers 1970–1983: Wounded Knee, 1973 Series*.

148 • CHAPTER 4

peoples, the abduction and enslavement of African peoples, and various forms of indenture, forced labor, and migration."[7] As I will show, US white possessive empire-building has been anchored in and advanced by destroying, patholo-gizing, and appropriating Indigenous and racialized immigrant foodways, as well as the bodies that produce and are produced by comestibles. While settler colonialism organizes Indigenous peoples and people of color differentially and unevenly through policy and media, the end of establishing, protecting, or increasing white possession is constant. At the same time, Indigenous and immigrant foodways are powerful sites of revolt, as in Indigenous and global peasant food sovereignty movements.

Unpacking the history of Thanksgiving further illuminates the gendered, racialized alimentary throughline of US empire. The 1621 meal shared between the Wampanoag (Pokanoket) and Pilgrims solidified their political alliance and a treaty and was a prelude to Indigenous genocide and the management of differentially racialized groups in connection with foodways to serve white possession. Patuxet was the Wampanoag name for the settlement the Pil-grims called "New Plymouth," which for centuries was a developed landscape with fields for corn and other crops such as beans and squash. Game hunt-ing was also practiced. While the Wampanoag had been a large, powerful nation, organized in sixty-nine villages in present-day Massachusetts, when the Pilgrims arrived, their population was decimated by smallpox and other diseases brought by earlier settlers, the area was abandoned, and they were in tension with the neighboring Narragansetts. While the Pilgrims stole food and other things from Indigenous peoples in the area, a political alliance with them was advantageous to the Wampanoag. In 1621 head sachem Massasoit and Tisquantum formed a treaty of peace and mutual protection with Pil-grims, and Tisquantum taught them Indigenous planting techniques.[8] Of the two extant primary sources about the "First Thanksgiving"—both penned by white male settlers—only a short description of the event, in Edward Win-slow's journal, *Mourt's Relation,* mentions Indigenous peoples' participation: upon hearing the settlers shooting guns as part of a harvest celebration, Mas-sasoit and ninety men arrived and joined the festivities; for three days they feasted together, sealing their alliance and treaty.[9] Neither primary text men-tions the word "thanksgiving."

---

7. Goldstein, "Ground Not Given," 83.

8. Dunbar-Ortiz and Gilio-Whitaker, *"All the Real Indians Died Off,"* 33–36.

9. "Primary Sources for 'The First Thanksgiving' at Plymouth," Pilgrim Hall Museum, accessed August 3, 2023, https://pilgrimhall.org/pdf/TG_What_Happened_in_1621.pdf.

FOOD, FARMING, FAT, AND NATIONAL(IST) DYSPEPSIA · 149

Two instances of brutal colonial violence offer a more comprehensive picture of early British settlers' relations with Indigenous peoples in relation to "thanksgiving" as a concept and as a national holiday revolving around a feast based on (small "n") native US American foodways. Some sources trace the first mention of a "thanksgiving" by Euro-American settlers in relation to Indigenous peoples to the Pequot War (1636–37) in what is now Connecticut. British settlers, with Mohegan and Narraganset mercenaries, attacked, murdered, and ostentatiously mutilated the Pequot in response to their resistance to colonial encroachment. In an attack during a harvest celebration that led to colonial victory, at least 400 Pequot, including an estimated 175 women and children, were killed, half of whom were burned to death. Many more Pequot were killed attempting to flee on boats. In the following months settlers pursued the remaining Pequot, killing leaders, fighting men, and enslaving women and children.[10] In *Of Plymouth Plantation*, Bradford—"honored" guest at the *Peanuts*' version of the first Thanksgiving—described the brutality of the attack on the Pequot and his gratitude for its success:

> Those that scaped the fire were slain with the sword, some hewed to pieces, others run through with rapiers, so as they were quickly dispatched and very few escaped. It was conceived they destroyed about 400 at this time. It was a fearful site [sic] to see them thus frying in the fire and the streams of blood quenching the same, and horrible was the stink and scent thereof; but the victory seemed a sweet sacrifice, and they gave the praise thereof to God.[11]

New England and other northeastern colonists periodically celebrated "thanksgivings," days of prayer and gratitude for a military victory, abundant harvest, safe travel, or another "blessing."[12] Many Native (and some non-Native) writers identify this Pequot massacre as the origin of the first "Thanksgiving,"[13] attributing the declaration of a "day of celebration and thanks giving for subduing the Pequots" to either Bradford or John Winthrop,

---

10. Kevin McBride, "Pequot War," *Encyclopedia Britannica*, September 5, 2022. https://www.britannica.com/topic/Pequot-War.

11. Bradford, *Of Plymouth Plantation, 1620–1647,* 296.

12. Brian Handwerk, "Thanksgiving 2012 Myths and Facts," *National Geographic*, November 21, 2012, https://www.nationalgeographic.com/news/2012/11/121120-thanksgiving-2012-dinner-recipes-pilgrims-day-parade-history-facts/#close.

13. Christopher Moraff, "Should We Rename Thanksgiving 'National Ethnic Cleansing Day'?," City Life, *Philadelphia*, November 20, 2012, https://www.phillymag.com/news/2012/11/20/dark-origins-thanksgiving/.

150 • CHAPTER 4

Governor of Massachusetts Bay Colony.[14] In his award-winning novel *There There* (2019) Tommy Orange (Cheyenne and Arapaho Tribes of Oklahoma) writes of the Pequot massacre that "the next day the Massachusetts Bay Colony had a feast in celebration, and the governor declared it a day of Thanksgiving. Thanksgivings like these happened everywhere, whenever there were what we have to call 'successful massacres.'"[15]

From this history of colonial brutality, the modern conception of the US national holiday of Thanksgiving accrued in stages. The US Continental Congress first proclaimed a national thanksgiving—a day of prayer—after enacting the Constitution in 1789. Because some viewed the days of thankful prayer unfavorably as a New England custom, or opposed national imposition of religious observance and the possibility of partisan public celebrations, observance was left to states' discretion. In 1821 Boston publisher Alexander Young printed Winslow's description of the 1621 shared feast, christening it the "First Thanksgiving."[16] But not until 1863 did President Abraham Lincoln, in the hopes of promoting national unity in the midst of the Civil War, and at the behest of Sarah Josepha Hale, editor of the popular *Godey's Lady Book* magazine, declare "Thanksgiving" a national holiday. Every subsequent president declared the national holiday, and in 1942 Franklin Delano Roosevelt designated the fourth Thursday in November for it.[17] Traditions have evolved from there, with religious and secular gratitude, feasting on foods and dishes considered "native" to the US, and a distorted story about the "friendship" of Indigenous peoples and settlers as the kernel of US democracy as consistent threads. While the veracity of the brutal massacre of Pequot people as *the* "Thanksgiving" may be debatable, as a matter of record, early thanksgivings celebrated military victories, many of which were against Indigenous peoples, and Bradford thanked God for the successful massacre of the Pequot dur-

---

14. Vincent Schilling, "6 Thanksgiving Myths and the Wampanoag Side of the Story," *Indian Country Today,* September 13, 2018, https://ictnews.org/archive/6-thanksgiving-myths-share-them-with-someone-you-know. Some Indigenous writers and organizations such as AIM cite the research of William B. Newell, a member of the Penobscot Tribe and former chairman of the Anthropology Department at University of Connecticut, to support this assertion, though this is a matter of internet debate. For example, see "Origins of Thanksgiving," American Indian Movement Grand Governing Council, AIM Movement, November 23, 2005, https://www.aimovement.org/moipr/thanksgiv.html; Laura Elliff, "Holy Day," *Republic of Lakotah,* (blog), August 26, 2010, https://lakotas-rep.livejournal.com/1359.html; and Allen Salway, "Thanksgiving: The National Day of Mourning," *Paper,* November 21, 2018, https://www.papermag.com/thanksgiving-native-american-history#rebelltitem2.

15. Orange, *There There.*

16. Brian Handwerk, "Thanksgiving 2012 Myths and Facts," *National Geographic,* November 21, 2012, https://www.nationalgeographic.com/news/2012/11/121120-thanksgiving-2012-dinner-recipes-pilgrims-day-parade-history-facts/#close.

17. David J. Silverman, "Thanksgiving Day," *Encyclopedia Britannica,* July 3, 2023. https://www.britannica.com/topic/Thanksgiving-Day.

ing their foodways celebration. The facts and debates surrounding the "first Thanksgiving" reveal that the United States would not be the United States without Indigenous genocide and dispossession; it is no wonder UAINE declared Thanksgiving a National Day of Mourning. As I will show, the linking of settler colonialism, racial capitalism, and foodways has long been explicit; the public pedagogy of US empire both feeds and is fed by foodways.

•

Historically the US government used starvation to subdue Indigenous peoples and erased their complex, varied geopolitical sustenance systems to rationalize dispossession and the forcing of Euro-American farming, dietary, and heteropatriarchal kinship models upon Indigenous peoples. Proximally, gendered, racialized policy channeled immigrants into indentured agricultural labor and work in the food industries, dispossessed Mexican and Asian American farmers, and demanded immigrants' dietary assimilation, including banning certain foods.

While into the nineteenth and early twentieth centuries, pedagogies of empire pathologized Indigenous peoples and racialized immigrants (and enslaved and formerly enslaved Black people) via their culinary practices, such as eating foods considered "savage," eating with one's hands, and consuming animals Euro-Americans viewed as pets, appropriating foodways has also always been a key part of US empire-building. To forge a distinct identity in contrast to British colonizers, early US Americans appropriated Indigeneity in connection with the alimentary realm. Taking a page from earlier US settlers' blend of food-related appropriation, pathologization, and gendered violence against Indigenous peoples, characterizing "ethnic" foods like tacos and Chinese takeout as quintessentially US American is emblematically neoliberal, combining gendered, racialized labor importation and exploitation and exclusion with selective consumptive incorporation. The food industries are targeted for immigration raids, even on "Taco Tuesday."

Neoliberal food systems also devastate economies and environments, necessitating migration, and food insecurity and food deserts are disproportionately prevalent on reservations and within impoverished communities of color, as are health disparities created by a lack of access to healthy food that is culturally and environmentally appropriate. Extant mainstream nutritional and health metrics are also rooted in white possessive logics. Anti-fat policy and media targets Indigenous women and women of color as personal failures, often in relation to mothering and poverty, as these communities disproportionately suffer from food insecurity, impoverishment, and diet-related illnesses created by centuries of US policy.

152 · CHAPTER 4

Therefore, as Indigenous activists and Critical Indigenous Studies scholarship emphasize, foodways are key to decolonization. The global food sovereignty movement challenges how colonization, assimilationist policies, and gendered stereotypes about mothering produce hunger, barriers to food access, poverty, and environmental degradation. It cohered in the 1990s in response to neoliberal policies that devastated small farmers and degraded the environment in gendered, racialized terms.[18] But long before the widespread use of the language of "food sovereignty," Indigenous leaders, activists, and scholars stressed the interconnection of Indigenous nation-based and food sovereignty, as traditional foods and foodways are the pillars of many Indigenous cultures, feeding physical bodies as well as spirits, entwined with specific lands and precolonial histories.[19] Defining and controlling Indigenous foodways and ensuring access to fresh, healthy, culturally and environmentally appropriate and sustainable food is often centered in current Indigenous decolonial movements.[20]

Additionally, a growing body of scholarship examines the links between foodways and the production of colonial, racial, and other systemic inequalities,[21] and immigration scholars interrogate racialization, nationalism, and foodways as sites of domination, adaptability, and resistance.[22] Feminist theorists have long studied the heteropatriarchal and racialized construction of food, cooking, and body size;[23] fat studies links the gendered production of anti-fat bias and "health" and "wellness" to race, dis/ability, and other axes of power.[24] After all, colonization devalues all aspects of the colonized, including their food and their physicality.

Drawing from and intervening in these bodies of knowledge, I argue that national(ist) dyspepsia—the "digestive" discomfort of a white possessive nation forced to reckon with the ongoing presence of Indigenous peoples and people of color—was and continues to be assuaged by controlling, in gendered, sexualized terms, Indigenous and racialized immigrant foodways. In short, from "The First Thanksgiving," entangled foodways public pedagogies about Indigenous peoples and racialized immigrants have been a potent tool

---

18. Patel, "What Does Food Sovereignty Look Like?," 663–706; and Grey and Patel, "Food Sovereignty as Decolonization," 431–44.

19. Gilio-Walker, *As Long as Grass Grows,* 87.

20. Mihesuah and Hoover, *Indigenous Food Sovereignty in the United States*; and Corntassel, "Toward Sustainable Self-Determination," 118.

21. See Tompkins, *Racial Indigestion.*

22. See Ku, Manalansan, and Mannur, "Alimentary Introduction"; and Diner, *Hungering for America.*

23. Bordo, *Unbearable Weight*; and Negrón-Muntaner, "Jennifer's Butt," 289–98.

24. Rothblum and Solovay, *Fat Studies Reader.*

of US empire. After chronicling the throughline of foodways pedagogies of empire in several historical moments, I conclude with discussion of Indigenous and racialized immigrant foodways and bodies, cast as revolting by US policies, institutions, and media, as powerful sites of revolt against US empire.

COMMODIFYING KIN: PRE- TO EARLY COLONIAL INDIGENOUS FOODWAYS

Food was vital to all aspects of Indigenous lives prior to colonization and in turn was vital to US empire-building. Broadly, precolonial Indigenous foodways shared what ethnobotanist Enrique Salmon (Rarámuri [Tarahumara]) calls a "kin-centric" relation to the natural world: foodways, spirituality, botanical and ecological knowledge, culture, and socioeconomic and political power were interconnected in largely if not universally nonviolent, nonexploitative ways. Animals and plants, including those used for medicine and food, and the land from where they and humans emerge as kin, were viewed as relatives.[25] According to an Indigenous worldview, land is responsibility and reciprocity, not a commodity or property. A "healthy landscape" is "whole and generous enough to be able to sustain its partners. It engages land not as a machine but as a community of respected nonhuman persons to whom we humans have a responsibility."[26]

Over two thousand years before Europeans knew that Indigenous peoples existed,[27] Indigenous kincentric relations with the natural world engendered vast bodies of botanical and ecological knowledge that along with bodies and minds, nourished economies and politics anchored in innovative, complex subsistence systems. Indigenous peoples in the Americas (Mesoamerica; South-Central Andes in South America; eastern North America) were some of the first to develop agriculture, based on corn. A parallel domestication of animals, as in other early agricultural centers throughout the world, was eschewed for game management. Some regions were arid, requiring intricate irrigation systems. Beans, squash, pumpkins, cocoa, and other regionally based food crops were also cultivated to support thriving societies. For example, the economic basis of the Aztec empire was hydraulic agriculture with corn as the main crop.[28] Corn was also the staple crop of nations in the northeastern part of North America, such as the matrilineal Haudenosaunee

---

25. Salmon, *Eating the Landscape*, 2.
26. Kimmerer, *Braiding Sweetgrass.*
27. Dunbar-Ortiz, *Indigenous Peoples' History*, 16.
28. Dunbar-Ortiz, *Indigenous Peoples' History*, 15–21.

154 • CHAPTER 4

confederacy, or Six Nations of the Iroquois Confederacy, including the Seneca, Cayuga, Onondaga, Oneida, and Mohawk Nations, and from the early nineteenth century, the Tuscaroras. Other nations had systems of farming and bison hunting, such as the Lakota and Dakota Sioux, or seafaring and fishing in the Pacific Northwest, for instance the Tlingit in Alaska.[29] Among Indigenous whaling nations in the Arctic such as the Inuit, the adage "I am what I am because of what I eat" illuminates how "whaling serves to link the Inuit materially, symbolically, and spiritually to their cultural heritage and ancestral knowledge."[30]

In precolonial Indigenous societies, foodways also determined gendered status and a complementary and an often-egalitarian gendered division of labor[31] (including gender-variant persons in societies that recognized them, as discussed in the conclusion). For instance, men might be responsible for hunting and fishing, and women for gathering other food sources, such as plants, and processing foods for storage, consumption, or trade. Women often held and transmitted immense and sophisticated knowledge about the harvesting, use, and sustainable stewardship of nutritive and medicinal plants,[32] and in some nations such as the matrilineal Seneca, this included political power. Clans distributed land to households according to their size and clan mothers, the oldest women from each extended clan, controlled distribution of household stores of food and other items. A chief matron was elected annually to direct work, and sick and injured community members received aid in this communal agricultural land stewardship model. Women also had their own councils, represented by a male speaker in the council of civil rulers, and elected civil rulers.[33] Thus precolonial kincentric Indigenous foodways were, in their immense variety, central to Indigenous survival and geopolitics.

•

Accordingly, settler coloniality was largely accomplished through inherently gendered attacks on Indigenous foodways—what John Grenier calls "feedfights,"[34] the destruction of all food resources. Settlers' claims that land was unused and naturally bountiful (see chapter 1) also undermined Indigenous people's careful stewardship and foodways, helping to rationalize this

---

29. Dunbar-Ortiz, *Indigenous Peoples' History,* 24–25.
30. Coté, "'Indigenizing' Food Sovereignty," 10.
31. Dunbar-Ortiz and Gilio-Whitaker, *"All the Real Indians Died Off,"* 138–39.
32. Grey and Patel, "Food Sovereignty as Decolonization," 438.
33. Jensen, "Native Women and Agriculture," 423, 425–26.
34. Grenier, *First Way of War.*

FOOD, FARMING, FAT, AND NATIONAL(IST) DYSPEPSIA · 155

powerful tool of nascent US empire-building. Moreover, inaugural feedfights opened the door wider for slavery and racial capitalism in what became the US, and the subsequent differential racialization, exploitation, and exclusion of im/migrants to further white heteropatriarchal property accumulation. For example, in 1609 John Smith, reinvented as a heroic heartthrob in Disney's *Pocahontas,* attempted to murder all Powhatan women and children and destroy their agricultural resources when Powhatan Confederacy leaders refused Smith's demand to feed and clothe the Jamestown settlers and give them land and labor. Bacon's Rebellion (1676), still celebrated by many US historians as a populist victory, was driven by an attack on Indigenous agriculture by a coalition of white farmers and landless indentured Black and white servants. Plantation-owing elites, troubled by the multiracial coalition, passed a law that made enslavement a permanent status for Africans,[35] binding Blackness to enslavement, linking Indigenous genocide and dispossession with racial capitalism and white possessive Euro-American wealth creation.[36] Early colonial feedfights, underpinned by gendered, racialized understandings of land as a commodity that should be individually owned and cultivated,[37] also included colonists' weaponization of alcohol, deliberately brought into Indigenous communities to weaken them.[38]

Feedfights were also built into foundational US governmentality. For example, because the Seneca allied with the British, George Washington instructed the military to take preemptory action against the Haudenosaunee. In 1779 the new Continental Congress ordered three armies to burn and loot all villages and destroy food supplies. To incentivize enlistment, the Pennsylvania assembly offered a bounty on Seneca scalps, regardless of sex or age.[39] Feedfight policies would continue to be a potent tool of empire-building.

Simultaneously, a white, heteropatriarchal US identity was forged in and through public pedagogy about "Indian" foodways, as hunger—and its alleviation—often motivated immigration to what would become the US. From the sixteenth and through the nineteenth century, in England and Europe the "agricultural revolution" entailed the enclosure of common lands, the rise of capitalist notions of property, new colonial crops, crop rotation, increased agricultural productivity, and market integration. It "work[ed] in tandem with colonial conquest and the outmigration of dispossessed peasants who in turn

---

35. See Allen, *Invention of the White Race,* vols. 1 and 2; and Painter, *History of White People.*

36. Dunbar-Ortiz, *Indigenous Peoples' History,* 60–62.

37. Goldstein, "Ground Not Given," 86; and Bhandar, *Colonial Lives of Property,* 8.

38. Dunbar-Ortiz, *Indigenous Peoples' History,* 69.

39. Dunbar-Ortiz, *Indigenous Peoples' History,* 76–77.

156 • CHAPTER 4

populated the front lines of settler colonization."[40] Sam Grey and Raj Patel noted that "capitalism's search for cheap food was a principle animus for imperialism—indeed, the modern food system's genealogy can be traced to the needs of the urban hungry in Europe and North America in the eighteenth and nineteenth centuries." A system of food production, processing, and consumption developed for the inhabitants of colonial metropoles that hinged on violence against people of color in the Global South and violence against Indigenous peoples in the Global North.[41] In the former, resources and labor were violently exploited and/or imported. In the latter, Indigenous peoples were violently dispossessed of land and natural resources.

Against this backdrop, from the early republic forward, foreign visitors and guidebooks for prospective, hungry European immigrants emphasized the abundance of food for "everyone" in the US, especially working men.[42] That food was sometimes explicitly characterized as "Indian" in gendered terms. As noted in chapter 1, white male settlers reinvented the Delaware leader Tamenend as "Tammany" in men's clubs and plays and songs that celebrated his hunting prowess to politicize the bountiful land/landscape, meat consumption, and revolutionary egalitarianism.[43] Similarly, Benjamin Franklin defended "Indian corn" in response to a British newspaper article mocking proto-US colonists' food habits, etiquette, and manners. Franklin reversed negative connotations of corn as "savage" animal feed or food for the very poor to assert that eating corn and political agency united all proto-US Americans. Following the revolution, corn became a signature national food, eaten by both rich and poor. Like meat and hunting, corn allowed early US Americans to imagine themselves as a community and begin to form a gendered, sexualized, racialized national identity.[44]

"Indian corn" and the Indigenous genocide and dispossession that made it possible for colonists to eat it was thus the beginning of a national cuisine, which was also foundationally shaped by chattel slavery. A national cuisine comprises specific dishes, and preparation and rules for eating on holidays as well as daily eating represent the history, ambitions, and territory of a unified nation.[45] Kyla Wazana Tompkins examines the nineteenth-century production of white nationalist mythologies through the politics of eating and

---

40. Goldstein, "Ground Not Given," 86.

41. Grey and Patel, "Food Sovereignty as Decolonization," 437; see also Davis, *Late Victorian Holocausts*.

42. Diner, *Hungering for America*, 12–13.

43. P. Deloria, *Playing Indian*, 18–20.

44. Balogh, Connolly, and Freeman, "What's Cooking?," *Back Story* podcast.

45. Vester, *Taste of Power*, 22–23.

the pathologization of what and how enslaved Black people, often starving or undernourished while forced to farm and prepare food for the white subjects of nationalism, ate. Because attempts to regulate eating are attempts to regulate embodiment,

> nationalist foodways—and the objects fetishized therein—in turn become allegories through which the expanding nation and its attendant anxieties play out. What we see in the nineteenth century—as indeed we do today in such racialized discourses as obesity, hunger, and diabetes—is the production of social inequality at the level of the quotidian functioning of the body.[46]

As eighteenth-century scientific discourses began to attempt to control US Americans' diets, early US cuisine, which included indigenous ingredients, continued to be linked to republicanism through gendered, racialized regulation of the body. Katharina Vester explains, "Living frugally, remaining temperate, and being committed to one's work and nation were crucial to the success of the republic. Eating, cooking, and providing certain foods became part of a citizen's commitment to the nation, as they were associated with the moral fiber and material well-being of the nation."[47] The first US American cookbook, Amelia Simmons's *American Cookery,* published in 1796 in Hartford, Connecticut, featured recipes with cornmeal ("Indian meal"). It was peppered with republicanism, offering recipes for "all grades of life," and was dedicated to US women.[48] A gendered, racialized regulation of eating was therefore embedded in US nationalism as Indigenous peoples were systematically attacked and starved off their land and as enslaved Africans were forced to cultivate that stolen land and prepare "American" foods as they too were systematically starved and malnourished. To bolster nascent US nationalism, some Indigenous foodways were also appropriated and both groups—and soon also im/migrants of color—were pathologized for their foodways and culinary habits, many of which were innovative ways to survive colonization and enslavement.

Prior to colonization, Indigenous foodways, geopolitics, spiritualities, cultural practices, and kincentric relations to the natural world were intertwined, and many Indigenous societies were gender-balanced if not equitable, with some granting women immense socioeconomic power and status in connection with foodways. Therefore, attacking, appropriating, and pathologizing Indigenous (and Black) foodways was crucial to anchoring the white

---

46. Tompkins, *Racial Indigestion,* 4.
47. Vester, *Taste of Power,* 19.
48. Vester, *Taste of Power,* 29–30.

158 • CHAPTER 4

possessive logics of US empire, destroying what Kyle Whyte (Citizen of the Potawatomi Nation) calls the capacities that Indigenous societies "rely on for the sake of exercising their own collective self-determination over their cultures, economics, health, and political order."[49]

FEEDING "AMERICAN" EMPIRE IN THE NINETEENTH AND EARLY TWENTIETH CENTURIES

To serve the manifesting destiny of the United States, settler colonial modes of Indigenous dispossession through foodways provided a template for and intersected with racialized immigration control and global imperialism. In this phase of empire-building, different, sometimes overlapping, but always entangled forms of foodways violence against Indigenous peoples and immigrants of color continued to bolster white possession. First, multimodal colonial feed-fights against Indigenous peoples persisted, sickening Indigenous peoples and further alienating them from their "land-based food and political systems."[50]

In numerous ways agriculture was a significant method of and rationale for Indigenous dispossession and the differential racialization of immigrants. The Civilization Act of 1819 anticipated allotment and compulsory boarding schools, centering on "civilizing" Indigenous nations near frontier settlements through missionary schools with curriculum that imposed a gendered division of farm labor: boys were taught to plow and plant; girls were taught to sew, spin, weave, and keep house. In a throughline from starvation as a tactic of colonial warfare, material supports were withheld from uncooperative Indigenous people.[51] Additionally, two Marshall Trilogy rulings, *Cherokee Nation v. Georgia* (1831) and *Worcester v. Georgia* (1832), justified Indigenous dispossession by characterizing Indigenous peoples as "wandering hordes" in a "savage state"[52] (the former) and bellicose hunters who "had made little progress in agriculture or manufactures"[53] (the latter). Then, to address the agricultural crisis provoked by the Civil War (75 percent of international exports came from Southern agriculture) and help consolidate the nation and economy, the federal government more explicitly made the frontier the *agricultural frontier*. In 1862 the US Department of Agriculture (USDA) was established, and

---

49. Whyte, "Food Sovereignty, Justice, and Indigenous Peoples," 349.

50. Martens et al., "Understanding Indigenous Food Sovereignty through an Indigenous Research Paradigm," 21.

51. Goldstein, "Ground Not Given," 87–88.

52. Cherokee Nation v. Georgia, 30 U.S. 1 (1831).

53. Williams, *Like a Loaded Weapon*, xvii; and Worcester v. Georgia, 31 US 515 (1832).

the first Homestead Act granted stolen land to non-Native would-be farmers to encourage westward migration and settlement. The Pacific Railway Act also gave incentives to farmers, many of whom were European immigrants, to settle on the Great Plains.[54] Under the Dawes Act (1887) white possessive logics found an especially pernicious structural foothold "in the fields and gardens of Indigenous Peoples."[55] Heteropatriarchal nuclear families received larger allotments as men were forced to take on the main role in foodways, and much of women's knowledge and structural power was rendered obsolete. Again, rations and other annuities were withheld from Indigenous peoples who refused to farm allotments according to Euro-American norms.[56] In compulsory schools, Native children were subjected to gendered curriculum and fed packaged, processed foods alien to them such as white flour, sugar, and dairy products. Physical abuse, including malnourishment and non-consensual nutritional experiments, was also prevalent at US and Canadian boarding schools,[57] as was sexual abuse (see chapter 3).

Direct colonial warfare against Indigenous peoples through foodways also persisted during relocation and incarceration until the 1890 Massacre at Wounded Knee, when US cavalry attacked unarmed, starving Lakota refugees who, accepting incarceration, were attempting to reach Pine Ridge reservation. Starvation was also part of forced relocation marches, as in 1864 when eight thousand Diné civilians were subjected to the Long Walk, a three-hundred-mile forced march to a military concentration camp in the southeastern New Mexico desert. At least one-fourth of incarcerated Diné died from starvation before 1868, when Congress decided that holding them was too expensive.[58]

To support westward expansion, the US government also encouraged and incentivized the army and civilians to kill bison, often commonly referred to as buffalo,[59] a main food source for White Plains nations such as the Lakota and Cheyenne. The so-called "Indian Problem" and "buffalo problem" was understood as linked,[60] for "in addition to the fortunes made in buffalo hides, their demise would starve various Indian nations onto reservations while

---

54. Goldstein, "Ground Not Given," 88–90.

55. Grey and Patel, "Food Sovereignty as Decolonization," 438.

56. Deloria and Lytle, *American Indians, American Justice.*

57. Coté, "'Indigenizing' Food Sovereignty," 3.

58. Dunbar-Ortiz, *Indigenous Peoples' History,* 138–39.

59. Bison and buffalo are distinct animals, both bovine. Bison reside in North America and Europe, buffalo in South Asia and Africa. US American bison are often referred to as buffalo, a misnomer often attributed to colonizers (Amy Tikkanen, "What's the Difference between Bison and Buffalo?," *Encyclopedia Britannica,* May 12, 2016. https://www.britannica.com/story/whats-the-difference-between-buffalo-and-bison).

60. Weber-Smith, "Burgers?," *American Hysteria* podcast.

simultaneously making way for a preferred (and now iconic) food system: the American cattle ranch."[61] In ten to fifteen years, twelve to fifteen million bison were killed.[62] Tasha Hubbard describes this "buffalo genocide" as part of the war on nature endemic to US settler colonialism.[63] Cattle ranches replaced the multispecies relations of the prairies, further imperiling Indigenous food security and the natural world. The developing beef industry targeted Indigenous populations with federal commodities programs distributing canned meat made of livestock raised on stolen Indigenous lands.[64] Meat-packing companies also exploited local ranchers and racialized immigrant labor, and beef became an iconic, very gendered part of national(ist) cuisine.[65]

Additionally, Indigenous foodways were destroyed by relocation to new and alien geography and climates—often arid and nonarable—and colonial and industrial expansion. Devon A. Mihesuah (Choctaw Nation) notes that "the plants and animals Indians once used for sustenance and medicine diminished. The ecosystems were transformed by damns, mines, deforestation, invasive species, and ranching."[66] Incarcerated on reservations, Indigenous peoples' movement was also restricted, and they were forced to rely on treaty-stipulated government rations of foods that were foreign to them, such as lard, white flour, sugar, cheese, and beef, or on insufficient treaty annuities.[67]

Meanwhile, pedagogies of empire in media framed the killing and consumption of bison and its conservation as patriotic and emblematic of an idealized US masculinity. Buffalo Bill Cody, the former Union solider, sharpshooter, and Pony Express rider, allegedly roamed the West and killed thousands of bison in just one year. Cody's vaudevillian Wild West Show (1882–1913) performed "buffalo" hunts with some of the few remaining bison.[68] Published prior to his tenure as president, Theodore Roosevelt's book, *Hunting Trips of a Ranchman* (1885), supplanted Turner's notion of an agrarian frontiersman with the new white male ideal, the "hunter/Indian fighter." While he mourned the likely extinction of bison and enjoyed hunting the animal, "its destruction was the condition precedent upon the advance of white civilization in the West."[69]

---

61. Grey and Patel, "Food Sovereignty as Decolonization," 437–38.

62. Balogh and Connolly, "Darkness over the Plain," *Backstory* podcast; and Isenberg, *Destruction of the Bison*.

63. Hubbard, "Buffalo Genocide in Nineteenth-Century North America," 292–305.

64. Barnard, "Bison and the Cow," 387; and LaDuke, *All Our Relations*.

65. Weber-Smith, "Burgers?,"

66. Mihesuah, "Searching for Haknip Achukma," 96.

67. For a primary text see Standing Bear, *My People the Sioux*, 71–81. See also Wiedman, "Native Embodiment," 595–612.

68. Weber-Smith, "Burgers?"

69. Roosevelt, *Hunting Trips of a Ranchman*, 248.

In popular literature and painting, the bison also somewhat ironically became "a charismatic emblem for a wild ecosystem and 'primitive' way of life that was inevitably disappearing as the nation expanded." As *part of* the nascent conservation movement, settlers could experience an "authentic" Indigeneity through the ritual killing and consumption of bison, a correlate for the "vanishing Indian."[70] As president, Roosevelt and other elite white men such as J. P. Morgan founded the Bison Society in 1905 to "preserve" bison in zoos: viewing the animals there and hunting them for sport on private ranches gave white men a "taste of the frontier."[71] Exceptionalist pedagogies of empire continue to claim bison, as in the National Bison Legacy Act (2016) and nationalist and consumerist discourses celebrating bison meat as a sustainable, authentically US American food.[72] Again, elite white men forged national identity by selectively appropriating Indigenous foodways in the midst of brutal feedfights against Indigenous peoples, claiming both beef and bison for their own.

As I discuss below, turn-of-the-century feedfights devastated Indigenous peoples' holistic health in enduring ways. As with sterilization abuse and un/rapeability, these foodways public pedagogies illuminate how the white possessive logics of US empire necessitate the ongoing violation of Indigenous bodies and lands.

•

US empire was proximally furthered via gendered foodways violence against im/migrants of color and newly colonized overseas racialized populations.[73] This wave of feedfights, defined by juridical and extralegal violence concentrated in the agricultural, restaurant, and food production industries and justified by stereotypes about food and eating habits and including selective appropriation, built on and was entangled with tactics used against Indigenous peoples, positioning Indigenous peoples and people of color differently—and often at odds—to further white possession.

Discussion of nineteenth- and early twentieth-century coloniality and anti-immigration through feedfights necessitates some contextualization and discussion of overseas colonization, especially that of the Philippines, which

---

70. Barnard, "Bison and the Cow," 377–402, 377–85.

71. Balogh and Connolly, "Darkness over the Plain."

72. Barnard, "Bison and the Cow," 377–85.

73. Although beyond the scope of this analysis, it bears repeating that foodways are an epicenter of anti-Blackness and the development of racial capitalism. For histories of Black American foodways, see Tompkins, *Racial Indigestion*; Twitty, *Cooking Gene*; and Chatelain, *Franchise*.

162 • CHAPTER 4

the US maintained as a formal colony from 1898 to 1946. Daniel Immerwahr explores how the tensions between a republican commitment to equality, white supremacy, and overseas expansion, the new frontier, were resolved by separating new colonies such as the Philippines, Puerto Rico, Guam—and their substantial nonwhite populations—as embryonic states. While the US had been annexing territory for over a century, it had not incorporated substantial nonwhite populations (the Louisiana, Florida, Oregon, Texas, and Mexican cessations included only small "foreign" populations of mostly Indigenous peoples and Mexicans, Spaniards, French, and some free Black people). With merely rhetorical republican commitments to equality, newly colonized, geographically distant overseas populations remained "foreign," unincorporated parts of the United States. To reflect this change (and silence critics), pedagogies of empire rebranded the US: prior to 1898, the word "America" does not appear in the public papers—or proclamations—of presidents or in patriotic songs. Teddy Roosevelt, in his first annual presidential message, referred to the US as "America." He continued to frequently use the term, as has every president since. Anthems such as "God Bless America" and "America the Brave" crystalized this national rebranding[74] that has since been naturalized.

Foodways public pedagogy was a powerful tool of empire-building in various, expanding US American contexts. For example, following the Treaty of Guadalupe Hidalgo (1848) annexation of parts of Mexico and before the regulation of Western Hemisphere im/migration, to safeguard white possession, Mexicans were first dispossessed and then exploited via various feedfights. This included taxation, privatizing communal grazing lands, and border control, which forced Mexican men into migratory labor across the new, relatively porous Mexico–US border, first as sheepshearers and vaqueros, and soon as laborers in railroad construction, mining, and agriculture. Many Mexican women remained in villages, maintaining domestic production and subsistence agriculture. Meanwhile, Progressive Era projects prepared Mexican children to bolster white possession. While schools and campaigns were often de facto rather than compulsorily segregated like those for Indigenous children, similar gendered curricula aimed to "civilize" Mexicans and prepare them for lives as laborers. This included replacing Mexican language and culture with the English language and US norms.[75]

Foodways public pedagogies about Asian immigrants also supported white possessive empire-building, and Asian immigrants used foodways to negotiate white supremacy. The editors of *Eating Asian America: A Food Studies Reader*

---

74. Immerwahr, *How to Hide an Empire*, 74–81.

75. Ruiz, "Confronting 'America,'" 343–47. For more on gendered curricula in schools, see Glenn, "Settler Colonialism as Structure," 61–63; and Velez-Ibanez, *Border Visions*.

describe how the differential racialization of foodways has "circumscribed Asians materially and symbolically in the alimentary realm, forcing them into indentured agricultural work and lifetimes spent in restaurants and other food service and processing industries."[76] Within China, diets are regionally diverse. While many immigrant groups have been characterized as masses of vermin, Chinese immigrants especially have been racialized through this stereotype, in explicit connection with foodways: the notion that Chinese people ate weird animals and disease-carrying vermin such as rats suggested that they were uncivilized *and* disease-carriers, justifying draconian policies, policing, and outright violence. In connection with the Chinese Exclusion Act (1882), in California white working men's fears of labor competition crystalized in foodways. Anti-Chinese activists and pundits first averred Chinese laborers were the center of a new slave system that degraded US labor, their alleged consumption of mice and rats evidence of their lower standard of living. Rice was also a gendered problem: Samuel Gompers, president of the American Federation of Laborers (AFL), asked, "Meat or Rice—American Manhood vs. Asiatic Coolieism. Which Shall Survive?"[77] Additionally, from the Gold Rush, Chinese immigrants opened restaurants catering to Chinese and non-Chinese customers,[78] and white US Americans responded with various degrees of xenophobia and patronage. Labor unions and moral crusaders attempted to eliminate Chinese restaurants and food industry workers. Middle- and upper-class white people visited Chinatowns for exotic spectacle that some eateries capitalized on with lurid displays and actors performing stereotypical Chinese vices such as smoking opium. Young white women also sought new freedoms in the liminal spaces of Chinese restaurants.[79] Meanwhile, minstrel songs such as Luke Schoolcraft's "Heathen Chinee" identified Chinese people with eating mice and rats, and dogs and cats.[80] An infamous nineteenth-century advertisement for "Rough on Rats," a pest control product, depicts a Chinese man, dressed in silk and a pointed hat, and with a long braid, visual signifiers of Chinese-ness at the time, eating a rat. Through the stereotype of Chinese people eating and therefore eliminating rats, the ad suggests the product is effective.[81]

---

76. Ku, Manalansan, and Mannur, "Alimentary Introduction," 1.

77. E. Lee, *At America's Gates*, 26.

78. Ku, Manalansan, and Mannur, "Alimentary Introduction," 3–4.

79. Chin and Ormonde, "War against Chinese Restaurants," 681–741; and Lancaster, "Plan to Kill," *Proof* podcast.

80. R. Lee, *Orientals*, 38–39.

81. E. Lee, *America for Americans*.

164 • CHAPTER 4

Simultaneously, Chinese immigrants became a powerful force in the restaurant industry, working within a racist system that excluded them from other industries and occupations, repeatedly reinventing and marketing Chinese food for US palates, and providing a critical lifeline for their community.[82] Chinese immigrants manipulated a 1915 exclusion policy exception that added "high grade" restaurants to the list of business ownership that allowed Chinese immigrants entry under "merchant" status. They pooled money and worked with white vendors to secure restaurant visas (two white witnesses were needed for visa applications). The number of US Chinese restaurants quadrupled by 1930.[83] A smaller Chinese population, increasing perception of Chinese restaurants as clean,[84] and the affordability of Chinese food also helped ease the Chinese restaurant strain of the "yellow peril."[85] But to be clear, gendered, racialized labor exploitation and exoticization persisted. In the post-1915 Chinese restaurant boom, New York City cooks worked for low wages for ten or more hours, seven days a week, over stoves kept as hot as possible to quickly prepare meals for white customers and reported being too tired to eat or sleep.[86] Late night "dine & dances" continued to capitalize on stereotypes of Chinese "foreignness" and "exoticness" and provided spaces where young mostly white people could experiment with gender roles.[87] Some Chinese restaurants were also glamourous places that included music, dancing, and entertainment, popular among white patrons and celebrities into the mid-twentieth century.[88]

As the continental frontier closed and to support the global expansion of US empire, foodways pedagogies of empire racialized Filipinxs as both "savage" colonial subjects and immigrants of color. Prior to US colonization, people in the Philippines ate a regionally diverse Southeast Asian diet, with influences from China, Spain, and Mexico.[89] Filipinx savagery and consequent inability to self-rule was evidenced by their consumption of dogs, a stereotype

---

82. Chen, *Chop Suey, USA*.

83. Maria Godoy, "Lo Mein Loophole: How US Immigration Law Fueled a Chinese Restaurant Boom," Food History & Culture, *NPR*, February 22, 2016, https://www.npr.org/sections/thesalt/2016/02/22/467113401/lo-mein-loophole-how-u-s-immigration-law-fueled-a-chinese-restaurant-boom.

84. Chin and Ormonde, "War against Chinese Restaurants," 731–33; and Lancaster, "Plan to Kill."

85. Chen, *Chop Suey, USA*.

86. H. Lee, "Life Cooking for Others," 54–55.

87. Graber and Twilley, "United States of Chinese Food," *Gastropod* podcast.

88. Chin and Ormonde, "War against Chinese Restaurants," 731–33; and Lancaster, "Plan to Kill."

89. Mabalon, "As American as Jackrabbit Adobo," 149.

FOOD, FARMING, FAT, AND NATIONAL(IST) DYSPEPSIA · 165

extended to Asian people. At the 1904 World's Fair, held just after the US victory in the Philippine–American War, the "Philippine Reservation" exhibit was designed with input from the US government to mitigate anti-imperialist opposition to overseas colonization and affirm white supremacy. Continuing with a Euro-American tradition of displaying "savage" peoples for entertainment, the fair's most expensive foreign exhibit included villages of Indigenous Filipinxs. In the Igorot section, naked Igorot, described as "head-hunters" in promotional materials and media coverage, daily killed and consumed a dog to amuse eager spectators. At the time, the Igorot people consumed dogs ritually and only occasionally.[90] Some people/people(s) in China, Korea, Vietnam, and the Philippines also consume dog. This varies further among generations and regions.[91] Soleil Ho notes that most Asians, especially those living in diaspora, tend to emphatically say "no" as a blanket statement to the question of whether Asians eat dog[92] because, "in places like the United States where the distinction between what is pet and what is food is understood as affectively stable," the question is about "determining who is a 'real' American and who is not, what sort of cultural practice is 'mainstream' and what is exotic, and what sort of food is disgusting and what is palatable."[93] At the risk of stating the obvious, dietary taboos are arbitrary and distinctions between food and pet are unstable, yet food choices are more than shorthand for identity: a population's actual, imagined, or force-fed diet justified colonization, exclusion, and exploitation.

Moreover, the distinct systems of settler and overseas colonialism were concretely linked via Native American boarding schools and US Philippine education, which included foodways. Schools had similar gendered, sexualized curricula and ideology, Filipinx students in the US were incorporated at some schools for Indigenous peoples, such as Carlisle, and schools shared administrators and teachers. Carlisle himself was deeply invested in colonial efforts in the Philippines.[94] Schools in the Philippines cultivated belief in the hygienic, pragmatic, and "modern" superiority of US packaged, processed foods and red meat, especially beef,[95] as consumer food products flooded the nation.[96] Negative health outcomes and gendered bodily pathologization

---

90. Castro, "Food, Morality, and Politics."
91. Wu, "Best 'Chink' Food," 39.
92. Soleil Ho, "Do You Eat Dog?," *Taste*, July 12, 2018, https://www.tastecooking.com/the-dog-question/.
93. Ku, Manalansan, and Mannur, "Alimentary Introduction," 2.
94. Hunziker, "Playing Indian, Playing Filipino," 425.
95. Fernandez, "Food and War," 241.
96. Orquiza, "*Lechon* with Heinz, Lea & Perrins with *Adobo*," 179–80.

followed. Additionally, shifts from subsistence farming, the norm prior to US colonial rule, engendered large-scale US migration and subsequent disproportionate low wage employment in food processing industries.[97]

In contrast, public pedagogies about white ethnic immigrant foodways fed turn-of-the-century US empire by becoming the bedrock of the "nation of immigrants" / multiculturalism mythos that rearticulated white possession for US neoliberal empire. Many if not most Irish and Eastern and Southern European immigrants migrated to alleviate hunger traced to the colonization of the Americas. In the eighteenth century, the introduction of corn, potatoes, and other colonial crops such as sugar, coffee, tea, and chocolate prompted a population increase and transformed economies and eating in Europe, enabling the Industrial Revolution. This ultimately exacerbated rather than alleviated hunger. White ethnic immigrants were, as Hasia Diner puts it, "hungering for America" given the US's global reputation as a place where food was available at relatively low cost. Many US Americans, perhaps especially newly immigrated ones, believed in their right to an acceptable standard of living that did not include hunger;[98] a right to "a piece of the pie" and often more pie (upward mobility). Who was invited to eat at the abundant US table, however, was determined by white possessive logics. Moreover, as in the early colonial period, the modern global reputation of the US as a land of plenty for *some* immigrants coalesced *because* Indigenous peoples had been and were still being starved, their foodways destroyed, pathologized, and selectively appropriated to support US empire expansion, and Black and other racialized groups' exploited labor, often in connection with food production and preparation, continued to build white heteropatriarchal wealth on that stolen Indigenous land.

Italian immigrant history perhaps most emblematically illustrates how white ethnic foodways public pedagogies reinvigorated white possessive empire-building (and arguably continue to). Following the national unification of Italy (1861), approximately four million mostly southern Italians immigrated between 1880 and 1920.[99] While poverty, labor exploitation, and a measure of systemic racialized discrimination (for instance, the Johnson–Reed Act [1924] nation-based quotas) shaped Italian immigrants' lives, alleviation of hunger underscored by increasing access to white possession ultimately came to define Italian American identity and discourse about it. Italian and other white ethnic immigrant laborers were initially exploited in the food processing industries, which Upton Sinclair famously dramatized

---

97. Mabalon, "As American as Jackrabbit Adobo," 151; 153.

98. Diner, *Hungering for America*, xvi–xvii; 15–16. See also Mintz, *Sweetness and Power*.

99. Diner, *Hungering for America*, 2.

FOOD, FARMING, FAT, AND NATIONAL(IST) DYSPEPSIA · 167

in his novel *The Jungle* (1906), and Italian men were recruited to replace formerly enslaved Black people on Southern sugar and corn plantations.[100] They often cultivated subsistence plots and, free from the dominance of a landlord as in Italy, became street vendors of fruits, vegetables, bread, and sweets. Discriminatory laws targeted Italian immigrant as well as Black food vendors, but Italians eventually rented or purchased commercial spaces for grocery stores that eventually fed other US Americans.[101] In regionally mixed Italian enclaves the first Italian restaurants were attached to small hotels or boarding houses for Italian men, who initially did their own cooking. As more women migrated, they took over, often commodifying household cooking and housekeeping skills to feed single Italian men.[102] Foods of affluence for southern Italians such as pasta and meat became staples for immigrants.[103] Pizza and spaghetti and meatballs, a purely US dish, also began to become popular among middle-class unhyphenated US Americans.[104] As with Indigenous peoples and Mexicans, Progressive reformers aimed to mitigate white ethnics' ostensible biological inferiority to white Anglo-Saxon Protestants via the intimate domains. They visited Italian immigrant homes to offer women lessons on cooking, nutrition, housekeeping, childrearing, and sanitation.[105] But unlike Indigenous peoples and Mexican and Asian immigrants, in the shadow of policies such as the Homestead Act that began to welcome white ethnics into white possessive empire-building, not feedfights and pernicious, racialized stereotypes but rather eating well (in comparison to experiencing hunger in Italy) and the ostensible abundance of food, shorthand for freedom, choice, and prosperity in the US, was and still is centered in public pedagogy about Italian immigrants and the multicultural "nation of immigrants" writ large.

As in the past, mainstream discourses about national cuisine and nutrition likewise supported white possessive empire-building. According to Sylvester Graham, the first well-known health reformer of the nineteenth century, now bread grown from wheat on the frontier, taken by conquest, was the (post-corn) literal stuff of US empire: "They who have never eaten bread made of wheat, recently produced by a pure, virgin soil have but a very imperfect notion of the deliciousness of good bread; such as is often to be met with in the comfortable log houses in our western country."[106] Cookbooks written to

---

100. Pelaccio, "Cries of Street Food Vendors," *Taste of the Past* podcast.
101. Pelaccio, "Cries of Street Food Vendors."
102. Diner, *Hungering for America,* 75–76.
103. Dickie, *Delizia!,* 47–57.
104. Mariani, *How Italian Food Conquered*; and Cinotto, *Italian American Table.*
105. Laurino, *Italian Americans,* 79–80.
106. Graham quoted in Vester, *Taste of Power,* 49–52.

168 • CHAPTER 4

and by white women continued to teach readers that eating "right" gave the eater/consumer health, social stability, and legitimated their class and racial privilege.[107] Experts also stressed the importance of nutrition for the nation. For men this required, as in the early republic, meat consumption. Ranching was also booming, giving more people access to more meat and especially beef than their European counterparts. Again, gendered, racialized "meat consumption became a source of national pride and an important element of an imagined American cuisine, commonly cited as proof of America's superiority over other nations."[108]

At the turn of the twentieth century, US continental and global empire was very much a culinary matter, exerted in the entanglement of foodways pedagogies of empire that targeted Indigenous peoples, immigrants of color, and overseas colonial subjects, and included beginning to incorporate white ethnic immigrants into white possession. Foodways public pedagogy is more "American" than apple pie: not everyone gets a piece, nor is everyone meant to.

MIDCENTURY APPETITES FOR EMPIRE

Throughout the mid-twentieth century, foodways pedagogies of empire managed Indigenous peoples and differentially racialized im/migrants in distinct, sometimes overlapping but always entangled ways. This section discusses flashpoints that paved the way for US neoliberal empire as a foodways project and for revolt against neoliberalism via foodways.

When the Indian Citizenship Act (1924) passed, ending allotment with procedures to restore some Indigenous land and governance, starvation, malnutrition, illness, and poverty were ubiquitous.[109] These fruits of centuries of colonial violence were exacerbated by foodways public pedagogy that continued to dispossess Indigenous peoples by circumscribing their ability to feed themselves, something even the US medical establishment, itself a powerful agent of empire, recognized.

For example, a 1927 study of nutrition on a Sioux reservation found that fry-bread (made from white flour and fried in some form of fat, one of many "creative reactions to the impositions of colonial provisions" and sometimes considered a "traditional" food[110]) was the dietary staple; vegetables and other plant and animal food sources were limited or absent, and government rations

---

107. Vester, *Taste of Power*, 63.
108. Vester, *Taste of Power*, 80.
109. Dunbar-Ortiz, *Indigenous Peoples' History*, 169.
110. Grey and Patel, "Food Sovereignty as Decolonization," 438.

(mass produced packaged foods) insufficient. The nutritionists attributed the prevalence of health issues, such as numerous over- and underweight (both are indicative of malnutrition and poverty) men, women, and children, as well as the prevalence of tooth decay, blindness, and high infant and child mortality rates, to poor nutrition.[111] A 1928 article in *Journal of the American Medical Association* (JAMA) observed that "the conquest by civilized man has brought about a change from the natural outdoor, nomadic life to one of restricted physical exertion and of indoor housing on the reservations," hastening "the extinction of the earliest American races."[112] Merging the "vanishing Indian" and "noble savage" stereotypes, the article, while clearly problematic, points to settler colonialism as the cause of the poor health and "decline" of Indigenous peoples. The necropolitical effects of US attacks on Indigenous peoples through foodways would become increasingly apparent throughout the twentieth century in epidemic rates of digestive and other diet-related illnesses.[113]

Termination, which further impoverished Indigenous peoples with the loss of millions of acres of land in tax forfeiture sales, included widespread food insecurity in urban relocation and on reservations[114] where environmental change and pollution continued to impede access to traditional foods and Indigenous peoples' ability to feed themselves. For example, with the damning of the Missouri River in the 1940s and 1950s most arable land on the Standing Rock, Cheyenne River, Crow Creek, and Fort Berthold Reservations in the Dakotas was lost. Damns in the Northeast and Northwest disrupted fisheries and flooded Indigenous lands. Industrial contaminants and pollutants also increasingly damaged Indigenous food systems. As traditional Indigenous food systems continued to decline, so too did the traditions and cultures associated with them.[115]

Colonial and racialized dispossession also persisted in midcentury US farming policies, with the USDA earning a reputation as the "last plantation." From the 1820s US agriculture was predicated on credit and cycles of indebtedness that became more prevalent in the mid-twentieth century when mechanization and government policy encouraged capital-intensive farming and expanded acreage economies of production. World War I exacerbated debt among Native, Black, and Latinx farmers, forcing many to sell their

---

111. Stene and Roberts, "Nutrition Study of an Indian Reservation," 217–21; and Levenstein, *Revolution at the Table*, 179–80.

112. "Diet and Deterioration Among the American Indians."

113. Mihesuah, "Searching for Haknip Achukma," 94–123; 96.

114. Jernigan, "Addressing Food Security and Food Sovereignty in Native American Communities," 113–32.

115. Mihesuah and Hoover, introduction to *Indigenous Food Sovereignty,* 5–7.

170 • CHAPTER 4

farms. Then New Deal USDA farm loans, debt services, and "resettlement" for poor landless farmers were disproportionately denied to racial minorities and women and granted to white men.[116]

•

Midcentury foodways public pedagogies concomitantly differentially racialized im/migrants to support the white possessive logics of US empire. While white ethnic racialization peaked with the Johnson–Reed Act, Mexican and Asian immigrants were subsequently more emphatically racialized and exploited and/or dispossessed in connection with foodways.

The racialization of Mexicans as permanently foreign and unassimilable "illegal aliens" and/or "alien citizens" was anchored in agricultural labor. Mostly male Mexican laborers were recruited and "repatriated"—that is, deported, often regardless of citizenship status—when their labor was no longer needed during the Great Depression,[117] following the World War II Bracero Program (1942–64), which also created the enduring "wetback" stereotype, and following the Korean War via Operation Wetback (1954).[118] This "imported colonialism" modernized the "legacy of the nineteenth-century American conquest of Mexico's northern territories"[119] by creating an easily exploitable gendered, racialized labor pool to further white heteropatriarchal property interests.

Foodways pedagogies of empire also continued to racialize Asian immigrants and citizens as aliens. To justify Japanese internment as an extraordinary wartime necessity, the World War II iteration of the "yellow peril" cast Japanese people as dangerous military hordes, forcing 120,000 Japanese Americans to abandon their homes, businesses, and possessions from 1942 to 1946.[120] Foodways loomed large in internment in several ways.

Prior to internment and in defiance of the intent of California's Alien Land Laws, which from 1913 attempted to bar Asians, still "aliens ineligible for citizenship" under federal law, from owning agricultural land or leasing it long-term, Japanese Americans dominated the strawberry industry and had significant stakes in the production of other crops such as lettuce and tomatoes. In fact, following the announcement of incarceration under Executive Order 9066, USDA officials and media feared wartime food supplies would

---

116. Goldstein, "Ground Not Given," 93–95.
117. Hoffman, *Unwanted Mexican Americans in the Great Depression,* 86–87.
118. Camacho, *Migrant Imaginaries,* 109.
119. Ngai, *Impossible Subjects,* 129.
120. Daniels, *Prisoners without Trial;* and R. Lee, *Orientals,* 146–47.

FOOD, FARMING, FAT, AND NATIONAL(IST) DYSPEPSIA · 171

dwindle without Japanese American farmers, prompting the government to survey and appraise Japanese American–owned properties and farms.[121] As the state dispossessed Japanese Americans, World War I victory gardens were revived to maintain food supplies for the (rest of) the nation. While products such as sugar and meat were rationed, by 1943 twenty million victory gardens produced 40 percent of US produce.[122]

Farming was both a means of survival and dispossession for interned Japanese Americans. Many interned Japanese Americans farmed to make camps self-sustaining. The War Relocation Authority (WRA) and media also depicted internal camp farm work, outside contract farm labor, and enlistment and resettlement—that is, purposeful ethnic dispersal—as patriotic, even as WRA reports fretted over camp communal mess hall eating routines undermining Japanese American nuclear families.[123] Additionally, most landowning Japanese American farmers in California lost their property during internment; those with tenant, cropper, or manager relationships with landowners lost everything. Agricultural laborers were replaced. Not surprisingly, the US government offered only a pittance of aid following the war.[124] World War II–era foodways public pedagogy about Japanese Americans thereby also furthered white possessive empire-building.

Chinese immigrants too continued to navigate and be disciplined by foodways public pedagogy. Amid wartime politics that recast Chinese people as World War II allies, then as Cold War enemies, and the ascent of the "model minority" stereotype, the affordability of Chinese food, which Chinese American restauranteurs and cooks continued to adapt for US palates (like combining sweet and spicy flavors and militarism in General Tso's chicken), democratized dining out. By 1980 Chinese food became the most popular cuisine in the US.[125]

Simultaneously stereotypes about Chinese people eating vermin or animals considered pets were rearticulated (this also forcefully resurged after the first cases of the COVID-19 pandemic were identified in China and blamed by some US senators on a "culture where people eat bats and snakes and dogs"[126]). Fears of "Chinese Restaurant Syndrome," a term coined in

---

121. Ichikawa, "Giving Credit Where It Is Due," 275.

122. Levenstein, *Paradox of Plenty*, 85.

123. Kim, "Incarceration, Cafeteria Style," 125–31.

124. Aoki, "No Right to Own?," 64.

125. Chen, *Chop Suey, USA*.

126. Nicolas Wu, "GOP Senator Says China 'to Blame' for Coronavirus Spread Because of 'Culture Where People Eat Bats and Snakes and Dogs,'" *USA Today*, March 19, 2020, https://www.usatoday.com/story/news/politics/2020/03/18/coronavirus-sen-john-cornyn-says-chinese-eating-bats-spread-virus/2869342001/.

the 1960s to describe symptoms such as headache and sweating that some people claimed to experience after eating Chinese food, were published in a 1968 letter to the *New England Journal of Medicine*. The journal subsequently published a spate of similar complaints. While the term is considered outdated and offensive, Chinese food is still associated with monosodium glutamate (MSG), a food additive, despite no scientific evidence linking MSG to alleged symptoms.[127] Moreover, the additive is in many foods, including some McDonald's items. Nonetheless, in 1993 Merriam Webster added "Chinese Restaurant Syndrome" to its dictionaries. It remains despite a 2020 campaign to remove or at least update the entry.[128] The insinuation that Chinese and "Asian" foods (and therefore Asian people) are foreign, dirty, and potentially harmful to US Americans, assumed to be white, was therefore rebranded in spurious medicalized MSG discourse.

Like Mexicans, Filipinxs were recruited for food industry labor and repatriated, another plain instance of "imported colonialism," especially given that Filipinx people were colonial subjects until 1946. In the 1910s and 1920s, working class and poor Filipinxs, impoverished and influenced by colonial public education, migrated to the US, initially unchecked by Asian exclusion as US nationals. One hundred and fifty thousand Filipinxs migrated by 1946. Before World War II, most migrants were men, often recruited to work in agriculture on the West Coast and in Hawai'i, in salmon canneries in Alaska, and as busboys and domestics in cities.[129] The Tydings–McDuffie Act or Philippine Independence Act (1934) established a ten-year independence process and reclassified all Filipinxs, including those in the US, as aliens, bringing Filipinxs into the Johnson–Reed system with an annual quota of just fifty immigrants. The Filipino Repatriation Act (1935) financed return to the Philippines. The laws ended Filipinx family reunification as the federal government permitted larger numbers of male agricultural laborers to immigrate. Filipinxs were thus "transformed from colonial subjects to undesirable aliens"[130] whose foodways labor, but not full incorporation into the US, was wanted. Additionally, during the Depression when farm labor wages shrank and service-sector work was sparse, Filipinxs lived in crowded communal spaces, shared expenses, and cooked food unfamiliar to white US Americans. In newspapers, white male

---

127. LeMesurier, "Uptaking Race."

128. Amelia Nierenberg, "Chinese Restaurant Syndrome," Food, *New York Times*, January 16, 2020, updated June 2020, https://www.nytimes.com/2020/01/16/dining/msg-chinese-restaurant-syndrome-merriam-webster-dictionary.html.

129. Mabalon, "As American as Jackrabbit Adobo," 154.

130. Ngai, *Impossible Subjects*, 97.

FOOD, FARMING, FAT, AND NATIONAL(IST) DYSPEPSIA • 173

pundits cast Filipinxs as culturally unassimilable and racially unfit for citizenship given their "low standard mode of housing and feeding."[131]

Simultaneously, via foodways, Italian Americans more fully "integrated" into white possession. In the 1920s and 1930s Italian American restaurants were popular among non-Italians in cities such as New York City, especially given the availability of homemade wine, beer, and other alcoholic drinks during Prohibition and the affordability of pasta. Although restaurants initially boiled pasta in large window cauldrons to ameliorate suspicions about Italian Americans' faltering commitments to US sanitary standards, by the 1930s full-service Italian restaurants proliferated, spreading from Italian enclaves into downtown business districts.[132] Mediated foodways flashpoints such as *Good Housekeeping* magazine's 1935 declaration that "Everybody seems to know a Tony's or Joe's where one can get the best spaghetti in town" also signaled Italian Americans' inclusion in white possession. After all, "everybody"—that is, the white middle-class female readers and their families—had a discerning enough palate for Italian American food to have a favorite restaurant.[133] So too did Disney's canine lovers in the animated children's film *Lady and the Tramp* (1955), who shared a romantic kiss over a plate of spaghetti and meatballs.

Public pedagogy about national cuisine concurrently served white possessive empire in a changing political and economic climate. As technological advances allowed convenience and other mass-produced foods and food-related goods—including animals for slaughter—to become cheaper to produce and market and therefore more accessible to consumers, the wartime independence that many (white) women found working outside of the home was quelled as popular media (for instance Betty Crocker advertising campaigns; women's magazines such as *Good Housekeeping, McCall's,* and *Better Homes and Gardens*; cookbooks; and 1950s family sitcoms such as *Father Knows Best*) framed white women's unpaid domestic labor and especially food preparation as essential to a strong nuclear family and nation. "Bringing home the bacon" was the realm of the white patriarch.[134] As nationalist discourse relegated white women to the kitchen (again), cooking and especially grilling and carving meat returned to the realm of proper white masculinity, especially in connection to beef, which the nascent fast food industry rehabilitated as the hamburger.[135]

---

131. Judge D. W. Rohrback, quoted in Mabalon, "As American as Jackrabbit Adobo," 155.

132. Levenstein, *Paradox of Plenty,* 51.

133. McFadden, "Let's Have Spaghetti," *Good Housekeeping,* March 1935, 89, cited in Levenstein, *Paradox of Plenty,* 52.

134. Levenstein, *Paradox of Plenty,* 102–5.

135. Weber-Smith, "Burgers?"

174 • CHAPTER 4

As part and parcel of midcentury empire-building, entangled foodways public pedagogies sickened, pathologized, and exploited Indigenous peoples and immigrants of color while incorporating white ethnic groups and cuisines into the US diet and body politic. This set the table for "health disparities," environmental destruction, labor exploitation, and selective foodways appropriation/incorporation as a central tool of US neoliberal empire.

REVOLTING NEOLIBERAL FOODWAYS

Jodi Byrd (a citizen of the Chickasaw Nation of Oklahoma) observes that in the neoliberal moment, "the financialized social relations created by colonialism continue to pay dividends at the ends of empire."[136] By the late twentieth century, the consequences of white possessive feedfights against Indigenous peoples and immigrants of color were evident in the disproportionate poverty, food insecurity, diet-related health disparities and bodily pathologization (framed as results of personal irresponsibility, excess, and laziness), and resource and/or labor exploitation among each group. In fact, neoliberalism could be considered a feedfight or foodways project: as neoliberal globalization calcified after World War II, food was hypercommoditized and food systems were globalized. Decision-making power over food production and distribution was concentrated in nation-states and supranational and transnational companies and organizations, with policies designed to serve agribusiness and other corporations rather than human beings. Consequently, "this neo-colonial process impoverished millions of peasants and Indigenous peoples by displacing them from the land, resulting in many of them being forced into wage labor to serve the global food economy"[137] and often necessitating migration.

Neoliberal policies also subject both Indigenous and communities of color to environmental racism, intensifying environmental degradation / climate change with investments in fossil fuels and industrial agriculture, which creates approximately one-fourth of greenhouse gas emissions.[138] Due to centuries of colonial and racialized impoverishment and segregation, both groups often live and work in the most polluted urban and rural areas, and Native lands have been invaded by extractive industries with processes such as fracking, causing severe pollution and earthquakes.[139]

---

136. Byrd, "'Variations under Domestication,'" 138.

137. Coté, "'Indigenizing' Food Sovereignty," 7.

138. McMichael, "Food Sovereignty in Movement," 168–85.

139. For examples of scholarship on environmental racism, see Cole and Foster, *From the Ground Up*; Checker, *Environmental Racism*; and Sze, *Noxious New York*.

FOOD, FARMING, FAT, AND NATIONAL(IST) DYSPEPSIA • 175

In numerous ways, neoliberal feedfights uniquely position Indigenous peoples to further the white property interests underpinning US empire. Regarding environmental degradation / climate change, by the late twentieth century, half of Indigenous communities in the US lived on or near reservations. In many of those communities, over 80 percent of people were on or below the poverty line and unable to use their lands for economic self-sufficiency except for those who agreed to exploitative forms of development and use.[140] Often the only jobs available on reservations are in extractive industries. Neoliberal investments in extractive industries and industrial agriculture consequently often also force Indigenous peoples to "cannibalize our own mother," the earth, as scholar and activist Winona LaDuke (Anishinaabe) put it.[141]

Simultaneously, neoliberal policies such as the North American Free Trade Agreement (NAFTA, 1994) continued to dispossess Indigenous agriculture within the US and Mexico, and Indigenous farmers seeking to sustain or revive traditional foodways and crops were hindered by "rigid patent laws and accompanying private claims on traditional knowledge; labeling conventions that favor non-Indigenous varieties of traditional foods," and traditional crops were rendered vulnerable to genetic contamination from neighboring industrial farms.[142] The USDA also continued to disproportionately deny or delay farm loans to Indigenous farmers.[143]

Neoliberal feedfights also caused epidemic rates of health disparities or health inequalities among Indigenous communities, many if not most of which are diet-related.[144] The World Health Organization (WHO) defines health inequalities as "*avoidable* inequalities in health between groups of people within countries and between countries [. . .] social and economic conditions and their effects on people's lives determine their risk of illness and the actions taken to prevent them becoming ill or treat illness when it occurs."[145] In 2003, the US Commission on Civil Rights found Indigenous peoples are twenty to twenty-five years behind the general population in health status.[146] Then the 2015 report, "Feeding Ourselves: Food Access, Health Disparities, and

---

140. Barker, "Territory as Analytic," 30.

141. LaDuke quoted in Waziyatawin, "Paradox of Indigenous Resurgence," 74.

142. Grey and Patel, "Food Sovereignty as Decolonization," 441.

143. Goldstein, "Ground Not Given," 93–97.

144. Echo Hawk Consulting, "Feeding Ourselves," 36. A longer eponymous report was produced by the University of Arkansas School of Law's Indigenous Food and Agriculture Initiative in partnership with the American Heart Association, the Robert Wood Foundation, and Echo Hawk Consulting along with another private Indigenous organization, Pipestem Law. All citations refer to the report published by Echo Hawk Consulting.

145. "Social Determinates of Health," WHO Team, World Health Organization, May 17, 2013, https://www.who.int/social_determinants/thecommission/finalreport/key_concepts/en/.

146. US Commission on Civil Rights, "A Quiet Crisis."

the Pathways to Healthy Native Communities," produced by Echo Hawk Consulting, a firm created by Crystal Echo Hawk (Pawnee Nation of Oklahoma), traced "the extent of the problem of Native health disparities and its deep interconnections to US Native American policy, poverty, historical trauma and food systems" with a focus on reservations and in rural areas. "Feeding Ourselves" argued that restoring Indigenous peoples' abilities to feed themselves was the key to their physical, spiritual, psychic, and economic health and made policy and funding recommendations.[147] As the report emphasizes, impoverishment is indivisible from a population's ability to feed itself. In 2010, 28 percent of Native Americans lived in poverty, compared to 15.3 percent for the rest of the US. In 2012, one in four American Indians and Alaskan Natives (AI/AN) lived in poverty. Of the ten poorest US counties, eight were on reservations or have reservations within them, or have 90 percent or more Indigenous people living within them.[148] Indigenous peoples living in urban areas are also impoverished at higher rates than any other racial group.[149] Therefore, food insecurity was and continues to be significantly higher among Indigenous peoples in comparison to the US average.[150] The USDA currently stipulates that a community's access to healthy and affordable food is measured by distance to a store or the number of stores in an area; individual-level resources such as family income or vehicle availability; and neighborhood level resources such as average income and the availability of public transportation.[151] Echo Hawk Consulting found that "virtually *all* of Indian Country resides within a 'food desert' as defined by the United States Department of Agriculture."[152] Some reservations are "super food deserts" as with the Osage reservation in Osage County, Oklahoma, which has only four grocery stores within its 2,251 miles. Most land is used for livestock ranching, not agriculture, and there is no public transportation.[153]

Additionally, US government rations during removal and allotment gave way to food stamps and other federal food distribution programs that, built upon earlier colonial feedfights, perpetuated hunger and diet-related health

---

147. Echo Hawk Consulting, "Feeding Ourselves," 10.

148. Echo Hawk Consulting, "Feeding Ourselves," 22–23.

149. Suzanne Macartney, Alemayehu Bishaw, and Kayla Fontenot, "Poverty Rates for Selected Detailed Race and Hispanic Groups by State and Place, 2007–2011," US Census Bureau, February 2013, https://www.census.gov/library/publications/2013/acs/acsbr11-17.html.

150. Mihesuah and Hoover, introduction to *Indigenous Food Sovereignty*, 6.

151. "Documentation," Economic Research Service, US Department of Agriculture, accessed on August 2, 2023, https://www.ers.usda.gov/data-products/food-access-research-atlas/documentation/.

152. Echo Hawk Consulting, "Feeding Ourselves," 32.

153. Mihesuah, "Searching for Haknip Achukma," 94–121; 97.

issues while damaging if not deliberately undermining Indigenous sovereignty, social relations, economies, spirituality, and kincentric relations with the natural world. Initiated in 1973, the Food Distribution Program on Indian Reservations (FDPIR) "provides USDA Foods to income-eligible households living on Indian reservations, and to American Indian households residing in approved areas near reservations or in Oklahoma." It is an alternative to other federal food assistance programs such as the Supplemental Nutrition Assistance Program (SNAP) for Native households without "easy access to SNAP offices or authorized food stores." The federal program is administered locally by Indian Tribal Organizations (ITOs) or state government agencies.[154] While Indigenous peoples have worked assiduously to add traditional and regionally relevant food such as frozen sockeye salmon, bison meat, and blue cornmeal to the FDPIR,[155] in 2023, highly processed, mass-produced, shelf-stable foods such as canned fruits and vegetables, cereals, grains, vegetable oils, and instant or evaporated milk comprise the bulk of the list. Through another USDA program recipients might be able to receive fresh fruits and vegetables.[156] Furthermore, many if not most foods require electricity and a kitchen or at least some culinary tools, as well as time and some measure of cooking skill, to prepare. Indigenous peoples' disproportionate impoverishment and struggle to feed themselves often includes a lack of modern appliances and facilities in which to store and prepare food.[157]

Therefore, there is a clear throughline from foodways pedagogies of empire targeting Indigenous peoples to epidemic levels of general and especially diet-related health issues among them.[158] According to Indian Health Service (IHS), which delivers health services to approximately 2.56 million of the 5.2 million AI/AN, AI/AN life expectancy is 5.5 years less than the US population as a whole (73 years to 78.5 years). Heart disease, diabetes, malignant neoplasm, and unintentional injuries are the leading causes of death among Indigenous peoples, who also die at higher rates than other US Americans from diabetes, chronic liver disease, and cirrhosis, as well as from unintentional injuries, assault/homicide, intentional self-harm/suicide, and chronic lower respiratory diseases.[159] Over 80 percent of AI/AN adults ages 20

---

154. "What Is FDPIR?," US Department of Agriculture, last updated January 1, 2018, https://www.fns.usda.gov/fdpir/fdpir-fact-sheet.

155. Mihesuah and Hoover, introduction to *Indigenous Food Sovereignty*, 6.

156. "FDPIR Program Fact Sheet," US Department of Agriculture, accessed August 2, 2023, https://www.fns.usda.gov/fdpir/fdpir-fact-sheet.

157. Echo Hawk Consulting, "Feeding Ourselves," 22–23.

158. Mihesuah and Hoover, introduction to *Indigenous Food Sovereignty*, 6–7.

159. "Disparities," Indian Health Service, October 2019, accessed August 2, 2023, https://www.ihs.gov/newsroom/factsheets/disparities/.

to 74 are overweight or obese. Among children and youth, between 45 and 51 percent are not of a healthy weight, and childhood obesity rates often exceed 50 percent in Indigenous communities; childhood obesity rates are twice as high among Indigenous peoples compared to other racial and ethnic populations. Prediabetes and type 2 diabetes are also disproportionately prevalent in AI/AN communities, with a 110 percent increase in diagnosed diabetes from 1990 to 2009 in AI/AN youth aged 15 to 19 years.[160] According to Centers for Disease Control (CDC) data, AI/AN are more likely to have diabetes than any other racial or ethnic group in the US (and at a rate of twice as likely as whites), and experience kidney failure from diabetes at a higher rate than any other race.[161] "Feeding Ourselves" notes that no word for diabetes existed in Indigenous languages prior to colonization. Rare among Natives into the 1940s, diabetes became common in the 1960s, exploding in the 1970s.[162] Diabetes and other diet-related health issues like obesity also translate directly into oral, maternal, child, and mental health issues, as well as higher instances of cancer, heart disease, amputations, strokes, and other health traumas.[163] As social demographer Desi Rodriguez-Lonebear (Cheyenne) emphasized in the early days of the COVID-19 pandemic, which was infecting and killing Indigenous, Black, and Latinx people at the highest rates, "Health disparities are nice words for systematic racism . . . it's the residual effects of the founding of this country."[164]

At the same time, biological markers of "health," obesity, and fatness as defined by colonial institutions are themselves pedagogies of empire, borne of and often further institutionalizing colonialism and white supremacy. After all, science/medicine does not read nature to find truths to apply to the social world; rather, social relationships structure and interpret the "natural."[165] For instance, the Body Mass Index (BMI), a measure of body fat based on height and weight, framed by medical and other social institutions such as the CDC as an objective measure of health, was invented in the nineteenth century by Belgian mathematician Adolphe Quetelet, whose research helped establish racist pseudoscience and criminology. The BMI, which he developed to statistically measure the health of white Western European populations, not

---

160. Echo Hawk Consulting, "Feeding Ourselves," 25.

161. "Native Americans with Diabetes," Vital Signs, Centers for Disease Control, last updated November 15, 2018, https://www.cdc.gov/vitalsigns/aian-diabetes/index.html.

162. Echo Hawk Consulting, "Feeding Ourselves," 30.

163. Echo Hawk Consulting, "Feeding Ourselves," 25.

164. Rebecca Nagle, "Native Americans Being Left out of US Coronavirus Data and Labeled as 'Other,'" *The Guardian*, April 24, 2020, https://www.theguardian.com/us-news/2020/apr/24/us-native-americans-left-out-coronavirus-data?CMP=share_btn_tw.

165. Fausto-Sterling, *Sexing the Body*, 116.

individuals, was quickly embraced by eugenicists to measure fitness to parent and justify the systemic sterilization of the disabled, racialized immigrants, people of color, and the impoverished. Since 1985, the US National Institute of Health, at the behest of insurance companies, adopted the BMI to measure obesity among individuals. Insurance companies often charge higher premiums for people with higher BMIs, though the BMI marker of "obese" has also changed over time.[166] The adoption of the BMI to categorize persons as unhealthily overweight therefore emblematizes the weaponization of neoliberal personal responsibility politics to structurally disadvantage people categorized as too fat and benefit corporations. Moreover, the meaning of fatness has also changed to continuously support white possession: in the late nineteenth and early twentieth centuries, among white US Americans fatness signified prosperity—that a person could afford to eat well. Industrialization, mass production and availability of food, and fatter immigrants (specifically white ethnics at the peak of their racialization as biologically inferior whites) democratized fatness. White slenderness came to represent class and status, harkening back to Puritan ideals of self-abnegation and denial. Fatness in turn signified overindulgence and gluttony, with science and medicine perpetuating this ideology.[167] Fat phobia is akin to other identity-based oppressions because fat people are structurally disadvantaged, disciplined, and blamed for being fat, making the state of fatness itself a problem and "fat" a negative identity. Fat activists therefore work to reclaim and rehabilitate fatness to pursue rights and decolonization of body-size ideals. As they point out, in the neoliberal context, the weight loss industry and medicine/health industry profits enormously from the dominant belief that fat is ugly and unhealthy.[168]

Indigenous women and women of color, mothers especially, are disciplined by medicalized neoliberal pedagogies of empire that cast fatness, obesity, and diet-related health issues as failures to take "personal responsibility" for one's body and/or one's children's bodies. For example, from the 1970s, studies published in medical journals about Indigenous health in Oklahoma claimed corpulence was a feminine ideal among nations such as the Comanche because they were ignorant about the health risks of being overweight. Traditionally the Comanches were nomadic hunters, without an agricultural tradition, and prevalent weight gain and associated health issues arose in connection with incarceration on reservations and the influx of white flour, sugar, lard, and other federal ration foods. An ideal of fatness or corpulence among some Comanche was thus shaped, pun intended, by US empire and

---

166. Hobbes and Gordon, "Body Mass Index," *Maintenance Phase* podcast.

167. Fraser, "Inner Corset," 11–14.

168. Wann, "Foreword: Fat Studies: An Invitation to Revolution," ix–xxv.

180 • CHAPTER 4

by *surviving* US empire, yet a host of US establishment medical texts viewed fatness as embodied evidence of Indigenous peoples' ignorance. Some studies even used fatness to mock Indigenous peoples as uncivilized.[169] Pathologization of Indigenous and nonwhite women's appetites to support neoliberal white possessive logics persists in policies and debates about regulating how women and especially mothers use welfare and food stamps. Moreover, the white female slender ideal excludes and pathologizes body types more prevalent among Indigenous women and women of color,[170] also resulting in eating disorders[171] that are also part of the throughline of the use of foodways as a tool of US empire.

To be clear, Indigenous peoples suffer disproportionately from diet-related illness, disease, and death. People of color also suffer disproportionately from diet-related health disparities and, like Indigenous peoples, are more likely to experience food insecurity and to live in food deserts.[172] Public pedagogy that divorces diet-related illnesses from the structural inequalities that produce them at elevated and epidemic rates among certain populations is—hand in glove with public pedagogy about body size and beauty ideals—necropolitical: "health disparities" and especially those that are diet-related are a powerful, extant thread of gendered neoliberal feedfights against Indigenous peoples and people of color, and so too is fat-phobia. Human bodies are different sizes for a variety of reasons, none of which warrant punishment and pathologization, and all of which are embedded in systemic power relations.

Based on her 2014 study of Alaska Native foodways, Melanie M. Lindholm uses the term "nutritional colonialism" to "describe the values and practices of the dominant food system that affect all areas of Native well-being." This includes a focus on profits and

> negation of subsistence lifestyles, cultural suppression or marginalization, removal of control over resources, lack of food sovereignty, fostered dependence, environmental degradation, increase in chronic diseases, and negation of any dominant sense of responsibility. Products of nutritional colonialism contribute to sedentary lifestyles, require cash, contain suboptimal nourishment, and are culturally insignificant.[173]

---

169. Mihesuah, "Comanche Traditional Foodways," 242–44.

170. Barrera, "Hottentot 2000," 407–20; Beltran, "Hollywood Latina Body," 71–86; and Negron-Mutaner, "Jennifer's Butt," 182–95.

171. Demby and Meraji, "Pretty Hurts," *Code Switch* podcast.

172. Odoms-Young and Bruce, "Examining the Impact of Structural Racism," S3–S6.

173. Lindholm, "Alaska Native Perceptions of Food," 161–62.

FOOD, FARMING, FAT, AND NATIONAL(IST) DYSPEPSIA · 181

Nutritional colonialism, including the notion of "health" itself, is a tool and effect of US neoliberal empire in ways that mirror and are part of flexible accumulation to serve white possession. Foodways pedagogies of empire continue to be an incredibly potent, pernicious means of Indigenous dispossession.

·

To protect and further white possession, US neoliberal foodways pedagogies of empire position racialized immigrants in ways that are distinct from but always entangled with Indigenous dispossession. Here I focus primarily on Latinx im/migrants given that US neoliberal empire is significantly produced and reproduced through various kinds of feedfights against Latinx immigrants, who are disproportionately employed, exploited, and racialized in the food industries.

Inaugural neoliberal immigration policy guaranteed a gendered, racialized labor pool in agricultural and food and service industries. The amnesty provision of the Immigration Reform and Control Act (IRCA) was another instance of "imported colonialism," binding applicants to employers during a long waiting period (making them vulnerable to abuses) and including the Seasonal Agricultural Worker (SAW) program for temporary laborers. Reagan, sympathetic to agribusiness, championed both as Mexican im/migrants were targeted by nativist and organized labor xenophobia (hence IRCA's increased border security and militarization alongside amnesty). As discussed in chapter 2, most SAW participants were Mexican men.[174]

An IRCA provision that penalized undocumented workers' employers was also written and implemented to serve employers and especially agribusiness while exploiting Latinx laborers: the penalty for employers was a civil offense, with a fine of $250 to $2,000 for each undocumented worker "knowingly" employed.[175] Employers could claim unknowingness and were exempt from penalization for employees who entered after the 1982 amnesty cut-off date, though it continued to be illegal for undocumented immigrants to work, and INS needed an owner's consent and warrant to enter an outdoor operation.[176] INS implementation of sanctions also gave southwestern employers and especially agribusinesses, where most undocumented laborers were employed, wide leeway, completing just over half of its inspection goals in its first two years (12,000 of a 20,000 goal of inspections in 1988 and 1989).[177]

---

174. Daniels, *Guarding the Golden Door,* 229.
175. The Immigration Reform and Control Act of 1986.
176. The Immigration Reform and Control Act of 1986.
177. Zolberg, *Nation by Design,* 373.

Neoliberal trade polices such as NAFTA devastated both Indigenous peoples and racialized groups throughout the Americas, making internal, regional, and international migration a survival strategy for people from Latin America and especially Mexico and Central America (and from the Global South),[178] and like immigration policy, channeling Latinx im/migrants into low-wage agricultural, food industry, and service jobs. NAFTA reduced or eliminated tariffs and opened Mexico to imports of US products, including agricultural goods, and reduced trade barriers and liberalized certain industries. Structural adjustment policies (SAPs) that began in the 1970s and picked up steam under Reagan crystalized under the Clinton administration.[179] Despite the positive, often multicultural rhetoric framing neoliberal policies as key to global prosperity for all, NAFTA bolstered only the US economy and big business in gendered, racialized terms. Mexico was required to cease protectionist agricultural policies that had allowed subsistence farmers to keep their own land as imported US goods flooded the market and wages and government spending on social services were cut. Within two years of NAFTA's implementation, over two million jobs were lost in Mexico.[180] Goldstein notes that "US-initiated neoliberal trade policies have reactivated and deepened particular imperial transits of racialization and Indigeneity in the Americas," rendering migrant farm labor nearly compulsory. Most farmworkers in states with large agricultural sectors are "Mexican and Central American migrants—often from Mixtec, Zapotec, or other Indigenous communities—who were farmers forced to seek work in the United States once neoliberal trade agreements undercut the viability of their own farms at home."[181]

As with Indigenous peoples and other racially marginalized groups, poverty rates among Latinxs are high, making Latinx im/migrants and especially women and the undocumented evermore vulnerable to labor exploitation in the food (and other) industries where they are employed, and to diet-related and other health disparities. Between 2007 and 2011 the highest national poverty rates were for AI/AN at 27 percent and Black Americans at 25.8 percent. Many Latinx groups had rates just below that but still higher than the overall US rate of 14.3 percent: Salvadorans and Cubans at 18.9 percent and 16.2 percent, respectively, and Mexicans and Guatemalans at about 25 percent, with similar rates among Puerto Ricans (25.6 percent) and Dominicans (26.3 percent). The white poverty rate was just 11.1 percent.[182] In terms of how

---

178. Toro-Morn and Alicea, *Migrations and Immigration*.
179. Steger and Roy, *Neoliberalism*, 55–56.
180. Heredia, "Downward Mobility," 34–40.
181. Goldstein, "Ground Not Given," 90.
182. Macartney, Bishaw, and Fontenot, "Poverty Rates."

this disproportionate impoverishment connects to labor exploitation, a 2008 survey of over 4,000 low-wage workers and labor law violations in three US cities found Latinxs and especially Latinx im/migrants suffered the highest number of workplace minimum wage violations at 32.8 percent overall, with 16.1 percent of the Latinx people surveyed US born, 35.1 percent foreign born, and 37 percent of the foreign born undocumented. In comparison, Black workers were at 19.1 percent, Asians at 15.1 percent, and whites at 7.8 percent. The minimum wage violation for foreign-born Latinxs at 35 percent was just over double the rate of US-born Latinxs and nearly 5 times the rate of US-born whites. Violations were also gendered, with Latina workers at a rate of 40 percent, and men at 24 percent. Violation rates for foreign-born workers were also concentrated among women.[183] In urban food industries and occupations, grocery stores violated minimum wage regulations at 23.5 percent; cooks, dishwashers, and food preparers suffered violations at a rate of 23.1 percent. Overtime violations were high in the food industries: 69.7 percent in restaurants and hotels; 65 percent in grocery stores; and 59.1 percent in food and furniture manufacturing, transportation, and warehousing. Occupational rates were at 77.9 percent for waiters, cafeteria workers, and bartenders and 67.8 percent for cooks, dishwashers, food preparers.[184]

Agribusiness is especially rife for employment abuses because farm work is not covered by other labor protections and employs a concentration of undocumented, racialized low-wage workers,[185] and by design US immigration and trade policy protects white property interests, not racialized workers. Of all US industries, agriculture has the highest share of undocumented workers,[186] who since the 1970s have continued to be disproportionately Latinx (while undocumented migration from Mexico has declined since the mid-2000s, undocumented migration from El Salvador, Guatemala, and Honduras has increased).[187]

---

183. Bernhardt et al., "Broken Laws, Unprotected Workers," 41–43.

184. Bernhardt et al., "Broken Laws, Unprotected Workers," 31; 34.

185. "US Labor Law for Farmworkers," Farmworker Justice, last updated 2023, https://www.farmworkerjustice.org/advocacy-and-programs/us-labor-law-farmworkers.

186. Jeffrey S. Passel and D'Vera Cohn, "Industries of Unauthorized Immigrant Workers," *Pew Research Center*, November 3, 2016, https://www.pewresearch.org/hispanic/2016/11/03/industries-of-unauthorized-immigrant-workers/.

187. Jeffrey S. Passel and D'Vera Cohn, "Unauthorized Immigrants Became a Smaller Share of US Foreign-Born Population," *Pew Research Center*, November 27, 2018, https://www.pewresearch.org/hispanic/2018/11/27/unauthorized-immigrants-became-a-smaller-share-of-u-s-foreign-born-population/.

As migration has become increasingly feminized,[188] the neoliberalization of foodways makes women and girls especially vulnerable to exploitation within as well as in crossing US borders. For instance, the informal economy of street-vending food in Los Angeles offers Latina immigrants flexibility that allows them to work and care for their families. In keeping with established gender norms that define the street as a space for men, women have carved out culturally acceptable feminine spaces in vending by selling only food.[189] At the same time, children may be forced to juggle work, school, and home responsibilities to help their family's business, working what Emir Estrada and Pierrette Hondagneu-Sotelo call the "third shift." Daughters often also experience unequal divisions of labor, particularly in food preparation labor gendered as feminine, and girls are vulnerable to sexism and sexual harassment from customers. Unlike children who work in formal-sector family ethnic enclave businesses such as Chinese and Korean restaurants, street-vending children also lack safety, protection, and respect from the larger society and government authorities.[190] This neoliberal food economy therefore renders Latina children multivalently precarious even as Latinas negotiate gendered expectations working in the masculine sphere of the street.

Neoliberal feedfights also imperil Latinx immigrant workers' health, particularly within agribusiness. Not surprisingly, low-wage food industry jobs do not provide health insurance and rarely provide paid sick leave. Along with the inherent precarity of undocumented status, this severely circumscribes low-wage and certainly immigrant workers seeking healthcare that they need in general and *because* of their jobs. As the League of United Latin American Citizens (LULAC) web page on health disparities notes, lower income workers are more likely to be exposed to noxious chemicals and physical hazards such as noise, heat, heavy lifting, long work hours, and unstable shift assignments, putting them at greater risk for injury. Overall, Latinxs have the highest rates of fatal work injuries. Agricultural labor puts workers and their families at a higher risk of illness and death from pesticides. Farm workers are also exposed to high rates of antibiotic-resistant bacteria due to consistent use of low-level antibiotics on livestock.[191] In 2004, Oxfam reported that globally farmworkers suffer elevated levels of chemical poisonings and illnesses, and a decades-long medical study also found that California's United Farmwork-

---

188. Toro-Morn, Guevarra, and Flores-González, "Introduction: Immigrant Women and Labor Disruptions," 3.

189. Munoz, "From Street Child Care to Drive-Throughs," 133–43.

190. Estrada and Hondagneu-Sotelo, "Living the Third Shift," 148–49.

191. "Latino Health Disparities," *League of United Latin American Citizens*, accessed August 2, 2023, https://lulac.org/programs/health/health_disparities/.

ers members had elevated rates of leukemia and cancers linked with pesticide exposure. Furthermore, US pesticide exposure standards are based on the adult male body, failing to consider the higher risks for pregnant female agricultural workers, which include spontaneous abortion and birth defects.[192] Thus, Latinx im/migrants' food industry work is functionally necropolitical in gendered terms.

As Latinx immigrants labor to provide other US Americans with food, food insecurity and hunger and diet-related health disparities are also disproportionately elevated among Latinxs. A 2007 study of Latinx migrant farmworkers in California, with 394 native Spanish-speaking respondents and 60 native Mixteco-speaking respondents, found 45 percent experienced food insecurity, with rates of food insecurity, hunger, and poor diet higher among marginalized groups such as undocumented workers, migrant workers, and native Mixteco speakers.[193] Diet-related illnesses are also prevalent: Latinxs have higher rates of obesity than non-Latinx whites.[194] Latinx adults are 70 percent more likely than non-Latinx whites to be diagnosed with diabetes, and in 2018 Latinxs were 1.3 times more likely than non-Latinx whites to die from diabetes.[195] In a recent poll, nearly one in five Latinxs said diabetes was the biggest health concern for them in their families. Diabetes also impacts Latinx children at higher rates, with Latinx children born today with a 50 percent chance of developing diabetes from main risk factors like obesity and physical inactivity.[196] A throughline from neoliberal polices like NAFTA to an obesity epidemic in Mexico is also evident: a 2017 *New York Times* article observed that neoliberal policy "transform[ed] the Mexican diet and food ecosystem to increasingly mirror those of the United States." In 1980, only 7 percent of Mexicans were obese. By 2016 that number tripled to 20.3 percent. Diabetes is now the top cause of death in Mexico, taking 80,000 lives a year, according to WHO.[197]

---

192. Oxfam, "Trading Away Our Rights: Women Working in Global Supply Chains," 27.

193. Wirth, Strochlic, and Getz, *Hunger in the Fields*.

194. "Profile: Hispanic/Latino Adults," US Department of Health and Human Services Office of Minority Health, last modified February 23, 2023, https://minorityhealth.hhs.gov/omh/browse.aspx?lvl=3&lvlID=64.

195. "Diabetes and Hispanic Americans," US Department of Health and Human Services Office of Minority Health, last modified March 1, 2021, https://minorityhealth.hhs.gov/omh/browse.aspx?lvl=4&lvlid=63.

196. "Latino Health Disparities," *League of United Latin American Citizens*, accessed August 2, 2023, https://lulac.org/programs/health/health_disparities/.

197. Andrew Jacobs and Matt Richtel, "A Nasty, Nafta-Related Surprise: Mexico's Soaring Obesity," *New York Times*, December 11, 2017.

Finally, public pedagogy about Mexican food also serves white possessive neoliberal empire-building. "Taco Tuesday" is a multicultural cultural institution; Mexican-themed fast food restaurants Taco Bell and Chipotle are wildly popular; and white US Americans have an appetite for "authentic" Mexican food. As Phil Deloria notes, Mexican food is a more palatable ethnic gift from Mexico then agricultural stoop labor, which clearly expresses social inequality, racism, and physical distance, yet the latter defines any authenticity in tortillas and frijoles.[198] Moreover, the widespread popularity of Mexican food coexists with widespread anti-Mexican and Latinx xenophobia, pointing to how the commoditization of "diverse" or "multicultural" products and especially foods does not translate to a welcoming, acceptance, or even tolerance of the human beings connected to those products any more than a predilection for cheap Latinx immigrant labor does. Feedfights against Latinx im/migrants, comprising gendered immigration and trade policy, labor exploitation, health disparities and bodily pathologization, and selective incorporation and intersecting with Indigenous dispossession sometimes explicitly, as in the fields of California, literally and metaphorically feed US neoliberal empire.

Feedfights against Asian immigrants as tactics of neoliberal empire also persist. In 2008 there were over 40,000 Chinese restaurants in the country, outnumbering US fast food giants McDonald's, Burger King, and KFC combined.[199] More recent industry statistics indicate that all of the McDonald's, Wendy's, Burger King, and other fast food giants like KFC, Arby's, and Taco Bell, must be combined to reach 40,000.[200] Chinese restaurants are thus more US American than "native" fast food restaurants, yet they continue to be targeted for immigration raids; the exploitation of Asian immigrant labor persists in food industries; and Asians continue to be rendered pathologically "foreign" through stereotypes about their "strange" and allegedly barbaric and unsanitary foods. For example, the casting of Asians as "savage" via the "dog eater" stereotype underpinned a 1989 California law that, following public outrage over an incident with two Cambodian immigrants, made it illegal to eat any animal kept as a pet or companion.[201] Extant panic about MSG, which Korean American celebrity chef David Chang emphasizes is a persistent form

---

198. P. Deloria, *Playing Indian,* 176–77.

199. J. Lee, *Fortune Cookie Chronicles,* 9.

200. Graber and Twilley, "United States of Chinese Food."

201. Soleil Ho, "Do You Eat Dog?," *Taste,* July 12, 2018, https://www.tastecooking.com/the-dog-question/; and Katherine Bishop, "California Journal; USA's Culinary Rule: Hot Dogs Yes, Dogs No," *New York Times,* October 5, 1989, section A, 22, https://www.nytimes.com/1989/10/05/us/california-journal-usa-s-culinary-rule-hot-dogs-yes-dogs-no.html.

FOOD, FARMING, FAT, AND NATIONAL(IST) DYSPEPSIA • 187

of anti-Asian racism,[202] and the common casting of Asian foods as "stinky" and disgusting endures as part of the throughline of weaponizing foods and smells against people of color and racialized immigrants: "Social hierarchies of power have been inscribed on bodies by categories created and maintained by other human senses besides sight, namely taste and smell."[203] While deodorization as a thread of white supremacy is perhaps most striking in 1950s movements to deodorize public spaces in connection to suburbanization as segregation,[204] it has long been grafted onto immigrants through their foods too. The stereotype that Italians and Greeks smelled like garlic was prevalent at the height of white ethnic xenophobia. Anti-Asian smell racism is still so common that Jenny Yang's "Bad Appetite" initiative invites people of color to bring "stinky" food to work to challenge it.[205] Recent children's books also challenge the food shaming that Asian American school children are often subject to because of their "stinky" and "gross" homemade lunches.[206]

In sum, to further US neoliberal empire, entangled gendered public pedagogies about Indigenous and racialized immigrant foodways transform economies and diets via land and agricultural dispossession and climate degradation, impoverishment, labor exploitation, and the diet-related sickening and pathologization of bodies. Tommy Orange eloquently states of contemporary Indigenous peoples, "Stray bullets and consequences are landing on our unsuspecting bodies even now."[207] This is an apt metaphor for and description of extant foodways pedagogies of empire that continue to imperil the bodies of Indigenous peoples and immigrants of color.

CONCLUSION: REVOLTING AGAINST NEOLIBERAL FOODWAYS

To resist neoliberal feedfights and neoliberal foodways pedagogies of empire, Indigenous peoples, racialized immigrants, and marginalized groups throughout the world formed food sovereignty movements, democratizing the

---

202. Paula Forbes, "Watch David Chang's MAD Talk on the Stigma of MSG," September 25, 2012, Eater, https://www.eater.com/2012/9/25/6542147/watch-david-changs-mad-talk-on-the-stigma-of-msg.

203. Padoongpatt, "Oriental Cookery," 189.

204. Classon, Howes, and Synnott, Aroma.

205. Demby and Bates, "Ask Code Switch," Code Switch podcast.

206. Ashia, "Don't Yuck My Yum: Kids Books That Dismantle Anti-Asian Racism & Food Shaming," Raising Luminaries: Books for Littles, May 1, 2017, last updated December 27, 2022, https://booksforlittles.com/orientalism-food-shaming/.

207. Orange, There There.

188 · CHAPTER 4

production, distribution, and consumption of culturally appropriate and nutritious food to address historical, structural injustices and their current manifestations in hunger, poverty, the unsustainability of industrial food production, and climate change.[208] I conclude with a brief discussion of some food sovereignty efforts to reclaim and reframe food, farming, and fat as avenues to decolonial and antiracist social justice. I also touch on an intersectional initiative to decolonize gendered body size and beauty ideals for Black, Indigenous, and other communities of color.

While understandings of and decisions about food sovereignty vary, it is a continuation of anti-colonial struggles and "consonant with a core set of principles (including women's rights, a shared opposition to genetically modified crops, and a demand for agriculture to be removed from current international trade agreements)."[209] The global food sovereignty movement was founded in 1996 by La Via Campesina, a transnational organization of peasants, to challenge the globalized, neoliberal model of agriculture that created economic policies and environmental damage that forced small-scale farmers into the global market economy as laborers.[210] At a 1996 conference in Tlaxcala, Mexico, La Via Campesina, a collective of small-scale farmers, introduced the concept of food sovereignty to counter the neoliberal food security movement, the latter of which sought to end global hunger only by continuing state and corporate control over food production and distribution and promoting agricultural practices that benefited transnational corporations and harmed small-scale farmers.[211] At the 2007 Nyéléni International Forum for Food Sovereignty held in Sélingué, Mali, the Nyéléni Declaration further defined food sovereignty as

> the right of peoples to healthy and culturally appropriate food produced through ecologically sound and sustainable methods, and their right to define their own food and agricultural systems. It puts the aspirations and needs of those who produce, distribute and consume food at the heart of food systems and policies rather than the demands of markets and corporations.[212]

Claims about rights and democracy, the cornerstones of liberal—and neoliberal—governance within the new language of "food sovereignty" was strategic

---

208. Mihesuah and Hoover, introduction to *Indigenous Food Sovereignty*, 9.

209. Grey and Patel, "Food Sovereignty as Decolonization," 431–44; 431.

210. "Food Sovereignty," US Food Sovereignty Alliance, accessed August 2, 2023, http://usfoodsovereigntyalliance.org/what-is-food-sovereignty/.

211. Patel, "What Does Food Sovereignty Look Like?," 665.

212. "Nyéléni Declaration on Food Sovereignty," 673.

when US neoliberal hegemony was unquestioned, and states refused to consider the problematic means by which food security would be achieved.[213]

Indigenous peoples with various foodways traditions connected with the food sovereignty movement's assertion that peoples should be able to define strategies and policies and develop food systems and practices that reflect their own cultural values around producing, consuming, and distributing food.[214] However, the movement's conceptualizations of sovereignty and "rights" occludes Indigenous peoples' "very particular cultural connections to land and the political relationships to settler-colonial governments."[215] The concept of sovereignty, after all, implies state authority and control, including the arbitration of "rights" from a colonial system predicated on ongoing Indigenous dispossession and domination over land.[216] Charlotte Coté (Tseshaht/Nuu-chah-nulth First Nation) asserts that "to indigenize the term sovereignty thus means reframing it within Indigenous people's struggles for autonomy, self-sufficiency, and self-determination rather than within assertions of domination, control, and authority over ancestral homelands."[217] As Devon Mihesuah and Elizabeth Hoover state, "Put simply, Indigenous food sovereignty 'refers to a re-connection to land-based food and political systems,' and seeks to uphold 'sacred responsibilities to nurture relationships with our land, culture, spirituality, and future generations.'"[218] (And therefore, it is not surprising that what is today understood as Indigenous food sovereignty has long if not always been key to various Indigenous decolonial struggles.[219])

Current examples of Indigenous food sovereignty efforts, which are pan-Indigenous, nation-based, community specific, and varied in method, reflect the belief among many Indigenous activists, scholars, medical professionals, and community members that, as Waziyatawin (Wahpetunwan Dakota from the Pezihutazizi Otunwe [Yellow Medicine Village]) asserts, to combat US empire "it is crucial that we re-institute land practices that re-connect us with our lands, that direct us back to our food sources, and that allow us to actively protect and defend the remaining integrity of our homelands as well as take action to restore lost integrity. [. . .] Our survival will depend on it."[220] "Feeding Ourselves" highlights efforts such as the Mvskoke Food Sovereignty

---

213. Patel, "What Does Food Sovereignty Look Like?," 665.
214. Coté, "'Indigenizing' Food Sovereignty," 8.
215. Mihesuah and Hoover, introduction to *Indigenous Food Sovereignty*, 11.
216. Barker, "For Whom Sovereignty Matters," 19.
217. Coté, "'Indigenizing' Food Sovereignty," 7.
218. Mihesuah and Hoover, introduction to *Indigenous Food Sovereignty*, 11.
219. Gilio-Walker, *As Long as Grass Grows*, 87.
220. Waziyatawin, "Paradox of Indigenous Resurgence," 74.

190 • CHAPTER 4

Initiative and the partnering of The Native Organizers Alliance (NOA), a project of the Alliance for a Just Society, with the Communities Creating Healthy Environments (CCHE). CCHE is a public health initiative focused on addressing the structural causes of childhood obesity, such as economic disadvantage, crime, food inequity, and lack of safe recreational spaces for children to play (as opposed to promoting healthy behaviors on an individual basis, a neoliberal "solution" that has had minimal health improvements in communities of color).[221] Seed revitalization projects are also prevalent. Diane Wilson (Rosebud Sioux) directs Dream of Wild Health Farm, one of many farms in which traditional Indigenous crops are grown in traditional and sustainable ways. In an interview on the *Gastropod* podcast, Wilson highlighted the aptly named "Cherokee Trail of Tears Poll Bean" crop. During relocation women sewed seeds into their clothing, preserving them even when their families and communities were starving. Seeds and the crops they generate are therefore a powerful remaining connection to Indigenous peoples' original homelands (and women's knowledge),[222] illuminating the interconnection of Indigenous food sovereignty, gender justice, and decolonization.

Chefs and cooks are also an important part of the Indigenous Food Movement (IFM).[223] Dina Gilio-Whitaker (Colville Confederated Tribes) emphasizes that "Indian 'survivance' has always been a matter of Native ingenuity aided by allies and accomplices working against the genocidal impulse of the State—sometimes within the State governmental structure itself but often outside it—in support of tribal self-determination." IFM, which includes some state and corporate partnerships (for instance, some funding for corporate food system projects filters down to Indigenous-run granting organizations such as the First Nations Development Institute, which provides tribal nations with grants) as well as tribal-nation and community-based efforts, "may be the epitome of these partnerships, with organizations born from, or at least influenced by, the environmental justice movement."[224]

In the Americas, examples of Indigenous revolt against neoliberalism centering or incorporating foodways—and at times im/migration and im/migrants—include the Zapatista Army of National Liberation. This Indigenous movement in Mexico has since 1994 linked local issues of racism, sexism, and economic inequality to neoliberal economic policies such as NAFTA and transnational organizations such as the World Trade Organization and challenged the Mexican state through armed and civil measures. Idle No More, founded in 2012 by three First Nations women in response to Canada's Bill

---

221. Echo Hawk Consulting, "Feeding Ourselves," 62–64.
222. Graber and Twilley, "What Is Native American Cuisine?," *Gastropod* podcast.
223. Mihesuah and Hoover, introduction to *Indigenous Food Sovereignty*, 18.
224. Gilio-Walker, *As Long as Grass Grows*, 88–90.

C-45, which eliminated many environmental laws and opened Indigenous lands to development, also necessarily encompasses decolonizing foodways.

Some US movements for im/migrant labor justice draw on the food sovereignty movement to address food industry labor practices, but racialized im/migrants remain largely outside of the food sovereignty movement per se. As detailed above, to profit agribusiness and other corporations, US immigration and labor policy isolates workers to exploit them. The neoliberal criminalization of undocumented migration exacerbates vulnerability to exploitation and other forms of violence. Many unions in the US labor movement, perceiving im/migrants of color as threats to "native" labor, and/or difficult to organize given the threat of deportation, also exclude them.[225] Therefore, as the particularities of im/migration and especially deportation pose unique threats to im/migrant laborers of color (and as US empire often positions them at odds with Indigenous peoples), numerous im/migrant organizations often fight for the rights of workers and against environmental racism, food insecurity, and health disparities within the framework of US law. Such efforts, varied and crucial to im/migrants' survival, are distinct from the food sovereignty movement and therefore beyond the scope of this analysis but are clearly complex and often overlap with Indigenous and peasant food sovereignty movement concerns, as exemplified by the exploitation of dispossessed, displaced, and often food-insecure Indigenous migrant laborers in US food industries. Suffice to say that Indigenous and global peasant food sovereignty movements and US im/migrant struggles for justice in relation to foodways are connected in their aims to challenge or navigate the white possessive logics of US neoliberal empire. Those connections are promising areas for the building of decolonial alliances, coalitions, and for further research.

Additionally, some community-based efforts to decolonize body size and beauty ideals explicitly confront together colonial and white supremacist foodways pedagogies of empire. Nalgona Positivity Pride (NPP) is a "grassroots movement dedicated to meeting the unique needs of Black, Indigenous, and communities of color (BICC) affected by eating disorders." Founded by Mexican American activist and public speaker Gloria Lucas in 2014, NPP, "drawing on indigenous matriarchal wisdom and punk influences," addresses the connections between historical violence, systems of oppression, and eating disorders to

> empowe[r] those who have been historically marginalized in the fight for body liberation & mental health equity. Refusing solely biomedicalized & oppressive healthcare, NPP is transforming the approach to eating disorder

---

225. Brent, Schiavoni, and Alonso-Fradejas, "Contextualizing Food Sovereignty," 618–35.

support using art, education, and activism. This new perspective challenges white cultural dominance and prioritizes cultural affirmation and community-building.[226]

NPP offers workshops and courses to individuals and healthcare providers and has a substantial social media following.

In conclusion, an array of uneven, entangled foodways public pedagogies have historically and into the neoliberal context furthered US empire, assuaging the white heteropatriarchal dyspepsia Indigenous peoples and populations of color provoke. And as historically, Indigenous peoples and racialized groups are, through various food sovereignty and other efforts rooted in or including foodways, resisting the use of foodways as a tool of white possession. In connecting these vexed matters of food, farming, and fat—that is, matters of corporal sustenance, size, and survival—this chapter reveals how, as part of a colonial throughline, foodways are essential to both the public pedagogy of US empire and revolting against it.

---

226. "About Nalgona Positivity Pride," *Nalgona Positivity Pride*, accessed December 27, 2023, https://www.nalgonapositivitypride.com/about-npp.

CONCLUSION

Queer Empire and the Public Pedagogy of Decoloniality

Like the partial, pixelated illumination cast by a spinning disco ball, historicizing Felipe Ortiz Rose's performances as "the Indian" in the Village People, the iconic disco group that targets a gay male audience, sheds some light on how public pedagogy about US American sexuality functions as a potent tool of US empire. Even when ostensibly queer and multicultural, as in the neoliberal context, policy and mainstream media sexuality discourses contain and manage Indigenous peoples and populations of color to further what Aileen Moreton-Robinson (Goenpul) calls the "white possessive logics"—assemblages of Indigenous dispossession, white supremacy, and heteropatriarchy—underpinning settler nations.[1] Consequently, decolonizing sexuality—and decolonization writ large—necessitates reterritorialization and horizontal solidarities. Following discussion of Rose and the Village People, I explore precolonial Indigenous traditions of gender and sexuality variance. I then trace the throughline of the entanglement of Indigenous dispossession and racialized anti-immigration via public pedagogies about sexuality from colonization into the ascendant neoliberal context, with careful attention to the selective incorporation of Indigenous, multicultural, and queer bodies and discourses as an important facet of neoliberal empire. I end with examples of Indigenous-led coalitional resistance to pedagogies of empire.

---

1. Moreton-Robinson, *White Possessive*.

194 • CONCLUSION

To no small extent, Rose's and the Village People's performances and catalog emblematize how public pedagogy about Indigeneity, race, gender, and sexuality exoticizes and appropriates, incorporating Indigeneity, populations of color, and/or queer people in distinct but entangled ways to further neoliberal empire. Rose's father was Lakota Sioux and his mother was Puerto Rican, and he identifies as gay. In the 1970s, he wore tribal regalia in homage to his Indigenous ancestry while working as a dancer and bartender in New York City nightclubs.[2] In 1977 producers Jacques Morelli and Henri Belolo recorded the first Village People album with Black American singer Victor Willis and professional background singers.[3] The name references New York City's Greenwich Village, one of a handful of cities that LGBTQ+ people migrated to en masse in the 1970s, seeking safety, belonging, and community,[4] and their songs feature suggestive lyrics. Responding to the album's popularity and demand for live appearances, Morelli and Belolo composed an actual group. They recruited Rose[5] and, inspired in part by his queer performance of a stereotypical, costumed Indigeneity (headdresses, war paint, etc.), populated the group with "macho" US archetypes—"Indian," cowboy, police officer, naval captain, soldier, construction worker, biker, and Leatherman. Morelli, who identified as gay, and Belolo, a straight ally, wanted the group to challenge homophobia in a provocative, subversive way.[6] The Village People, the first gay mainstream group, has sold millions of records and continues to perform.

Rose's performances with the Village People and as a solo artist cannot be reduced to a simple matter of costumed Indigenous affiliation, appropriation, or individual(ized) profiteering given his mixed Indigenous and Latinx heritage and deep investments in Indigenous and Latinx communities and cultures. (Though as I will discuss, the relationship between queer Indigenous peoples and queer people of color is sometimes fraught even as all are subject to the colonial-imperial forces of US empire.) Over the course of his lengthy career, Rose, who performed with the Village People until 2017, formed the Tomahawk Group record label, which focuses on contemporary Indigenous music, has won multiple NAMMYs (Native American Music Awards) for his

---

2. Hank Stuever, "Village Person Donates 'Y.M.C.A.' Record," *NBC News*, January 13, 2005, https://www.nbcnews.com/id/wbna6819496.

3. "A Great Concept . . . ," *Village People*, last updated 2022, https://www.villagepeople.com/history.html.

4. Jeff Perlman, "'Y.M.C.A.' (An Oral History)," Spotlight, *Spin*, May 27, 2008, https://www.spin.com/2008/05/ymca-oral-history/.

5. "A Great Concept . . ."

6. Frank Broughton, "Interview: Henri Belolo, Disco Producer and DJ," *Red Bull Music Academy*, April 13, 2016, https://daily.redbullmusicacademy.com/2016/04/henri-belolo-interview.

QUEER EMPIRE AND THE PUBLIC PEDAGOGY OF DECOLONIALITY • 195

solo work, and is a NAMMY Hall of Fame inductee.[7] In 2005 he donated the gold record for "Y.M.C.A."—one of the Village People's biggest hits, which from the 1990s had a second surge of popularity, becoming a wedding, party, and sporting events staple—to the National Museum of the American Indian (NMAI). Following initial misgivings, NMAI accepted the gift.[8] At the donation ceremony, which opened with a Lakota prayer and included dancing to "Y.M.C.A.," Rose, resplendent in a turquoise buckskin vest and Lakota-style hair plume, was enthusiastically welcomed with a birthday cake.[9] Rose also trained with the Ballet de Puerto Rico as a teen, has performed with Tito Puente and other Latinx groups, and sat on Indigenous and Latinx music organization boards. Rose and the Village People have also raised money for many charities, including organizations that support Native Americans.[10]

Simultaneously and as some Indigenous activists have noted,[11] Rose publicly performed and profited from a harmful colonial stereotype, and the Village People's hit song, "Go West," the title track of their fourth album (1979), baldly illustrates how queer modernities engender "settler homonationalism." Jasbir Puar defines homonationalism as the process through which whiteness and imperialism selectively incorporate US queer subjects to justify neoliberal projects at home and abroad, often at the expense of the most vulnerable groups (for instance, US military interventions into overtly anti-queer nations are justified as pro-LGBTQ+ actions).[12] Scott Lauria Morgensen, building on Puar's work, argues that queer politics create "settler homonationalism," which hinges on Indigenous dispossession by drawing on a universalized "Native" gender and sexual diversity for inspiration (primitivism) and predicating racialized queer citizenship, modernity, and the like on settled, stolen land (globalism).[13] "Go West" references the 1970s view of California as the preeminent site of Gay Liberation, a movement that often appropriated traditions of Indigenous gender and sexual diversity to advance mostly white lesbian and gay inclusion and belonging in the settler state. For example, media, usurping

---

7. "Hall of Fame," *Native American Music Awards,* 2022, https://nativeamericanmusicawards.com/hall-of-fame.

8. Teja Anderson, "Felipe Rose: Village People's Macho Man," *Living Media,* October 25, 2008, https://web.archive.org/web/20081231225538/http://livinginmedia.com/article/felipe_rose_village_peoples_macho_man.html; and Hank Stuever, "Celebrity Artifact: Felipe Rose, Village Person and Lakota, Donates 'Y.M.C.A.' Record to the Indian Museum," *Washington Post,* January 13, 2005, https://www.washingtonpost.com/archive/lifestyle/2005/01/13/celebrity-artifact/65ea7b22-1ac5-46ea-9637-49691f898ece/.

9. Stuever, "Celebrity Artifact."

10. Anderson, "Felipe Rose."

11. Stuever, "Celebrity Artifact."

12. Puar, *Terrorist Assemblages.*

13. Morgensen, "Settler Homonationalism," 105–6.

Indigenous and Muslim epistemologies, cast San Francisco and especially the Castro district as the "homeland" and "mecca" for queer people.[14] To be clear, the need for safe places for LGBTQ+ people was very real: violence against LGBTQ+ people in that very space, among others, was prevalent, with the 1978 assassination of Harvey Milk, the first openly gay elected politician, and what came to be termed "gay bashing" coming to fruition in San Francisco. Yet framing San Francisco as a queer homeland "ignores the genocide, deracination, and displacement of California's Indigenous peoples, in order for the very same lands and waters to become havens for other peoples fleeing oppression elsewhere."[15] (New York City, the site of the Stonewall Riots often heralded as the start of Gay Liberation, is Lenape land and similarly fraught.) While, as I will show, "a white and national heteronormativity formed by regulating Native sexuality and gender while appearing to supplant them with the sexual modernity of settlers," queer modernities too comprise "settler sexuality," including queer of color and queer migrant activism and critique that pursues settler state inclusion.[16]

"Go West," written by Morelli, Belolo, and lead singer Victor Willis, offers a similar pedagogy of empire to non-Native queer people. The song repurposes the nineteenth-century colonial imperative, widely attributed to *New York Tribune* founder and editor Horace Greely, to "Go West, young man," to invite queer people to seek settler citizenship on the West Coast. Thus the "kings of disco [. . .] took up the doctrine of manifest destiny on their own terms," creating a "gay anthem."[17] Settler homonationalism also underpins the album's other hit single, "In the Navy," a campy celebration of US naval militarism and imperialism. The Navy even considered using the song and a video shot with the group for recruitment purposes.[18]

While settler homonationalism surfaced in other instances of non-Native LGBTQ+ politics and performance in the ascending neoliberal context, biopolitical and territorial enforcements of heteronormativity, which names not an object choice but rather "entail[s] sexual and gender norms that are inextricable from racial, economic, and colonial logics that structure property relations, resource distribution, public/private distinctions, and the differential

---

14. Howe, "Queer Pilgrimage," 35–61.

15. Lee-Oliver et al., "Imperialism, Settler Colonialism, and Indigeneity," 251.

16. Morgensen, *Spaces between Us*, 31.

17. Harriet Fitch Little, "How the US Doctrine of Manifest Destiny Became the Gay Anthem 'Go West,'" *Financial Times*, June 26, 2017, https://www.ft.com/content/65131be4-5805-11e7-80b6-9bfa4c1f83d2.

18. Ed Vulliamy, "Everyday People," The Observer, *The Guardian*, November 11, 2006, accessed January 15, 2021, https://www.theguardian.com/music/2006/nov/12/popandrock8.

QUEER EMPIRE AND THE PUBLIC PEDAGOGY OF DECOLONIALITY · 197

valuation of people,"[19] were simultaneously predominant. Policy that used sexuality to advance white possessive neoliberal empire included governmental inaction and negligence regarding the AIDS crisis, which some queer activists and theorists viewed as a genocidal effort against gay men akin to systemic genocidal efforts against racialized groups.[20] A "modern" throughline of state coercion of heteropatriarchy as a mode of Indigenous dispossession is also evident from mid-twentieth century Termination and Relocation policy to Self-Determination policy that (re)rendered Indigeneity reprosexual and racial rather than geopolitical, and in some Indigenous nations' homophobic and anti-queer laws. Proximally, immigration policy explicitly banned LGBTQ+ migrants and privileged racialized reprosexual family reunification.

As in so many other instances, Indigenous communities (and communities of color and queer communities) challenged oppressive policies and politics, including those that appeared to be progressive. While in practice conversations about gender and sexuality were sometimes polemical, queer Indigenous people developed community-based modes of transnational decolonial resistance and revitalization that drew on precolonial Indigenous traditions of gender and sexual variance and diversity, strategically revising public pedagogy about Indigeneity, gender, sexuality, and often racism and migration as well. In the wake of earlier Termination policy that compelled urban migration and given the confluence of Self-Determination and Gay Liberation, in the 1970s many LGBTQ+ Indigenous people also migrated to cities, organizing "spaces of respect and support by and for Native GLBTQ people, even as they sought to educate non-Native and Native communities in GLBTQ people's existence."[21]

I have shown that in the often unexamined or understudied spheres of welfare, rape, and foodways, historically and into the neoliberal context, pedagogies of US empire crystalize in the gendered, sexualized entanglement of Indigenous genocide and dispossession, and racialized anti-immigration. Moreover, I have shown how, in tandem with media, "colonial regimes of control migrate from laws imposed on Indigenous Nations to regulations that govern immigrants"[22] and, as a white possessive strategy, often position Indigenous peoples and people of color antagonistically. I conclude the book with

---

19. Luibhéid, "'Treated neither with Respect nor with Dignity,'" 20.

20. Kiki Mason, "Manifesto Destiny: 'I am someone with AIDS and I want to live by any means necessary,'" *POZ Magazine* June–July 1996, Act UP, accessed on August 3, 2023, https://actupny.org/diva/CBnecessary.html#:~:text=here%20it%20is%3A-,%22I%20am%20someone%20with%20AIDS%20and%20I%20want%20to%20live,be%20helping%20people%20with%20AIDS.

21. Morgensen, "Unsettling Queer Politics," 135.

22. Lee-Oliver et al., "Imperialism, Settler Colonialism, and Indigeneity," 238.

198 • CONCLUSION

an analysis of how public pedagogy about understudied aspects of another tool of US empire, hegemonic American sexuality, positions Indigenous peoples, im/migrants of color, and queer people. I also consider instances of Indigenous, decolonial, coalitional knowledge production and praxis in and across various Indigenous spaces that migrate beyond (pun intended) the colonial and racial violences structuring US empire.

MORE THAN TWO: INDIGENOUS GENDER AND SEXUAL VARIANCE AND DIVERSITY

Prior to colonization of the Americas, many Indigenous nations systemically recognized gender and sexual variance and diversity (and as previously discussed, nonheteropatriarchal geopolitical kinship structures prevailed in many if not most Indigenous societies). *Living the Spirit: A Gay American Indian Anthology* (1988), compiled by members of one of the first community-based support groups for LGBTQ+ Native people, Gay American Indians (GAI), and edited by San Francisco–based white gay activist and writer Will Roscoe, was the first collection to examine gender, sexual diversity, and homophobia within Native communities. In 1987 the GAI History Project documented "alternative gender roles involving cross-gender or same-sex behavior" in over 135 North American tribes, showing that before colonization and into the early reservation period, gender and sexual variance and diversity was common in Indigenous societies. In the preface of the anthology, a continuation of GAI's queer decolonial recovery project, GAI cofounder Randy Burns (Northern Paiute) wrote, "For centuries before and after the arrival of Europeans, gay and lesbian American Indians were recognized and valued members of tribal communities."[23]

While systems, understandings, and expressions of gender and sexual diversity varied among Indigenous tribal nations, there are some commonalities. Generally, Indigenous epistemologies do not perceive gender and sex as binaries and instead "typically connote anything close to a gender identity as existing in a range of identities and, in many tribes, identification features are malleable and not fixed, not pure or impure in their biological form."[24] As part of kincentric relations with the natural world, Indigenous worldviews emphasize and appreciate transformation, ambiguity, and change. For instance, in numerous origin and didactic narratives humans and animals

---

23. Burns, Preface to *Living the Spirit*, 1; see also 217–22.
24. Lee-Oliver et al., "Imperialism, Settler Colonialism, and Indigeneity," 235.

QUEER EMPIRE AND THE PUBLIC PEDAGOGY OF DECOLONIALITY • 199

transform into each other, intermarry, and include human-animal hybrids. In some Indigenous societies, gender and sexual variance was therefore part of the transformation and fluidity endemic to nature.[25] Indigenous societies that recognized gender variance also often used specific terminology to refer to gender-variable persons, reflecting the institutionalized status of third, or third and fourth, genders.[26] A community's recognition of a person as gender diverse was determined by several factors, such as an individual's occupational preferences within a place-based gendered division of labor. For example, biologically female persons who took on the typical roles of biologically male persons might as children show interest in masculine occupations, as with Diné *nádleeh*. Biologically female Cocopa *warrhameh* played with cis boys, made arrows and bows for themselves, and hunted rabbits and birds.[27] Parents might make the decision to raise a favored child as gender diverse, or in connection to foodways. For instance, Inuit diets were mostly meat-based, and male-gendered people hunted. Inuit families and communities in need of additional hunters might raise daughters as sons. Other factors such as a vision calling a child to a gender-variant role and beliefs in reincarnation also shaped a family or community's decision to raise a child as gender variable.[28] Gender-variable people were important to their communities' sustenance and sustainability, arts, spirituality, healing, mediation, and warfare. They sometimes practiced specialized occupations and were believed to have special powers. Among the Achomawi, Klamath, Tolowa, and some Mohave, for instance, "men-women" were healers.[29] *Winkte*, recognized and respected members of Sioux communities, had special roles in religious ritual and childcare.[30] Additionally, classifications of sexual partner choice were based on the gender rather than the physical sex of partners, while gender and sexual taboos varied among Indigenous societies.[31] And a gender-variable person's gender and sexual expression was just one aspect of them rather than a defining and marginalizing trait, though to be clear, gender-variant and what we might call queer people were not universally recognized with a specific linguistic marker, honored, accepted, or raised "to be the way they are."[32]

---

25. Lang, "Native American Men-Women, Lesbians, Two-Spirits," 305.

26. Hall, "You Anthropologists Make Sure You Get Your Worlds Right," 273.

27. Lang, "Native American Men-Women, Lesbians, Two-Spirits," 305–6.

28. Lang, "Native American Men-Women, Lesbians, Two-Spirits," 306.

29. Lang, "Native American Men-Women, Lesbians, Two-Spirits," 307.

30. Lang, *Men as Women, Women as Men*.

31. See Williams, *Spirit and the Flesh*; Medicine, *Learning to Be an Anthropologist*; Rifkin, *When Did Indians Become Straight?*, 174; and Lang, "Native American Men-Women, Lesbians, Two-Spirits," 309–10.

32. Jacobs, Thomas, and Lang, introduction to *Two-Spirit People*, 5.

200 • CONCLUSION

In sum, Indigenous precolonial gender and sexual variance and diversity were entwined with specific Indigenous societies' geopolitical systems of sustenance, labor, kinship, health, and spirituality. Consequently, public pedagogies that criminalized Indigenous sexuality were crucial to the formation of US settler colonialism.[33]

QUEERING, QUEERNESS, AND CONQUEST

To establish and expand white possession, pedagogies of empire racially police gender and sexuality. This began with Indigenous peoples, and hegemonic discourses of sexuality are an ongoing axis of Indigenous dispossession. As Cathy Cohen powerfully argued, to great consequence people of color's failure to practice heteropatriarchal or conjugal domesticity is equated with a racial inclination toward perversity regardless of sexual object choice.[34] Euro-American colonial policy and discourse framed Indigenous peoples as "queer" to white civilization: the lack of heteropatriarchy and gender- and sexual-variant systems and persons especially evidenced Indigenous godlessness, debauchery, disorder, and incapacity for self-governance. Racialized queering and queerness therefore rationalized conquest and colonization.[35]

To justify sexualized violence against Indigenous peoples and colonial violence in general, from the start of European colonization of the Americas "explorers," travelers, missionaries, and colonial officials chronicled—usually with disdain and abhorrence—the absence of heteropatriarchy and presence of gender diverse persons and what they perceived as homosexual relationships in Indigenous societies. Regarding the former, the political importance of often nonheteropatriarchal and nonnuclear family and household formation was discounted as "official and popular narratives from the early Republic onward demeaned and dismissed the kinds of social relations around which native communities were structured, denying the possibility of interpreting countervailing cultural patterns as principles of geopolitical organization."[36] Regarding the latter, the distinct subject, the *berdache*, which in translation means "kept boys" or "boy slaves," originated in early European and British Orientalist accounts of perceived gender transgressions among Middle Eastern and Muslim men. The term also inflected early modern Spanish, French,

---

33. Denetdale, "Return to 'The Uprising at Beautiful Mountain in 1913,'" 69–98.

34. Cohen, "Punks, Bulldaggers, and Welfare Queens," 437–65.

35. Smith, *Conquest*; Smith, "Queer Theory and Native Studies," 43–65; and Rifkin, *When Did Indians Become Straight?*.

36. Rifkin, *When Did Indians Become Straight?*, 7.

QUEER EMPIRE AND THE PUBLIC PEDAGOGY OF DECOLONIALITY · 201

and British interactions with Indigenous peoples in the Americas, most often naming "male-bodied gender-different people."[37] *Berdache* and the societies that produced them were rendered sinful "and primitive," and "modern" Euromerican sexuality was comparatively defined as heteropatriarchal. The category indicated "a logic of sexual primitivity and civilization that created Indigenous people and colonists in relation to each other. In the process, colonial discourses of race and sexuality came to mark transgressive individuals and entire communities when they meted out spectacular death to educate Native peoples in the moral order of colonization."[38] Gendercide of gender-variant persons through overt violence was part of this early Euro-American settler colonialism.[39] (And as discussed in chapter 3, the rape of Indigenous women is a potent tool of white possessive empire-building).

As discussed in previous chapters, nineteenth-century pedagogies of empire were increasingly enforced by more administrative rather than overtly violent heteropatriarchal disciplinary regimes in US policy, agencies, missionary churches, and schools and reinforced in media. Under the Code of Indian Offenses (1883), a federal law adopted to address misdemeanors on reservations, dances and feasts, "medicine men" and other spiritual roles and practices, polyamory, and other customary Indigenous practices became illegal. Penalties included imprisonment, forced labor, and withholding rations.[40] Government "Indian agents" and missionaries used the code to destroy Indigenous sexual and marriage practices.[41] Punishment and humiliation of gender-diverse children and adults that functionally continued gendercide was also common. For example, in 1879 a local government agent forcibly stripped the last surviving Hidatsa *miati* (biologically male gender-variant person) of their feminine clothing and forced them to wear masculine clothing and cut off their braids.[42]

Moreover, the contemporaneous scientific pathologization of Indigenous gender variance enduringly shaped Euro-American understandings of sexuality and some Indigenous understandings as well. Foucault famously argued that homosexual identity and "the homosexual" as a category of person cohered in the nineteenth century as a new site for state discipline. As sexology developed as a "scientific" field of study, the category of the "invert," later

---

37. Gilley, *Becoming Two-Spirit*, 8.

38. Morgensen, *Spaces between Us*, 36–37.

39. Miranda, "Extermination of the Joyas," 253–84.

40. Code of Indian Offenses, Department of the Interior, Office of Indian Affairs.

41. Gilley, *Becoming Two-Spirit*, 14–15.

42. Bowers, "Hidatsa Social and Ceremonial Organization"; and Lang, "Native American Men-Women, Lesbians, Two-Spirits," 300.

the "homosexual," emerged as something akin to a third sex. Sexologists such as Havelock Ellis cited the presence and acceptance of gender variance and queerness in Indigenous societies as evidence of their primitivity and of the universal existence of "inversion" as a congenital defect.[43] Sexology cemented a link between "inversion," deviance, primitivity, white supremacy, and coloniality, building on the religious colonial pedagogical archive with science to queer Native peoples and people of color—and LGBTQ+ people of all races—to "civilization," justifying the ongoing policing of their sexuality, lives, and access to property and other resources. Indeed, the Euro-American conception of "sexuality" is colonial, presuming liberal individualism and divisions between public and private spaces.[44]

Queering all Indigenous peoples—often through the existence and societal acceptance of queer Natives and nonheteropatriarchal kinship/geopolitics—was thereby weaponized in a variety of ways to rationalize genocide and dispossession. Following more overt forms of early colonial sexualized violence, in the nineteenth century, colonization was carried out in and through policing intimate domestic spaces, destroying Indigenous forms of kinship and therefore politicality, governance, and territoriality. By the second half of the nineteenth century at the latest, the special roles and statuses of Indigenous gender-variant persons markedly declined.[45] Over time "heteropatriarchy has become so natural in many Native communities that it is internalized and institutionalized as if it were traditional."[46]

For example, Jennifer Nez Denetdale (Diné/Navajo) shows that despite previous resistance, matrilineality, the recognition of diverse genders, and k'e (the traditional Diné concept of belonging based on kinship), in the wake of colonization, Diné linked nationhood with heteropatriarchal notions of family, marriage, and sexuality and framed heteropatriarchy as "traditional."[47] Tradition is thus "not without political context,"[48] as with the Diné Marriage Act of 2005, which tried to enforce heteronormative marriage within the Navajo Nation, modeling its national sovereignty upon the US settler state.[49] Brian Gilley's ethnography of Two-Spirit men and social acceptance also chronicles negotiations of the identities "gay" and "Indian" given homophobia within

---

43. Ellis, *Studies in the Psychology of Sex.*
44. Rifkin, "Erotics of Sovereignty," 186.
45. Williams, *Spirit and the Flesh.*
46. Finley, "Decolonizing the Queer Native Body (and Recovering the Native Bull-Dyke)," 34.
47. Denetdale, "Return to 'The Uprising at Beautiful Mountain in 1913,'" 88.
48. Denetdale, "Chairmen, Presidents, and Princesses," 10.
49. Denetdale, "Carving Navajo National Boundaries," 289–94.

Indigenous communities, internalized homophobia, and racism against and within Indigenous communities.[50]

•

To further white possessive empire-building, the US immigration apparatus structurally positions some im/migrants similarly to Indigenous peoples, queering them as emblems of collective racial degradation[51] and positioning others as ideal or future settlers. The organizing of federal immigration control around sexuality and intersecting with gender, race, and class criteria also contributed to the production of modern US sexuality[52] as a tool of US empire. In addition to codifying differentially racialized tracks for exclusion, temporary labor, or heteropatriarchal settlement, turn-of-the-twentieth-century immigration policies and practices systemized bans on migrants perceived as threating to heteronormativity, including "sex workers; those deemed immoral; men who had sexual, erotic, and romantic relationships with other men; women who had sexual, erotic, and romantic relationships with other women; and anarchists, labor organizers, and political dissidents, among others."[53] Although terms such as "gay" and "queer" were not always used as an identity label by migrants who had "homosexual" relationships,[54] perception of migrants as queer and/or self-identification as LGBTQ+ has had marked consequences: "In the process of migration, LGBTQI people, especially those who are trans and gender non-conforming, face exacerbated risks of violence, policing, and containment at the hands of state and non-state entities."[55] With the Immigration and Nationality Act (1917), Congress expanded the Likely to Become a Public Charge (LPC; 1882) grounds for exclusion to include "persons of psychopathic inferiority" in connection with the category "mentally or physically defective." This codified sexologists' pathologization of LGBTQ+ people (or those perceived as such) as a form of border control. The term was the precursor to others immigration officials and courts, often in connection with public health officials, used to "medically" exclude LGBTQ+ migrants throughout the twentieth century.[56] Policing

---

50. Gilley, *Becoming Two-Spirit.*
51. Morgensen, *Spaces between Us,* 43.
52. Luibhéid, *Entry Denied,* xii.
53. Luibhéid, "'Treated neither with Respect nor with Dignity,'" 21.
54. Cantu, *Sexuality of Migration,* 21–22.
55. Chávez and Luibhéid, introduction to *Queer and Trans Migrations,* 3.
56. Poznanski, "Propriety of Denying Entry to Homosexual Aliens," 334.

im/migrants' sexuality according to racialized and heteronormative standards therefore worked co-constitutively with the policing of Indigenous peoples' sexuality to gatekeep the US as a white possessive territory.

As discussed in preceding chapters, media such as travel diaries, captivity narratives, and early cinema queered Indigenous peoples and the "frontier" where they resided through a focus on Natives' nonheteropatriarchal practices, both real and imagined. Proximally, racialized immigrants, the nations they hailed from, and the spaces they inhabited in the US (Chinatowns, for instance) were similarly queered in media, as in D. W. Griffith's silent film *Broken Blossoms or The Yellow Man and the Girl* (1919). The protagonist, Chinese immigrant Cheng Huan (played in "yellow face" by Richard Barthelmess), shelters a white woman (Lillian Gish) from her abusive father who ultimately causes her death attempting to rescue her from the "heathen." Cheng is portrayed as sympathetic to the extent that he is the desexualized and effeminized protector of the white woman (there is no sexual intimacy between them). However, homesick Cheng becomes addicted to opium (in a Chinatown, of course) and his relationship with the white woman leads to her death and his suicide. The film therefore taught spectators about the deadly risks of interracial relationships, people of color's inability to assimilate, and the queer abjection of racialized spaces.

Inaugural public pedagogy about sexuality in the US systemically and ideologically cast Indigenous peoples and racialized immigrants as queer threats to or at best incompatible with white heteropatriarchal possession. As such, the uneven policing of Indigenous peoples' and immigrants' sexuality—and the formation of normative US American sexuality in contrast to that of Indigenous peoples and people of color—was key to the territorially acquisitive project of US empire.

MID- TO LATE CENTURY MODERN SETTLER SEXUALITY

From the mid-twentieth century, US American sexuality continued to support white possessive US empire-building, pathologizing Indigenous peoples and racialized immigrants and comparatively producing "modern" or "settler sexuality." Although the wielding of pedagogies of empire about sexuality occurred most clearly through state impositions and coercions of heteronormativity, in ostensibly progressive institutions and communities, neoliberal pedagogies of empire incorporated queer modernities, queer people of color, and queer migrant activism and critique that pursues inclusion in the settler state.[57] Settler sexuality diversified to continue to accumulate and protect white property interests.

In terms of policy for Indigenous peoples, the Indian Reorganization Act (IRA; 1934), framed as a path to Indigenous autonomy and reversal of prior assimilationist policy through creating and supporting self-directed tribal economies, defined and legislated Indigeneity according to the heteronormative logics of allotment. Bureau of Indian Affairs (BIA) oversight over Indigenous affairs persisted, and the nuclear family, firm separation between public and private spheres, and privatization of land and resources continued to structure Native collectivity and governance.[58]

Termination and the urban migration it coerced unabashedly sought to obliterate tribal nations, lands, governance, and any remaining nonheteropatriarchal epistemologies and practices. This included gendered relocation of Native peoples from rural reservations to urban areas. In 1951 BIA Commissioner Dylan S. Myer (who also oversaw Japanese internment, another explicitly white possessive law) initiated a relocation program to certain cities. Government funds incentivized diaspora and displacement: the mostly cis male relocatees received a one-way bus ticket to a city with a field office such as Chicago, Denver, or Los Angeles, and food and housing expenses for one month. It was assumed that men would bring their (nuclear) families with them or send for them later. Meanwhile development on tribal lands was disincentivized by the precarity created and/or exacerbated by termination policies and the lack of work on or near reservations.[59] (Incidentally Felipe Rose's father moved to New York from "near the site of the Wounded Knee massacre"[60] in the 1940s, part of a wave of Indigenous people migrating for construction work. Given the timing, that migration may have been connected to impending termination.[61]) While only 31,000 of the 120,000 people who left reservations for cities between 1940 and 1960 received federal relocation funding, suggesting that many Indigenous people moved for other reasons such as unemployment, the 1976 American Indian Policy Review Commission report found the US government used relocation to terminate its trust responsibility to Indigenous peoples.[62] At the same time, in pushing Indigenous peoples

---

57. Morgensen, *Spaces between Us*, 31.

58. Rifkin, *When Did Indians Become Straight?*, 41.

59. Rifkin, *When Did Indians Become Straight?*, 248–49; 259; 264.

60. Vulliamy, "Everyday People."

61. Stuever, "Celebrity Artifact."

62. Rifkin, *When Did Indians Become Straight?*, 264; *American Indian Policy Review Commission: Final Report, Task Force No. 9, Law Consolidation, Revision And Codification*, 7.

into urban spaces, US termination policy also helped create the conditions for the formation of queer Indigenous communities and decolonial revitalization and resistance.

Self-Determination policy, framed as a reversal of termination and relocation policy, continued to wield sexuality as a tool of white possessive empire. As discussed previously, the Indian Child Welfare Act and *Oliphant v. Suquamish Indian Tribe* (1978) rendered Indigeneity racial/reprosexual rather than geopolitical as "a means of differentiating tribes from other populations but in ways that do not undermine the authority of the US government to superintend them and to assert the a priori internality of Indigenous territory with respect to the settler state."[63]

●

Discourse about sexuality in roughly concurrent US immigration policy and policing also furthered the white heteropatriarchal property interests underpinning US empire. Alongside and sometimes as part of the midcentury racialized immigration policy and policing examined throughout this book, the Immigration and Naturalization Service (INS) and the Public Health Service (PHS) implemented anti-queer policy and policing.[64] The McCarran–Walter Act (1952), in accordance with increasing Cold War tensions and conflation of anti-Communist and anti-queer politics, banned from entry those deemed "subversive" and "aliens afflicted with psychopathic personality, epilepsy, or mental defect," phrasing designed to include LGBTQ+ immigrants.[65] In the Congressional debates preceding the passing of the law, a Senate Judiciary Committee report recommended adding "homosexuals and other sex perverts" to the list of medically excludable aliens. After consulting with PHS on the difficulty of substantiating a diagnosis of homosexuality, the finalized bill used the phrase "psychopathic personality and mental defect." As PHS suggested, it was broad enough to provide for the exclusion of homosexuals and sex perverts.[66] As previously discussed, while the McCarran–Walter Act ended Asian exclusion and removed race as a bar to immigration, it continued to favor white Northern European immigration by maintaining 1920s national

---

63. Rifkin, "Around 1978," 179. On blood quantum, see TallBear, *Native American DNA*.

64. Poznanski, "Propriety of Denying Entry to Homosexual Aliens," 331–59.

65. Swetha Sridharan, "The Difficulties of US Asylum Claims Based on Sexual Orientation," *Migration Policy Institute*, October 29, 2008, https://www.migrationpolicy.org/article/difficulties-us-asylum-claims-based-sexual-orientation#:~:text=A%201965%20amendment%20contained%20more,the%20Immigration%20Act%20of%201990.

66. 82 Cong. Rec. S.1137 (1951); and Poznanski, "Propriety of Denying Entry to Homosexual Aliens," 334–35.

origins quotas. Anti-Semitism and discomfort with "indigestible blocs" of white ethnics were also explicit in McCarran's Congressional defense of the law,[67] making it another clear example of the coloniality, white supremacy, and heteropatriarchy structuring the public pedagogy of US empire.

The ostensibly antiracist watershed 1965 Immigration and Nationality Act (INA) made heteronormative family reunification the cornerstone of US immigration policy, and racial exclusion persisted in the intent if not the outcome of the policy. While ending nation-based quotas, lawmakers assumed most family reunification slots would be filled by Eastern and Southern Europeans (the "white ethnics" fully incorporated into white possession at this point). However, slots were filled by mostly Asian and Latinx immigrants. The law also more explicitly barred LGBTQ+ immigrants, adding "sexual deviation" as grounds for exclusion to make the intent of Congress to exclude LGBTQ+ immigrants abundantly clear.[68] Although the American Psychiatric Association (APA) removed homosexuality from its list of mental illnesses in 1973, and PHS denied INS medical certification as the basis for LGBTQ+ immigrant exclusion in 1979, INS continued to exclude LGBTQ+ immigrants under INA's "sexual deviation" clause. Courts had varied responses to INS's exclusion of LGBTQ+ migrants without medical certification.[69]

While appearing to be somewhat more inclusive, pedagogies of empire about sexuality persisted in neoliberal immigration policy and in popular culture. The 1986 Immigration Reform and Control Act (IRCA) included an amnesty program that, while framed by lawmakers and in media as a humanitarian watershed, captured a pool of disproportionately Mexican male laborers. Additionally, IRCA maintained heterosexual family reunification as the cornerstone of immigration policy despite some lawmakers' straightforwardly gendered, racist objections to the increase in Latinx and Asian immigration under INA. Family-sponsored migration also created the largest group of "unskilled workers," increasing im/migrant laborers' precarity,[70] as did increased militarization of the US–Mexico border. Racialized anti-immigration and labor exploitation worked hand in glove with heteronormative multicultural politics of recognition/inclusion to make IRCA emblematically neoliberal immigration policy.[71] Along similar lines, while INA's sexual deviation clause was overturned in the 1990 Immigration Act (and 1990s policy began

---

67. 83 Cong. Rec. S.518 (1953).

68. Immigration and Nationality Act of 1965, Pub. L. 89-236, 79 Stat. 911 (1965); and Poznanski, "Propriety of Denying Entry to Homosexual Aliens," 338.

69. Poznanski, "Propriety of Denying Entry to Homosexual Aliens," 331–32.

70. Reddy, "Asian Diasporas, Neoliberalisms, and Family."

71. Perry, Cultural Politics of US Immigration.

to include gender and sexuality as loci of persecution and therefore grounds for asylum or refugee status), ever-increasing neoliberal border militarization and illegalization, detention, and deportation continued to make LGBTQ+ migrants especially precarious. Into the present day, LGBTQ+ migrants, especially when they are trans women of color coming from Latin America or the Caribbean and/or are poor, are especially vulnerable to violence in the countries from which they came and during crossing, from the state and individuals or gangs. Upon arrival in the US, they are also hypervulnerable to being detained and abused and/or neglected in detention and to "being pushed into homelessness, survival sex work, and the underground economy." Additionally, HIV-positive migrants are particularly vulnerable to violence and neglect, especially in jurisdictions that criminalize HIV-positive status, and they frequently struggle to access healthcare in detention. Sexual abuse, especially of transgender women, is rampant in detention centers.[72] And yet, the selective inclusion of some LGBTQ+ people or im/migrants in the state bolsters US empire: public pedagogy that frames sending nations as homophobic and therefore "backward" justifies the imperial coercion of migrant labor and/or US military intervention. Thus, settler homonationalism and hetero- and homonormative multicultural politics of recognition occlude the ongoing Indigenous dispossession, racialized anti-immigration, heterosexism, and economic exploitation driving US neoliberal empire.

In these ways, mid- and especially late twentieth century public pedagogies about sexuality continued to police Indigenous peoples and im/migrants as a tool of US empire. Moreover, efforts to gatekeep the US as a white possessive space via sexuality have been exacerbated rather than alleviated or mitigated by ostensibly evermore progressive public pedagogy. Jodi Byrd (a citizen of the Chickasaw Nation of Oklahoma) emphasizes that "liberalism is designed to maintain settler colonialism through dialectical and competing modes of inclusion and exclusion." Neoliberal biopolitics "expand access only to ensure incorporation as non-transformation," effectively managing racial, gender, and Indigenous differences.[73] This is always-already territorial, what Byrd describes as a

> movable frontier now figured as the cauldron of integration. Matters of race, subjectivity, and citizenship are only temporarily resolved so that boundaries and borders can be established, violated, and exceeded in a never-ending push toward a civil and civilizing horizon. In this process, however, indige-

---

72. Luibhéid, "'Treated neither with Respect nor with Dignity,'" 29–30.
73. Byrd, "*Loving* Unbecoming," 208.

QUEER EMPIRE AND THE PUBLIC PEDAGOGY OF DECOLONIALITY · 209

neity collapses into race and is then supposedly remediated through a racial liberalism that offers incorporation into the imperial nation as the fulfillment of humanity's struggle against oppression.[74]

•

In the shadow of ascending neoliberal policy and policing, in scholarship and media created in "small-p" progressive academic and queer countercultures, respectively, Indigenous gender and sexual diversity was appropriated and instrumentalized to make a case for settler citizenship. Proximally, an idealized heteropatriarchal nuclear immigrant family, which selectively included "diverse" families of color, became a fixture in popular culture, together furthering white possession *as part of* the liberal zeitgeist of the late twentieth century.

Morgensen meticulously chronicles how mid- to late twentieth-century gay and lesbian anthropology and queer assimilationist and radical activists embraced the colonial category *berdache* to redefine sexual minorities' "nature and purpose as an indigenized minority ready for integration into settler freedom," particularly for white men.[75] For example, Harry Hay and the Mattachine Society, founded in 1950 as the first US advocacy organization for sexual minority rights, used "emancipationist discourse on berdache as a model for modern social acceptance of sexual diversity" with "white men argu[ing] on behalf of all sexual minorities that their civil rights and national belonging were affirmed by the berdache."[76] Gay and lesbian radicals such as the Radical Faeries also universalized and instrumentalized Indigenous gender and sexual variance to challenge heteropatriarchal capitalism, racism, and imperialism. Like earlier back-to-nature gay and lesbian collectives, the Faeries, formed in 1979, coded rural space as "Native." Non-Natives could connect with their "primitive" queer natures through rituals allegedly rooted in Indigenous traditions, as with evocations of queer "shaman," and return to their often urban homes rejuvenated and perhaps enlightened.[77] As in the broader counterculture, queer academic and activist appropriations of Indigenous spirituality granted queer non-Natives connection with but no accountability to Indigenous peoples and decolonization—a potentially guilt-free way for them to

---

74. Byrd, "*Loving* Unbecoming," 211.
75. Morgensen, *Spaces between Us*, 45.
76. Morgensen, *Spaces between Us*, 48.
77. Morgensen, *Spaces between Us*, 128–31.

210 • CONCLUSION

"play Indian"[78] while accessing and furthering the white property interests underpinning neoliberal empire.

Mainstream pedagogies of empire also began fetishizing and commodifying queer Indigeneity even before the Village People urged LGBTQ+ people to "Go West." Popular revisionist Western and antiwar film *Little Big Man* (1970) was directed by Arthur Penn and based on the eponymous 1964 novel by Thomas Berger. Given contemporaneous high profile Indigenous decolonial activism and policy changes, mainstream audiences were primed to perceive Indigenous peoples as US citizens, ecologists/mystics, and heroic antiestablishment warriors, allowing non-Native filmmakers such as Penn to "use sympathy toward and notoriety of the Native American to entertain" and to make their own political statements.[79] In the satire, in a series of narrated flashback vignettes 121-year-old white man, Jack Crabb / Little Big Man (Dustin Hoffman) narrates his life among Indigenous peoples and Euro-Americans during imperial conquest of the West. Adopted by the Cheyenne as a young pioneer child following a Pawnee wagon train attack, he has an idyllic childhood. He is then "rescued" by US soldiers and returned to white society where he tries on numerous white identities. After once again "going West" in the Greely sense, he returns to the Cheyenne, who are eventually massacred by US calvary. He then becomes a hermit in the wilderness and is the sole white survivor of Custer's Last Stand. Lest there is any confusion who spectators should sympathize with, the Cheyenne refer to themselves as the Human Beings, whereas whites are depicted as glibly violent, amoral, duplicitous, hypocritical, and greedy; Custer is insane, a departure from most other previous filmic representations of him as a hero; and the Cheyenne massacre is an allegory for US militarism in Vietnam.

The film, which met with mixed reviews from Indigenous scholars,[80] arguably went further than others at the time in attempting to accurately represent some Cheyenne traditions, casting some Indigenous people in some Indigenous roles, and clearly depicting Natives as the heroes. *Little Big Man* also featured nuanced depictions of Indigenous and Indigenized gender and sexual variance.

---

78. P. Deloria, *Playing Indian,* 156–57.

79. Kilpatrick, *Celluloid Indians,* 77.

80. Vine Deloria Jr. (Standing Rock Sioux) critiques the film's representation of Indigenous passivism in the face of white colonial violence, among other things ("American Indian Image in North America," xii). Rebecca Kugel (Ojibwe and Shawnee), on the other hand, argues that the counternarrative of the West "satirized nearly all the 'Indian movie' conventions" and ultimately "asserts that America was built on economic rapacity justified in the name of white racial and male sexual hierarchy" ("Little Big Man [1970]," 80, 82).

Little Horse (Robert Little Star), Jack's childhood friend, became a *heme-nah,* a gender-different person. As a child, Little Horse, lacking the temperament for warfare, preferred to stay behind with the women, which Crabb narrates, "was all right with the Human Beings." Reflecting on reuniting with his childhood friend upon returning to the Cheyenne, Crabb says Little Horse had "become a *hemane,* for which there ain't no English word. And he was a good un' too. The Human Beings thought a lot of him." In precolonial Cheyenne society a *hemenah's* third-gender status or gender neutrality made them respected "go-betweens." They bridged personal and spiritual gaps between cis men and cis women, providing, for instance, courtship and marriage services.[81] The film therefore represents Indigenous gender variance with some accuracy, emphasizing the Human Beings' acceptance of and respect for gender-variant persons and the lack of an English translation for the Cheyenne word for gender-variant persons. This also counteracts contemporaneous attempts to equate Indigenous gender and sexual variance to homosexuality or LGBTQ+ identity in academic and activist communities and instrumentalize it.

Yet the film ultimately affirms public pedagogy about sexuality that serves US empire with its abundance of hackneyed stereotypes of "Indian savagery," primitivism, and mysticism, as well as historical inaccuracies and problematic gender and sexual politics. In terms of the former, the Pawnee are represented as bloodthirsty savages; the Cheyenne use sticks in battle against the US military, casting them as unsophisticated at best; Chief / Little Big Man's adoptive grandfather, Old Lodge Skins (Chief Dan George), has prescient dreams and visions. In terms of the latter, while some of the male Native characters are developed and complex, Native women are two-dimensional, "naturally" sexual, and connected to the natural world. White women are also the butt of an array of misogynistic jokes. Polygamy, which Crabb embraces at the insistence of Sunshine (Amy Eccles), his first Indigenous wife, a "hippie-like child/woman of nature enmeshed in the earth around her,"[82] is presented as unprecedented among the Cheyenne. Yet traditional Cheyenne society included monogamous and polygamous marriages.[83] Moreover, Custer's calvary kills Crabb's wives and all their children (another example of the death of the "primitive" Celluloid Indian Maiden) along with nonheteropatriarchal kinship and Indigenous futurity,[84] so that white possessive US empire can thrive. As Phil Deloria (Dakota) notes, while Indigenous peoples in the film are generally depicted as "flexible boundary hoppers with multiple modes and

---

81. Gilley, *Becoming Two-Spirit,* 11; and Kugel, "Little Big Man (1970)," 81.
82. Marubbio, *Killing the Indian Maiden,* 180–82.
83. Grinnell, *Cheyenne Indians.*
84. Marubbio, *Killing the Indian Maiden,* 183.

meanings [. . .] funny, smart, and sexy," spectators are positioned to identify with the "white-Indian" protagonist and *his* crossing of the boundaries of race, gender and sexuality, and nation.[85] Furthermore, the "white Indian" survives and lives to an absurdly old age as the Cheyenne and their queer gender and sexual politics and practices vanish. Within this larger plot, the film's portrayal of Indigenous and *Indigenized* gender and sexual variance exemplifies liberal and "progressive" non-Natives' claiming of queer Indigeneity—and Indigenized oppositional political culture—for themselves, advancing rather than challenging pedagogies of empire that in the neoliberal context incorporate queerness and multiculturalism to an extent.

While no parallel mainstream media representations of queer im/migrants were produced at this time, media that idealized immigrant heterosexual nuclear families abounded, particularly in the 1980s during debates about IRCA, and the AIDS crisis in the 1990s, as a key part of neoliberal multicultural politics of recognition. In a host of TV shows and films, from *Who's the Boss* and *Golden Girls* to *Greencard* and *Moscow on the Hudson,* the modern, ideal immigrant subject was fetishized as self-sufficient, hardworking, heterosexual, and part of or seeking to build a nuclear family, and usually white. Fetishization of some immigrant families of color and especially Asian "model minority" nuclear families also gained traction in the popular news media of the day.[86]

Some mainstream media and academic and activist discourses about queer im/migrants and queer people of color that instrumentalized Indigeneity also functioned as settler homonationalist pedagogies of empire, though how and to what extent varied. In academic and activist pedagogies, Indigeneity was sometimes treated problematically. Although "queer migration analyses and activisms require critically engaging settler colonialisms and Native American and First Nations' sovereignty," they rarely do.[87] Women of color feminism, cohering in the late twentieth century at the "interstices between ethnic and indigenous studies, race-based social movements, and indigenous sovereignty movements, on the one hand, and feminism and the women's movement, on the other,"[88] generated groundbreaking knowledge production and praxis and often included Indigenous feminists. For example, the anthology *This Bridge Called My Back* (1981), edited by Chicanx queer feminists Gloria Anzaldua and Cherrie Moraga, centers on themes of interdependence and building bridges and alliances across differences. This text and other women of color feminist

---

85. P. Deloria, *Playing Indian,* 161.

86. Perry, *Cultural Politics of US Immigration.*

87. Lee-Oliver et al., "Imperialism, Settler Colonialism, and Indigeneity," 226.

88. Hames-Garcia, "What's after Queer Theory?," 386.

QUEER EMPIRE AND THE PUBLIC PEDAGOGY OF DECOLONIALITY · 213

work has influenced queer Indigenous knowledge production and activism. Yet tensions and debates arose around Chicanx claiming Indigenous roots, the distinctiveness of Chicanx and Indigenous racialization in the US and Mexico, and Chicanx nationalism superseding Indigenous sovereignty.[89] Anzaldua's borderlands theory, for example, challenges colonialism and white supremacy by rejecting the pejorative racialization of *mestizo/a* identities (*mestizaje* translates as "mixing" and refers to the racialized blending of European colonizers and Indigenous peoples in what is now Mexico), celebrating Chicanx indigeneity, and calling for intersectional alliances and coalitions.[90] She also casts Indigenous peoples and Europeans in a conflictual binary (primitive vs. rigid and intolerant of sexual difference, respectively) rectified with the modern border-crossing *mestizaje*.[91] Additionally, Anzaldua's evocation of Aztec culture in her *mestizo/a* nationalism aligns with Mexican state efforts to promote an ancient Mexican pan-Indigeneity as nationalism, occluding settler colonialism and living Indigenous peoples. Alongside her incredibly valuable, seminal contributions to radical intersectional scholarship and justice, Anzaldua's pursuit of an emancipatory queer Chicanx identity affirms US and Mexican settler colonialism.[92]

Additionally, some more recent queer of color / queer migration critique instrumentalizes Indigeneity by valorizing a complex, mature diasporic or mixed, hybrid queer subject juxtaposed against a primitive, simple Indigenous subject and overlooks settler colonialism and Indigenous dispossession. For example, often the noncitizen refugee or immigrant of color queers the heteronormativity of the state. This fails to recognize that not all peoples are in a postcolonial relationship to the state and that for Indigenous peoples nationhood/nationalism is a distinct, territorial or landed matter that, prior to colonization, often *held space* for gender and sexual variance and nonheteropatriarchal and nonhomonormative kinship in general.[93]

Inadvertently reproducing Indigenous dispossession is also prevalent in queer migrant activism. Monisha Das Gupta observes that legalization and a pathway to citizenship as the goals of the im/migrant rights movement are rarely questioned, except within some radicalized migrant-led spaces. Moreover, policy proposals supported by the mainstream im/migrant rights movement link legalization to increased interior enforcement and border

---

89. Morgensen, "Unsettling Queer Politics," 140; and Contreras, *Bloodlines*.

90. Anzaldua, *Borderlands*.

91. Smith, "Queer Theory and Native Studies," 49–50; and Anzaldua, *Borderlands*.

92. See Saldana-Portillo, *Revolutionary Imagination*; and Morgensen, *Spaces between Us*, 181.

93. For critique of queer of color / queer migration theorization, see Smith, "Queer Theory and Native Studies," 56–58; and Morgensen, *Spaces between Us*, 178–79.

militarization. This puts migrant communities and especially queer migrants at greater risk of harm and violence and threatens "the self-determination and territorial integrity of borderland Native American tribal governments."[94] Simultaneously, mainstream LGBTQ+ organizations tend to include immigration issues only in relation to same sex marriage, normalizing what kinds of kinship deserve protection and incorporation. Das Gupta also points out that through "settling stories," immigration justice struggles reinscribe "genocidal American exceptionalism," as with the pro-immigration framing of the US as a "nation of immigrants" and portrayal of young undocumented people as estranged from their homeland.[95] Some queer youth in antideportation struggles reject the hegemonic assimilative tropes common in pro-im/migration discourse, skeptical about belonging in a colonized space, focusing instead on imagining and opening up spaces for queer borderless futures, as with some Undocuqueer projects.[96] However, tension with Indigenous justice remains prevalent given distinctly Indigenous understandings of territoriality, land, nationalism, and borders and their significance to Indigenous decolonial struggles. As Leece Lee-Oliver (Blackfeet/Choctaw/Cherokee/Wyandot) points out, finding a sense of belonging and place in a colonized space requires perpetually defending that belonging, and any defense that does not consider Indigenous peoples is a stance of oppression.[97]

In sum, the throughline of the public pedagogy of US American sexuality as a tool of white possessive empire-building requires moving bodies and rationalizing that movement: dispossessing/relocating Indigenous peoples; displacing, excluding, and/or exploiting the labor of racialized im/migrants while regulating the domestic spaces of both groups; and supporting/incentivizing white and select nonwhite settlers to occupy, cultivate, and commodify stolen Indigenous lands. Public pedagogy about modern sexual identities and politics, including liberal, more inclusive, ostensibly progressive policy, scholarship, activism, and media, also furthers US neoliberal empire through the fundamentally territorial multicultural politics of recognition and settler homonationalism. This might be understood as the public pedagogy of queer empire.

However, in the late twentieth century, Indigenous activists and scholars engaged non-Native queer and multicultural modernities to form pragmatic, enduring, coalitional critiques of US empire and its many tools. Indigenous coalitional public pedagogies of decoloniality remade and reterritorialized US American sexuality, and the US itself.

---

94. Lee-Oliver et al., "Imperialism, Settler Colonialism, and Indigeneity," 226–27.
95. Lee-Oliver et al., "Imperialism, Settler Colonialism, and Indigeneity," 226–27.
96. White, "Documenting the Undocumented," 976–97.
97. Lee-Oliver, "Imperialism, Settler Colonialism, and Indigeneity," 247.

QUEER INDIGENOUS HUBS AND MIGRATING
BEYOND QUEERING EMPIRE

Rayna Ramirez's work shows how Indigenous peoples negotiate settler diasporas by forming "Native hubs" where they reconnect with tribal identities while forming pantribal solidarities.[98] In the wake of termination, urban relocation, and migration, in the late twentieth century queer Indigenous people formed transnational networks in cities and at gatherings across US and Canadian borders, and they distinguished themselves from and within non-Native sexual minority politics. These new queer Indigenous organizations created and dispersed decolonial public pedagogies through educational booths at powwows, testimonials in Indigenous media, working with Indigenous health agencies to address HIV/AIDS, and other initiatives to educate civic agencies and the broader LGBTQ+ community on historical and contemporary Indigenous gender and sexual diversity.[99] LGBTQ+ Indigenous activists, scholars, and writers also produced texts about Indigenous understandings and practices of gender and sexuality in and across different Indigenous spaces (urban, rural, reservation, and nation; past and present) and often dialogically addressed the erasure and/or appropriation of Indigenous gender and sexual variance and lack of support for contemporary queer Natives in non-Native spaces.[100]

GAI, founded in San Francisco in 1975 by Randy Burns (Northern Paiute) and Barbara Cameron (Lakota Sioux), was one of, if not the first, support group for queer Indigenous people. GAI's work was grounded in the notion that given Indigenous cultural traditions of gender and sexual diversity, contemporary LGBTQ+ Natives should be accepted and welcomed in Native communities. GAI also sought to educate non-Native queers about those traditions while avoiding absorption into sexual minority politics. Actions included collaboration with urban Indigenous activist and service groups, outreach at regional events like powwows and rodeos, promoting Indigenous inclusion in mainstream gay politics and events such as pride parades, and raising awareness of queer Indigenous people in mainstream media.[101] As mentioned above, the GAI History Project also led to the groundbreaking *Living the Spirit: A Gay American Indian Anthology* (1988). While the book was to an extent organized around the term and concept of the *berdache,* soon

---

98. Ramirez, *Native Hubs.*

99. Gilley, *Becoming Two-Spirit,* 26–29.

100. For example, see Kenny, "Tinselled Bucks"; Brandt, *Mohawk Trail*; Allen, *Sacred Hoop*; and Gay American Indians and Roscoe, *Living the Spirit.* For a literature review see Barker, "Introduction: Critically Sovereign," 1–44.

101. Morgensen, "Unsettling Queer Politics," 135–36.

problematized for its male-centric, pantribal generalizations and misrepresentation and appropriation among non-Natives, contributors reflected on queer Indigenous people's historical experiences and lived realities,[102] and engaged non-Native sexual minorities and LGBTQ+ theorization, providing scaffolding for later queer Indigenous decolonial critiques and praxis. Additionally, pantribal urban support and activist groups like GAI subsequently formed throughout and across the US and Canada.

Queer Indigenous critique and activism sharpened with the successive formation of Two-Spirit identity and politics. The term was coined in 1990 at an international gathering of gay and lesbian First Nations / Indigenous peoples to replace *berdache*. Based on a term from Northern Algonquin language, *niizh manitoag*, participants at the Gathering of American Indian and First Nations Gay and Lesbians defined Two-Spirit as "the presence of both a masculine and a feminine spirit in one person," and initially including "gay, lesbian, transvestite, transexual, transgender, drag queens, and butches, as well as *winkte, nádleeh,* and other appropriate tribal terms."[103] Two-Spirit identity and activism strategically connects precolonial Indigenous traditions of gender and sexual variance and modern-day LGBTQ+ Indigenous people. Two-Spirit therefore bridges past and present and tribal-nation specificity and pan-Indigeneity. Two-Spirit persons may cross gender roles, gender expression, and sexual identities and often emphasize their spiritual and communal roles rather than their gender presentation and/or sexual identity. Developed in urban spaces, Two-Spirit has been adopted across tribal-nation borders, in reservation and rural spaces.[104] From the start, Two-Spirit activists mobilized their communities, for example, making AIDS prevention work more compatible with queer Indigenous lives and cultures and reshaping academic work on queer Indigenous people.[105] Since the 1990s, Indigenous Lesbian, Gay, Bisexual, Transgender, Queer, and Two-Spirit people (LGBTQ2S) have continued to tease out and debate its meanings given differences between traditions of gender and sexual variance and modern understandings of gender and sexual identity.[106]

•

---

102. Barker, "Introduction: Critically Sovereign," 18–19.

103. Morgensen, *Spaces between Us,* 81.

104. Terra Matthews-Hartwell, "LGBTQ2 Well-Being Education Series: LGBTQ2S Advocacy, and Nativeout," *Native Out,* accessed on August 4, 2023, https://www.ihs.gov/sites/telebehavioral/themes/responsive2017/display_objects/documents/slides/lgbt/lgbtnativeout.pdf; and Jacobs, Thomas, and Lang, introduction to *Two-Spirit People,* 2–3.

105. Driskill et al., introduction to *Queer Indigenous Studies,* 10–13.

106. Tony Enos, "8 Things You Should Know About Two Spirit People," *Indian Country Today,* March 28, 2017, updated September 13, 2018, https://indiancountrytoday.com/archive/8-things-you-should-know-about-two-spirit-people-294cNoIj-EGwJFOWEnbbZw.

QUEER EMPIRE AND THE PUBLIC PEDAGOGY OF DECOLONIALITY • 217

I end my interrogation of the entanglements of Indigenous dispossession and racialized anti-immigration constituting the public pedagogy of US empire with examples of Indigenous-led, coalitional decolonial public pedagogy. Corey Snelgrove, Rita Kaur Dhamoon, and Jeff Corntassel (Cherokee Nation) assert that solidarity between Indigenous and non-Indigenous people must be anchored in actual practices and place-based relationships,[107] the pragmatic and spatialized baseline for what Karma Chávez describes in her work on queer migration politics as "coalitional moments" that open up options for radical change.[108] First, regarding community-based queer Indigenous coalitional praxis, Morgensen described how in 1989 Leota Lone Dog (Lakota), Curtis Harris (San Carlos Apache), and Kent Lebsock (Lakota) drew from prior organizing work with the American Indian Cultural House and especially its HIV/AIDS program, to form WeWah and BarCheeAmpe, the first NYC group for Indigenous lesbians and gays (which adopted Two-Spirit upon its proposition). Members also joined Cairos Collective, a citywide coalition of LGBTQ+ people of color. Media-based decolonial pedagogy was key to both group's activism, with the former releasing the newsletter *Buffalo Hide* as the collective published the magazine *COLORLife!* announcing its formation. Between 1990 and 1992, in both texts WeWah and BarCheeAmpe members called on queer people of color to critique settler colonialism and recognize that Two-Spirit people and queer Indigenous people "were members of sovereign peoples with histories and cultures that remained distinct from all non-Natives. Their insistence on national difference was not a barrier to coalition, but its condition."[109] Ultimately Cairos Collective included Two-Spirit people among those whom it sought to represent, its mission described as serving "LGBTST people of color." Its successor, the Audre Lorde Project (ALP), named for the queer Black feminist scholar and activist, took up the phrase. This Indigenous-led coalitional movement "formed the first context in which Two-Spirit identity politically aligned with sexual minority identities while remaining distinct" and with Cairos Collective's commitment to challenge settler colonialism, racism, and homophobia.[110]

The legacy of this decolonial coalition lives on in ALP. According to its mission statement, ALP is

a Lesbian, Gay, Bisexual, Two Spirit, Trans and Gender Non Conforming (LGBTSTGNC) People of Color center for community organizing, focusing on the New York City area. Through mobilization, education and capacity-

---

107. Snelgrove, Dhamoon, and Corntassel, "Unsettling Settler Colonialism," 3.
108. Chávez, *Queer Migration Politics*.
109. Morgensen, "Unsettling Queer Politics," 136.
110. Morgensen, "Unsettling Queer Politics," 136–37.

building, we work for community wellness and progressive social and economic justice. Committed to struggling across differences, we seek to responsibly reflect, represent and serve our various communities.[111]

ALP's core commitment is to support and pursue justice for LGBTSTGNC People of Color primarily through community organizing, as with the 3rd Space Support program, which provides sustainable support around issues of employment, education, health care, and immigration status. Confronting oppressive policy and creating media to support queer people of color is also an important facet of ALP's work. For example, "Say What: How to Talk about Trans and Gender Non-Conforming People, LGBTQ People, Youth and People in the Sex Trade Respectfully," edited by Elliott Fukui, Audre Lorde Project trans justice coordinator, and collaborated on in partnership with FIERCE as well as Streetwise and Safe (SAS), was "developed to support journalists, reporters, activists and organizers in using more inclusive and transformative language and frameworks when addressing issues that relate to our most vulnerable community members' experiences of discriminatory policing."[112]

More recently, in 2017, the protest slogan "No Bans on Stolen Lands," coined by Indigenous activists responding to the Trump administration's Muslim Bans, recognized the inextricable entanglement of Indigenous dispossession and racialized anti-immigration underpinning US empire as well as the consequent inextricable entanglement of decolonization and im/migrant justice. Anti-immigrant, gendered, sexualized racism was arguably the spark that ignited Trumpism, the rallying cry for Trump's base, and the centerpiece of much of his administration's policy and media discourse: Trump infamously announced his successful 2016 presidential campaign with a televised speech that tacitly elaborated on the originary, gendered, sexualized stereotype of Native savagery and alienage in its characterization of Mexican immigrants as drug dealers, criminals, and rapists imminently threatening white US America. His administration's policies included multiple bans of immigrants from Muslim-majority nations, immigration officials separating im/migrant babies and children from their parents and imprisoning them in cages and concentration camps, aggressive immigration raids, systematic rape and sexual abuse at the hands of guards and other immigration and law enforcement personnel in detention centers, and ramped up Mexico–US border militarization, including sending military troops to police it. There is also Trump's personal,

111. "History," About ALP, The Audre Lorde Project, accessed February 7, 2023, https://alp.org/about.

112. "Say What? Media Guide," Resources, Audre Lorde Project, June 26, 2015, https://alp.org/resources/from-alp.

QUEER EMPIRE AND THE PUBLIC PEDAGOGY OF DECOLONIALITY · 219

frenzied obsession with building a border wall; his cavalier response to the devastation of Puerto Rico following Hurricane Maria, notably including viral footage of him tossing paper towels into a crowd in San Juan; and his administration's negligence, to put it mildly, regarding the COVID-19 pandemic and its disproportionate impact on Indigenous communities and communities of color. All the while Trump overtly supported and defended white supremacist violence, including inciting a violent insurrection at the US capitol in 2021. He also literally personifies rape culture. While the ethnonationalist, far right dismantling of existing structures and blatant embrace of white possessive logics departs from the norms of US neoliberal empire to an extent, Trump and his administration carried on and furthered the kinds of necropolitical anti-Indigenous and racialized anti-immigrant US American traditions of empire-building analyzed throughout this book.

Additional recent examples of the ongoing force of pedagogies of empire that precede and succeed the Trump administration, from across the political spectrum, abound. Since 9/11, in policy and media explicit links have been drawn between "Indian savagery" and always-already Muslim terrorists, as with military codes calling Osama Bin Laden "Geronimo." The Trump administration attempted to continue dispossessive extractive construction projects on Indigenous lands such as the Dakota Access Pipeline, and the suppression of non-Christian and racialized religious freedom long at play in US history intersected in the Muslim Bans as well as the pipelines and fracking that disrupt sacred Indigenous sites. Systematically removing Indigenous children from their families during allotment and the compulsory boarding school system also established the paradigm of alien/citizen divisions used to rationalize the Trump administration's use of kidnapping and incarcerating children as border control. At the time of writing, Biden administration Native American and immigration policy appears to be a (predictable) more inclusive return to the "normalcy" of US neoliberal multicultural liberal democracy. A blend of gendered, sexualized Indigenous pathologization and appropriation in popular culture, politics, and academia and racialized anti-immigration / "nation of immigrants" hetero- and homonormative multiculturalism also persists.

Some media flashpoints include Senator Elizabeth Warren's claiming of Indigenous ancestry and Trump's mocking of her; Andrea Smith's false claims of Indigenous identity even as she produced pathbreaking queer feminist Critical Indigenous Studies (CIS) scholarship and worked as an activist for Indigenous justice; and viral images of the "QAnon Shaman," a white cisgendered man who outfitted himself in furs, horns, and war paint evocative of "Native" regalia during white nationalist protests, including the violent 2021 riot at the US Capitol. Hackneyed images of Latinx drug dealers and criminals and

CONCLUSION

Muslim terrorists continue to proliferate in various media, including social media, of which the Trump's Twitter feed stands as an archive. Simultaneously, im/migrant stories of hard work and upward mobility continue to imagine the US as the exceptionally multicultural "nation of immigrants."

This collective of public pedagogy shows that gendered, sexualized entanglements of Indigenous dispossession and racialized anti-immigration continue to structure US empire, the major tropes rationalizing white possession enduring even as the post-9/11 "War on Terror" reconfigured discourse about Indigenous peoples and immigrants and as Trumpism continues to metastasize as a perhaps post-neoliberal phenomenon. Recent pedagogies of empire also remind us that decolonization and im/migrant justice are necessarily interconnected.

Recognizing this interconnection, Melanie Yazzie (Navajo Nation) began using the hashtag #NoBanOnStolenLand in response to hearing the US National anthem and hearing and seeing "nation of immigrants" rhetoric at Muslim Ban protests, with hashtags and protest signs proclaiming #weareallimmigrants and #heretostay. She stated that "'Native people were here before, and we can't be counted in that immigrant category that's glorified through the 'U.S.A.' chant that is happening." She views the hashtag and protest signs as education for non-Natives that accurately reflects the history of US colonization and racialized exclusion. Nick Estes, who is from the Lower Brulé Indian Reservation in South Dakota, expressed similar sentiments regarding Indigenous protests against the Muslim Ban, stating, "It's not that we have to say we're pro-immigration for people to come and steal our lands. It means that if people are gonna come here and coexist peacefully, it has to be on the terms of the people whose land it is to begin with." He noted that the Tongva people, the original Indigenous peoples of the Los Angeles area, held a welcoming ceremony at the airport for people detained under the travel ban. Indigenous peoples quickly popularized the No Bans on Stolen Lands slogan on social media, on protest signs, and in artwork, and it was embraced beyond US borders.[113] The slogan also inspired teach-ins such as a 2017 event organized by the NYC Stands with Standing Rock Collective and cosponsored by the New York University (NYU) Department of Social and Cultural Analysis, the NYU Native American and Indigenous Students' Group, the Native Studies Forum, and the Asian/Pacific/American Institute at NYU, called "No Bans on Stolen Lands: A #NODAPL Teach-in for Standing Rock & Muslim/Immigrant/Refugee

---

113. Lenard Monkman, "'No Ban on Stolen Land,' Say Indigenous Activists in US," *CBS News*, February 6, 2017, https://www.cbc.ca/news/indigenous/indigenous-activists-immigration-ban-1.3960814.

Bans."[114] Artist, activist, and scholar Dylan A. T. Miner's (Métis Nation of Ontario) graphic of the phrase "No Bans on Stolen Lands" in the shape of the continental US visualizes the interconnection of Indigenous dispossession and anti-immigration.[115] In another visual interpretation, the protest slogan frames an outline of the continental US with tribal-nations' lands named and shaded in various colors within its borders, rather than US states.

Again, Indigenous peoples generated coalitional, decolonial public pedagogy with practical, place-based, mediated critiques of the coloniality and racialized anti-immigration foundational to the United States of America and its ongoing white possessive imperial projects. As Indigenous feminist and queer critiques have shown, decolonial remapping of Indigenous lands, nationalisms, and bodies necessitates dismantling the assemblages of heteropatriarchy, Indigenous dispossession, and white supremacy that together compose white possession.[116] Although not explicitly queer or gendered, the place-based relationality and pragmatism of the "No Bans on Stolen Lands" slogan, activism, and art seems spacious enough to encompass Indigenous justice, im/migrant justice, and gender justice.

Public pedagogies of decoloniality reject and remap the settler colonial, white supremacist, heteropatriarchal, and homonational logics of US empire historically and into the neoliberal context. The queer coalitions formed between WeWah and BarCheeAmpe, Cairos Collective, and ALP, and the coalitional praxis of "No Bans on Stolen Land" activism and art exemplify decolonial horizontal solidarities that embrace movement while being anchored in actual communities, practices, and place-based relationships that center and honor the specificity of Indigenous knowledges, spaces, and reterritorializations. These examples of Indigenous-led coalitions provide powerful teachings and lessons to those within and outside of US borders, literally grounding decolonial public pedagogy and antiracist resistance, creating bridges between Indigenous peoples and im/migrant communities of color to move us all beyond the gendered, sexualized, racialized entanglements of US empire.

---

114. "No Bans on Stolen Lands: A #NODAPL Teach-in for Standing Rock & Muslim/Immigrant/Refugee Bans," A/P/A Institute at NYU, https://apa.nyu.edu/event/no-bans-on-stolen-lands-a-nodapl-teach-in-for-standing-rock-muslimimmigrantrefugee-bans/.

115. "Graphics//Prints," Dylan Miner, accessed on August 4, 2023, https://dylanminer.com/artworks.

116. Goeman, "Notes Towards a Native Feminism's Spatial Practice," 169–70.

BIBLIOGRAPHY

Abourezk, James G. *Papers 1970–1983: Wounded Knee, 1973 Series.* University of South Dakota, Special Collections. https://www.usd.edu/library/special/wk73hist.htm.

Abramovitz, Mimi. *Regulating the Lives of Women.* Cambridge, MA: South End Press, 1988.

Acs, Gregory. "Does Welfare Promote Out-of-Wedlock Childbearing?" In *Welfare Reform: Analysis of the Issues,* edited by Isabel V. Sawhill. Washington, DC: Urban Institute, 1995.

Aksikas, Jaafar, and Sean Johnson Andrews. "Neoliberalism, Law and Culture: A Cultural Studies Intervention after 'The Juridical Turn.'" In "Cultural Studies and/of the Law," edited by Jaafar Aksikas and Sean Johnson Andrews. Special issue, *Cultural Studies* 28 nos. 5–6 (2014): 742–80.

Alexander, Michelle. *The New Jim Crow: Mass Incarceration in the Age of Colorblindness.* New York: New Press, 2010.

Aliess, Angela. *Making the White Man's Indian: Native Americans and Hollywood Movies.* Westport, CT: Praeger, 2005.

Allen, Paula Gunn. *Off the Reservation: Reflections on Boundary-Busting, Border-Crossing Loose Cannons.* Boston: Beacon Press, 1998.

———. *The Sacred Hoop: Recovering the Feminine in American Indian Traditions.* Boston: Beacon Press, 1986.

Allen, Theodore. *The Invention of the White Race, Volume 1: Racial Oppression and Social Control.* London: Verso, 1994.

———. *The Invention of the White Race, Volume 2: The Origin of Racial Oppression in Anglo-America.* London: Verso, 1994.

Alonso, Ana Maria, and Maria Teresa Koreck. "Silences: 'Hispanics,' AIDS, and Sexual Practices." In *The Lesbian and Gay Studies Reader,* edited by Henry Abelove, Michele Aina Barale, and David M. Halperin, 110–26. New York: Routledge, 1992.

BIBLIOGRAPHY

American Indian Policy Review Commission: Final Report, Task Force No. 9, Law Consolidation, Revision and Codification. Washington: US Government Printing Office, 1976.

Amnesty International. *Invisible Victims: Migrants on the Move in Mexico.* London: Amnesty International Publications, 2010.

———. *Maze of Injustice: The Failure to Protect Indian Women from Sexual Violence in the USA.* London: Amnesty International Publications, 2007.

———. *The Never-Ending Maze: Continued Failure to Protect Indigenous Women from Sexual Violence in the USA.* London: Amnesty International Publications, 2022.

Amott, Teresa L. "Black Women and AFDC: Making Entitlement out of Necessity." In *Women, the State, and Welfare,* edited by Linda Gordon, 280–98. Madison: University of Wisconsin Press, 1990.

Anderson, Benedict. *Imagined Communities: Reflections on the Origin and Spread of Nationalism.* New York: Verso, 1991.

Anzaldua, Gloria. *Borderlands/La Frontera: The New Mestiza.* San Francisco: Aunt Lute Books, 1987.

Anzaldua, Gloria, and Cherrie Moraga, eds. *This Bridge Called My Back: Writings by Radical Women of Color.* Berkeley, CA: Third Woman Press, 1981.

Aoki, Keith. "No Right to Own?: The Early Twentieth-Century 'Alien Land Laws' as a Prelude to Internment." *Boston College Third World Law Journal* 19, no. 37 (1998): 37–50.

Balogh, Brian, and Nathan Connolly. "Darkness over the Plain: The Bison in American History." Produced by Virginia Foundation for the Humanities. *Back Story.* October 4, 2019. Podcast. https://www.backstoryradio.org/shows/darkness-over-the-plain/#transcript.

Balogh, Brian, Nathan Connolly, and Joanne Freeman. "What's Cooking? A History of Food in America." Produced by Virginia Foundation for the Humanities. *Back Story.* December 28, 2018. Podcast. https://www.backstoryradio.org/shows/whats-cooking.

Barker, Joanne, ed. *Critically Sovereign: Indigenous Gender, Sexuality, and Feminist Studies.* Durham, NC: Duke University Press, 2017.

———. "For Whom Sovereignty Matters." In *Sovereignty Matters: Locations of Contestation and Possibility in Indigenous Struggles for Self-Determination,* edited by Joanne Barker. 1–32. Lincoln: University of Nebraska Press, 2006.

———. "Introduction: Critically Sovereign." In Barker, *Critically Sovereign,* 1–44.

———. "Territory as Analytic: The Dispossession of Lenapehoking and the Subprime Crisis." In "Economies of Dispossession: Indigeneity, Race, Capitalism," edited by Jodi A. Byrd, Alyosha Goldstein, Jodi Melamed, and Chandan Reddy. Special issue, *Social Text* 36, no. 2 (June 2018): 19–39.

Barnard, John Levi. "The Bison and the Cow: Food, Empire, Extinction." *American Quarterly* 72, no. 2 (June 2020): 377–402.

Barrera, Magdalena. "Hottentot 2000: Jennifer Lopez and Her Butt." In *Sexualities in History: A Reader,* edited by Kim M. Phillips and Barry Reay, 407–20. New York: Routledge, 2002.

Bell, Derrick J., Jr. *And We Are Not Saved: The Elusive Quest for Racial Justice.* San Francisco: Harper San Francisco, 1989.

———. "Racial Realism." In *Critical Race Theory: The Key Writings That Formed the Movement,* edited by Kimberle, Neil Gotanda, Gary Peller, and Kendall Thomas. New York: New Press, 1995.

Beltran, Mary. "The Hollywood Latina Body as Site of Social Struggle: Media Constructions of Stardom and Jennifer Lopez's 'Cross-Over Butt.'" *Quarterly Review of Film and Video* 19, no. 1 (Jan.–Mar. 2002): 71–86.

BIBLIOGRAPHY · 225

Berger, Bethany. "After Pocahontas: Indian Women and the Law, 1830–1934." School of Law, Faculty Articles and Papers 113 (1997). http://digitalcommons.uconn.edu/law_papers/113.

Berglund, Jeff. "Pocahontas." *Seeing Red: Hollywood's Pixelated Skins*, edited by LeAnne Howe, Harvey Markowitz, and Denise K. Cummings, 40–56. East Lansing: Michigan State University Press, 2013.

Bernhardt, Annette, Ruth Milkman, Nik Theodore, Douglas Heckathorn, Mirabai Auer, James DeFilippis, Ana Luz González, Victor Narro, Jason Perelshteyn, Diana Polson, and Michael Spiller. "Broken Laws, Unprotected Workers: Violations of Labor and Employment Laws in America's Cities." Center for Urban Economic Development, University of Chicago, National Employment Law Project, UCLA Institute for Research and Employment, 2009.

Bhandar, Brenna. *Colonial Lives of Property: Law, Land, and Racial Regimes of Ownership.* Durham, NC: Duke University Press, 2018.

Bird, S. Elizabeth. "Gendered Construction of the American Indian in Popular Media." *Journal of Communication* 49, no. 3 (1999): 61–83.

Blackhawk, Ned. *Violence over the Land: Indians and Empires in the Early American West.* Cambridge, MA: Harvard University Press, 2006.

Block, Sharon. *Rape and Sexual Power in Early America.* Durham: University of North Carolina Press, 2006.

Bold, Christine. *Selling the Wild West: Popular Western Fiction, 1860 to 1960.* Indianapolis: Indiana University Press, 1987.

Bordo, Susan. *Unbearable Weight: Feminism, Western Culture, and the Body.* 2nd ed. Oakland: University of California, 2004.

Bowers, Alfred W. "Hidatsa Social and Ceremonial Organization." *Bureau of American Ethnology, Bulletin 194.* Washington, DC: Smithsonian Institution Press, 1965.

Bradford, William. *Of Plymouth Plantation, 1620–1647,* edited by Samuel Eliot Morison. New York: Alfred A Knopf, 2002.

Brandt, Beth. *Mohawk Trail.* Ithaca, NY: Firebrand Books, 1985.

Brent, Zoe W., Christina M. Schiavoni, and Alberto Alonso-Fradejas. "Contextualizing Food Sovereignty: The Politics of Convergence among Movements in the USA." *Third World Quarterly* 36, no. 3 (2015): 618–35.

Brownmiller, Susan. *Against Our Will: Men, Women, and Rape.* New York: Ballantine Books, 1975.

Bruyneel, Kevin. "Challenging American Boundaries: Indigenous People and the 'Gift' of U.S. Citizenship." *American Political Development* 18, no. 1 (April 2014): 30–43.

Bual, Harman. "Native American Rights & Adoption by Non-Indian Families: The Manipulation and Distortion of Public Opinion to Overthrow ICWA." *American Indian Law Journal* 6, no. 2, Article 6 (2018). https://digitalcommons.law.seattleu.edu/ailj/vol6/iss2/6/.

Buff, Rachel Ida. *The Deportation Terror: Organizing for Immigrant Rights in the Twentieth Century.* Philadelphia: Temple University Press, 2018.

Burns, Randy. Preface to *Living the Spirit: A Gay American Indian Anthology,* edited by Gay American Indians and Will Roscoe. New York: St. Martin's Press, 1988.

Burrows, Edwin G., and Mike Wallace. *Gotham: A History of New York City to 1898.* New York: Oxford University Press, 1999.

Byrd, Jodi A. "Arriving on a Different Shore: US Empire at Its Horizons." *College Literature: A Journal of Critical Literary Studies* 41, no. 1 (Winter 2014): 174–81.

———. "*Loving* Unbecoming: The Queer Politics of the Transitive Native." In Barker, *Critically Sovereign,* 207–28.

———. *The Transit of Empire: Indigenous Critiques of Colonialism*. Minneapolis: University of Minnesota Press, 2011.

———. "'Variations under Domestication:' Indigeneity and the Subject of Dispossession." In "Economies of Dispossession: Indigeneity, Race, Capitalism," edited by Jodi A. Byrd, Alyosha Goldstein, Jodi Melamed, and Chandan Reddy. Special issue, *Social Text* 36, no. 2 (June 2018): 123–41.

Byrd, Jodi A., Alyosha Goldstein, Jodi Melamed, and Chandan Reddy. "Predatory Value: Economies of Dispossession and Disturbed Relationalities." In "Economies of Dispossession: Indigeneity, Race, Capitalism," edited by Jodi A. Byrd, Alyosha Goldstein, Jodi Melamed, and Chandan Reddy. Special issue, *Social Text* 36, no. 2 (June 2018): 1–18.

Cacho, Lisa. "Civil Rights, Commerce, and U.S. Colonialism." In "Economies of Dispossession: Indigeneity, Race, Capitalism," edited by Jodi A. Byrd, Alyosha Goldstein, Jodi Melamed, and Chandan Reddy. Special issue, *Social Text* 36, no. 2 (June 2018): 63–82.

———. *Social Death: Racialized Rightlessness and the Criminalization of the Unprotected*. New York: New York University Press, 2012.

Camacho, Alicia Schmidt. *Migrant Imaginaries: Latino Cultural Politics in the U.S.–Mexico Borderlands*. New York: New York University Press, 2008.

Cannon, Lou. *President Reagan: The Role of a Lifetime*. New York: Simon & Schuster, 1991.

Cantu, Lionel, Jr. *The Sexuality of Migration: Border Crossings and Mexican Immigrant Men*, edited by Nancy A. Naples and Salvador Vidal-Ortiz. New York: New York University Press, 2009.

Carpio, Myla Vicenti. "The Lost Generation: Indian Women and Sterilization Abuse." *Social Justice* 31, no. 4 (2004): 40–53.

Castellanos, Bianet, Lourdes Gutiérrez Nájera, and Arturo Aldama, eds. *Comparative Indigeneities of the Américas: Toward a Hemispheric Approach*. Tucson: University of Arizona Press, 2012.

Castro, Bel S. "Food, Morality, and Politics: The Spectacle of Dog-Eating Igorots at the 1904 St. Louis World Fair." In *Food and Morality: Proceedings of the Oxford Symposium on Food and Cookery 2007*, edited by Susan R. Friedland, 70–81. Blackawton, Totnes, Devon, UK: Prospect Books, 2008.

Chang, Grace. *Disposable Domestics: Immigrant Women Workers in the Global Economy*. Cambridge, MA: South End Press, 2000.

Charlie Brown Thanksgiving, A. directed by Bill Melendez and Phil Roman, Chicago, United Feature Syndicate, 1973.

Chatelain, Marsha. *Franchise: The Golden Arches in Black America*. New York: Liveright, 2020.

Chávez, Karma R. *Queer Migration Politics: Activist Rhetoric and Coalitional Possibilities*. Urbana: University of Illinois Press, 2013.

Chávez, Karma R., and Eithne Luibhéid. Introduction to Chávez and Luibhéid, *Queer and Trans Migrations*, 1–18.

Chávez, Karma R., and Eithne Luibhéid, eds. *Queer and Trans Migrations: Dynamics of Illegalization, Detention, and Deportation*. Urbana: University of Illinois Press, 2020.

Chavez, Leo R. *The Latino Threat: Constructing Immigrants, Citizens, and the Nation*. Stanford: Stanford University Press, 2008.

Checker, Melissa. *Environmental Racism and the Search for Justice in a Southern Town*. New York: New York University Press, 2005.

Chen, Yong. *Chop Suey, USA: The Story of Chinese Food in America*. New York: Columbia University Press, 2014.

BIBLIOGRAPHY • 227

Chin, Gabriel J., and John Ormonde. "The War against Chinese Restaurants." *Duke Law Journal* 67 (2018): 681–741. https://scholarship.law.duke.edu/dlj/vol67/iss4/1.

Cinotto, Simone. *The Italian American Table: Food, Family and Community in New York City.* Urbana: University of Illinois Press, 2013.

Classon, Constance, David Howes, and Anthony Synnott, eds. *Aroma: The Cultural History of Smell.* New York: Routledge, 1994.

Code of Indian Offenses, Department of the Interior, Office of Indian Affairs. 1883.

Cohen, Cathy. "Punks, Bulldaggers, and Welfare Queens: The Radical Potential of Queer Politics?" *GLQ* 3, no. 4 (1997): 437–65.

Cole, Luke W., and Sheila R. Foster. *From the Ground Up: Environmental Racism and the Rise of the Environmental Justice Movement.* New York: New York University Press, 2001.

Commissary General of Subsistence. *Correspondence on the Subject of the Emigration of Indians.* Washington, DC: Duff Green, 1834.

Comptroller of the United States. *Investigations of Allegations Concerning Indian Health Services.* Washington, DC: Government Printing Office, 1976.

Contreras, Shelia Marie. *Bloodlines: Myth, Indigenism, and Chicana/o Literature.* Austin: University of Texas Press, 2008.

Cook, Samuel R. "Ronald Reagan's Indian Policy in Retrospect: Economic Crisis and Political Irony." *Policy Studies Journal* 24, no. 1 (1996): 11–26.

Corntassel, Jeff. "Toward Sustainable Self-Determination: Rethinking the Contemporary Indigenous-Rights Discourse." *Alternatives* 33 (2008): 105–32.

Coté, Charlotte. "'Indigenizing' Food Sovereignty: Revitalizing Indigenous Food Practices and Ecological Knowledges in Canada and the United States." *Humanities* 5, no. 57 (2016): 1–14.

Cothran, Boyd. *Remembering the Modoc War: Redemptive Violence and the Making of American Innocence.* Chapel Hill: University of North Carolina Press, 2014.

Coulthard, Glen. *Red Skin, White Masks: Rejecting the Colonial Politics of Recognition.* Minneapolis: University of Minnesota Press, 2014.

Daniels, Roger. *Guarding the Golden Door: American Immigration Policy and Immigrants since 1882.* New York: Hill and Wang, 2004.

———. *Prisoners without Trial: Japanese Americans in World War II.* New York: Hill and Wang, 1993.

Das Gupta, Monisha, and Sue Haglund. "Mexican Migration to Hawai'i and US Settler Colonialism." *Latino Studies* 13, no. 4 (2015): 455–80.

Davila, Arlene. *Latinos Inc.: The Marketing and Making of a People.* New York: New York University Press, 2008.

Davis, Angela Y. *Freedom Is a Constant Struggle: Ferguson, Palestine, and the Foundations of a Movement,* edited by Frank Barat. Chicago: Haymarket Books, 2016.

———. "Rape, Racism, and the Capitalist Setting." *The Angela Y. Davis Reader,* edited by Joy James, 129–37. Malden: Blackwell Publishing, Inc., 1998.

———. *Women, Race, Class.* 1981. New York: Knopf Doubleday Publishing Group, 2011.

Davis, Mike. *Late Victorian Holocausts: El Nino Famines and the Making of the Third World.* New York: Verso, 2001.

Day, Iyko. *Alien Capital: Asian Racialization and the Logic of Settler Colonialism.* Durham, NC: Duke University Press, 2016.

———. "Racial Capitalism, Colonialism, and Death-Dealing Abstractionism." *American Quarterly* 72, no. 4 (December 2020): 1033–46.

Deer, Sarah. *The Beginning and End of Rape: Confronting Sexual Violence in Native America.* Minneapolis: University of Minnesota Press, 2015.

——. "Decolonizing Rape Law: A Native Feminist Synthesis of Safety and Sovereignty." In "Native Feminisms: Legacies, Interventions, and Indigenous Sovereignties," edited by Mishuana R. Goeman and Jennifer Nez Denetdale. Special issue, *Wicazo Sa Review* 24, no. 2 (2009): 149–67.

——. "Toward an Indigenous Jurisprudence of Rape." *Kansas Journal of Law and Public Policy* 14 (2004): 121–54.

Delgado, Richard. "The Imperial Scholar: Reflections on a Review of Civil Rights Literature." *University of Pennsylvania Law Review* 132, no. 3 (March 1984): 561–78.

Delgado, Richard, and Jean Stefanic, eds. *Critical Race Theory: An Introduction.* Philadelphia: Temple University Press, 2001.

——. *The Derrick Bell Reader.* New York: New York University Press, 2005.

Deloria, Philip J. *Playing Indian.* New Haven, CT: Yale University Press, 1998.

Deloria, Vine, Jr. "The American Indian Image in North America." In *The Pretend Indians: Images of Native Americans in the Movies,* edited by G. M. Bataille & C. L. Silet. Ames: Iowa State University Press, 1974.

——. *Custer Died for Your Sins: An Indian Manifesto.* New York: Macmillan, 1969.

——. *God Is Red: A Native View of Religion.* Golden, CO: Fulcrum, 1973.

Deloria, Vine, Jr., and Clifford M. Lytle. *American Indians, American Justice.* Austin: University of Texas Press, 1983. Kindle version.

——. *The Nations Within: The Past and Future of American Indian Sovereignty.* New York: Pantheon Books, 1984.

Deloria, Vine, Jr., and Daniel Wildcat. *Power and Place: Indian Education in America.* Golden, CO: Fulcrum Publishing, 2001.

Demby, Gene, and Karen Grigsby Bates. "Ask Code Switch: You Are What You Eat." Produced by Leah Donella and Sami Yenigun. *Code Switch.* March 27, 2019. Podcast. https://www.npr.org/transcripts/704861884.

Demby, Gene, and Shereen Marisol Meraji. "Pretty Hurts." Produced by Kumari Devarajan, Leah Donnella, Maria Paz Gutierrez, Sami Yenigun, and Shreen Marisol Meraji. *Code Switch.* January 30, 2019. Podcast. https://www.npr.org/transcripts/689687288?storyId=689687288?storyId=689687288.

Denetdale, Jennifer Nez. "Carving Navajo National Boundaries: Patriotism, Tradition, and the Diné Marriage Act of 2005." *American Quarterly* 60 (2008): 289–94.

——. "Chairmen, Presidents, and Princesses: The Navajo Nation, Gender, and the Politics of Tradition." *Wicazo Sa Review* 21, no. 1 (2006): 9–28.

——. "Return to 'The Uprising at Beautiful Mountain in 1913': Marriage and Sexuality in the Making of the Modern Navajo Nation." In Barker, *Critically Sovereign,* 69–98.

Derounian-Stodola, Kathryn Zabelle. "The Captive and Her Editor: The Ciphering of Olive Oatman and Royal B. Stratton." *Prospects* 23 (1998): 171–92.

——. "The Indian Captivity Narratives of Mary Rowlandson and Olive Oatman: Case Studies in the Continuity, Evolution, and Exploitation of Literary Discourse." *Studies in the Literary Imagination* 27, no. 1 (Spring 1994): 33–46.

Dickie, John. *Delizia!: The Epic History of Italians and Their Food.* New York: Free Press, 2008.

"Diet and Deterioration among the American Indians." *JAMA: The Journal of the American Medical Association* 90, no. 25 (1928): 2020–21. https://doi.org/10.1001/jama.1928.02690520032013.

BIBLIOGRAPHY • 229

Diner, Hasia R. *Hungering for America: Italian, Irish, and Jewish Foodways in the Age of Migration*. Cambridge, MA: Harvard University Press, 2001.

Driskill, Qwo-Li, Chris Finley, Brian Joseph Gilley, and Scott Lauria Morgensen. Introduction to Driskill et al., *Queer Indigenous Studies*, 1–28.

———, eds. *Queer Indigenous Studies: Critical Interventions in Theory, Politics, and Literature*. Tucson: University of Arizona Press, 2011.

Duffy, Jennifer. *Who's Your Paddy? Racial Expectations and the Struggle for Irish American Identity*. New York: New York University Press, 2014.

Duggan, Lisa. *The Twilight of Equality: Neoliberalism, Cultural Politics, and the Attack on Democracy*. Boston: Beacon Press, 2003.

Dunbar-Ortiz, Roxanne. *An Indigenous Peoples' History of the United States*. Boston: Beacon Press, 2014.

———. *Not a Nation of Immigrants: Settler Colonialism, White Supremacy, and a History of Erasure and Exclusion*. Boston: Beacon Press, 2021.

Dunbar-Ortiz, Roxanne, and Dina Gilio-Whitaker. *"All the Real Indians Died Off" and 20 Other Myths about Native Americans*. New York: Beacon Press, 2016.

Echo Hawk Consulting. *Feeding Ourselves: Food Access, Health Disparities, and the Pathways to Healthy Native American Communities*. Longmont, CO: Echo Hawk Consulting, 2015.

Ellis, Havelock. *Studies in the Psychology of Sex, Volume 2: Sexual Inversion*. Project Guttenberg, 1927. http://www.gutenberg.org/files/13611/13611-h/13611-h.htm.

Estrada, Emir, and Pierrette Hondagneu-Sotelo. "Living the Third Shift: Latina Adolescent Street Vendors in Los Angeles." In *Immigrant Women Workers in the Neoliberal Age*, edited by Nilda Flores-González, Anna Romina Guevarra, Maura Toro-Morn, and Grace Chang, 144–63. Urbana: University of Illinois Press, 2013.

Fausto-Sterling, Ann. *Sexing the Body: Gender Politics and the Construction of Sexuality*. New York: Basic Books, 2000.

Fernandez, Doreen. "Food and War." In *Vestiges of War: The Philippine American War and the Aftermath of an Imperial Dream*, edited by Angel Velasco Shaw and Luis H. Francai. New York: New York University Press, 2002.

Finley, Chris. "Decolonizing the Queer Native Body (and Recovering the Native Bull-Dyke): Bringing 'Sexy Back' and Out of Native Studies' Closet." In Driskill et al., *Queer Indigenous Studies*, 31–42.

Fletcher, Matthew L. M., Wenone T. Singel, and Kathryn E. Fort, eds. *The Indian Child Welfare Act at 30*. East Lansing: Michigan State University Press, 2008.

Foucault, Michel. *The History of Sexuality, Volume 1*. New York: Vintage, 1990.

———. *Society Must Be Defended*. New York: Picador, 1997.

Frank, Gillian, and Lauren Gutterman. "Against Our Will." Produced by Saniya Lee Ghanoui. *Sexing History*. November 15, 2019. Podcast. https://www.sexinghistory.com/sexinghistory?format=RSS.

Fraser, Laura. "The Inner Corset: A Brief History of Fat in the United States." In Rothblum and Solovay, *The Fat Studies Reader*, 11–14.

Fregoso, Rosa Linda. *MeXicana Encounters: The Making of Social Identities on the Borderlands*. Berkeley: University of California Press, 2003.

Fujikane, Candace. "Introduction: Asian Settler Colonialism in the U.S. Colony of Hawai'i." In *Asian Settler Colonialism: From Local Governance to the Habits of Everyday Life in Hawai'i*, edited by Candace Fujikane and Jonathan Y. Okamura, 9–11. Honolulu: University of Hawai'i Press, 2008.

Gabler, Neal. *An Empire of Their Own: How the Jews Invented Hollywood.* New York: Anchor Books, 1988.

Gardener, Martha. *The Qualities of a Citizen: Women, Immigration, and Citizenship, 1870–1965.* Princeton: Princeton University Press, 2005.

Gay American Indians and Will Roscoe, eds. *Living the Spirit: A Gay American Indian Anthology.* New York: St. Martin's Press, 1988.

Gerken, Christina. *Model Immigrants and Undesirable Aliens: The Cost of Immigration Reform in the 1990s.* Minneapolis: University of Minnesota Press, 2013.

Gilley, Brian Joseph. *Becoming Two-Spirit: Gay Identity and Social Acceptance in Indian Country.* Lincoln: University of Nebraska Press, 2006.

Gilmore, Ruth Wilson. *Abolition Geography: Essays Toward Liberation,* edited by Brenna Bhandar and Alberto Toscano. London: Verso, 2022.

———. *Golden Gulag: Prisons, Surplus, Crisis, and Opposition in Globalizing California.* Berkeley: University of California Press, 2007.

Gilmore, Ruth Wilson, and Leopold Lambert. "Making Abolition Geography in California's Central Valley with Ruth Wilson Gilmore." *Funambulist* 21 (2019): 14–19.

Gilio-Walker, Gina. *As Long as Grass Grows: The Indigenous Fight for Environmental Justice, from Colonization to Standing Rock.* Boston: Beacon Press, 2019.

Glenn, Evelyn Nakano. "Settler Colonialism as Structure: A Framework for Comparative Studies of U.S. Race and Gender Formation." *Sociology of Race and Ethnicity* 1, no. 1 (2015): 52–72.

Goeman, Mishuana R. "Notes Towards a Native Feminism's Spatial Practice." In "Native Feminisms: Legacies, Interventions, and Indigenous Sovereignties," edited by Mishuana R. Goeman and Jennifer Nez Denetdale. Special issue, *Wicazo Sa Review* 24, no. 2 (2009): 169–87.

———. "Ongoing Storms and Struggles: Gendered Violence and Resource Exploitation." In Barker, *Critically Sovereign,* 99–126.

Goeman, Mishuana R., and Jennifer Nez Denetdale. "Guest Editor's Introduction." In "Native Feminisms: Legacies, Interventions, and Indigenous Sovereignties," edited by Mishuana R. Goeman and Jennifer Nez Denetdale. Special issue, *Wicazo Sa Review* 24, no. 2 (2009): 9–13.

Goeman, Mishuana R., and Jennifer Nez Denetdale, eds. "Native Feminisms: Legacies, Interventions, and Indigenous Sovereignties." Special issue, *Wicazo Sa Review* 24, no. 2 (2009).

Goldstein, Aloysha. "The Ground Not Given: Colonial Dispositions of Land, Race, and Hunger." In "Economies of Dispossession: Indigeneity, Race, Capitalism," edited by Jodi A. Byrd, Alyosha Goldstein, Jodi Melamed, and Chandan Reddy. Special issue, *Social Text* 36, no. 2 (June 2018): 83–106.

Gonzalez, Evelyn. *The Bronx.* New York: Columbia University Press, 2006.

González-López, Gloria. *Erotic Journeys: Mexican Immigrants and their Sex Lives.* Berkeley: University of California Press, 2005.

Graber, Cynthia, and Nicola Twilley. "The United States of Chinese Food." Produced by Cynthia Graber and Nicola Twilley. *Gastropod.* August 25, 2015. Podcast. https://gastropod.com/the-united-states-of-chinese-food/.

———. "What Is Native American Cuisine?" Produced by Cynthia Graber and Nicola Twilley. *Gastropod.* November 1, 2016. Podcast. https://gastropod.com/?s=native+american+cuisine.

Green, Joyce, ed. *The White Possessive: Making Space for Indigenous Feminisms.* London: Zed Books, 2007.

Green, Rayna. "The Pocahontas Perplex: The Image of Indian Women in American Culture." *Massachusetts Review* 16, no. 4 (1975): 698–714.

Grenier, John. *The First Way of War: American War Making on the Frontier, 1607–1814.* New York: Cambridge University Press, 2005.

Grey, Sam, and Raj Patel. "Food Sovereignty as Decolonization: Some Contributions from Indigenous Movements to Food Systems and Development Politics." *Agriculture & Human Values* 32 (2015): 431–44.

Grinnell, George Bird. *The Cheyenne Indians: Their History and Ways of Life.* 2 Vols. New York: Cooper Square Publishers, 1962.

Gutiérrez, Elena. *Fertile Matters: The Politics of Mexican-Origin Women's Reproduction.* Austin: University of Texas Press, 2008.

Hall, Clyde M. "You Anthropologists Make Sure You Get Your Worlds Right." In *Two-Spirit People: Native American Gender Identity, Sexuality, Spirituality,* edited by Sue-Ellen Jacobs, Wesley Thomas, and Sabine Lang, 272–75. Urbana: University of Illinois Press, 1997.

Hames-Garcia, Michael. "What's after Queer Theory? Queer Ethnic and Indigenous Studies." *Feminist Studies* 39, no. 2 (2013): 384–404.

Haney Lopez, Ian F. *White by Law: The Legal Construction of Race.* New York: New York University Press, 1996.

Harris, Cheryl I. "Whiteness as Property." *Harvard Law Review* 106, no. 8 (June 1993): 1707–91.

Hartman, Saidiya. *Scenes of Subjection: Terror, Slavery, and Self-Making in Nineteenth-Century America.* New York: Oxford University Press, 1997.

Harvey, David. *A Brief History of Neoliberalism.* New York: Oxford University Press, 2005.

Heredia, Carlos A. "Downward Mobility: Mexican Workers after NAFTA." *North American Congress on Latin America (NACLA)* 30, no. 3 (November/December 1996): 34–40.

Herman, Diane F. "The Rape Culture." In *Women: A Feminist Perspective,* 4th ed., edited by Jo Freeman, 45–52. Mountain View, CA: Mayfield, 1989.

Hertzberg, Hazel W. "Reaganomics on the Reservation." *New Republic,* November 2, 1982, 15–18.

Hobbes, Michael, and Aubrey Gordon. "The Body Mass Index." Produced by Michael Hobbes and Aubrey Gordon. *Maintenance Phase.* August 3, 2021. Podcast. https://www.maintenancephase.com/.

Hoffman, Abraham. *Unwanted Mexican Americans in the Great Depression: Repatriation Pressures, 1929–1939.* Tucson: University of Arizona Press, 1974.

Hong, Grace Kyungwon. *Death beyond Disavowal: The Impossible Politics of Difference.* Minneapolis: University of Minnesota Press, 2015.

———. *The Ruptures of American Capital: Woman of Color Feminism and the Culture of Immigrant Labor.* Minneapolis: University of Minnesota Press, 2006.

———. "Speculative Surplus: Asian American Racialization and the Neoliberal Shift." In "Economies of Dispossession: Indigeneity, Race, Capitalism," edited by Jodi A. Byrd, Alyosha Goldstein, Jodi Melamed, and Chandan Reddy. Special issue, *Social Text* 36, no. 2 (June 2018): 107–22.

Howe, Alyssa. "Queer Pilgrimage: The San Francisco Homeland and Identity Tourism." *Cultural Anthropology* 16, no. 1 (2001): 35–61.

Hubbard, Tasha. "Buffalo Genocide in Nineteenth-Century North America: 'Kill, Skin, and Sell.'" In *Colonial Genocide in Indigenous North America,* edited by Alexander Laban Hinton, Andrew Woolford, and Jeff Benvenuto, 292–305. Durham, NC: Duke University Press, 2014.

Hunziker, Alyssa A. "Playing Indian, Playing Filipino: Native American and Filipino Interactions at the Carlisle Indian Industrial School." *American Quarterly* 72, no. 2 (June 2020): 423–48.

232 · BIBLIOGRAPHY

Hurtado, Albert L. "When Strangers Met: Sex and Gender on Three Frontiers." *Frontiers: A Journal of Women Studies* 17, no. 3 (1996): 52–75.

Hutchinson, E. P. *Legislative History of Immigration Policy, 1798–1965.* Philadelphia: University of Pennsylvania Press, 1981.

Ichikawa, Nina F. "Giving Credit Where It Is Due: Asian American Farmers and Retailers as Food System Pioneers." In Ku, Manalansan, and Mannur, *Eating Asian America,* 274–87.

Ignatiev, Noel. *How the Irish Became White.* New York: Routledge, 1996.

Immerwahr, Daniel. *How to Hide an Empire: The History of the Greater United States.* New York: Picador, 2019.

Indiana General Assembly, *1907 Laws of the Indiana General Assembly.* Indianapolis: William B. Burford: 1907. 377–78. https://scholarworks.iupui.edu/items/b9edd72e-c1c9-4efe-bc12-816ae55552e6.

Isenberg, Andrew. *The Destruction of the Bison: An Environmental History 1750–1920.* Cambridge: Cambridge University Press, 2000.

Jacobs, Sue Ellen, Wesley Thomas, and Sabine Lang. Introduction to *Two-Spirit People: Native American Gender Identity, Sexuality, Spirituality,* edited by Jacobs, Thomas, and Lang, 1–20. Urbana: University of Illinois Press, 1997.

Jacobson, David. *Rights across Borders: Immigration and the Decline of Citizenship.* Baltimore: Johns Hopkins University Press, 1996.

Jacobson, Matthew. *Roots Too: White Ethnic Revival in Post-Civil Rights America.* Cambridge, MA: Harvard University Press, 2006.

———. *Whiteness of a Different Color: European Immigrants and the Alchemy of Race.* Cambridge, MA: Harvard University Press, 1998.

Jacobson, Robin Dale. *The New Nativism: Proposition 187 and the Debate over Immigration.* Minneapolis: University of Minnesota Press, 2008.

Jensen, Joan M. "Native Women and Agriculture: A Case Study." *Sex Roles* 3, no. 5 (1977): 423–41.

Jernigan, Valerie Blue Bird. "Addressing Food Security and Food Sovereignty in Native American Communities." In *Health and Social Issues of Native American Women,* edited by Jennie Joe and Francine Guachupin, 113–32. Santa Barbara, CA: Praeger, 2012.

Johnson, Lyndon P. "Remarks at the Signing of the Immigration Bill, Liberty Island, New York, October 3, 1965." In *Public Papers of the Presidents of the United States: Lyndon Johnson, 1965, Book 2: June 1–December 31, 1965.* Washington, DC: Government Printing Office, 1967.

Jun, Helen. *Race for Citizenship: Black Orientalism and Asian Uplift from Pre-Emancipation to Neoliberal America.* New York: New York University Press, 2011.

Kanstroom, Daniel. *Deportation Nation: Outsiders in American History.* Cambridge, MA: Harvard University Press, 2007.

Kaplan, Sydney. "Historical Efforts to Encourage White–Indian Intermarriage in the United States and Canada." *International Social Science Review* 65, no. 3 (Summer 1990): 126–32.

Karuka, Manu. *Empire's Tracks: Indigenous Nations, Chinese Workers, and the Transcontinental Railroad.* Berkeley: University of California Press, 2019.

Kellner, Douglas. "Cultural Studies, Multiculturalism, and Media Culture." In *Gender, Race, and Class in Media: A Critical Reader,* 6th ed., edited by Gail Dines, Jean M. Humez, Bill Yousman, and Lori Bindig Yousman, 6–16. Thousand Oaks, CA: Sage Publications, 2018.

———. *Media Culture: Cultural Studies, Identity, and Politics between the Modern and the Postmodern.* New York: Routledge, 1995.

Kenny, Maurice. "Tinselled Bucks: An Historical Study of Indian Homosexuality." *Gay Sunshine: A Journal of Gay Liberation* 26/37 (1975/76): 15–17.

Kilpatrick, Jacquelyn. *Celluloid Indians: Native Americans and Film.* Lincoln: University of Nebraska Press, 1999.

Kim, Heidi Kathleen. "Incarceration, Cafeteria Style: The Politics of the Mess Hall in the Japanese American Incarceration." In Ku, Manalansan, and Mannur, *Eating Asian America,* 125–46.

Kim, Jodi. *Ends of Empire: Asian American Critique and Cold War Compositions.* Minneapolis: University of Minnesota Press, 2010.

Kimmerer, Robin Wall. *Braiding Sweetgrass: Indigenous Wisdom, Scientific Knowledge, and the Teachings of Plants.* Minneapolis, MN: Milkweed Editions, 2013.

King, Tiffany Lethabo. *The Black Shoals: Offshore Formations of Black and Native Studies.* Durham, NC: Duke University Press, 2019.

———. "Labor's Aphasia: Toward Antiblackness as Constitutive to Settler Colonialism." *Decolonization: Indigeneity, Education, and Society.* June 10, 2014. https://decolonization.wordpress.com/2014/06/10/labors-aphasia-toward-antiblackness-as-constitutive-to-settler-colonialism/.

———. "Racial Ecologies: Black Landscapes in Flux." In *Racial Ecologies,* edited by Leilani Nishime and Kim D. Hester Williams. Seattle: University of Washington Press, 2018.

Kosasa, Karen A. "Sites of Erasure: The Representation of Settler Culture in Hawai'i." In *Asian Settler Colonialism: From Local Governance to the Habits of Everyday Life in Hawai'i,* edited by Candace Fujikane and Jonathan Y. Okamura, 95–208. Honolulu: University of Hawai'i Press, 2008.

Ku, Robert Ji-Song, Martin F. Manalansan IV, and Anita Mannur. "An Alimentary Introduction." In Ku, Manalansan, and Mannur, *Eating Asian America,* 1–10.

Ku, Robert Ji-Song, Martin F. Manalansan IV, and Anita Mannur, eds. *Eating Asian America: A Food Studies Reader.* New York: New York University Press, 2013.

Kugel, Rebecca. "Little Big Man (1970)." In *Seeing Red—Hollywood's Pixeled Skins: American Indians and Film,* edited by Leanne Howe, Harvey Markowitz, and Denise K. Cummings, 79–82. East Lansing: Michigan State University Press, 2013.

Kuhl, Stefan. *The Nazi Connection: Eugenics, American Racism, and German National Socialism.* New York: Oxford University Press, 1994.

Kupperman, Karen Ordahl. *Pocahontas and the English Boys.* New York: New York University Press, 2019.

LaDuke, Winona. *All Our Relations: Native Struggles for Land and Life.* Chicago: Haymarket Books, 1999.

Lancaster, Bridget. "The Plan to Kill the Chinese Restaurant." Produced by America's Test Kitchen. *Proof.* July 18, 2019. Podcast. https://www.americastestkitchen.com/podcasts/proof.

Landsberg, Alison. *Prosthetic Memory: The Transformation of Remembrance in the Age of Mass Culture.* New York: Columbia University Press, 2004.

Lang, Sabine. *Men as Women, Women as Men: Changing Gender in Native American Cultures.* Austin: University of Texas Press, 1998.

———. "Native American Men-Women, Lesbians, Two-Spirits: Contemporary and Historical Perspectives." *Journal of Lesbian Studies* 20, nos. 3–4 (2016): 299–323.

Laurino, Maria. *The Italian Americans: A History.* New York: W. W. Norton, 2014.

Lawrence, Jane. "The Indian Health Service and the Sterilization of Native American Women." *American Indian Quarterly* 24, no. 3 (Summer 2000): 400–419.

Le, Quynh Nhu. *Unsettled Solidarities Asian and Indigenous Cross-Representations in the Américas*. Philadelphia: Temple University Press, 2019.

Lee, Erika. *America for Americans: The History of Xenophobia in the United States*. New York: Basic Books, 2021.

———. *At America's Gates: Chinese Immigration during the Exclusion Era, 1882–1943*. Chapel Hill: University of North Carolina Press, 2003.

Lee, Heather. "A Life Cooking for Others: The Work and Migration Experiences of a Chinese Restaurant Worker in New York City, 1920–1946." In Ku, Manalansan, and Mannur, *Eating Asian America*, 53–77.

Lee, Jennifer 8. *The Fortune Cookie Chronicles: Adventures in the World of Chinese Food*. New York: Twelve, 2008.

Lee, Robert. *Orientals: Asian Americans in Popular Culture*. Philadelphia: Temple University Press, 1999.

Lee-Oliver, Leece, Monisha Das Gupta, Katherine Fobear, and Edward Ou Jin Lee. "Imperialism, Settler Colonialism, and Indigeneity." In Chávez and Luibhéid, *Queer and Trans Migrations*, 226–55.

Leff, Mark. "Consensus for Reform: The Mothers' Pension Movement in the Progressive Era." *Social Service Review* 47 (1973): 397–417.

LeMesurier, Jennifer L. "Uptaking Race: Genre, MSG, and Chinese Dinner." *Poroi* 12, no. 2 (February 2017). https://doi.org/10.13008/2151-2957.1253.

Levenstein, Harvey. *Paradox of Plenty: A Social History of Eating in Modern America*. Berkeley: University of California Press, 2003.

———. *Revolution at the Table: The Transformation of the American Diet*. Berkeley: University of California Press, 2003.

Lew, Janey. "Intimacies between Empires: New Directions in Critical and Comparative Ethnic Studies." *College Literature: A Journal of Critical Literary Studies* 41, no. 1 (Winter 2014): 189–94.

Lewis, Oscar. *The Children of Sanchez: Autobiography of a Mexican Family*. New York: Vintage, 1963.

———. *La Vida: A Puerto Rican Family in the Culture of Poverty—San Juan and New York*. New York: Vintage, 1966.

Lindholm, Melanie M. "Alaska Native Perceptions of Food, Health, and Community Well-Being: Challenging Nutritional Colonialism." In Mihesuah and Hoover, *Indigenous Food Sovereignty in the United States*, 155–72.

Lopez, Ana. "Are All Latins from Manhattan? Hollywood, Ethnography, and Cultural Colonialism." In *Unspeakable Images: Ethnicity and the American Cinema*, edited by Lester Friedman, 404–24. Urbana: University of Illinois Press, 1991.

Lopez, Iris. "Agency and Constraint: Sterilization and Reproductive Freedom among Puerto Rican Women in New York City." In *Situated Lives: Gender and Culture in Everyday Life*, edited by L. Lamphere, H. Ragone, and Patricia Zavella, 155–71. New York: Routledge, 1993.

Lopez, Lori Kido. "Notes on Terminology." In *Race and Media: Critical Approaches*, edited by Lori Kido, vii–xii. New York: New York University Press, 2020.

Luibhéid, Eithne. *Entry Denied: Controlling Sexuality at the Border*. Minneapolis: University of Minnesota Press, 2002.

———. "'Treated neither with Respect nor with Dignity': Contextualizing Queer and Trans Migrant 'Illegalization,' Detention, and Deportation." In Chávez and Luibhéid, *Queer and Trans Migrations*, 19–40.

BIBLIOGRAPHY · 235

Luibhéid, Eithne, and Lionel Cantu Jr., eds. *Queer Migrations: Sexuality, U.S. Citizenship, and Border Crossing*. Minneapolis: University of Minnesota Press, 2005.

Mabalon, Dawn Bohulano. "As American as Jackrabbit Adobo: Cooking, Eating, and Becoming Filipina/o American before World War II." In Ku, Manalansan, and Mannur, *Eating Asian America*, 147–76.

Mariani, John F. *How Italian Food Conquered the World*. New York: St. Martin's Press, 2011.

Martens, Tabitha, Jamie Cidro, Michael Anthony Hart, and Stephanie McLachlan. "Understanding Indigenous Food Sovereignty through an Indigenous Research Paradigm." *Journal of Indigenous Social Development* 5, no. 1 (2016): 18–37.

Marubbio, M. Elise. *Killing the Indian Maiden: Images of Native American Women in Film*. Lexington, KY: The University Press of Kentucky, 2006.

May, Larry. *Screening Out the Past: The Birth of Mass Culture and the Motion Picture Industry*. Chicago: University of Chicago Press, 1980.

McClintock, Anne. *Imperial Leather: Race, Gender, and Sexuality in the Colonial Contest*. New York: Routledge, 1995.

———. "No Longer in a Future Heaven: Gender, Race, and Nationalism." In *Dangerous Liaisons: Gender, Nation, and Postcolonial Perspectives*, edited by Anne McClintock, Aamir Mufti, and Ella Shohat. Minneapolis: University of Minnesota Press, 1997.

McDonnell, Janet. *The Dispossession of the American Indian, 1887–1934*. Bloomington: Indiana University Press, 1991.

McMichael, Philip. "Food Sovereignty in Movement: Addressing the Triple Crisis." In *Food Sovereignty: Reconnecting Food, Nature and Community*, edited by Hannah Wittman, Anette Aurelle Desmarais, and Nettie Wiebe, 68–185. Oakland, CA: Food First Books, 2010.

McRobbie, Angela. *The Aftermath of Feminism: Gender, Culture, and Social Change*. New York: Sage, 2009.

Medicine, Beatrice. *Learning to be an Anthropologist and Remaining "Native": Selected Writings*. Edited with Sue-Ellen Jacobs. Urbana: University of Illinois Press, 2001.

Melamed, Jodie. "Reading Tehran in *Lolita*: Making Racialized Gendered Difference Work for Neoliberal Multiculturalism." In *Strange Affinities: The Gender and Sexual Politics of Comparative Racialization*, edited by Grace Kyunghwon Hong and Roderick Ferguson, 76–112. Durham, NC: Duke University Press, 2011.

———. *Represent and Destroy: Rationalizing Violence in the New Racial Capitalism*. Minneapolis: University of Minnesota Press, 2011.

Mendible, Myra, ed. *From Bananas to Buttocks: The Latina Body in Popular Film and Culture*. Austin: University of Texas Press, 2007.

Merskin, Debra. "The S-Word: Discourse, Stereotypes, and the American Indian Woman." *Howard Journal of Communications* 21, no. 4 (2010): 345–66.

Mifflin, Margot. *The Blue Tattoo: The Life of Olive Oatman*. Lincoln: University of Nebraska Press, 2011.

Mihesuah, Devon A. *American Indians: Stereotypes and Realities*. Regina, Saskatchewan: Clarity, 1996.

———. "Comanche Traditional Foodways and the Decline of Health." In Mihesuah and Hoover, *Indigenous Food Sovereignty in the United States*, 223–52.

———. *Indigenous American Women: Decolonization, Empowerment, Activism*. Lincoln: University of Nebraska Press, 2003.

———. "Searching for Haknip Achukma (Good Health): Challenges to Food Sovereignty Initiatives in Oklahoma." In Mihesuah and Hoover, *Indigenous Food Sovereignty in the United States*, 94–121.

Mihesuah, Devon A., and Elizabeth Hoover. Introduction to Mihesuah and Hoover, *Indigenous Food Sovereignty in the United States,* 3–25.

———, eds. *Indigenous Food Sovereignty in the United States: Restoring Cultural Knowledge, Protecting Environments, and Regaining Health.* Norman: University of Oklahoma Press, 2019.

Mink, Gwendolyn. "The Lady and the Tramp: Gender, Race, and the Origins of the American Welfare State." In *Women, the State, and Welfare,* edited by Linda Gordon, 92–122. Madison: University of Wisconsin Press, 1990.

Mintz, Sydney W. *Sweetness and Power: The Place of Sugar in Modern History.* New York: Penguin, 1985.

Miranda, Deborah A. "Extermination of the Joyas: Gendercide in Spanish California." *GLQ: A Journal of Gay and Lesbian Studies* 16, no. 1–2 (January 2010): 253–84.

Molina-Guzman, Isabel. *Dangerous Curves: Latina Bodies in the Media.* New York: New York University Press, 2010.

———. *Latinas and Latinos on TV: Colorblind Comedy in the Post-Racial Network Era.* Tucson: University of Arizona Press, 2018.

Moloney, Deirdre M. "Women's Sexual Morality and Economic Dependency in Early U.S. Deportation Policy." *Journal of Women's History* 18, no. 2 (2006): 95–122.

Montejano, David. *Anglos and Mexicans in the Making of Texas, 1836–1986.* Austin: University of Texas Press, 1987.

Moreton-Robinson, Aileen. *Talkin' Up to the White Woman: Indigenous Women and Feminism.* Queensland, AU: University of Queensland Press, 2002.

———. *The White Possessive: Property, Power, and Indigenous Sovereignty.* Minneapolis: University of Minnesota Press, 2015.

Morgensen, Scott Lauria. "Settler Homonationalism: Theorizing Settler Colonialism within Queer Modernities." *GLQ: A Journal of Lesbian and Gay Studies* 16, no. 1 (2010): 105–31.

———. *The Spaces between Us: Queer Settler Colonialism and Indigenous Decolonization.* Minneapolis: University of Minnesota Press, 2011.

———. "Unsettling Queer Politics: What Can Non-Natives Learn from Two-Spirit Organizing?" In Driskill et al., *Queer Indigenous Studies,* 132–52.

Morris, C. Patrick. "Termination by Accountants: The Reagan Indian Policy." In *Native Americans and Public Policy,* edited by Fremont J. Lyden and Lyman H. Lagters, 63–69. Pittsburgh: University of Pittsburgh Press, 1992.

Moynihan, Patrick. *The Negro Family: The Case for National Action.* Washington, DC: Office of Policy Planning and Research, Department of Labor, March 1965. http://www.dol.gov/oasam/programs/history/webid-meynihan.htm.

Munoz, Lorena. "From Street Child Care to Drive-Throughs: Latinas Reconfigure and Negotiate Street Vending Spaces in Los Angeles." In *Immigrant Women Workers in the Neoliberal Age,* edited by Nilda Flores-González, Anna Romina Guevarra, Maura Toro-Morn, and Grace Chang, 133–43. Urbana: University of Illinois Press, 2013.

Nagle, Rebecca. *This Land.* Produced by Crooked Media. 2019–21. Podcast. https://crooked.com/podcast-series/this-land/.

Native American Solidarity Committee in coordination with the American Indian Treaty Council Information Center. "Documentation of Current (20th Century) Genocidal Policy: Sterilization Abuse." June 1977.

Negron-Mutaner, Frances. "Jennifer's Butt." *Aztlan* 22, no. 2 (2000): 182–95.

Ngai, Mae M. *Impossible Subjects: Illegal Aliens and the Making of Modern America.* Princeton, NJ: Princeton University Press, 2004.

Nichols, Robert. "Theft Is Property! The Recursive Logic of Dispossession." *Political Theory* 46, no. 1 (2018): 3–28.

Nixon, Richard. "Special Message to the Congress on Indian Affairs." *The American Presidency Project,* July 8, 1970. http://www.presidency.ucsb.edu/ws/?pid=2573.

Noriega, Chon. "Citizen Chicano: The Trials and Titillations of Ethnicity in the American Cinema, 1935–1962." In *Latin Looks: Images of Latinas and Latinos in the U.S. Media,* edited by Clara E. Rodriguez, 85–103. Boulder, CO: Westview, 1997.

Norton, Henry K. *The Story of California from the Earliest Days to the Present.* Chicago: A. C. McClurg, 1924.

"Nyéléni Declaration on Food Sovereignty, 27 February 2007." In "Food Sovereignty," edited by Raj Patel. Special issue, *Journal of Peasant Studies* 36, no. 3 (July 2009): 673–706.

O'Brien, Jean M. *Firsting and Lasting: Writing Indians out of Existence in New England.* Minneapolis: University of Minnesota Press, 2010.

Odoms-Young, Angela, and Marino Bruce. "Examining the Impact of Structural Racism on Food Insecurity." *Family & Community Health* 1 (April/June 2018): S3–S6. https://doi.org/10.1097/FCH.0000000000000183.

Orange, Tommy. *There There.* New York: Penguin-Random House, 2018. Kindle version.

Ordover, Nancy. *American Eugenics: Race, Queer Anatomy, and the Science of Eugenics.* Minneapolis: University of Minnesota Press, 2003.

Orquiza, René Alexander, Jr. "*Lechon* with Heinz, Lea & Perrins with *Adobo*: The American Relationship with Filipino Food, 1898–1946." In Ku, Manalansan, and Mannur, *Eating Asian America,* 177–85.

O'Sullivan, Meg Devlin. "Informing Red Power and Transforming the Second Wave: Native American Women and the Struggle Against Coerced Sterilization in the 1970s." *Women's History Review* 25, no. 6 (2016): 965–82.

Oxfam. "Trading Away Our Rights: Women Working in Global Supply Chains." Oxford, UK: Oxfam International, 2004. https://www.ituc-csi.org/IMG/pdf/cr-trading-away-rights-women-global-supply-chains-10404-en.pdf.

Padoongpatt, Mark. "'Oriental Cookery': Devouring Asian and Pacific Cuisine during the Cold War." In Ku, Manalansan, and Mannur, *Eating Asian America,* 186–207.

Painter, Nell Irvin. *The History of White People.* New York: W. W. Norton, 2010.

———. "Soul Murder and Slavery: Toward a Fully Loaded Cost Accounting." In *US History as Women's History: New Feminist Essays,* edited by Linda K. Kerber, Alice Kessler-Harris, and Katheryn Kish Sklar, 125–46. Chapel Hill: University of North Carolina Press, 1995.

Patel, Leigh. "Nationalist Narratives, Immigration and Coloniality." *Decolonization: Indigeneity, Education, and Society.* September 15, 2015. https://decolonization. wordpress.com/2015/09/17/ nationalist-narratives-immigration-and-coloniality/.

Patel, Raj. "What Does Food Sovereignty Look Like?" In "Food Sovereignty," edited by Raj Patel. Special issue, *Journal of Peasant Studies* 36, no. 3 (July 2009): 663–73.

Pelaccio, Linda. "The Cries of Street Food Vendors: 19th C. Public Culture of Food in New Orleans." Produced by Heritage Radio Network. *Taste of the Past.* December 6, 2018. Podcast. https://heritageradionetwork.org/podcast/the-cries-of-street-food-vendors-19thc-public-culture-of-food-in-new-orleans.

Perez, Gina M. *The Near Northwest Side Story: Migration, Displacement, and Puerto Rican Families.* Berkeley: University of California Press, 2004.

Perez, Gina M., Frank A. Guridy, and Adrian Burgos Jr. Introduction to *Beyond El Barrio: Everyday Life in Latina/o America,* edited by Perez, Guridy, and Burgos Jr. New York: New York University Press, 2010.

Perez, Richie. "From Assimilation to Annihilation: Puerto Rican Images in U.S. Films." In *Latin Looks: Images of Latinas and Latinos in the U.S. Media,* edited by Clara E. Rodriguez, 142–63. Boulder, CO: Westview, 1997.

Perry, Leah. *The Cultural Politics of U.S. Immigration.* New York: New York University Press, 2016.

———. "'I Can Sell My Body If I Wanna': Riot Grrrl and Performing Shameless Feminist Resistance." *Lateral: Journal of the Cultural Studies Association* 4 (2015). https://csalateral.org/issue/4/i-can-sell-my-body-if-i-wanna-riot-grrrl-body/.

Piatote, Beth. *Domestic Subjects: Gender, Citizenship, and Law in Native American Literature.* New Haven, CT: Yale University Press, 2013.

"Policies of General Applicability: Provision of Sterilization in Federally Assisted Programs of the Public Health Service." *Federal Register* 43, no. 217. Washington, DC: Office of the Federal Register, National Archives and Records Service, General Services Administration, Supt. of Docs, US GPO. November 8, 1978.

Poznanski, Robert. "The Propriety of Denying Entry to Homosexual Aliens: Examining the Public Health Service's Authority Over Medical Exclusions." *University of Michigan Journal of Law Reform* 17 (1984): 331–59.

Puar, Jasbir K. *Terrorist Assemblages: Homonationalism in Queer Times.* Durham, NC: Duke University Press, 2007.

Raj, Anita, and Jay Silverman. "Violence against Immigrant Women: The Roles of Culture, Context, and Legal Immigrant Status on Intimate Partner Violence." *Violence against Women* 8, no. 3 (March 2002): 367–98.

Ralstin-Lewis, D. Marie. "The Continuing Struggle against Genocide: Indigenous Women's Reproductive Rights." *Wicazo Sa Review* 20, no. 1 (2005): 71–95.

Ramirez, Renya K. *Native Hubs: Culture, Community, and Belonging in Silicon Valley and Beyond.* Durham, NC: Duke University Press, 2007.

———. *Standing Up to Colonial Power: The Lives of Henry Roe and Elizabeth Bender Cloud.* Lincoln: University of Nebraska Press, 2018.

Reddy, Chandan. "Asian Diasporas, Neoliberalism, and Family: Reviewing the Case for Homosexual Asylum in the Context of Family Rights." *Social Text* 23, nos. 3–4 (Fall–Winter 2005): 101–19.

Reel Injun: On the Trail of the Hollywood Indian. Directed by Neil Diamond, Catherine Bainbridge, and Jeremiah Hayes. New York: Lorber Films, 2010.

Rifkin, Mark. "Around 1978: Family, Culture, and Race in the Federal Production of Indianness." In Barker, *Critically Sovereign,* 169–206.

———. "The Erotics of Sovereignty." In Driskill et al., *Queer Indigenous Studies,* 172–89.

———. *Settler Common Sense: Queerness and Everyday Colonialism in the American Renaissance.* Minneapolis: University of Minnesota Press, 2014.

———. *When Did Indians Become Straight? Kinship, the History of Sexuality, and Native Sovereignty.* New York: Oxford University Press, 2011.

Roberts, Dorothy E. "Who May Give Birth to Citizens? Reproduction, Eugenics, and Immigration." In *Immigrants Out! The New Nativism and the Anti-Immigrant Impulse in the United States,* edited by Juan E. Perea. New York: New York University Press, 1997.

Rodríguez, Juana María. *Sexual Futures, Queer Gestures, and Other Latina Longings.* New York: New York University Press, 2014.

Roediger, David. *Working toward Whiteness: How America's Immigrants Became White: The Strange Journey from Ellis Island to the Suburbs.* New York: Basic Books, 2005.

Rogin, Michael. *Ronald Reagan: The Movie and Other Episodes in Political Demonology.* Berkeley: University of California Press, 1987.

Rollins, Peter C., ed. *The Columbia Companion to American History on Film.* New York: Columbia University Press, 2003.

Roosevelt, Theodore. *Hunting Trips of a Ranchman: Sketches of Sport on the Northern Cattle Plains.* New York: G. P. Putnam's Sons, 1885.

Rosay, Andre B. *Violence against American Indian and Alaska Native Women and Men: 2010 Findings from the National Intimate Partner and Sexual Violence Survey.* Washington, DC: National Institute of Justice, 2016.

Rothblum, Esther, and Sondra Solovay, eds. *The Fat Studies Reader.* New York: New York University Press, 2009.

Rottenberg, Catherine. "The Rise of Neoliberal Feminism." *Cultural Studies* 28, no. 3 (May 2014): 418–37.

Rowe, John Carlos. "Reading 'Reading Lolita in Tehran' in Idaho." *American Quarterly* 59, no. 2 (June 2007): 253–75.

Rowland, Robert C., and John M. Jones. *Reagan at Westminster: Foreshadowing the End of the Cold War.* College Station: Texas A&M University Press, 2010.

Ruiz, Vicki L. "Confronting 'America': Mexican Women and the Rose Gregory Settlement." In *American Dreaming, Global Realities: Rethinking US Immigration History,* edited by Donna R. Gabaccia and Vicki L. Ruiz, 343–60. Urbana: University of Illinois Press, 2006.

Sadowski-Smith, Claudia. *The New Immigrant Whiteness: Race, Neoliberalism, and Post-Soviet Migration to the United States.* New York: New York University Press, 2018.

———. "Unskilled Labor Migration and the Illegality Spiral: Chinese, European, and Mexican Indocumentados in the United States, 1882–2007." In "Nation Past and Future," edited by David G. Gutierrez and Pierrette Hondagneu-Sotelo. Special issue, *American Quarterly* 60, no. 3 (September 2008): 779–804.

Said, Edward. *Culture and Imperialism.* New York: Vintage, 1993.

Saldaña-Portillo, Maria Josefina. *Indian Given: Racial Geographies across Mexico and the United States.* Durham, NC: Duke University Press, 2016.

———. *The Revolutionary Imagination in the Americas and the Age of Development.* Durham, NC: Duke University Press, 2003.

Salmon, Enrique. *Eating the Landscape: American Indian Stories of Food, Identity, and Resilience.* Tucson: University of Arizona Press, 2012.

Sánchez, Rosaura, and Beatrice Pita. "Rethinking Settler Colonialism." *American Quarterly* 66, no. 4 (December 2014): 1039–55.

Santa Ana, Otto. *Brown Tide Rising: Metaphors of Latinos in Contemporary Public Discourse.* Austin: University of Texas Press, 2002.

Schaller, Michael. *Reckoning with Reagan: America and Its President in the 1980s.* New York: Oxford University Press, 1992.

Schuland-Vials, Cathy J., Linda Trinh Vo, and K. Scott Wong, eds. *Keywords in Asian American Cultural Studies.* New York: New York University Press, 2015.

Shaw, Susan M., and Janet Lee. "Sexual Assault and Rape." In *Women's Voices, Feminist Visions: Classic and Contemporary Readings,* 6th ed., edited by Susan M. Shaw and Janet Lee, 550–54. New York: McGraw-Hill, 2015.

Simpson, Audra. *Mohawk Interruptus: Political Life Across the Borders of Settler States.* Durham, NC: Duke University Press, 2014.

240 • BIBLIOGRAPHY

Simpson, Leanne Batasamosake. "Land as Pedagogy: Nishnaabeg Intelligence and Rebellious Transformation." *Decolonization: Indigeneity, Education, and Society* 3, no. 3 (2014): 1–25.

Sklar, Robert. *Movie-Made America: A Cultural History of American Movies.* New York: Vintage, 1994.

Slotkin, Richard. *Gunfighter Nation: The Myth of the Frontier in Twentieth-Century America.* New York: Atheneum, 1992.

———. *Regeneration through Violence: The Mythology of the American Frontier, 1600–1860.* Middletown, CT: Wesleyan University Press, 1973.

Smith, Andrea. *Conquest: Sexual Violence and American Indian Genocide.* Durham, NC: Duke University Press, 2005.

———. "Queer Theory and Native Studies: The Heteronormativity of Settler Colonialism." In Driskill et al., *Queer Indigenous Studies,* 43–65.

Smith, Andrea, and J. Kehaulani Kauanui. "Introduction: Native Feminisms Engage American Studies." *American Quarterly* 60, no. 2 (June 2008): 241–50.

Smits, David D. "The S—Drudge." In *Native Women's History in Eastern North America before 1900: A Guide to Research and Writing,* edited by R. Kugel and L. Eldersveld Murphy, 27–49. Lincoln: University of Nebraska Press, 2007.

Snelgrove, Corey, Rita Kaur Dhamoon, and Jeff Corntassel. "Unsettling Settler Colonialism: The Discourse and Policy of Settlers, and Solidarity with Indigenous Nations." *Decolonization: Indigeneity, Education & Society* 3, no. 3 (2014): 1–32.

Speed, Shannon. "States of Violence: Indigenous Women Migrants in an Era of Neoliberal Multicriminalism." *Critique of Anthropology* 36, no. 3 (June 2016): 280–301.

Spiritu, Yen Le. *Asian American Panethnicity: Bridging Institutions and Identities.* Philadelphia: Temple University Press, 1993.

Spruhan, Paul. "A Legal History of Blood Quantum in Federal Indian Law to 1935." *South Dakota Law Review* 51, no. 1 (2006): 1–50.

Standing Bear, Luther. *My People the Sioux.* 1928. Lincoln: University of Nebraska Press, 2006.

Steger, Manfred B., and Ravi K. Roy. *Neoliberalism: A Very Short Introduction.* New York: Oxford University Press, 2010.

Stene, Jessie A., and Lydia J. Roberts. "A Nutrition Study of an Indian Reservation." *Journal of the American Dietetic Association* 3, no. 4 (March 1928): 217–21.

Stern, Alexandra Minna. *Eugenic Nation: Faults and Frontiers of Better Breeding in Modern America.* Berkeley: University of California Press, 2005.

———. "Sterilized in the Name of Public Health: Race, Immigration, and Reproductive Control in Modern California." *American Journal of Public Health* 95, no. 7 (July 2005): 1128–38. https://doi.org/10.2105/AJPH.2004.041608. PMID: 15983269; PMCID: PMC1449330.

Stevens, Scott Manning. "Tomahawk: Materiality and Depictions of the Haudenosaunee." *Early American Literature* 53, no. 2 (2018): 475–511.

Stoler, Laura Ann. *Race and the Education of Desire.* Durham, NC: Duke University Press, 1995.

———. "Tense and Tender Ties: The Politics of Comparison in North American History and (Post) Colonial Studies." *Journal of American History* 88, no. 3 (2001): 829–65.

Stratton, Royal B. *Captivity of the Oatman Girls.* New York: Carlton and Porter, 1859.

Strong, Pauline Turner. "What Is an Indian Family? The Indian Child Welfare Act and the Renascence of Tribal Sovereignty." *American Studies* 46, no. 3–4 (2005): 205–31.

Sze, Julie. *Noxious New York: The Racial Politics of Urban Health and Environmental Justice.* Cambridge, MA: MIT Press, 2006.

TallBear, Kim. *Native American DNA: Tribal Belonging and the False Promises of Genetic Science.* Minneapolis: University of Minnesota Press, 2013.

Thaggert, Miriam. "Marriage, Moynihan, Mahogany: Success and the Post–Civil Rights Black Female Professional in Film." *American Quarterly* 64, no. 4 (December 2012): 715–40.

Tompkins, Kyla Wazana. *Racial Indigestion: Eating Bodies in the 19th Century.* New York: New York University Press, 2012.

Toro-Morn, Maura, Anna Romina Guevarra, and Nilda Flores-González. "Introduction: Immigrant Women and Labor Disruptions." In *Immigrant Women Workers in the Neoliberal Age,* edited by Nilda Flores-González, Anna Romina Guevarra, Maura Toro-Morn, and Grace Chang, 1–16. Urbana: University of Illinois Press, 2013.

Toro-Morn, Maura, and Marixsa Alicea. *Migrations and Immigration: A Global View.* Westport, CT: Greenwood Press, 2004.

Torpy, Sally J. "Native American Women and Coerced Sterilization: On the Trail of Tears in the 1970s." *American Indian Culture and Research Journal* 24, no. 2 (2000): 1–22.

Trask, Haunani-Kay. "Settlers of Color and 'Immigrant' Hegemony: 'Locals' in Hawai'i." In *Asian Settler Colonialism: From Local Governance to the Habits of Everyday Life in Hawai'i,* edited by Candace Fujikane and Jonathan Y. Okamura, 45–65. Honolulu: University of Hawai'i Press, 2008.

"Treaty with the Delawares, 1778." In *Indian Affairs: Laws and Treaties Vol II (Treaties),* edited by Charles J. Kappler. Washington, DC: Government Printing Office, 1904.

Tuan, Mia. *Forever Foreigners or Honorary Whites? The Asian Ethnic Experience Today.* New Brunswick, NJ: Rutgers University Press, 1998.

Twitty, Michael W. *The Cooking Gene: A Journey through African American Culinary History in the Old South.* New York: Amistad, 2017.

"United States: Report of the President's Committee on Population and Family Planning." *Studies in Family Planning* 1, no. 40 (1969): 1–4. https://doi.org/10.2307/1965283.

US Commission on Civil Rights. "A Quiet Crisis: Federal Funding and Unmet Needs in Indian Country." Washington, DC: US Commission on Civil Rights, July 2013.

Valdivia, Angharad. "Is Penelope to J. Lo as Culture Is to Nature? Eurocentric Approaches to 'Latin' Beauties." In Mendible, *From Bananas to Buttocks,* 129–48.

———. *A Latina in the Land of Hollywood.* Tucson: University of Arizona Press, 2000.

Velez-Ibanez, Carlos. *Border Visions: Mexican Cultures of the Southwest United States.* Tucson: University of Arizona Press, 1996.

Vered, Karen Orr and Sal Humphreys. "Postfeminist Inflections in Television Studies." *Continuum* 28, no. 2 (2014): 155–63.

Vester, Katharina. *A Taste of Power: Food and American Identities.* Oakland: University of California Press, 2015.

Volscho, Thomas W. "Sterilization Racism and Pan-Ethnic Disparities of the Past Decade: The Continued Encroachment on Reproductive Rights." *Wicazo Sa Review* 25, no. 1 (Spring 2010): 7–31.

Wagner, Bill. "Lo the Poor and Sterilized Indian." *America* 136 (January 29, 1977): 75.

Wald, Gale. "Just a Girl? Rock Music, Feminism, and the Cultural Construction of Female Youth." *Signs: Feminisms and Youth Cultures* 23, no. 3 (Spring 1998): 585–610.

Wann, Marylin. "Foreword: Fat Studies: An Invitation to Revolution." In Rothblum and Solovay, *The Fat Studies Reader,* ix–xxv.

Waziyatawin. "The Paradox of Indigenous Resurgence at the End of Empire." *Decolonization: Indigeneity, Education & Society* 1 (2012): 68–85.

Weber-Smith, Chelsey. "Burgers?" Produced by Chelsey Weber-Smith and Miranda Zickler. *American Hysteria.* February 17, 2020. Podcast. https://www.chelseywebersmith.com/.

Wheeler, Charles, and Beth Zachovic. "The Public Charge Ground of Exclusion for Legalization Applicants." *Interpreter Releases* 64 (September 14, 1987).

White, Melissa Autumn. "Documenting the Undocumented: Toward a Queer Politics of No Borders." *Sexualities* 17, no. 8 (2014): 976–97.

Whyte, Kyle Powys. "Food Sovereignty, Justice, and Indigenous Peoples: An Essay on Settler Colonialism and Collective Continuance." In *Oxford Handbook of Food Ethics,* edited by Ann Barnhill, Tyler Doggett, and Mark Budolfson. Oxford, UK: Oxford University Press, 2018.

Wiedman, Dennis. "Native Embodiment of the Chronicities of Modernity: Reservation Food, Diabetes, and the Metabolic Syndrome Among the Kiowa, Comanche, and Apache." *Medical Anthropology Quarterly* 26, no. 4 (2012): 595–612.

Williams, Joyce. "Rape Culture." In *Blackwell Encyclopedia of Sociology.* Oxford: Blackwell Publishing, 2007.

Williams, Robert A. *Like a Loaded Weapon: The Rehnquist Court, Indian Rights, and the Legal History of Racism in America.* Minneapolis: University of Minnesota Press, 2005.

Williams, Walter L. *The Spirit and the Flesh: Sexual Diversity in American Indian Culture.* Boston: Beacon Press, 1986.

Wirth, Cathy, Ron Strochlic, and Christy Getz. *Hunger in the Fields: Food Insecurity among Farmworkers in Fresno Country.* Sacramento, CA: California Institute for Rural Studies, 2007.

Wolfe, Patrick. "Recuperating Binarism: A Heretical Introduction," *Settler Colonial Studies* 3, nos. 3–4 (2013): 257–79.

———. "Settler Colonialism and the Elimination of the Native." *Journal of Genocide Research* 8, no. 4 (December 2006): 387–409.

———. *Traces of History: Elementary Structures of Race.* London: Verso, 2016.

Wu, Frank H. "The Best 'Chink' Food: Dog Eating and the Dilemma of Diversity." *Gastronomica* 2, no. 2 (2002): 38–45. https://doi.org/10.1525/gfc.2002.2.2.38.

Zangwill, Israel. *The Melting Pot.* New York: Macmillan, 1909.

Zolberg, Aristide R. *A Nation by Design: Immigration Policy in the Fashioning of America.* Cambridge, MA: Harvard University Press, 2006.

INDEX

Abbott and Costello Show, The (TV series), 64

abortion, 85

Abourezk, James, 88, 91–92

"abstinence only" public school programs, 105

Achomawi, 199

African American, as term, 8–9. *See also* Black people

agricultural frontier, 158–59

agricultural labor: and allotment policy, 42, 159; of Black women, 83; credit programs and debt cycles, 169–70, 175; of Filipinx people, 172; seasonal, 52, 57–58, 181; and trade policies, 175, 182; undocumented, 183; wartime, 170–71; and workplace hazards, 184–85

agricultural revolution, 155–56

agriculture, Indigenous, 153–54

Ahn, Mihi, 111

Aid to Families with Dependent Children (AFDC) program, 83, 104

AIDS crisis, 197, 215, 216

aliens and alienation, defined, 34

Aliess, Angela, 54

Allen, Paula Gunn, 113

Alliance for a Just Society, 190

allotment policy, 42, 46, 56, 120–21, 159, 205

American Indian Civil Rights Act (1968), 65

American Indian Cultural House, 217

American Indian Movement (AIM), 147, 150n14

American Indian Policy Review Commission for Congress, 91, 205

Amherst, Jeffrey, 78

amnesty, 103–4, 181, 207

Amnesty International, 130, 131, 136

anchor babies, 93, 104, 134

Anderson, Benedict, 36n21

anti-rape movement, 139–43

anti-Semitism, 55, 207

Anzaldúa, Gloria, 212, 213

Apaches, 123

Asians and Asian Americans: citizenship of, 45, 48, 51; foodways, 162–65, 170–73, 186–87; media representations of, 48, 55, 59–60, 63, 68–69, 111; "model minority" rhetoric, 19–20, 65, 68, 84; terminology, 9. *See also specific groups*

244 • INDEX

assimilation: at boarding schools, 42, 49, 67, 72, 83, 121, 158, 159, 162, 165; incompatibility with, 68, 123, 128, 173, 204; and intermarriage, 43, 63, 116; and "model minority" rhetoric, 19; and "vanishing Indian" myth, 41

asylum and refugees, 21, 61, 218, 220–21

Audre Lorde Project (ALP), 217–18

"authenticity" rhetoric, 70, 99

Avildsen, John, 68

Aztecs, 153, 213

Bacon's Rebellion (1676), 155

Badge 373 (film), 69

Baldwin, Douglas, 106

bandito/greaser trope, 49–50, 54

Barker, Joanne, 11, 27, 75, 110

Barthelmess, Richard, 204

Bear Comes Out, Mary Ann, 90

beauty ideals, 179–80, 191

beef industry, 156, 160, 161, 168, 173. *See also* meat consumption

Belolo, Henri, 194, 196

berdache label, 200–201, 209, 216

Berger, Thomas, *Little Big Man,* 210

Bhandar, Brenna, 26, 36n21

BIA (Bureau of Indian Affairs): and boarding school system, 121n65; establishment of, 39–40, 78; funding for, 101; vs. Immigration Bureau, 51; programs, overview, 77, 78; and relocation, 127; and Wounded Knee occupation, 147

Biden, Joe, 20, 21, 137, 143

Biggers, Earl Derr, *A House without a Key,* 55

Bin Laden, Osama, 20

biopower, 50, 76–79, 87, 91–92

birth control clinics, 80, 81, 84–85. *See also* sterilization

bison and buffalo, 159–61

Bison Society, 161

Black fungibility, 3, 6

Black people: in the Bronx, 2, 4–5; citizenship of, 41, 48; and "cultural difference" rhetoric, 62; enslavement of, 3, 9, 24, 34n3, 35n11, 38, 43, 64, 79, 118, 138, 140, 155, 157; foodways, 161n73; one drop rule, 43; par-

allels with Indigenous dehumanization, 24, 25–26; poverty rates, 182; poverty rhetoric, 68, 83; and rape law, 118–19, 139, 140; segregation of, 61; terminology, 8–9. *See also* women, Black

Block, Susan, 119

blood quantum requirements, 42–43, 46, 101, 117

BMI (Body Mass Index), 178–79

boarding schools: for Indigenous children, 42, 49, 67, 72, 83, 121, 158, 159; for Mexican children, 162; including Filipinx children, 165

Bogue, Donald, 93

border dynamics: for Indigenous peoples, eighteenth-century, 36; for LGBTQ+ people, 203–4, 208, 214; for Mexicans, 49, 51–52, 104; rape, 123–24, 135–36, 138, 208; and Trumpism, 218–19

Border Patrol: establishment of, 51–52; rape culture, 124, 136; and Texas Rangers, 123–24

Border Patrol Sex (web series), 138

Bordertown (film), 59

Bracero Program (1942–64), 57–58, 170

Bradford, William, 146, 149, 150

Brando, Marlon, 63

Broken Arrow (film), 69

Broken Blossoms or The Yellow Man and the Girl (film), 204

Broken Doll, The (film), 123

Broken Rainbow (film), 98

Bronx, Jonas, 4

Bronx, New York City, 2, 4–5

Brown v. Board of Education, 61–62

Brownmiller, Susan, *Against Our Will: Men, Women and Rape,* 139–40

Buck v. Bell, 80

buffalo and bison, 159–61

Buffalo Bill, 45, 48, 53, 62–63, 160

Buffalo Bill (film), 62–63

Bureau of Immigration and Naturalization, 51

Bureau of Indian Affairs. *See* BIA

Burke, Tarana, 141

Burns, Randy, 198, 215

Bush, George H. W., 98

INDEX · 245

Byrd, Jodi A., 5, 25, 26, 41, 70, 116–17, 174, 208–9

Cacho, Lisa Marie, 25

Cairos Collective, 217

Calhoun, John C., 78

California Coalition for the Medical Rights of Women, 95

California Gold Rush (1848–59), 120

California's Alien Land Laws, 170

California's Proposition 187 (1994), 104

Camacho, Keith L., 25

Cameron, Barbara, 215

Canada's Bill C-45, 190–91

captivity narratives, 44–45, 140

Carter, Jimmy, 96

casinos, on reservations, 16, 107

Catholic immigrants, 47

Cattle Queen of Montana (film), 97

cattle ranches, 160, 168, 176

"Caucasian" label, 62

Cayuga, 154

Celluloid Maiden figure, 72, 122–23, 125, 132–33, 211

Chae Chan Ping v. United States, 46

Chan, Charlie, character, 55, 59–60, 63

Chang, David, 186–87

Chapman, Leonard F., 66

Charbonneau, Toussaint, 115

Charlie Brown Thanksgiving, A (short film), 145–47

Charo, 94

Chávez, Karma R., 26, 217

Chavez, Leo, 69

Cherokee Nation v. Georgia, 40, 46, 78–79, 158

Cheyenne, 159, 210–11

Cheyenne Autumn (film), 69

Cheyenne River Reservation, 169

Chicana/o, as term, 9. *See also* Latinx people

children: anchor babies, 93, 104, 134; boarding schools for Indigenous, 42, 49, 67, 72, 83, 121, 158, 159; boarding schools for Mexican, 162; boarding schools including Filipinx, 165; custody of, in sterilization

coercion, 88, 89, 90, 92; health disparities, 178, 185, 190; labor of, 184; mixed-race, 43, 72; in neoliberal ideology, 14, 21; schools in the Philippines, 165

Chinese Exclusion Act (1882), 45–46, 58, 74, 81, 163

Chinese immigrants: foodways, 163–64, 171–72; immigration restrictions, 45–46, 74, 123, 163; media representations of, 48, 55, 59–60, 63, 68–69, 163, 204; as wartime allies, 58

"Chinese Restaurant Syndrome," 171–72

Chino, Maya, 111

Cho, Margaret, 111

citizenship: of Black people, 41, 48; ceremonies, 53; of immigrants, 21, 37, 38, 45, 48, 51, 52–53; of Indigenous peoples, 37, 41, 42, 48, 52–53; of Mexicans, 49; of Puerto Ricans, 69n171; and whiteness, 24, 35n11, 37, 51

Civil Rights Act (1964), 65, 82

civil rights movement, 61, 65

Civilization Act (1819), 158

"civilization" rhetoric: and fatness, 180; and hunter figure, 160; and "s—" stereotype, 73; and "savage" label, 5, 22, 35–36, 40, 41, 44–45, 48, 58, 72, 122; and "vanishing Indian" myth, 18–19, 41. *See also* assimilation

Clinton, Bill, 142

Coalition for Immigrant and Refugee Rights Services (CIRRS), 137

Cocopa, 199

Code of Indian Offenses (1883), 201

Cody, Buffalo Bill, 45, 48, 53, 62–63, 160

Cody, Iron Eyes, 15n53

Cohen, Cathy, 200

Cohen's Advertising Scheme (film), 55

Cohen's Fire Sale (film), 55

Colorado Territory (film), 125

"colorblindness" rhetoric, 61–62, 65–66

Colors (film), 19

Columbus, Christopher, 114

Comanches, 123, 179–80

Commission on Public Growth and the American Future, 85

246 • INDEX

Committee on Population Control and Family Planning, 84–85

Committee to End Sterilization Abuse, 95

Communities Creating Healthy Environments (CCHE), 190

Comprehensive Employment and Training Act (CETA), 101

Congress of Industrial Organizations (CIO), 57

consumerism, 98, 99

continental imperialism, 10–11, 119

Cooper, James Fennimore, *Last of the Mohicans*, 44

corn consumption, 153, 156

Corntassel, Jeff, 217

Coté, Charlotte, 189

Coulthard, Glen, 23

COVID-19 pandemic, 171, 219

criminalization: and capitalization, 142; of Mexicans, 49, 51–52, 59, 66, 69, 100, 104; and rape, 119; of undocumented immigration, 51, 104

Crow Creek Reservation, 169

Cubans, 182

cultural appropriation, 70, 109–11, 209–10

"cultural difference" rhetoric, 62

Custer's Revenge (video game), 133

Cyr, Lillian St., 71

Dakota Access Pipeline, 219

Dakota Sioux, 154

Dances with Wolves (film), 18–19, 99

Daniels, Victor, 59

Darnell, Linda, 125

Darwin, Charles, 79

Darwinism and natural selection, 41, 50–51, 80. *See also* eugenics; "vanishing Indian" myth

Das Gupta, Monisha, 26, 213–14

Daughter of the Dragon (film), 59

Davis, Angela, 24, 119, 140

Dawes Act (1887), 42, 72, 159

Day, Iyko, 25, 26, 34n3, 46

Death Valley Days (TV series), 62, 97

Declaration of Independence, 36

decolonial coalitional praxis, 217–18, 220–21

Deer, Sarah, 113, 126

Deferred Action for Childhood Arrivals (DACA), 21

Del Rio, Dolores, 126

Deloria, Philip, 35, 37, 186, 211–12

Deloria, Vine, Jr., 42, 117, 210n80

DeMille, Cecil B., 71

Denetdale, Jennifer Nez, 27, 202

deodorization, 187

Department of Defense (DOD), 147

Department of Health, Education, and Welfare (HEW), 78, 85, 86, 87, 89, 92, 94–95

Department of Homeland Security (DHS), 135

Department of Justice (DOJ), 147

Department of Justice, Office on Violence Against Women, 142

deportation: and eugenics, 47, 56, 94; Indigenous peoples as first deportees, 40; and labor exploitation, 25, 46, 57–58, 104, 137, 191; legislation on, 104, 135

Dhamoon, Rita Kaur, 217

diabetes, 177, 178, 185

Diamond, Neil, 100

diet. *See* foodways

Dillingham Commission, 51

Diné, 159, 199, 202

Diné Marriage Act (2005), 202

Diner, Hasia, 166

dirtiness/uncleanliness/impurity rhetoric, 73, 115

divorce by abandonment, 121

Doctrine of Discovery (1492–1600), 34, 39, 114

dog consumption, 163, 164–65, 186

domestic subjects, 52–53

Dominicans, 182

"Dragon Lady" stereotype, 59

Dream of Wild Health Farm, 190

Dred Scott (1857), 41

Duel in the Sun (film), 125

Eastwood, Clint, 97

eating disorders, 180, 191–92

INDEX · 247

Echo Hawk Consulting, "Feeding Ourselves" report, 175–76, 178, 189–90

Economic Opportunity Act (1964), 82–83

Edison, Thomas, 53

Eisenhower, Dwight D., 60

Ellis, Havelock, 202

Emerald Forest, The (film), 99

Enlightenment thinking, 35–37

enslavement. *See* slavery

environment and environmentalism: Enlightenment ideas of, 37; and foodways, 174–75; and Indigenous stereotypes, 15, 69, 99

Estes, Nick, 220

Estrada, Emir, 184

"ethnicity" rhetoric, 62

eugenics: birth control clinics, 80, 81, 84–85; and blood quantum requirements, 42–43; and deportation, 47, 56, 94; and "Pocahontas Exception," 117; "positive" vs. "negative," 79–80; rebranded as family planning, 81–82; and "vanishing Indian" myth, 41, 50–51, 54, 80. *See also* sterilization

Executive Order 9066 (1942), 58, 170

extinction narrative, 18

extractive industries, 175

Family Planning Act (1970), 85

Family Support Act (1988), 104

fat phobia, 179

fat studies, 152

fatness and obesity, 178–80, 185

FBI (Federal Bureau of Investigation), 121, 147

federal aid. *See* welfare

Federation for American Immigration Reform (FAIR), 134

feedfights, 154–55, 158, 159–60, 161, 174, 184, 186

"Feeding Ourselves" report (Echo Hawk Consulting), 175–76, 178, 189–90

femininity, bodily pathologization of, 179–80

feminists: Indigenous/women of color, 22–23, 27, 212–13; white/mainstream, 28, 82, 84, 93, 95, 112, 139, 140–41

Filipino Repatriation Act (1935), 172

Filipinx people: foodways, 164–65, 172–73; terminology, 9

First Nations, as term, 8. *See also entries at Indigenous*

Flower Drum Song (film), 68–69

Fojas, Camilla, 25

Fong Yue Ting, 46

food assistance programs, 176–77, 180

food deserts, 176, 180

Food Distribution Program on Indian Reservations (FDPIR), 177

food insecurity, 160, 168–71, 175–76, 180, 185

food processing industries, 166–67

food sovereignty movements, 152, 187–91

food stamps, 103, 176, 180

foodways: agricultural frontier, 158–59; agricultural revolution, 155–56; bodily pathologization of, 174, 178–80, 191–92; buffalo genocide, 159–61; feedfights, 154–55, 158, 159–60, 161, 174, 184, 186; health disparities, 175–76, 177–78, 180, 184–85; hunger and starvation, 155, 157, 158, 159, 166, 168; labor exploitation, 162, 166–67, 170, 172, 175, 183–84; national(ist) cuisine, 156–57, 160, 161, 167–68, 173; nutritional colonialism, 180–81; precolonial Indigenous, 153–54, 199; racial pathologization of, 157, 163, 164–65, 171, 172–73, 186–87; restaurant industry, 163–64, 171–72, 173, 186; Thanksgiving, 145–51; and trade policies, 175, 182; in US empire-building, overview, 151–52; wartime, 170–71, 173

Forbes, Jack D., 24

Ford, Gerald, 96

Ford, John, 58–59, 125

Fort Apache, 4

Fort Apache, The Bronx (film), 1–3, 4, 5–6

Fort Berthold Reservation, 169

Fort Pitt, Treaty of (1778), 36

Foucault, Michel, 50, 76, 201

Franklin, Benjamin, 156

Friends of the Indian, 120

Frontier Myth, 39, 44–46, 53, 96–98, 107

Frontier Thesis, 39, 41, 58

Fu Manchu character, 55, 59–60, 63

Fukui, Elliott, 218

fur traders, 115–16, 123

Galton, Francis, 79

248 • INDEX

Gamble, James, 81

gaming industry, 16, 107

Gay American Indians (GAI), 198, 215–16

gays. *See* LGBTQ+ (LGBTQ2S) people

gender and sexual identity: activist and academic appropriation of Indigenous, 70, 209–10, 212–13; in neoliberal ideology, 12–13; scholarship on, 27–28; sexology field, 201–2; terminology, 10; variance and diversity of precolonial Indigenous, 198–200, 211, 216. *See also* LGBTQ+ (LGBTQ2S) people; *entries at women*

gendercide, 201

gendered labor roles, 49, 158, 162, 173, 184, 199

genocide: and AIDS crisis, 197; buffalo, 160; gendercide, 201; Indigenous, 40, 41, 53, 148, 149–50, 159; insufficient healthcare as, 91–92; justification of, 35, 53, 72, 116; sterilization as, 87, 92, 94

Gesell, Gerhard, 86

GI Bill, 77

Gilio-Whitaker, Dina, 190

Gilley, Brian, 202–3

Gilmore, Ruthie Wilson, 24, 107

Glazer, Nathan, 68

Glenn, Evelyn Nakano, 25

Goeman, Mishuana, 27, 122

Goldberg, Eric, 133

Goldbergs, The (radio show), 64

Golden Girls (TV series), 19

Goldstein, Alyosha, 25, 147–48, 182

Goldwater, Barry, 98

Gompers, Samuel, 163

Good Neighbor films, 125–26

Gordon, Glen, 63

Government Accounting Office (GAO), 88–90

Graham, Sylvester, 167

Greaser Act (1855), 49

"greaser" label, 49–50, 54

Great Depression, 56

Greely, Horace, 196

Green, Rayna, 95

Grenier, John, 154

Grey, Sam, 156

Grey, Zane, *Vanishing American,* 54

Griffith, D. W., 204

Guadalupe Hidalgo, Treaty of (1848), 49, 162

Guam, colonization of, 50, 162

Guatemalans, 182

Guevarra, Rudy P., 25

Gutierrez, Elena, 75, 94

Haaland, Deb, 20–21

Hale, Sarah Josepha, 150

Harajuku Girls, 110–11

Harris, Cheryl, 24, 35n11

Harris, Curtis, 217

Haudenosaunee confederacy, 153–54, 155

Hawaii, colonization of, 50

Hay, Harry, 209

Hayes (Motion Picture) Code, 58

health disparities, 175–76, 177–78, 180, 184–85

helper films, 122–23

Hidatsa, 201

Hill Street Blues (TV series), 2

Hispanic, as term, 9. *See also* Latinx people

Hitler, Adolf, 80

Ho, Soleil, 165

Holland, Sharon P., 24

Homestead Act (1862), 159, 167

homonationalism, 195

homosexual, as category, 201–2. *See also* LGBTQ+ (LGBTQ2S) people

Hondagneu-Sotelo, Pierrette, 184

Hong, Grace, 12

Hoover, Elizabeth, 189

House Concurrent Resolution 108 (1953), 60

Housing and Urban Development (HUD), 101

Hubbard, Tasha, 160

Human Rights Watch, 136

hunger and starvation, 155, 157, 158, 159, 166, 168

Hurricane Maria, 219

Hurtado, Albert, 114

Hyde Amendment (1976), 85

hyperfertility myths, 51, 56, 74, 93, 103, 123, 134

hypersexual stereotype, 54, 69, 74, 94, 103, 111, 125, 126, 128, 132–34, 138

Idle No More, 190–91

IHS (Indian Health Service): diet-related health statistics, 177–78; employee background checks, 121n65, 131; funding for, 78, 101, 102, 103; mission, 77; sterilization practices, 14, 87–93

illegal immigration, 51, 52, 57, 66, 93–94, 99, 104, 135, 137, 181, 183

Illegal Immigration Reform and Immigrant Responsibility Act (IIRIRA; 1996), 104, 135

Immerwahr, Daniel, 162

im/migrants: citizenship of, 21, 37, 38, 45, 48, 51, 52–53; in eighteenth-century policy, 37–38; in nineteenth-century media, 47–48, 49–50; in nineteenth-century policy, 38, 45–47, 48–50, 81; scholarship on, 28; terminology, 10; in twentieth-century media, early- and mid-, 54–55, 59–60, 62, 63–64, 172, 204; in twentieth-century media, neoliberal, 19–20, 68–69, 100; in twentieth-century policy, early-and mid-, 51–52, 56, 57–58, 61, 81, 125–26, 203, 206–7; in twentieth-century policy, neoliberal, 17–18, 21, 65–66, 99, 103–5, 181–82, 207–8, 218–19. See also eugenics; foodways; welfare; women, im/migrant; specific groups

Immigration Act (1882), 47

Immigration Act (1990), 207–8

Immigration and Customs Enforcement (ICE), 135

Immigration and Nationality Act (1917), 203

Immigration and Nationality Act (McCarran–Walter Act; 1952), 61, 206–7

Immigration and Nationality Act (INA; 1965), 65, 66, 82, 84, 207

Immigration and Naturalization Service (INS), 56, 103, 135, 181, 206

Immigration Reform and Control Act (IRCA; 1986), 17–18, 99, 103–4, 134, 135–36, 181, 207

imported colonialism, 57–58, 170, 172, 181

impossible subjects, 52–53

impurity/uncleanliness/dirtiness rhetoric, 73, 115

Indian, as term, 8

Indian Child Protection Act (1990), 121n65

Indian Child Welfare Act (ICWA; 1978), 14, 21, 67, 83, 206

Indian Citizenship Act (1924), 52, 124–25, 168

Indian Citizenship Act (Snyder Act; 1921), 78

Indian Civil Rights Act (ICRA; 1968), 128

Indian Country, defined, 129n95

Indian Health Service. See IHS

Indian Healthcare Improvement Act (IHCIA; 1976), 78, 91

Indian Intercourse Act (1790), 37

Indian Princess imagery, 37, 43, 54, 63, 73n7, 117, 122–23, 132–33

Indian Religious Freedom Act (1978), 14, 67

Indian Removal Act (1830), 40

Indian Reorganization Act (IRA; 1934), 43, 56–57, 124–25, 205

Indian Self-Determination and Education Assistance Act (1975), 14, 67

Indian Wars, The (film), 53–54

Indian Women United for Justice, 95

Indigenous dispossession: in colonial conquest policy, 34–35, 114, 155; in eighteenth-century policy, 35–36, 37–38, 155; and immigration scholarship, 28–29; in neoliberal ideology, overview, 11, 12–13; in nineteenth-century policy, 38–43, 46, 78–79, 120–22, 158–59, 201; scholarship on, 26–27; settler colonial logics of, overview, 22–23, 25–26; in twentieth-century policy, early- and mid-, 52–53, 56–57, 60, 127, 168, 205; in twentieth-century policy, neoliberal, 14–16, 20–21, 66–67, 82–83, 100–103, 205–6

Indigenous Food Movement (IFM), 190

Indigenous peoples: citizenship of, 37, 41, 42, 48, 52–53; decolonial coalitional praxis, 217–18, 220–21; in eighteenth-century media, 36–37; enslavement of, 24, 41, 115, 118, 120, 149; food insecurity, 160, 168–71, 175–76, 180; gender and sexual identity, variance and diversity of precolonial, 198–200, 211, 216; health disparities, 175–76, 177–78, 180; healthcare for (*see* IHS); Mexicans conflated with, 49; in nineteenth-century media, 43–45; parallels with Black dehumanization, 24, 25–26; poverty rates, 176; precolonial food culture, 153–54, 199; as racial vs. political group, 13, 14, 29, 43, 67, 206; spirituality of, 88, 153, 154, 199, 201, 209, 211, 216; terminology, 8; in twentieth-century media, early- and mid-, 53–54, 58–59, 62–63, 122–23, 125, 128; in twentieth-century media, neoliberal, 18–19, 69–70, 98–99, 109–10, 210–13. *See also* eugenics; foodways; welfare; women, Indigenous

Indigenous self-determination movement, 13

infantilization and paternalism, 40, 52, 72, 78–79, 87, 122

informed consent, for sterilization, 84, 85, 86, 88, 89, 90, 95

interimmigrant unities, 57

intermarriage and miscegenation, 42–43, 51, 63, 71–72, 114, 115–16, 121, 204

International Indian Treaty Council (IITC), 92–93

Inuit, 154, 199

Iola's Promise (film), 123

Irish immigrants, 9–10, 47, 48, 64, 166

Italian immigrants, 55, 59, 64, 68, 166–67, 173

Ivory Soap, 73

Jackson, Andrew, 40

Jacobson, Matthew Frye, 62, 68

January 6 insurrection (2021), 219

Japanese Americans: foodways, 170–71; internment of, 58, 81, 170–71; media representations of, 63; "model minority" rhetoric, 65; sterilization of, 81

Jefferson, Brian Jordan, 25

Jeremiah Johnson (film), 132

Jewish immigrants, 47, 55, 61, 64, 207

Jimmy Durante Show, The (TV series), 64

Johnson, Jed, 81

Johnson, Lyndon B., 12, 14, 65, 75, 82, 84

Johnson v. M'Intosh, 39

Johnson–Reed Act (1924), 51, 61, 74, 81, 166, 172

Jones Act (1917), 69n171

Kanal, Tony, 109

Kanstroom, Daniel, 25

Karuka, Manu, 10–11, 26, 119

Kellner, Douglas, 18

Kennedy, John F., *A Nation of Immigrants*, 64

King, Tiffany Lethabo, 24

Kita, Jennifer, 111

Kitayama, Mayuko, 111

Klamath, 199

Kosasa, Karen A., 34

Koshy, Susan, 25

Ku Ku Harajuku (TV series), 110–11

Kugel, Rebecca, 210n80

La Via Campesina, 188

labor exploitation: of Black women, 83; of Chinese immigrants, 45–46; and competition fears, 56; and deportation, 25, 46, 57–58, 104, 137, 191; of Filipinx people, 172; and imposed heteronormativity, 207; of Italian immigrants, 166–67; of Latinx people, 49, 57–58, 66, 99, 162, 170, 181, 184–85; minimum wage violations, 183; in neoliberal ideology, 17; and rape, 118, 137, 138; and reproduction, 79, 83, 118

LaDuke, Winona, 175

Lady and the Tramp (film), 173

Lakota, 41, 147, 154, 159

Last of the Mohicans, The (film), 18–19, 99

Last Outpost, The (film), 97

"Latina Threat" rhetoric, 103, 134, 135

Latina/o, as term, 9

Latinx people: in the Bronx, 2, 4–5; and DACA, 21; health disparities and food insecurity, 184–85; labor exploitation of, 49, 57–58, 66, 99, 162, 170, 181, 184–85; media representations of, 49–50, 54, 59, 63, 69, 94; poverty rates and minimum wage violations, 182–83; terminology, 9. *See also specific groups*

Laughing Boy (film), 125

Law and Order (film), 97

Lawrence, Jane, 88

Lazarus, Margaret, 139

Le, Quynh Nhu, 26

League of United Latin American Citizens (LULAC), 184

Lebsock, Kent, 217

Lee, Robert, 47, 63

Lee-Oliver, Leece, 26–27, 214

Legends of the Fall (film), 132

Lenape, 4, 36

lesbians. *See* LGBTQ+ (LGBTQ2S) people

INDEX · 251

Lewis, Oscar, 84, 123

Lewis and Clark expedition, 115

LGBTQ+ (LGBTQ2S) people: immigration restrictions, 61, 65, 206–7; imposed and coerced heteronormativity, 202, 205–6, 207; Indigenous hubs, 215–16; Indigenous-led coalitional resistance, 217–18; instrumentalized inclusion in the settler state, 70, 209–14; racialized queerness, 200–204; violence against, 136, 141, 143, 196, 201, 203, 208, 214. *See also* gender and sexual identity

Licking the Greasers (film), 49

Life with Luigi (radio show), 64

Lincoln, Abraham, 150

Lindholm, Melanie M., 180

Little Big Man (film), 132, 210–12

Little Ceaser (film), 59

Little House on the Prairie (TV series), 5

Living the Spirit: A Gay American Indian Anthology, 198, 215–16

Lone Dog, Leota, 217

Lone Ranger (film serial), 59

Lone Wolf v. Hitchcock, 46

Lonestar (film), 104

Long Walk, 159

LPC provisions, 47, 74, 81, 103, 123, 203

Lucas, Gloria, 191–92

Luibhéid, Eithne, 26

Lytle, Clifford, 42

Madrigal v. Quilligan, 94

mafia stereotype, 59

Major Crimes Act (MCA; 1885), 122, 127

Man Called Horse, A (film), 132

Man Who Loved Cat Dancing, The (film), 132

Manifest Destiny, 39

marriage: heteronormative, 202; intermarriage and miscegenation, 42–43, 63, 71, 114, 115–16, 121; rape in, 121, 124

Marshall Trilogy rulings, 39, 40–41, 46, 78–79, 129, 158

Martin, Dean, 64

Marubbio, M. Elise, 72, 125, 132

masculinity: and diet, 156, 163, 173; white male ideal of, 58–59, 96–98, 160

Massasoit, 146, 148

Mattachine Society, 209

McCarthyism, 64

McGowan, Rose, 141

meat consumption, 160, 161, 163, 165, 168

Medicaid, 85, 91, 103, 104

Medicare, 104

Melamed, Jodi, 25

mental illness, 51, 80, 86, 203, 206, 207

mestizo/a identities, 213

#MeToo movement, 141, 143

Mexican American Women's National Association (MANA), 95

Mexicans and Mexican immigrants: and border policy, 49, 51–52; citizenship of, 49; criminalization of, 49, 51–52, 59, 66, 69, 100, 104; foodways, 162, 170, 185, 186; immigration restrictions, 56, 99, 103–4, 134, 181; indigeneity, 213; labor exploitation of, 49, 57–58, 66, 99, 162, 170, 181; media representations of, 49–50, 54, 59, 63, 69, 74, 94, 104, 125–26, 138; poverty rates, 182; as racial category, 48; sterilization of, 93–94; welfare restrictions, 99, 103–4

Mi Familia (film), 104

Mi Vida Loca (film), 19

Miami Vice (TV series), 19

migrants. *See* im/migrants

Mihesuah, Devon Abbot, 27, 160, 189

Milano, Alyssa, 141

Miles, Tiya, 24

Milk, Harvey, 196

Miller, James C., III, 141–42

Miner, Dylan A. T., 221

minimum wage violations, 183

Miranda, Carmen, 59, 94, 126

miscegenation and intermarriage, 42–43, 51, 63, 71–72, 114, 115–16, 121, 204

mixed-race children, 43, 72

"model minority" rhetoric, 19–20, 65–66, 68, 84

Modoc, 3

Mohave, 199

Mohawk, 35, 73, 154

Mohegan, 149

Moraga, Cherrie, 27, 212

moral turpitude provisions, 47

Morelli, Jacques, 194, 196

Moreton-Robinson, Aileen, 3, 193

Morgan, J. P., 161

Morgensen, Scott Lauria, 17, 195, 209, 217

Moscow on the Hudson (film), 19

Moynihan, Daniel Patrick, 68, 104

Moynihan Report, The (1965), 68, 83

MSG (monosodium glutamate), 172, 186–87

multicultural politics of recognition: emergence of, 61–62, 63–64; in film industry, 126; in foodways, 167, 186; in neoliberal ideology, overview, 12–13, 17, 18, 19–20, 21, 65–66, 68, 70; and "Pocahontas Exception," 117; and tokenism, 65, 109; in welfare rhetoric and policy, 83–84, 99

Muni, Paul, 59

Muslim Bans, 218, 219, 220–21

Mvskoke Food Sovereignty Initiative, 189–90

My Darling Clementine (film), 125

Myer, Dylan S., 205

Nalgona Positivity Pride (NPP), 191–92

Narragansetts, 148, 149

"nation of immigrants" rhetoric, 64, 65–66, 68, 84, 99, 167

National Bison Legacy Act (2016), 161

National Congress of American Indians (NCAI), 92, 102–3, 106

National Organization for Women (NOW), 95

National Women's Health Network (NWHN), 95

Native American Solidarity Committee, 91

Native Organizers Alliance (NOA), 190

Native princess figure, 37, 43, 54, 63, 73n7, 117, 122–23, 132–33

Natives/Native Americans. *See entries at Indigenous*

natural selection and Darwinism, 41, 50–51, 80. *See also* eugenics; "vanishing Indian" myth

naturalization. *See* citizenship

Naturalization Act (1790), 37–38

Naturalization Act (1906), 51

neoliberalism: ideology, overview, 11–13; in media, overview, 15, 18–20; in US policy, overview, 14–18, 20–21, 65

neoliberalism ideology, overview, 11–13

New Deal programs, 57, 77, 83, 170

"New Federalism," 14, 15, 66, 75, 100

New York Radical Feminists, 141

Newell, William B., 150n14

Ngai, Mai, 52

Nixon, Richard, 14, 17, 66–67, 75, 84, 85, 87, 91–92, 96, 100

"No Bans on Stolen Lands" activism, 218, 220–21

No Doubt (rock band), "Looking Hot," 109–10

"noble greaser" figure, 50

"noble savage" figure, 15, 34, 35, 44, 59, 69, 132. *See also* Native princess figure

Norris, George W., 124

North American Free Trade Agreement (NAFTA), 175, 182

Northern Exposure (TV series), 19

Northwest Mounted Police (film), 125

nutrition. *See* foodways

nutritional colonialism, 180–81

Nyéléni Declaration, 188

obesity and fatness, 178–80, 185

O'Brien, Jean M., 18

Office on Economic Opportunity (OEO), 83, 85

Office on Violence Against Women, Department of Justice, 142

Oglala Lakota, 147

Oklahoma v. Castro-Huerta, 21

Oliphant v. Suquamish Indian Tribe, 14, 67, 129, 143, 206

one drop rule, 43

Oneida, 154

Onondaga, 154

Operation Blockade / Hold the Line, 135

Operation Bootstraps, 69n171

Operation Gate Keeper, 135

Operation Wetback, 58, 170

Orange, Tommy, *There There,* 150, 187

INDEX · 253

Osage, 121, 176

Ozawa v. United States, 51

Pacific Railway Act (1862), 159

Page Law (1875), 45, 74, 81, 123

Paiute, 120

pan-Indigenous imagery, 70, 99, 109

Patel, Raj, 156

paternalism and infantilization, 40, 52, 72, 78–79, 87, 122

Pawnee, 210, 211

Penn, Arthur, 210

Penn, William, 37

Pequot War (1636–37), 149–50

Perfect Strangers (TV series), 19

Personal Responsibility and Work Opportunity Reconciliation Act (PRWORA; 1996), 104

personal responsibility politics: in neoliberal ideology, overview, 13, 15–16, 20, 74–75; in welfare rhetoric, 84, 100–102, 104–5

Peter Pan (film), 128

Petrie, Daniel, 1

Philippines: colonization of, 9, 50, 161–62 (*see also* Filipinx people); independence of, 172

Piatote, Beth, 52, 120

Pilgrims, 145, 146, 148

Pine Ridge Reservation, 41, 147, 159

Pine Ridge Sioux, 53

Pinkerton-Uri, Constance, 88, 90, 95

Plains tribes, 54, 63

Plainsman, The (film), 58

Planned Parenthood, 80

"playing Indian," 35, 37, 109, 210

plenary power doctrine, 45, 46, 67

Pocahontas, 43, 63, 116–17

Pocahontas (film), 132–33, 155

"Pocahontas Exception," 117

Popeno, Paul, 50–51, 80

Population Council, 82

pornography industry, 133, 138, 141

poverty rates, 176, 182–83

Powhatan, 43, 116, 155

Presidential Commission on Indian Reservation Economies (PCIRE), 102

prestige pictures, 125

Production Code Administration, 126

Puar, Jasbir, 194

Public Health Service (PHS), 78, 205–6

Public Law 280 (1953), 60, 127, 128

public pedagogy, as concept, 3–7

Puerto Ricans: citizenship of, 69n171; media representations of, 69; poverty rates, 182; sterilization of, 81, 94–95

Puerto Rico: colonization of, 4, 50, 69n171, 81, 162; Hurricane Maria, 219

Puritans, 115, 179

"QAnon Shaman," 219

queer identity. *See* LGBTQ+ (LGBTQ2S) people

Quetelet, Adolphe, 178–79

racial capitalism, 5, 7–8, 22–26, 43, 68, 82, 112, 119, 151, 155, 161n73

racialized anti-immigration: in neoliberal ideology, overview, 11, 17–18, 19–20; settler colonial logics of, overview, 23–24, 25–26. *See also* im/migrants; *specific policies*

Radical Faeries, 209

ranching, 160, 168, 176

rape: anti-rape movement, 139–43; at the border, 123–24, 135–36, 138, 208; colonialism and/as, 113–16; defined, 108n1; and enduring legacy of colonialism, 116–18, 119–21; eroticization of, in media, 109–10, 138; and hypersexual stereotypes, 111, 125, 128, 132–34, 138; and labor exploitation, 118, 137, 138; laws on, as racialized and gendered, 117–19; laws on, definitions, 124, 141–42; laws on, rape shield, 141, 142; laws on, under federal vs. Indigenous jurisdiction, 122, 127, 128–29, 132, 142–43; marital, 121, 124; rarity of, in precolonial Indigenous cultures, 113, 140; and sex work, 114, 120, 128, 135, 138; statistics, 129–31, 136, 137; vulnerability to, 127–28, 134–35, 137

Rape Culture (documentary film), 139

rape culture, as term, 139

rape shield laws, 141, 142

254 • INDEX

rat consumption, 163

Razalan, Rino Nakasone, 111

Reagan, Ronald: in film and TV, 62, 96–97; and frontier mythology, 96–98; neoliberal policies, overview, 15–16, 17–18, 66, 75, 96; welfare policy and discourse, 99–107

Real Women Have Curves (film), 104

red face, 19, 54

Red Girl (film), 54, 94

Red Power, 92

Red Wing's Gratitude (film), 123

Reddy, Chandan, 25

refugees and asylum, 21, 61, 218, 220–21

Rehnquist, William, 67

Relf v. Weinberger, 86

religion and spirituality, Indigenous, 88, 153, 154, 199, 201, 209, 211, 216

relocation. *See* termination and relocation policy

reproduction. *See* eugenics; sterilization

restaurant industry, 163–64, 171–72, 173, 186

"rez girl," 133

rice consumption, 163

Riley, Angela R., 109–10

Riot Grrrl movement, 141

Roberts, Dorothy, 105

Rockefeller, John D., III, 82

Rocky (film), 68

Rodríguez, Juana María, 138

Rodriguez-Lonebear, Desi, 178

Rodríguez Trías, Helen, 95

Roediger, David, 57

Rogin, Michael, 97

Rohmer, Sax: *The Hand of Fu Manchu,* 55; *The Insidious Dr. Fu Manchu,* 55; *The Return of Fu Manchu,* 55

Rolfe, John, 43, 116

Rolfe, Thomas, 116, 117

Roosevelt, Franklin Delano, 12, 58, 81, 124, 125, 150

Roosevelt, Theodore, 98, 161; *Hunting Trips of a Ranchman,* 160

Rosay, Andre, 131

Roscoe, Will, 198

Rose, Felipe Ortiz, 193, 194–95, 205

Rowlandson, Mary, *A True History,* 37

Royle, Edwin Milton, *S— Man,* 71

S— Man (film), 71–72, 74, 122, 125

"s—" stereotype, 54, 72–74, 75, 87

Sacagawea, 115–16, 122–23

Said, Edward, 34

Saldaña-Portillo, Maria Josefina, 33–34, 35n11

Salmon, Enrique, 153

Salvadorans, 182

Sanchez, Marie, 90, 95

Sand Creek Massacre, 140

Sanger, Margaret, 80, 81, 84

"Savage as the Wolf" border policy, 36

"savage" label: and "civilization" rhetoric, 5, 22, 35–36, 40, 41, 44–45, 48, 58, 72, 122; and diet, 151, 156, 164–65; financial reframing of, 102; and gaming industries, 16; as justification of violence and dispossession, 35, 53, 109, 140, 158; and Mexicans, 49; vs. Native princess figure, 117; "noble savage" figure, 15, 34, 35, 44, 59, 69, 132; and sexualized maiden figure, 125; and uncleanliness, 73; vs. white womanhood, 37

Sayonara (film), 63

Scarface (film), 19, 59

school lunch programs, 104

Schultz, Charles M., *Peanuts,* 145–46

Seasonal Agricultural Worker (SAW) program, 181

Second National Conference on Race Betterment (SNCRB), 80

segregation, racial, 61

Seneca, 154, 155

Serena, Norma Jean, 92

settler citizenship, 17

settler colonialism: justification in public pedagogy, overview, 3–7; and neoliberal ideology, 11–21; and racial capitalism, 5, 22–26, 68, 119

settler homonationalism, 195

sex trafficking, 115–16, 120, 128, 135, 138

sex work, 45, 47, 74, 114, 120, 123, 128, 135, 138

sexology, as field, 201–2

sexual violence. *See* rape

sexuality. *See* gender and sexual identity; LGBTQ+ (LGBTQ2S) people

sexualized maiden stereotype, 125, 128

Shigematsu, Setsu, 25

Silent Tongue (film), 132

Simmons, Amelia, *American Cookery,* 157

Simon, Paul, 134

Simpson, Audra, 3

Sinatra, Frank, 64

Sinclair, Upton, *The Jungle,* 166–67

Sioux, 168–69, 199

Sioux Ghost Dance (short film), 53

"Sioux Uprising" (1862), 119

Siwanoy, 4

slavery: and *berdache* label, 200; of Black people, 3, 9, 24, 34n3, 35n11, 38, 43, 64, 79, 118, 138, 140, 155, 157; of Indigenous peoples, 24, 41, 115, 118, 120, 149; sex trafficking, 115–16, 120, 128, 135, 138

Slotkin, Richard, 2, 39, 98

SlutWalk, 141

smell racism, 187

Smith, Andrea, 219

Smith, John, 116, 155

Smith, Kenneth L., 102

Snelgrove, Corey, 217

Snyder Act (Indian Citizenship Act; 1921), 78

Social Security, 104

Social Security Act (1935), 83

Spanish colonial practice, 35–36, 114–15

spirituality and religion, Indigenous, 88, 153, 154, 199, 201, 209, 211, 216

Stagecoach (film, 1939), 18, 59

Stagecoach (film, 1986), 99

Stallone, Sylvester, 68

Standing Rock Reservation, 169

starvation and hunger, 155, 157, 158, 159, 166, 168

Steerage Act (1819), 38

Stefani, Gwen, 108–12

sterilization: abuse of, defined, 75; and BMI, 179; consent for, 81, 84, 85, 86, 88, 89, 90,
95; federal legislation and funding for, 14, 80, 81, 84–85; of immigrants, 81, 93–94; of Indigenous women, 14, 87–93, 95; methods, 85n64; and personal responsibility politics, 105; in state legislation, 51, 80, 85; welfare recipients as targets of, 14, 80, 81, 84–87, 89, 91

street-vending food, 167, 184

Strong, William, 120–21

structural adjustment policies (SAPs), 182

submissive stereotype, 63, 69, 111, 138

Supplemental Nutrition Assistance Program (SNAP), 177

supplemental security income (SSI), 105

Taka, Miiko, 63

Tamenend, 37, 156

Taylor, Linda, 100

Temporary Assistance to Needy Families (TANF), 104–5

termination and relocation policy: collective Indigenous resistance to, 13; and food insecurity, 169; and imposed heteronormativity, 205–6; and welfare, 14, 15, 60, 66, 75, 100–103, 106–7

Texas Rangers, 123–24

Thanksgiving, 145–51

Theodore Roosevelt Indian School, 4

This Bridge Called My Back, 212–13

Thunderheart (film), 132

Tisquantum, 148

Tlingit, 154

Tohono O'odham nation, 20

tokenism, 65, 109

Tolowa, 199

Tompkins, Kyla Wazana, 156–57

Tonto character, 59

trade policies, 175, 182

Trail of Tears (1838–39), 40

trans people. *See* LGBTQ+ (LGBTQ2S) people

Trask, Haunani-Kay, 23

Tribal Self-Governance Demonstration Project, 107

Truman, Harry, 61

256 · INDEX

Trump, Donald, 18, 28, 136–37, 218–19, 220

Turner, Frederick Jackson, 39, 41, 58

Tuscaroras, 154

Two-Spirit people, 10, 202, 216, 217

Tydings–McDuffle Act or Philippine Independence Act (1934), 172

uncleanliness/dirtiness/impurity rhetoric, 73, 115

undocumented immigration, 51, 52, 57, 66, 93–94, 99, 104, 135, 137, 181, 183

Undocuqueer projects, 214

United American Indians of England (UAINE), 147, 151

United States v. Kagama, 46

United States v. Thind, 51

US empire, as term, 10–11

US Marshals Service (USMS), 147

USDA (US Department of Agriculture), 158–59, 169, 170–71, 175, 176

US–Dakota War (1862), 119

Valentino, Rudolph, 64

Vanishing American, The (film), 123

"vanishing Indian" myth, 18–19, 34, 41, 50–51, 54, 58, 80, 99, 161, 169

Velez, Lupe, 59, 74, 94, 125, 126

Vester, Katharina, 157

victory gardens, 171

Village People (music group), 193, 194–96; "Go West," 195, 196; "In the Navy," 196; "Y.M.C.A.," 195

violence, against LGBTQ+ people, 136, 141, 143, 196, 201, 203, 208, 214. *See also* gendercide; genocide; rape; slavery

Violence Against Women Act (VAWA; 1994, 2022), 142

Violent Crime Control and Law Enforcement Act (1994), 142

Virginia Racial Integrity Act (1924), 117

Vitoria, Francisco de, 34

Wampanoag, 145, 148

War Department, 39, 51, 78

War on Drugs, 18, 100

War on Poverty, 14, 65, 66, 75, 82–83, 91, 93

War on Terror, 18, 20, 220

War Relocation Authority (WRA), 171

Warren, Elizabeth, 219

Washington, George, 36, 155

Watt, James, 16, 105–6

Wayne, John, 59

Waziyatawin, 189

welfare: as biopower, 76–79, 87, 91–92; and blood quantum requirements, 43, 101; food assistance programs, 176–77, 180; and immigration restrictions, 47, 74, 81, 103–5; and multicultural politics of recognition, 83–84, 99; vs. neoliberal ideology, overview, 14, 15–16, 20, 68, 74–75; New Deal policies, 57, 83, 170; and personal responsibility politics, 84, 100–102, 104–5; and sterilization, 14, 80, 81, 84–87, 89, 91; and termination, 14, 15, 60, 66, 75, 100–103, 106–7

"welfare queen" stereotype, 16, 75, 100, 106

West Side Story (film), 69

WeWah and BarCheeAmpe, 217, 221

white ethnic immigrants: foodways, 166–67, 173, 179; immigration restrictions, 46–47, 74, 81, 123, 206–7; media representations of, 48, 55, 59, 64; and multicultural politics of recognition, 64, 65, 68, 84; and "whiteness" category, 9–10

white women. *See* women, white

whiteness: vs. Black and Indigenous status, 24; as category, 9–10; and citizenship, 24, 35n11, 37, 51; and civilization, 45; in eugenics ideology, 79; and "Pocahontas Exception," 117

WHO (World Health Organization), 175

Whyte, Kyle, 158

Wiechquaesgecks, 4

Williams, Robert A., 36

Willis, Victor, 194, 196

Wilson, Diane, 190

Winslow, Edward, *Mourt's Relation,* 148, 150

Winthrop, John, 149–50

Wolfe, Patrick, 26

women, Black: rape of, 43, 79, 118, 138, 140, 141; sterilization of, 80, 86; in welfare policy, 83; "welfare queen" stereotype, 16, 75, 100, 106

women, im/migrant: hyperfertility myths, 51, 56, 74, 93, 103, 123, 134; hypersexual stereotype, 54, 69, 74, 94, 103, 111, 125, 126, 138; and immigration restrictions, 47, 74, 81, 99, 103–4; labor expectations, 162, 184; and sex work, 45, 47, 74, 123, 135, 138; sterilization of, 81, 93–95; submissive stereotype, 63, 69, 111, 138; "welfare queen" stereotype, 16, 75. *See also* rape

women, Indigenous: bodily pathologization of, 179–80; Celluloid Maiden figure, 72, 122–23, 125, 132–33, 211; enslavement of, 115, 118, 120, 149; murder of, 121; Native princess figure, 37, 43, 54, 63, 73n7, 117, 122–23, 132–33; in precolonial foodways, 154, 157, 199; "s—" stereotype, 54, 72–74, 75, 87; and sex work, 114, 120, 128; sexualized maiden stereotype, 125, 128; sterilization of, 14, 87–93, 95. *See also* rape

women, white: foodways, 173, 180; and rape law, 118–19, 124, 139, 140; reproductive rights of, 82, 84, 95; vulnerability and protection rhetoric, 37, 45, 49, 118–19, 204; in welfare policy, 80, 83

Women of All Red Nations (WARN), 92–93

Wong, Anna May, 59

Worcester v. Georgia, 41, 158

World's Fair (1904), 165

Wounded Knee: activist occupation of, 147; massacre (1890), 41, 53, 159

Wynter, Sylvia, 24

Yang, Jenny, 187

Yazzie, Melanie, 220

yellow face, 48, 63, 204

Young, Alexander, 150

Zambrano v. INS, 103–4

Zangwill, Israel, *The Melting Pot,* 55

Zapatista Army of National Liberation, 190

Zero Population Growth (ZPG), 134

RACE AND MEDIATED CULTURES
CAMILLA FOJAS, SERIES EDITOR

Race and Mediated Cultures provides a venue for innovative humanistic explorations of race and mediated culture, broadly defined to include screen cultures, social media, surveillance, data algorithms, fandom and media activism, propaganda, and other permutations of mediated life. Books in this new series interrogate mediations of race and racialization and their social and political contexts and ramifications.

Indigenous Dispossession, Anti-Immigration, and the Public Pedagogy of US Empire
  LEAH PERRY

Deflective Whiteness: Co-Opting Black and Latinx Identity Politics
  HANNAH NOEL